FAITH IN PUBLIC LIFE

William J. Collinge
Editor

**THE ANNUAL PUBLICATION
OF THE COLLEGE THEOLOGY SOCIETY
2007
VOLUME 53**

ORBIS

Maryknoll, New York

Founded in 1970, Orbis Books endeavors to publish works that enlighten the mind, nourish the spirit, and challenge the conscience. The publishing arm of the Maryknoll Fathers and Brothers, Orbis seeks to explore the global dimensions of the Christian faith and mission, to invite dialogue with diverse cultures and religious traditions, and to serve the cause of reconciliation and peace. The books published reflect the views of their authors and do not represent the official position of the Maryknoll Society. To learn more about Maryknoll and Orbis Books, please visit our website at www.maryknoll.org.

Copyright © 2008 by the College Theology Society.

Published by Orbis Books, Maryknoll, New York 10545-0308.
Manufactured in the United States of America.

Library of Congress Cataloging-in-Publication Data

Faith in public life / William J. Collinge, editor.
    p. cm. — (College Theology Society annual ; v. 53, 2007)
    ISBN-13: 978-1-57075-774-7
    1. Christian sociology—Catholic Church. 2. Church and social problems—Catholic Church.   I. Collinge, William J., 1947-
    BX1753.F25 2008
    261.7—dc22
                                                          2008000217

Contents

Introduction   1
William J. Collinge

PART I
RETRIEVING CATHOLIC TRADITIONS

The Bible and Public Life: Excuses, Abuses,
and Some Powerful Uses   15
Dennis Hamm

Implementing Catholic Social Teaching   39
John Sniegocki

Outside the Castle Walls: The Public Politics
of Teresa's Vision   62
Elizabeth Newman

Religious Liberty and the Common Good:
A Baptist Engagement with the Catholic Americanist
Tradition   81
Coleman Fannin

The "Princeton Statement" on Church-State Relations:
Reflections on a Little-Known Text   110
(Appendix: "The Princeton Statement"
of Jacques Maritain and Marston Morse   120)
Patrick Hayes

PART II
EXPLORING THE CONTEMPORARY
AMERICAN CONTEXT

Does Systematic Theology Have a Future? A Response
to Lieven Boeve   135
  William L. Portier

Religion as a Basis of Lawmaking under
the Nonestablishment Norm   151
  Michael J. Perry

How to "Vote Catholic": Dueling Catholic Voter
Guides in the 2006 Midterm Elections   179
  Harold E. Ernst

Table Fellowship in a Land of Gated Communities:
Virgilio Elizondo as Public Theologian   202
  Mary Doak

Intelligent Design "in the Public Square":
Neo-Conservative Opposition to Darwinian Naturalism   218
  Anne M. Clifford

PART III
BROADENING THE HORIZONS

Jus Post Bellum: Extending the Just War Theory   241
  Mark J. Allman and Tobias L. Winright

Living as "Risen Beings" in Pursuit of a Reconciled World:
Resources from Jon Sobrino   265
  Ernesto Valiente

Communal Penance and Public Life: On the Church's
Becoming a Sign of Conversion from Social Sin   284
  James T. Cross

Contributors   298

Introduction

William J. Collinge

"My faith doesn't influence my decisions, it drives them," declared former Arkansas governor Mike Huckabee, while a candidate for the Republican nomination for president in 2008.[1] Responding to Huckabee, *Washington Post* columnist Richard Cohen wrote, "When any issue, any question, becomes a matter of faith, it means it cannot be argued. That's not what we do in a democracy."[2] The present volume, consisting of papers delivered at the 2007 Annual Convention of the College Theology Society, held at the University of Dayton, stands as a refutation of Cohen, as fourteen authors—thirteen theologians and a legal scholar—argue over the implications of faith for public life.

"Faith," in this volume, means Christian faith and, in particular, Catholic faith. Most of the authors write as Catholics, and the two who write as Baptists draw on Catholic sources. Much of what is said here, however, has implications well beyond the Catholic sphere and to some extent beyond the Christian sphere. "Public" here means, first and foremost, the political domain, as in the classical term *res publica* or Richard Neuhaus's "public square."[3] However, the term "public" has a much broader extension, and some of the articles in this volume reach beyond the strictly political zone; I will do so myself toward the end of this introduction.

Theology and the Modern Secular State

Perhaps the most fundamental issue raised at the conference is that of the legitimacy of the modern state, from a Christian point of view. This question was the subject of David L. Schindler's keynote address, "Multiculturalism inside the Liberal State: The Problem of Truth, Natural Law, and Civil Community."[4] The modern liberal or "juridical" state, Schindler argues,

> understands itself to be about procedures necessary for adjudicating fairly between competing exercises of freedom by individuals in society, as distinct from defending, or calling to mind in an explicit way, any truth to which these individuals might already-anteriorly be "bound" *qua* human. Such a state thus tends toward displacing the notion of the common good by that of public order.[5]

It purports to offer a framework within which people from various cultures—Schindler has in mind chiefly those who belong to the great religions that *do* make substantive truth claims about the human being and the common good—can live freely and in peace.

Schindler argues that this offer is deceptive, in that the supposedly neutral state actually embodies implicit truth claims that are at odds with the religious traditions, and the Christian faith in particular. The liberal state, he says, construes freedom as "a primitively indifferent act of choice," according to which the other—the object of choice—"lacks an inherent worth that makes an *already-anteriorly given*, and thus ineliminable and non-arbitrary, demand upon the will and the intelligence."[6] This is an "instrumentalist" view of freedom, according to which freedom is understood as a neutral power of choice rather than as a power whereby rational beings adhere to an antecedent substantive good.

The juridical state, in a word, in the name of avoiding substantive truth about the nature of man, unconsciously embodies a "substantively" instrumentalist truth about the nature of man, one which, *prima facie*, is at odds with alternative notions of freedom, reason, and religion in (at least some of) the various traditional religious cultures.[7]

This leads unwittingly, says Schindler, to a "supremacy of the strong over the weak"[8]:

> Instrumentalist freedom and intelligence imply an original indifference to the other that renders the other without any inherent—that is, constitutively and not merely contractually given—dignity *as* other. Those who are not useful and cannot assert their rights through an exercise of their own freedom—the unborn, human embryos subject to destruction in scien-

tific research, the terminally ill—have no publicly-constitu-
tionally recognized worth; rather, their rights are contingent
on the good will of those who are able to exercise their
freedom and choose to enact laws to protect these vulnerable
ones.[9]

Schindler is not alone in his challenge to the modern public
order. Lieven Boeve groups Schindler's *Communio* school with
the associates of John Milbank's Radical Orthodoxy and George
Lindbeck's "Yale school" postliberalism as "anti-moderns."[10] To
that list one might add those influenced by Stanley Hauerwas, a
Yale graduate whose criticism of the liberal order resembles that
of Radical Orthodoxy. All such theologians object to the idea that
theology should adapt itself to the demands of the modern secular
order. As Elizabeth Newman quotes Stephen Long[11] in this volume, "Whether the assumed broader social reality is called 'the
public,' 'society,' 'civilization,' or 'the political,' to ask the question of theology's relevance to such a grand social reality inevitably subordinates the church to it."[12] Mary Doak quotes Milbank
in this volume on a similar point: that "Christian theologians
should oppose secular society on the grounds that Christian discourse must either 'master or be mastered by' all other forms of
discourse."[13]

Arrayed on the other side are the proponents of "public theology." This term was given its present meaning by Martin Marty
and championed especially by theologians associated with the
University of Chicago. Public theology aimed, according to Doak,
to "address issues of society, politics, and culture theologically,"
and "to articulate this theology in a manner accessible to the wider
population."[14] What was especially to be avoided was "sectarianism," the withdrawal of Christians from public discourse into the
discourse of separated (and probably small) communities.[15] Although William Portier is "tempted to say that the battle is over
and Yale has won"[16] (and I, as a Yale graduate, am tempted to say,
"boola, boola"), the paper in this volume by Doak, a Chicago
graduate, shows that there is life in "public theology" yet. The
present volume does not by any means settle the contest, but the
concern about the legitimacy and manner of adapting Christian
discourse to the modern secular order, especially in the United
States, pervades it, and several of the essays offer perspectives
that promise to lead beyond the standoffs of the past decades.[17]

Resources from Scripture and Tradition

The first set of articles in this volume returns to the Catholic tradition with an eye to its bearing on contemporary political affairs. I mean "tradition" here both in its normative sense—the Bible and the official teaching of the church, as with the articles by Dennis Hamm and John Sniegocki—and in the less formal sense of the thought and example of saints and scholars of the past, as with the articles by Elizabeth Newman, Coleman Fannin, and Patrick Hayes.

Dennis Hamm, S.J., looks at the use and misuse of the Bible in American public life. After rebutting the use of certain scripture passages as excuses for Christians to "dodge political responsibility," he examines a prominent abuse of the Bible in political discourse: the "dispensational premillenialism" of the "Left Behind" series of novels. He finds the practice of the U.S. bishops in their pastoral letters of the 1980s and their quadrennial "Faithful Citizenship" documents, along with certain documents of the Vatican, to provide a model, using the Bible not as a collection of maxims but as containing "narratives that teach a way of seeing that leads to a way of being."[18] Although he is attracted to Gerhard Lohfink's idea of the church as a "contrast community," he worries about its tendencies to "sectarianism," and desires not to let go of the bishops' aim to have a direct influence on public policy, or "convert Pharaoh" (as he quotes Norbert Lohfink).

John Sniegocki's concern is with the "way of being" that follows from the "way of seeing" developed in the great documents of Catholic social teaching. "How can [this vision] be translated from the realm of teaching into the realm of practice?" is his question.[19] He is less sanguine than Hamm about the effectiveness of what he labels a "chaplaincy model," which seeks to affect public policy through the moral formation of the leaders of society. While not dismissing the effort to influence those who hold power, he draws on the work of John Howard Yoder to defend a "bottom-up" or "grassroots" model for church social involvement. He rejects the label "sectarian," arguing that "church-sect typologies are generally not helpful, and often contribute to more confusion than clarity."[20] Far from encouraging withdrawal from social engagement, an accusation that often accompanies the label "sectarian," Sniegocki proposes a series of concrete steps for the church to respond to the Iraq War and the problem of economic globalization. In the words of one of the anonymous reviewers of Sniegocki's article, "Were bishops to take the recommendations in this essay seriously, the Church might actually change the world."

Since 1996, the National Association of Baptist Professors of Religion (NABPR) has met jointly with the College Theology Society. Baptists in the United States have a history in regard to faith in public life that is significantly different from that of Catholics. From the time of Roger Williams in the seventeenth century, Baptists have been among the strongest contributors to and defenders of the American project of separation of church and state. On the other hand, Baptists have been at the center of the "religious right," whose rise, usually dated from the late Baptist leader Jerry Falwell's establishment of the Moral Majority in 1979, is the factor that has most altered the debate about "faith in public life" in the last several decades.

Two members of the NABPR, Elizabeth Newman and Coleman Fannin, are contributors to this volume. Both turn to Catholic sources for alternatives to the individualism they see as prevalent in Baptist thought, particularly the popular idea of "soul competency," whereby "religion is a personal matter between the individual and God," as Newman quotes theologian Herschel H. Hobbs. [21] Newman reads Teresa of Avila's *Interior Castle* (*Las Moradas*) as developing a reading of the Bible much as Dennis Hamm would have it be read. Far from a private, inward-turning spirituality (as the word "interior" in the title of the English translation implies), Teresa's reading of scripture challenges, according to Newman, "the triumphalistic political tyranny of her day . . . as well as the political tyranny of our own day, which relegates faith to an apolitical sphere."[22]

Fannin, likewise reacting against a tendency in Baptist thought to privatize faith and also against a corresponding tendency to regard the nation-state as the custodian of the common good, turns to John Courtney Murray, the leading twentieth century American Catholic theorist of church-state relations. Murray, writing in the context of American Catholics' post-World-War-II emergence into full participation in American civic life, sought both to reassure Americans that Catholics were no threat to their religious liberty and to convince Catholics that American religious liberty was not contrary to Catholic teaching. To do so, he had to counter the "thesis-hypothesis" position then prevalent in Rome and among some American theologians, which held that ideally the Catholic Church should be the established church, but that religious liberty and a religiously neutral state could be accepted as an accommodation to particular circumstances. For Murray, the ideal of establishment was itself an accommodation to circumstances, and the natural law principle of human dignity implied religious freedom. Murray's thought later had a substantial influence on the position taken by the Second Vatican Council in *Dignitatis Humanae*, the "Declaration on Religious Freedom."

I once heard Bill Portier label the subsequent debates among American Catholics on church and state as "the battle for the bones of John Courtney Murray."[23] In that battle, Murray was both a "totem" for liberals and conservatives "and a target for radical critics who question whether the Catholic Church can indeed be reconciled with the American state."[24] Fannin himself, though expressing great respect for Murray's arguments, finds that they ultimately concede too much to the state and leave "little distinctive or substantive public role for the church."[25]

If this book were being published in French, the words *un inédit de Jacques Maritain* would stand out in advertisements for it. Next to Murray, Maritain, a French philosopher then living in Princeton, New Jersey, was probably the most influential figure in the immediate postwar period in American Catholic thought on church and state. In his research on the now-defunct Catholic Commission on Intellectual and Cultural Affairs, Patrick Hayes has discovered a previously unpublished 1949 statement on the church-state problem called "The Princeton Statement," written by Maritain, with an addendum by the mathematician Marston Morse. Maritain's statement challenges the "thesis-hypothesis" position, holding that the church's "universal, immutable principles" may well have supported an established church in earlier patterns of civilization, but that in "the historical climate of modern civilization," which acknowledges "the freedom of individual conscience," those same principles call for equal rights of all citizens to freedom of religion.[26] Hayes's article in this volume develops the context within which the statement was made and suggests that it influenced Murray's thought as well as anticipated Maritain's *Man and the State*.[27]

The Contemporary American Context

William Portier's paper is a transition between the first and second parts of this volume. In dialogue with Lieven Boeve, Portier addresses the broad question of theology's relation to modern secular culture. Between Boeve's labels of "correlationist" and "anti-modern," Portier unhesitatingly chooses "anti-modern." But he argues that seemingly theoretical positions about "modernity" may really rest on judgments about specific historical and political contexts. If he and Boeve disagree, he concludes, "it is more likely on judgments about the particularities of our present time of upheaval."[28] Portier characterizes his present American context as "an empire that makes war without end."[29] Were he in a different political setting (Canada, perhaps?), he might well sound less "anti-modern."

For constitutional scholar Michael J. Perry, the modern secular state is less secular than some have thought. In earlier works, Perry has argued philosophically that one of its central principles, the affirmation of human rights, requires a religious foundation.[30] He has also argued, against John Rawls and others, that it is not immoral in a liberal democracy for legislation to have a religious basis.[31] In this volume he argues, as a matter not of philosophy but of U.S. constitutional law, that the "nonestablishment norm," expressed in the First Amendment as "Congress shall make no law respecting an establishment of religion," does not prohibit religion-based lawmaking, although it does ban laws whose only discernible rationale is *certain kinds* of religious principle.

Harold Ernst focuses closely on one of the "particularities of our present time," namely, Catholic voter guides circulated during the 2006 congressional elections. The two guides he studies, one from the right and one from the left, could well be judged guilty, at least to some degree, of Stephen Long's charge of subordinating the church to the political. Like Dennis Hamm, Ernst judges that some documents of the U.S. bishops offer a more promising approach to "voting Catholic."

In my parish in Pennsylvania, two of the six Sunday masses are in Spanish. This local fact points to a wider reality for American Catholic theology: increasingly, both its spokespersons and its audience will be Hispanic. One of the leading American Latino theologians (and incidentally the winner of the 2007 John Courtney

Murray Award, bestowed by the Catholic Theological Society of America) is Virgilio Elizondo. In her article in this volume, Mary Doak shows how Elizondo's approach fulfills the demands of "public theology" while—as the "anti-moderns" would require—"thoroughly rooted in [a] particular ecclesial tradition,"[32] in this case that of Mexican-American Catholicism.

Anne Clifford's article opens another dimension of "public life." Scientific discourse is often said to be "public" in a way that religious discourse is not; scientific data are "scientific" precisely in being "publicly verifiable."[33] Clifford is concerned, however, not with the philosophy of science, but with the politics of science, specifically evolutionary biology, in the United States. She traces the rise of "Intelligent Design," ostensibly a scientific alternative to evolutionary theory, as part of a larger movement of "Christian neo-conservatism," whose purposes are social and political rather than scientific.

Broadening and Reconciling

The last section of this volume is titled "Broadening the Horizons" because each essay extends in a different direction the scope of the discussion of faith in public life. The directions of extension are diverse, but one common feature is that all three essays are centrally concerned with reconciliation.

Mark Allman and Tobias Winright extend the boundaries of Catholic thinking on war. The traditional just war theory addresses the questions of whether to go to war (*jus ad bellum*) and how to conduct warfare (*jus in bello*). The alternative tradition of pacifism is largely concerned with the questions of whether to go to war (answering in the negative) and what are the alternatives to war. What is missing in these traditions is consideration of the ethics of the conduct of the victors after the fighting is over (*jus post bellum*). Allman and Winright propose four *jus post bellum* criteria: just cause, reconciliation, punishment, and rehabilitation, with the latter three corresponding to phases of the post-war process.

Allman and Winright are aware of the hazards of a forced, false "reconciliation" of the "forgive and forget" variety that excuses human rights violations. A similar sort of "reconciliation theology" has been proposed by some church leaders as a response to social conflicts in Latin America; such theology, presented as an alternative to liberation theology, dismisses the liberationists' call for social change. In this volume, Ernesto Valiente broadens the horizons from North to Central America and examines the theology of reconciliation of a prominent liberation theologian, Jon Sobrino of El Salvador. According to Valiente, "Sobrino's Christology and particularly his interpretation of Jesus' resurrection offer important theological resources for the development of a spirituality that fosters social reconciliation as well as a ministry of reconciliation capable of successfully integrating the values of social justice with personal and social forgiveness."[34]

James Cross, finally, addresses a different kind of public life—the church's own public life of sacramental worship. The sacrament of reconciliation as usually celebrated, in the form of private confession, emphasizes individual sins. How ought the church to respond in worship and sacrament to social sin, prominent in Catholic thought (both magisterial and theological) since the Second Vatican Council? Cross argues that the communal celebration of penance is crucial to this response, and he offers several proposals for such celebrations.

There are other respects in which I would have liked to broaden the scope of "public life" in this volume. Well over a hundred papers were presented at the 2007 convention, and forty-eight were submitted for publication here. Among those that were in the end excluded were four on marriage and family life. For Catholic social thought, marriage and family life are not relegated to a private sphere,[35] nor are they purely civic matters. They are truly intermediate institutions, and Catholic thought on the family and on the larger social order should not be as far separated from one another as they now are in our curricula, in which Christian Marriage and Catholic Social Teaching are usually two separate courses.[36] One paper was submitted on Catholic thought in relation to the environment, and to have included it would have broadened our horizons to encompass at least a bit of the area from which the greatest challenges to American and global public life are likely to arise in the century to come.

Finally, no papers were submitted (or presented) on the market economy. And yet, increasingly, matters of the common good, both domestic and global, formerly decided by politics, are relegated to market forces instead. For some, this is an ideal. Douglas Besharov proposes, as one of "six principles that underlie a conservative approach to social problems":

Respect for private choice, often in the form of markets. Conservatives have great faith in the ability of individuals— including the poor—to make sound decisions about their lives. Private choice is a value in itself, but when properly channeled, the individual choices of thousands about the services they receive translate into market forces many times more efficient—and less political—than the top-down decision making of most social programs.[37]

Others, such as the historian Tony Judt, worry that "in forsaking public interest for private advantage, . . . we have also devalued those goods and services that represent the collectivity and its shared purposes."[38] The market—particularly its expansion into areas formerly considered public goods (for example, the privatization of formerly "public utilities")—is an area of public life very much in need of examination through the lenses provided by biblical thought and the tradition of Catholic social thought, an area to which theologians have as yet paid insufficient attention.[39]

Acknowledgments

I am indebted to many people for help with this volume and the process that led to it. I begin with the CTS "Dream Team" of Philip Rossi, the executive director of annual conventions; Bill Portier, the local coordinator of the convention at the University of Dayton; Sally Kenel, the chairperson and editor of research and publications; and Susan Perry of Orbis Books, whose tireless and all-seeing editorial eye caught many errors and stylistic lapses.

I wish to thank the fourteen authors of the articles in this volume for their patience in working with me and their promptness in responding to queries and suggestions. I am grateful to thirty-six other authors and co-authors for submitting papers that were not included; they too were patient, as they waited for final judgments on their papers, many of which will surely be published in other locations eventually.

I owe a special debt to the forty-two members of the CTS who served as anonymous reviewers of the papers submitted to this volume, doing as many as four of them. But those whose patience was tried the most, I suspect, were the sixty students in my two sections of Foundations of Theology (Honors) and one section of

Mysticism East and West in the fall semester of 2007, the grading of whose papers was delayed again and again by my work on this volume—thanks, all of you, for your good will. Finally, my wife, Susan Collinge, whose patience has likewise been tried in many ways, has given support in even more ways throughout this process, and I conclude with special thanks to her.

Notes

[1]Mike Huckabee for President website, http://www.mikehuckabee.com/?FuseAction=Issues.Home (accessed December 1, 2007).

[2]Richard Cohen, "You First, Governor Huckabee," *The Washington Post,* November 20, 2007, A17.

[3]Richard John Neuhaus, *The Naked Public Square: Religion and Democracy in America* (Grand Rapids: Eerdmans, 1986).

[4]Schindler's paper is part of a larger work in progress and is not included in this volume. For a brief presentation of Schindler's argument, see David Schindler, "Multiculturalism and Civil Community inside the Liberal State: Truth and (Religious) Freedom," *Revista Española de Teología* 67 (2007): 373-85.

[5]Ibid., 374.

[6]Ibid., 381.

[7]Ibid., 382.

[8]Ibid., 380.

[9]Ibid., 383.

[10]See William L. Portier, "Does Systematic Theology Have a Future? A Response to Lieven Boeve," below, 135.

[11]Both Newman and Long wrote their doctoral dissertations under the supervision of Stanley Hauerwas.

[12]D. Stephen Long, *John Wesley's Moral Theology: The Quest for God and Goodness* (Nashville: Kingswood Books, 2005), 210. Quoted in Elizabeth Newman, "The Public Politics of Teresa's Vision," below, 73.

[13]Mary Doak, "Table Fellowship in a Land of Gated Communities: Virgilio Elizondo as Public Theologian," below, 213, quoting John Milbank, *Theology and Social Theory: Beyond Secular Reason* (Oxford: Blackwell, 1990), 327.

[14]Doak, "Table Fellowship in a Land of Gated Communities," below, 202.

[15]This language originates in the church-sect typology of Ernst Troeltsch. See John Sniegocki, "Implementing Catholic Social Teaching," below, 47 and note 34.

[16]Portier, "Does Systematic Theology Have a Future?" below, 141.

[17]See also Kristin E. Heyer, *Prophetic and Public: The Social Witness of American Catholicism* (Washington: Georgetown University Press, 2006).

[18]Dennis Hamm, "The Bible and Public Life: Excuses, Abuses, and Some Powerful Uses," below, 25.

[19]Sniegocki, "Implementing Catholic Social Teaching," below, 39.

[20]Ibid., below, 47.

[21]Newman, "The Public Politics of Teresa's Vision," below, 63.

[22]Ibid., below, 73.

[23]Murray is mentioned or cited in six articles in this volume.

[24]Fannin, "Religious Liberty and the Common Good: An Engagement with the Catholic Americanist Tradition," below, 89. Fannin takes the word "totem" from Portier.

[25]Ibid., below, 97.

[26]Jacques Maritain in Maritain and Marston Morse, "The Princeton Statement," below, 122.

[27]Jacques Maritain, *Man and the State* (Chicago: University of Chicago Press, 1951).

[28]Portier, "Does Systematic Theology Have a Future?" below, 147.

[29]Ibid., below, 140.

[30]See Perry, *The Idea of Human Rights: Four Inquiries* (New York: Oxford University Press, 1997).

[31]See Perry, *Under God? Religious Faith and Liberal Democracy* (Cambridge: Cambridge University Press, 2006).

[32]Doak, "Table Fellowship in a Land of Gated Communities," below, 203.

[33]As Ian Barbour noted long ago, however, "They are 'publicly verifiable'—not because 'anyone' could verify them, but because they represent the common experience of the scientific community at a given time. For there is always an interpretive component present" (*Issues in Science and Religion* [New York: Harper & Row, 1966], 139).

[34]Ernesto Valiente, "Living as 'Risen Beings' in a Reconciled World: Resources from Jon Sobrino," below, 266.

[35]As in the bourgeois family system critically examined in Christopher Lasch's classic *Haven in a Heartless World: The Family Besieged* (New York: Basic Books, 1977).

[36]See Pope Benedict XVI's 2008 Message for World Day of Peace, "The Human Family, A Community of Peace," http://www.vatican.va/holy_father/benedict_xvi/messages/peace/.

[37]Douglas Besharov, "The Right Kind of Hand Up," *The Washington Post*, November 19, 2007, A17. Notice how, in the quotation, "political" is a pejorative term.

[38]Tony Judt, "The Wrecking Ball of Innovation," *The New York Review of Books*, December 6, 2007, 26.

[39]One recent examination of markets from a Catholic point of view is Daniel Finn, *The Moral Ecology of Markets: Assessing Claims about Markets and Justice* (Cambridge: Cambridge University Press, 2006).

Part I

RETRIEVING CATHOLIC TRADITIONS

The Bible and Public Life

Excuses, Abuses, and Some Powerful Uses

Dennis Hamm

Some Christians quote the Bible to *excuse* themselves from in-tegrating their faith with their life as citizens. They invoke sayings like "The poor you will always have with you" and "My kingdom is not of this world" to divorce faith from politics. Others, whose faith life is shaped by the doomsday scenario that surfaces in the "Left Behind" novel series, are convinced that biblical prophecy understood as Rapture and imminent catastrophe renders irrel-evant any concern for such earthly issues as global warming, pov-erty, and universal health care. Still others, such as recent popes and most Roman Catholic bishops, encouraged by a tradition of social teaching that integrates insights from the Bible with con-cepts from philosophy and the data of the social sciences, urge a *vigorous involvement* in public issues. Already, it must be evident that I consider the first two cases examples of *abuses* of scripture in relation to public life and the third one an example of a proper *use* of scripture in that regard.

A distinctly *non*-biblical anecdote helps me think about these things. In the opening pages of his *Situation Ethics* (1966), Joseph Fletcher tells this story:

> A friend of mine arrived in St. Louis just as a presidential campaign was ending, and the cab driver, not being above the battle, volunteered his testimony. "I and my father and grandfather before me, and their fathers, have always been straight-ticket Republicans." "Ah," said my friend, who is himself a Republican, "I take it that means you will vote for

15

Senator So-and-So." "No," said the driver, "there are times when a man has to push his principles aside and do the right thing."[1]

Quite apart from Fletcher's use of that anecdote, the cabbie's remark is a wonderful starting point for thinking about the sources of moral decision-making. The humor of the remark derives, of course, from the impossibility of ascertaining what's right without evaluating one's options against some principled framework. But I suspect that part of the humor also springs from the insight that most choices, in the thick of the competing claims in a person's daily life, private and public, are made quite spontaneously, drawing on the instincts of character informed by one's upbringing, formal education, social setting, status—especially those "habits of the heart" that comprise the focus of virtue ethics. In that mix, the language, imagery, and themes of the Bible may, or may not, have a significant place. Those of us who teach, preach, and otherwise minister in Christian communities usually work with the conviction that, for better or for worse, the biblical tradition plays a huge part in this formation process.

This paper probes some of the ways Christians use the Bible as they work out the relationship between faith and public life. It has three parts. First, I review two kinds of abuses of scripture in connection with public life—the citation of certain New Testament passages to divorce faith from politics, and the fundamentalist doomsday scenario that informs the "Left Behind" novels; second, I review three examples of what I consider some appropriate uses of scripture with regard to public life; and third, I offer seven practical conclusions.

Some Abuses of Scripture

Five Biblical Texts Often Used to Dodge Political Responsibility

In my experience, five New Testament texts frequently turn up as rationales for separating Christian faith from politics. I list them here and, in each case, show how using the passage as a warrant for divorcing Christian life from public involvement entails a misunderstanding of the biblical text.[2]

1. "The poor you will always have with you" (Mt 26:11; Mk 14:7; Jn 12:8). This statement by Jesus during a dinner in Bethany

is sometimes taken as an assurance from Jesus himself that poverty will always be part of the human condition, and that, therefore, it is futile to try to mitigate it. In fact, Jesus' words are not primarily about the poor but about himself. Mark likely expects his readers to make a connection between the (king-like) anointing of Jesus' head, the reference to his approaching death, and his status as Anointed One (Christ) to be achieved in death and resurrection. Further, Mark's inclusion of the words "and whenever you will you can do good to them" indicates that Jesus' words allude to the Jubilee legislation of Deuteronomy 15, especially verse 11: "The needy will never be lacking in the land; that is why I command you to open your hand to your poor and needy kinsman. . . ." The Deuteronomist's reference to the poor is clearly not a prediction of a permanent underclass. Rather, envisioning a situation in which "there should be no one of you in need" (verse 4), the text implies a mandate to help people in economic need *whenever* that circumstance occurs. There is no reason to deny that *Jesus'* allusion to that text carries the same meaning.

2. "Render to Caesar the things that are Caesar's, and to God the things that are God's" (Mk 12:17; Mt 22:21, and Lk 20:25, in the King James Version [KJV], Rheims, and New International Version [NIV] translations, the version that most people recall). This statement is sometimes taken to imply that God and civil authorities govern separate realities and that church leaders should confine themselves to the "things of God" and refrain from commenting on such Caesar-like things as taxation and other economic structures. But Jesus' reference to the emperor's image on the denarius raises an unspoken question: If the emperor's image on the Roman coin is a sign of his authority over the empire's monetary system, then what carries the *image of God* (indicating *God's* ownership and authority)? The answer of course, right out of the first chapter of Genesis, is that all human beings bear the image of God. What we have, then, in Jesus' famous remark about what is Caesar's and what is God's is not a demarcation of separate worlds but an assertion about the reign of God: the Creator is lord over all creation. And the details of social arrangements like taxation and social order are to be worked out by the faithful within that horizon of divine ownership—precisely what Jesus' adversaries were failing to do in their effort to have him killed. This Jewish and Christian worldview thus warrants both cooperation with, and critical scrutiny of, such things as the structures of taxation and governance.

3. "The kingdom of God is within you" (Lk 17:21b, KJV, Rheims, NIV). This verse, especially in this translation (*"within you"*), is sometimes used to argue that the kingdom proclaimed by Jesus pertains mainly to individual interiority *apart from any social dimension*. The alternative translation *"among* you"—recognizing that the Greek pronoun is plural—reflects the ambiguity of the phrase *entos hymôn*, which can be rendered either "within you" or "among you." While Jesus surely addresses the importance of interior disposition, the context of Luke 17, where the grateful Samaritan leper has just returned to acknowledge the power of God present *in their midst* in the person of Jesus, supports the translation *"among* you." It is a misunderstanding, then, to hijack this saying as a mandate for interpreting the kingdom sayings of Jesus in support of a privatized faith that distances itself from social involvement.

4. "My kingdom is not of this world" (Jn 18:36a, in the King James, Rheims and NIV versions, the wording that most people recall). While this translation is valid, the phrasing is open to the misunderstanding that Christ's kingdom has nothing to do with the world in which we live. The Greek phrase in question, *ek tou kosmou*, is best translated *"from* this world," as in the New Revised Standard Version. In the context of Jesus' conversation with Pilate, the issue is not the *reach* of Jesus' kingly authority but its *source*. The authority by which the risen Jesus endows the disciples with the Holy Spirit and sends them into the world as he had been sent by the Father (Jn 20:21-22) is surely an authority that has effect *here*, in this world. For exponents of the Catholic social tradition, this means that any issue of public policy impinging upon the dignity of persons must be addressed within the Christian perspective of Jesus' reign over our lives here and now.

5. "Let every person be subordinate to the higher authorities, for there is no authority except from God, and those that exist have been established by God" (Rom 13:1). While Romans 13:1-7 is rightly used by the Church to support obedience to civil authorities to pursue the common good, this passage has sometimes been invoked to support a passive and uncritical attitude toward public officials. The danger of such an interpretation became famously evident during the rise of Nazism in Germany, when some Christian pastors, urging their congregants to cooperate with Hitler and his agents, quoted Romans 13 as justification for that policy. Hitler was, after all, a legitimately elected official. Paul, however,

was making the case to the Roman Christians that, *normally*, civil authorities are servants of divine providence (knowingly or not). Obedience to such officials was a way of loving one's neighbor as oneself and of fostering the order necessary for harmony in society. Civic cooperation was, indeed, a way of being obedient to God. However, Paul was writing in the 50s, when the empire sponsored a civil order mainly benign with respect to the Christian movement. Some forty years later, though, when Roman officials in some quarters were trying to compel Christians to participate in local liturgies of emperor worship, the author of another document, the book of Revelation, could portray Rome as an instrument of Satan, indeed as all four evil empires of the vision of Daniel 7 rolled into one (Revelation 13). We can be grateful that the canon of the New Testament contains both Romans 13 and Revelation 13 (by happy coincidence, the same chapter number). The creative tension between the two passages serves as a reminder that Catholic tradition holds that Christian citizens are called to exercise intelligence and conscience in their collaboration with, and sometimes resistance to, public authorities. Proper respect for secular authority does not release Christians from the responsibilities of engaging as faithful citizens in political action and of advocating for justice and peace.

So much for New Testament passages often used to distance faith from public life. Now I'd like to address a particular kind of fundamentalism that encourages dangerous political attitudes and behavior, a phenomenon that often goes unrecognized by mainstream U.S. Catholics. I refer to the doomsday scenario embodied in the "Left Behind" series of novels.

The "Left Behind" Books: A Quasi-Biblical Fantasy, with Real-World Consequences

Most of us who work in religious studies and theology are at least vaguely familiar with the story of Premillennial Dispensationalism. Many, I suspect, dismiss it as an odd and recent growth on the Christian tradition that has found its way into some lucrative pop fiction and fringe films—in short, a phenomenon unworthy of serious study and curricular attention. That is a naïve assessment, on several counts. Odd and recent though it may be, this scenario has the *appearance* of biblical warrant and frames the faith of possibly millions of U.S. Christians. Those who subscribe to this scenario tend to denigrate ecumenism, to suspect any efforts at a systemic approach to the universal common good (such as the United Nations, the Kyoto treaty), to scoff at efforts to forestall nuclear proliferation, and to give uncritical support to the policies of the state of Israel. Allow me to review the kind of information we need to share with our students and faith communities if we are to help them think critically about this abuse of scripture.[3]

First, while it is put forth as, and *sounds like*, basic Christianity, this end-time scenario is a relatively recent and mainly North American development, traceable to John Nelson Darby (1800-1882), a former Anglican priest, founder of a sect called the Plymouth Brethren, and formulator of the worldview that scholars have dubbed Premillennial Dispensationalism (hereafter PD). A disciple of Darby, Cyrus Scofield, forty-three years his junior, systemized Darby's vision and incorporated it in an annotated version of the King James Bible, which came to be called *The Scofield Reference Bible*, first published in 1909. Hal Lindsey's *Late Great Planet Earth* published an updated version of the vision in 1970; it sold seven million copies. And now the same scenario, further updated, is finding an even wider public: in the forty million-plus copies sold of Tim LaHaye and Jerry B. Jenkins' "Left Behind" novel series, sixteen volumes so far.

How does the PD scenario unfold?[4] The Darby-Scofield schema finds in scripture seven "dispensations" in the story of God's relationship with human beings—seven "economies" of salvation, each with its own covenant and its example of ultimate human failure. The first four are found in Genesis—(1) Innocence (Gn 1-3), (2) Conscience (the Fall to the covenant with Noah), (3) Human Government (Gn 8:20-12:1, Noah to the Call of Abraham), and (4) Promise (Gn 12:1 to Moses). In terms of their theological and practical import, the final three dispensations are the most important: (5) Law (the Sinai covenant through the public ministry of Christ), (6) Grace (Christ's death to the present, also known as the Church Age) and, finally, (7) the Millennium (Revelation 20, beginning with Christ's return to earth, also known as the Kingdom Age).

In this scenario, the Age of Grace functions as a kind of parenthetical period that is closed with the onset of the seventh dispensation, the Millennium, a literal thousand-year period during which the Christian faithful reign on earth with Jesus *after* the Second

Coming.[5] Exponents of this premillennialist scenario understand us to be at the end of the dispensation of Grace and on the verge of the Millennium. Most of biblical prophecy, therefore, is interpreted in ways that virtually bypass the *first* coming of Jesus, including his life, teaching, death, and resurrection; for premillennialists, prophecy pertains mainly to events that are current and imminent in our day. (That is what "Prophecy Workshops" are about—how scripture is fulfilled in contemporary and future events.) Consequently, the most crucial features of the PD scenario involve the final years before the second coming.

These final years entail four movements. They begin with the Rapture of the truly faithful Christians; the rest—flawed Christians and non-Christians alike—are "left behind" and given a seven-year second chance (the period of Tribulation) to become true believers in Christ. Meanwhile, there are some preliminaries to the onset of the Second Coming[6]: the restoration of Israel (interpreted as the U.N.'s establishment of the modern state of Israel in 1948), the repossession of Jerusalem, the building of the third temple on the Temple Mount and the restoration of its liturgy, the revival of Rome (understood as the fourth kingdom of Daniel 2 and 7), the emergence of the Antichrist (Revelation 13, seen as pointing to a modern tyrant with a power base in Rome), the emergence of a one-world religious system (an unholy alliance between New Age occultism and liberal, ecumenical pseudo-Christianity), the conversion of one-third of the world's Jews to Christianity (Zec 13:8-9 = the 144,000 of Rv 7:1-8); the conversion of countless Gentiles by those Jewish Christians, the invasion of Israel by Russia and its allies (Armageddon, Rv 16:16), and finally the coming of Christ amidst a thermonuclear blast.

What's wrong with this picture? First, it violates the interpretation of prophecy provided by the New Testament itself:

• The gospel writers and Paul envisioned the end times, or the Jewish "Age to Come," as *already inaugurated* in the life, death, and resurrection of Jesus and the Pentecostal outpouring of the Spirit (see, for example, 1 Cor 10:11; Heb 1:1-2; Lk 11:20)—not two millennia in their future.

• For the New Testament authors, the end-time *restoration of Israel* occurred in the establishment of the Christian community beginning in Jerusalem on Pentecost (see, for example, Gal 6:16; Jas 1:1; Lk 22:28-30; Acts 1:1-2:47)—not in the future establishment of a secular state nineteen centuries later.

• Whereas the PD scenario requires the physical *construction of a third temple on the Temple Mount in Jerusalem* (currently occupied by the Muslim shrine of the Dome of the Rock and the Al-Aqsa Mosque), for the New Testament authors the expected end-time temple is the Christian community established after Easter (see, for example, 1 Cor 3:16-17 and 1 Pt 2:4-5).

• Whereas the PD scenario understands OT prophecy requiring a literal *restoration of temple worship*, for the NT writers, the renewal of the temple and its liturgy has been established through the death and resurrection of Jesus. The community is now the privileged locus of access to the presence of God, and the church's life in Christ constitutes the primary end-time form of worship.[7]

• Regarding the Rapture of the PD scenario, the seed of that unusual idea, 1 Thessalonians 4:17, expressed Paul's idea of what might happen to the living at the time of the Parousia using a combination of triumphal entry and assumption imagery, not to a "rapture" happening *seven years prior* to the Parousia. Paul imagines the Parousia moment in yet another way in 1 Corinthians 15:51-52: "We will all be *changed* [*allagēsometha*]"—that is, not a rapture but a transformation.

• The whole effort to discern signs of the imminence of the second coming flies in the face of Jesus' own teaching: "But of that day or hour, no one knows, neither the angels in heaven, nor the Son, but only the Father" (Mk 13:32).

In short, the best response to the misunderstanding of scripture embodied in this doomsday scenario is a careful study of the New Testament itself, especially its Christian interpretation of Old Testament prophecy as fulfilled in Jesus, the church, and its mission.

Does this scenario have political consequences? Yes, dangerous ones.

• Consider the consequences of trying to construct a third temple on the Temple Mount in Jerusalem. That would entail destroying the Muslim shrine and mosque that currently occupy what has been for thirteen hundred years the third most sacred place in Islam.[8]

• This left-behind scenario also leads to an uncritical support of the policies of the state of Israel, because of the role it plays in their plot (full geographical restoration, followed by the conversion of many Jews, worldwide, to Christianity, leading to *their* mission to the rest of the world). Incidentally, in the "Left Behind" books, the United Nations and the project of world peace through disarmament are tools of the Antichrist and instruments of Satan.[9]

• The conviction that the end of the world (as we know it) is approaching makes ecological responsibility irrelevant.

Having reviewed some abuses of scripture in efforts to divorce faith from public life, and that other kind of abuse embodied in the "Left Behind" doomsday scenario as a wrong-headed interpretation of faith's approach to public life,[10] let us ease our minds by considering some helpful examples of the appropriate use of the biblical tradition.

Three Helpful Models for Using Scripture to Relate Faith and Public Life

The Peace and Justice Pastorals of the 1980s

In the 1980s the U.S. Catholic bishops modeled for the universal church a new way of writing pastoral letters on social issues. This new way entailed two new processes: 1) broad consultation with both experts and "grass-roots" responses through several drafts and 2) a use of biblical traditions that focused more on broad vision and grand themes rather than on shoring up principles with apposite but atomistic quotations. It is the latter feature—the holistic reading of scripture—that invites our attention here. For example, in *The Challenge of Peace: God's Promise and Our Response—A Pastoral Letter on War and Peace*,[11] before the bishops take up the more philosophical questions of the nature of peace, the presumption against war, and the principle of legitimate self-defense, they spend some fifty paragraphs reviewing themes from scripture that pertain to war and peace, especially the kingdom of God, first in the Old Testament (conveyed through themes of God-given *shalom*, covenant, and prophetic hope) and then in the New Testament (as embodied in the person, teaching, and ministry of Jesus, the nonviolent Messiah). The section on "The Kingdom and History," then, sketches the church's efforts to respond to Jesus' teaching in theory and practice. This developmental approach—telling the "story" of the People of God as they respond to issues of war and peace over the centuries and interpreting their experience through reflection on biblical tradition—sets the scene for a fresh integration of Jesus' nonviolence and love of enemies with the criteria of the just war theory for our day, when the existence of weapons of mass destruction renders problematic the criteria of proportionality and discrimination between combatants and noncombatants. This method of approaching contemporary questions by first reviewing pertinent aspects of the biblical tradition and then the post-biblical historical experience provides a model for using scripture to relate faith to the issues of public life.

Three years later, our bishops did it again in *Economic Justice for All: Pastoral Letter on Catholic Social Teaching and the U. S. Economy*[12] (1986). Before they address specific contemporary issues, the bishops spend almost a third of the document on a chapter entitled "The Christian Vision of Economic Life." This vision is spelled out under two headings: first, "Biblical Perspectives," then "Ethical Norms for Economic Life" (in traditional terms, first the givens of *revelation*, then arguments from *reason*). The biblical part is a powerful elaboration of certain themes moving through the First and Second Testaments—creation, covenant, community, the reign of God, poverty, riches, the challenge of discipleship, and the preferential option for the poor. All of this unpacks the governing thesis: "*The dignity of the human person, realized in community with others, is the criterion against which all aspects of economic life must be measured. All human beings, therefore, are ends to be served by the institutions that make up the economy, not means to be exploited for more narrowly defined goals*" (par. 28). Already, we can hear a biblical theme elaborated by concepts from philosophy.

The theme of creation focuses on the dignity of human beings created in the image of God and given the role of stewarding creation for the common good, as portrayed in Genesis 1. The authors survey the range of justice language (*mishpat* and *sedaqah*), showing how biblical justice is more comprehensive than subsequent philosophical definitions, being concerned not simply with a strict definition of rights and duties but with the "richness of the human condition before God and within society"—life lived in covenant relationships.

The section on ethical norms, then, reviews the framework that philosophers have supplied regarding human relationships, in terms of duties and rights, and justice in its three dimensions as commutative, distributive, and social. The bishops stress that the common good requires not only the recognition of *civil* and *political* rights—already recognized in our culture—but also specifically *economic* rights not fully acknowledged in our system: the right to food, shelter, clothing, medical care, rest, and basic education, for example. All this is a way of spelling out biblical justice. Even the preferential option for the poor can be justified by reason as a sure means for society to meet the needs of *all*, for the condition of its weakest members is a sign of the health or illness of the whole body.

In the light of this biblical and philosophical elaboration of Catholic social teaching, the rest of the pastoral analyzes four specific issues: employment, poverty, food and agriculture, and the relationship of the U.S. economy to the developing nations. Then it proposes "a new American experiment—partnership for the common good."

Like the peace pastoral issued three years earlier, this document employs a new style of using scripture in an ecclesial document. Rather than using the more traditional mode of proof-texting and atomistic quotation, these documents preface their treatments of specific issues with extended presentations of pertinent biblical themes. By the way they use scripture, these pastoral letters on peace and economic justice teach that the Bible has more than maxims to offer; it contains narratives that teach a way of seeing that leads to a way of being.

In reviewing these pastoral letters at such length, I realize that I am rehearsing material quite familiar to most teachers of college theology. I remind us of these documents because they remain lucid examples of an important U.S. Catholic way of using the biblical tradition in relating Christian faith to the issues of public life. While some U.S. Christians use scripture alone in their approach to public life (whether to engage or to withdraw from the public arena) and others prefer to avoid religious language altogether in political discourse, these pastoral letters of the 1980s can serve as a reminder of two realities: 1) we are learning to read the biblical traditions whole and in a developmental way, culminating in Jesus; and 2) the mainstream Roman Catholic tradition is not content to be nurtured only with the themes, imagery, and narratives of the Bible; rather, it also draws on the tools of philosophy and the social sciences to integrate the "thick" biblical tradition into its theory and praxis.

"Faithful Citizenship: A Catholic Call to Political Responsibility"[13]

Since 1975, the U.S. Catholic bishops have issued a pastoral letter twelve months before each presidential election, reminding U.S. Catholic citizens that participating in the political processes of our country is a duty of faith, that we should base that participation, our voting especially, on judgments of conscience informed by the full range of Catholic social teaching. Given that the subject of this letter is precisely the relationship of faith to public life, it is instructive to examine its use of scripture. We shall look at the 2003 edition of this quadrennial letter, the seventh since the start of this process more than thirty years ago.[14] Though the document refers to scripture only sporadically, its use of the biblical theme of vocation and other biblical allusions clearly ground the letter's coherent vision of peace and justice. Already in Msgr. William P. Fay's prefatory statement expressing the purpose of the letter we hear biblically based language:

> The purpose of this statement is to communicate the church's teaching that every Catholic *is called* to an active and faith-filled citizenship, based on a properly informed conscience, in which each *disciple of Christ* publicly *witnesses* to the Church's commitment to human life and dignity with *special preference for the poor and vulnerable* [italics added].

Fay strikes four biblical notes in a single sentence here. The notion of "call" invokes the biblical category for the vocation of prophets. The reference to the U.S. Catholic population as "disciples of Christ" reflects a recent and growing appreciation for discipleship as a key theme in the New Testament's portrayal of the church as community of disciples, flawed learners, and followers of Jesus, as portrayed in the four gospels. That we are "called to *witness*" picks up a major theme from Acts defining the church's mission as precisely that, a witnessing community that embodies what it witnesses to. And the reference to a "special preference for the poor and vulnerable" picks up the biblically based theme that the universal church has learned from recent experience of the Latin American church: a preferential option for the poor.

As we move through the document, the scriptural theme of this "call" is developed. The claim for a biblically informed viewpoint comes with annotated allusions: "The *Word of God and the teachings of the Church* give us a particular way of viewing the world. Scripture calls us to 'choose life' [Dt 30:19-20], to serve 'the least of these' [Mt 25:34-35], to 'hunger and thirst' for justice and to be 'peacemakers' [Mt 5:3-12]." The call to engagement is also expressed in biblical allusions: "We are called to be moral leaven [Mt 13:33] and salt of the earth [Mt 5:13-16]."

The biblical foundation is also implicit in the exposition of seven themes of Catholic social teaching. Allusions to the Genesis creation accounts support the life and dignity of every human being ("created in the image and likeness of God"), the dignity of work ("continuing participation in God's act of creation"), and care for God's creation ("our stewardship of the Earth is a form of participation in God's act of creating and sustaining the world"). The theme of solidarity is supported by an ironic allusion to Genesis 4 ("we are our brothers' and sisters' keepers"). The authorial committee provides specific biblical references for the fourth theme, the option for the poor and vulnerable:

> Scripture teaches that God has a special concern for the poor and vulnerable [Ex 22:20-26, regarding widows, orphans, immigrants, and debtors]. The prophets denounced injustice toward the poor as a lack of fidelity to the God of Israel [Is 1:21-23; Jer 5:28]. Jesus, who identified himself with "the least of these" [Mt 25:40-45, the Last Judgment scenario] came to preach "good news to the poor, liberty to captives . . . and to set the downtrodden free" [Lk 4:18-19, phrases from Jesus' application of Isaiah 61 to himself during his "inaugural" homily in the Nazareth synagogue].

Having used allusions to the biblical tradition to join faith to public engagement and to elaborate seven themes that animate Catholic social teaching, the document then proceeds to name four "Moral Priorities for Public Life"—protecting human life, supporting families, pursuing social justice, and practicing global solidarity. To implement these priorities the bishops advocate some forty specific policies, addressing, for example, abortion, cloning, assisted suicide, euthanasia, the intentional targeting of civilians in war or terrorist attacks, biotechnology, preemptive and "preventive" use of military force, nuclear proliferation, anti-personnel landmines, the global trade in arms, and the death penalty; the protection of the institution of marriage, just wages, the nurturing and education of children; employment, just wage, discrimination, the right to unionize, economic freedom, initiative, and the right to own private property, child tax credits, appropriate welfare reform, affordable and accessible health care, affordable housing, food security for all, sustainable agriculture, a decent return for farmers, just wages for farm workers, alleviation of global poverty, the spread of nuclear, biological, and chemical weapons, support for appropriate United Nations programs, other international bodies, international law, and justice for immigrants.

In none of these policy statements is there any mention of the biblical traditions. Nor is any such mention necessary. The biblically based vision was already expressed in the introduction and in the seven themes, and anyone familiar with that vision will recognize that all of the issues named relate in some way to the Catholic understanding of the divine gift of life, the dignity of persons and human work, the virtue of solidarity, and the need for special attention to the poor and vulnerable—as these things are understood in the light of biblical revelation climaxing in Jesus Christ as model and enabler of the fullness of life with God.

Like the U.S. pastorals of the 1980s, the "Faithful Citizenship" letter shows that the place for Bible talk is not so much in the rhetoric of public discourse as in the inner life of the faith community as it orients itself, in catechesis and worship, to be sent into the larger culture of work, family life, and politics. The document presumes a biblically literate readership, for whom allusions are enough to make the connection between faith and public life.

The Catechism of the Catholic Church *and the* Compendium of the Social Doctrine of the Church

Some responses from the academy to the publication, in 1994, of the *Catechism of the Catholic Church*[15] were critical of its use of scripture, finding some treatments of the biblical traditions out-of-date with respect to contemporary scholarship. This apparent lapse is understandable, given that the purpose of the *Catechism* was the essentially conservative one of representing the teaching of the church, which necessarily entails some traditional uses of certain biblical texts. That said, on the question of the relationship of faith to public life and the developing tradition of Catholic social teaching, the *Catechism*'s use of scripture is, in my opinion, not only appropriate but pedagogically powerful. Following a long tradition of the moral manuals, the *Catechism* uses the Ten Commandments to organize the presentation of the specifics of Catholic social teaching. The topic of faith and public life is first addressed at length within the treatment of the Fourth Commandment. It may seem a stretch to move from "honor your father and your mother" to political responsibility. The rationale: the family is "the original cell of social life"[16] and, thus, the portal, both chronologically and rationally, to all the other social relationships and the exercise of authority they entail. When the *Catechism* takes up the duties of citizens in that section, it evokes the classic applications of Romans 13:7 and 1 Timothy 2:2. At the same time, it refers to Matthew 22:21 ("render to Caesar . . . and to God") to assert the primacy of conscience: "The citizen is obliged in conscience not to follow the directives of civil authorities when they are contrary to the demands of the moral order, to the fundamental rights of persons or the teachings of the Gospel."[17]

What becomes pedagogically powerful is the *Catechism*'s move to treat most of Catholic social teaching under the fifth and seventh commandments—"You shall not kill" and "You shall not steal." While the Catholic social tradition, particularly that of the past 110 years, has grown to be richly complex and philosophical, presenting that teaching under the rubric of the fifth and seventh commandments is a stunning reminder that our elaborate social tradition is indeed a spelling out of a basic biblical given, the mandates against killing and stealing. Thus, "The Challenge of Peace" unpacks "Thou shalt not kill" for our time, and "Economic Justice for All" does the same for "Thou shalt not steal."[18] A subsequent, equally authoritative Vatican document, *The Compendium of the Social Doctrine of the Church*,[19] mirrors the structure of the U.S. pastorals of the 1980s by prefacing each of the chapters on specific issues with two to four pages reviewing pertinent biblical themes.[20]

Some Practical Conclusions

In our efforts to relate faith to public life, we use scripture in two very different arenas: 1) the "insider" discourse within our community of faith—in catechesis, worship, preaching, formation of conscience, and communal deliberation regarding advocacy in the civic arena; and 2) the "public" discourse of advocacy within that civic arena. The first six practical conclusions pertain to our in-house discourse.

1. *The Catholic way of using scripture in relating faith to public life combines faith and reason.* Even in this brief sampling of recent church teaching pertaining to faith and public life, we can recognize that the Roman Catholic use of scripture is at home with an easy blend of the biblical tradition and philosophical reflection on experience and the data of the social sciences. Mainstream Christians are *not*, strictly speaking, "People of the Book." We are, first, "people of a *Person*"—Jesus of Nazareth, understood as Messiah, Son of God incarnate, sent by the Father, risen Lord, mediator of the Holy Spirit. We read the New Testament as the definitive post-Easter interpretation of that person, and we understand the Greek canon of the Hebrew Scriptures in the light of the person and teaching of Jesus. Although we accept the canon of scripture as the full revelation of what the Creator has done in Jesus, still the Bible is not for us an "answer book" regarding the social issues of our day. To arrive at decisions of praxis, we follow the model of the Jerusalem Council as reflected in Acts 15: we integrate reflection on experience with the biblical tradition to come up with policy decisions for the living out of faith in daily, public life. What seems to be emerging in church teaching since Vatican Council II is a more consistent and holistic use of scripture to ground our philosophical reflection and practical action. This is evident in the examples reviewed here, the U.S. pastorals of the 1980s, the *Catechism*, the "Faithful Citizenship" letter in its quadrennial redactions, and the Vatican *Compendium of the Social Doctrine of the Church*. The practical conclusion that I reach after considering this ready mix of reason and revelation is that our catechetics and homiletics need to emphasize this intimate connection. That will require a surge of effort in the direction of *biblical literacy* in our schools and churches.

2. *The biblical tradition of God as Creator is a rich but—at least in popular discourse—an underused and widely misunderstood source of the Catholic social tradition.* We need to learn, teach, and preach it better. In popular culture, references to Christian faith in a Creator typically surface in discussions of "creationism" (the biblical narratives understood in a literalistic and non-contextual way) and "intelligent design"—discussions that are preoccupied with the question of *origins* and framed largely in

denial of the theory of evolution. These discussions and debates have served to distract from the traditional faith in a Creator who has not only originated but *sustains* all that is (a notion compatible with the theory of evolution and closer to the intent of the implied authors of the biblical accounts). The uncoupling of creation from a fixation on explaining origins enables a Christian faith in the sustaining Creator to explore more fully other important aspects of the biblical creation accounts. I mean such themes as the equality of men and women as images of God, human beings as part of (not *apart from*) the rest of nature, human beings as stewards of the Earth whose ultimate owner is God, the universal destination of all goods, the dignity of work, and the place of Sabbath rest in one's life with God and one another.

Ecologists rightly lament our culture's way of making a dichotomy between humanity and nature. Non-human nature is spontaneously treated as something to be "tamed" by humanity, a mind-set warranting an exploitative and unjust use of the earth. And religious discourse often presents nature as simply the backdrop against which the drama of humanity's relationship to God is played out. Yet, the biblical accounts present humanity as *part* of nature—even as humanity is assigned a special ministerial role with respect to the rest of nature. It is a message the West needs to relearn.

We live at a moment when the human family is more and more using its arable land in a mode of industrialized farming that many experts judge unsustainable. The agrarian setting of much of the Hebrew Bible provides an opportunity for contemporary scholars and preachers to help their largely urban communities recognize that we post-moderns still live on food grown in the soil, and that our faith-understanding of creation calls us to see that the land is used to feed the hungry before it can be used to earn maximum profit for the satisfied.

3. *We need to learn, teach, and preach better the New Testament meaning of the kingdom of God.* Though most NT scholars agree that the reign of God is neither a code name for a particular social program nor a place name for the realm of God, this central symbol in Jesus' preaching surely has something to do with a social order created in response to the righteousness of God expressed in Jesus' life, sealed by his death and resurrection, and lived by people called to be his disciples. Submitting to God's reign surely entails a community ordered in justice and love. Jesus uses the kinship image to say this when he calls "brother and sister and

mother" everyone who does the will of God (Mk 3:35). Teaching and preaching the biblical meaning of this centerpiece of Jesus' teaching will remain one of the best things we can do to help people integrate gospel language with Catholic social teaching regarding issues of peace and justice.

4. *Biblical justice is more comprehensive than ethics and forensic justice; let us explore the rich complexity of biblical justice.* Though it has sometimes been a cause of confusion, it is a happy fact that the same semantic field of justice words (*tsedaqah, mishpat, dikaiosunē*) embraces both the range of human relationships in community (what we call commutative, distributive, and social justice) *and* God's saving fidelity to the covenant promises. The fact that biblical justice language covers both the horizontal and the vertical dimensions (both human justice and the process of divine justification) is a powerful reminder that the biblical vision of justice not only points to the content and duty of human relationships, it also proclaims the good news that the righteous presence of God is available to heal, liberate, and strengthen weak human beings in their fumbling efforts to live out that justice. We can help people understand that.[21]

Some people tend to speak of *biblical* justice *in contrast to* the justice of the *philosophers,* as if Jerusalem and Athens had nothing to say to each other. Some would even use that disjunction to argue that the justice talk of the Bible has nothing to do with the politics of today, as if *biblical* justice were somehow individualistically religious, as distinct from *secular* justice understood as a matter for the police and the law courts. The shapers of the Catholic tradition knew perfectly well that they were using the categories of philosophical reflection (rights, duties, and the analysis of relationships between individuals, between groups and society, between states and the world as a whole) to explicate the biblical vision of justice. As theological scholars, we can explore and teach that relationship.[22]

5. *Granted its dangers when interpreted fundamentalistically (as in the Doomsday scenario of the "Left Behind" series), the book of Revelation remains pertinent for Christians in the twenty-first century.* We can still embrace John the Seer's vision that Christian hope for the future is rooted in the past, the Easter victory of the Lamb that was slain. All subsequent struggles for peace and justice—past, present and future—are simply mop-up skirmishes after a victory achieved long ago. And while the literal target of

the recycled imagery of Daniel 7 is the Roman empire of the 90s of the first century, that imagery has enduring value as a caution against the temptations of empire—a crucial lesson for citizens of a nation holding the greatest military power on Earth and moved by an official policy of "Full Spectrum [land, sea, and air] Dominance" and readiness for preemptive strikes. In the long run, there is greater security to be found in adhering to the nonviolence of Jesus and the pursuit of the universal common good.

For teachers of college theology, the best antidote for the PD virus is a solid knowledge of the New Testament's interpretation of prophecy. For *those* Christian authors—and for us who claim the New Testament as our sacred scripture—the end times were inaugurated in the life, death, and resurrection of Jesus and the mission of his disciples; the church is the new temple, and the offering of one's body "as a living sacrifice" along with that of its risen Lord, is its worship; what is expressed in Holy War imagery in the Apocalypse is lived out as peacemaking entailing nonviolent love of enemies; the final judgment of evil-doers, sometimes pictured as done with a hail storm, sometimes as a fire storm, sometimes as a vulture feast, is an option for God and not for us. Whatever Armageddon points to, it is not a human battle but a saving act of God. Of the day, the hour, and the means of the Parousia and the final judgment, the Markan Jesus tells "the reader" not to speculate (Mk 13:32-33).

6. *The biblically based model of church as a "contrast society" exercising a "prophetic imagination" can inform our use of scripture in a way that enables us to better serve the world around us.* A community needs to form a distinctive identity and vision if it is to have something to offer to the culture surrounding it. I take this notion of "contrast society" from the German exegete Gerhard Lohfink, who developed it in collaboration with his brother Norbert, a Jesuit and an Old Testament exegete. The idea is that the people of God—in their covenant relationship with the God of Israel, whom they recognize to be the God of all nations—are both mediators of the relationship between the Creator and the rest of the nations and also models of a communal life whose interpersonal relationships are grounded in their collective and individual relationships with God, and whose relationships with God find expression in their relationships with one another. Israel of old is God's "social project" and the Law is "bread in the wilderness" because it shows them the concrete ways of living out

divine righteousness as a new kind of family and, in that way, becoming a "light to the nations." For the New Testament authors, the Christian movement assumes this identity.[23] This model of church as contrast society may seem, on the face of it, to block faith from relating to any "public life" larger than the internal life of the faith community itself. Indeed, it is a model that has led to sectarianism.[24] Yet, understood as illuminating an *aspect* of the church's life and mission, the model can encourage Christian communities to exercise what Walter Brueggemann has taught us to call "prophetic imagination" in a prophetic ministry, whose task he describes as "to nurture, nourish, and evoke a consciousness and perception alternative to the consciousness and perception of the dominant culture around us."[25]

7. *Rhetoric is not a dirty word: Bible talk in the public arena.* When we turn from the question of Bible-talk within the immediate faith community (I am still thinking in the context of U.S. Catholics) to focus on the question of using scriptural language in the public forum, it becomes obvious that we are dealing with the strategic question of rhetoric. I mean rhetoric in the classical sense, as Aristotle defines it—"the ability to see, in each particular instance, the available means of persuasion."[26] In some contexts, doing that will mean following John Courtney Murray's advice to maximize the use of the more publicly accessible language of reason—such as concepts of subsidiarity, common good, proportionality, noncombatant immunity, last resort, equality of access. In some other circumstances, when, for example, we are explicitly reaching out to other Christians beyond the Catholic pale, it may be strategic to use biblical language that we hold in common—like reference to the centrality of Jesus' teaching of love of God and neighbor understood in the light of the Good Samaritan parable and the mandate to love enemies, the primacy of service, the use of material goods to meet the needs of all, care for the poor, nonviolent response to hostility, and the sense of being fellow creatures with the animals and plants of the rest of nature, and members of a human family with a common origin.[27]

The better we teachers and preachers promote biblical literacy and join the Catholic social tradition to its biblical roots, the more likely that St. Louis cabbie is to recognize where his instinct for doing "the right thing" comes from, and the more likely he is to connect his faith with the whole of his life—public as well as private.

Notes

[1]Joseph Fletcher, *Situation Ethics: The New Morality* (Philadelphia: Westminster, 1966), 13.

[2]What follows in this section summarizes what I spelled out at greater length in "Dodging Faith's Call," *America*, March 2, 2006, 8-10; and "Faith's Call to Justice," *America*, July 31-August 7, 2006, 18-20.

[3]What follows is a summary of a fuller treatment of this material in Dennis Hamm, "The Doomsday Scenario of the 'Left Behind' Series: How Biblical Is It?" *The Creighton University Magazine*, Summer 2005, 45-49; available at www.creightonmagazine.org/files/Summer_2005/CUMag_SU05.pdf.

[4]For a comprehensive introduction to this scenario, see Leslie J. Hoppe, O.F.M., "Premillennial Dispensationalism: Fundamentalism's Eschatological Scenario," *Chicago Studies* 34 (1995): 222-35.

[5]That sequence—first the Parousia, then the Millennium—is the meaning of the adjective "*pre*millennial." If you expect a literal thousand-year era of messianic peace (before or after the Parousia), you are a *millennialist*. There are two different ways to be a millennialist. If you expect the second coming to occur prior to the millennium, you are a *pre*-millennialist; if you think of the millennium of peace on earth as a human achievement that *prepares* for the second coming, you are a *post*-millennialist. Most millennialists have been *pre*-millennialists. Throughout the past sixteen hundred years most Christians have been "*a*-millennialists"—that is, they don't hold for a literal millennium at all. Augustine settled the question for the mainstream Christian tradition; in book 22 of *The City of God*, taking his cue from the symbolic nature of *all* the numbers in Revelation, he argued that the millennium of Revelation 20 is a symbolic number designating the whole period between Easter and the Second Coming, however long it lasts.

[6]For Hal Lindsey, these events are preliminary to the Rapture; for LaHaye and Jenkins, they mainly occur during the seven-year Tribulation period.

[7]A series of passages in Mark—11:17 (Is 56:7), 12:10 (Ps 118:22), 13:1-2, 14:58, and 15:29, 38—points to Jesus fulfilling the expectations about a new temple. See also the Gospel of John and the Letter to the Hebrews for the theme that the meaning of Old Testament temple worship is now fulfilled in the sacrifice of Jesus.

[8]Can you think of a quicker way to start World War III? Yet there are groups raising the funds to do just that. I have seen liturgical vessels for the third temple already on display in the Old City of Jerusalem. And I have read that a Nebraska farmer has been contracted to breed the red heifer whose ashes Numbers 19 requires for the purification of the temple. Curiously, the construction of the third temple occurs without incident and with little narrative description in *The Tribulation Force*, the second book of the "Left Behind" series; even in fiction, LaHaye and Jenkins don't want to take the implications seriously.

⁹James Watt, President Reagan's Secretary of the Interior, asserted famously that concern about the sustainability of soil and forests lacked urgency in the light of the likely imminence of the Second Coming. And Mr. Reagan was clearly influenced by this worldview when he cited biblical commentators who identified Gog of the book of Revelation with Russia; that made the epithet "Evil Empire" easy to apply to that nation. This scenario promotes a social attitude of "If you are not with us, you are against us"—an attitude that makes enemies even of friendly critics. Some political analysts have claimed that, when it comes to U.S. foreign policy regarding the Middle East, fundamentalist Evangelicals comprise an even more formidable Congressional lobby than the American Israel Public Affairs Committee (AIPAC). Many Evangelicals base their uncritical support for the state of Israel on the role Israel has in the premillennial dispensationalist doomsday scenario. See the next note, regarding Gorenberg's book.

¹⁰For a fascinating review of this kind of fundamentalism among Christians, Jews, and Muslims, see Gershom Gorenberg, *The End of Days: Fundamentalism and the Struggle for the Temple Mount* (New York: Oxford University Press, 2000).

¹¹Washington, DC: U.S. Catholic Conference, 1983.

¹²Washington, DC: U.S. Catholic Conference, 1986.

¹³Formerly accessible online at http://www.usccb.org/faithfulcitizenship/bishopStatement.htm. As of November 26, 2007, it remains accessible at http://www.cscsisters.org/justice/pdf/FaithfulCitizenship2.pdf.

¹⁴As this volume goes to press, the USCCB has issued its 2007 version of the quadrennial teaching on faithful citizenship, "Forming Consciences for Faithful Citizenship: A Call to Political Responsibility from the Catholic Bishops of the United States" (available at http://www.usccb.org/bishops/FCStatement.pdf). It has been noted that references to scripture are scarce in this version. This is understandable, given that the focus of this document is on the more philosophical topic of the formation of conscience. In fact, the bishops do cite John 13:34 (par. 10) and Matthew 25:31-46 (par. 50 on the option for the poor), and they make a number of biblical allusions—for example, "the Scriptural call to welcome the stranger among us" (regarding immigrants, in par. 53), "the Gospel's invitation to be peacemakers" (par. 53), "our stewardship of God's creation," and "stewards called by God to share the responsibility for the future of the earth" (par. 54). For a readership already tutored by a thirty-year tradition of "faithful citizenship" teaching—and this document does not supersede but develops the prior faithful citizenship pastorals—a few citations and allusions suffice to call to mind the biblical bases of this teaching.

¹⁵Liguori, MO: Liguori Publications, 1994, available online from the U.S. Conference of Catholic Bishops at http://www.usccb.org/catechism/text/.

¹⁶*Catechism*, par. 2207.

¹⁷Ibid., par. 2242.

¹⁸The wisdom of keeping our social teaching close to the biblical framework of the Ten Commandments came home to me recently when I was trying

to identify why the U.S. government's stated goal of the "Full Spectrum Dominance" of land, sea, and space seemed so radically immoral to me (see *United States Space Long Range Plan* at http://www.fas.org/spp/military/docops/usspac/lrp/toc.htm). I came to realize that, prior to the issues of the threat to kill indiscriminately, the policy is a matter of the seventh commandment (and of course the tenth, nurturing the *desire* to break the seventh). For just as the domination of the seas by one nation is an immoral (and illegal) arrogation of what is understood to be a commons to be used cooperatively by all 180 sovereign nations of the planet, something understood by our tradition to be a violation of the commandment against stealing, so is one nation's domination of Earth-linked space a similar violation against the universal common good. No technical discussion of the physics and ballistics of the militarization of space should obscure the ancient and still essential reality of the biblical foundation of the moral understanding of the "common destination of goods." Ultimate dominion belongs to the Creator; any exercise of relative human dominion is to be an act of stewardship serving the common good.

[19]Pontifical Council for Justice and Peace, *Compendium of the Social Doctrine of the Church* (Libreria Editrice Vaticana; English trans., Washington, DC: United States Conference of Catholic Bishops, 2004).

[20]The *Compendium* thoroughly integrates the principles and the specific teachings of the Catholic social tradition with their biblical foundations. The first five chapters—1) God's Plan of Love for Humanity, 2) The Church's Mission and Social Doctrine, 3) The Human Person and Human Rights, 4) The Principles of the Church's Social Doctrine, and 5) The Family, The Vital Cell of Society—consistently integrate the post-biblical developments with biblical themes. And the next six chapters—6) Human Work, 7) Economic Life, 8) The Political Community, 9) The International Community, 10) Safeguarding the Environment, and 11) The Promotion of Peace—each begin with a section called "Biblical Aspects," devoting two to four pages relating biblical themes to the issue at hand.

[21]For a comprehensive review of these and other dimensions of the interface between scripture and Catholic social teaching, see John R. Donahue, S.J., "The Bible and Catholic Social Teaching: Will This Engagement Lead to Marriage?" in Kenneth R. Himes, O.F.M., ed., *Modern Catholic Social Teaching: Commentaries and Interpretations* (Washington, DC: Georgetown University Press, 2005), 9-40.

[22]I explore the relationship between biblical and forensic justice in "Preaching Biblical Justice," *Church* 12, no. 1 (Spring 1996): 17-21.

[23]See Gerhard Lohfink, *Jesus and Community: The Social Dimension of Christian Faith* (New York: Paulist Press, 1984). For an excellent contemporary assessment of various Catholic postures vis-à-vis the surrounding culture, see Kristin E. Heyer, *Prophetic and Public: The Social Witness of U.S. Catholicism* (Washington, DC: Georgetown University Press, 2007).

[24]I thought I heard a hint of that possibility in a comment of Norbert Lohfink. In Rome, around 1985, I happened to encounter him and asked him

what he thought of the U.S. bishops' emerging pastoral letter on the U.S. economy. He said something like, "I am afraid your bishops are trying to convert Pharaoh." The situation didn't allow for a probing of that remark, but the allusion to Exodus seemed clear enough. I took him to mean that our church ought not to try to convert the alien culture but, rather, should get on with the ecclesial exodus—shaking off the effects of the alien culture to become a contrast society. I heard this as the reflection of a European whose best hope was to nurture a minority group of Catholics in a post-Christian Europe. As an American, I preferred, rather, to share the hope of the U.S. bishops that the substantial minority of U.S. Roman Catholics, properly informed and inspired by their church's rich social tradition regarding the common good in matters of war, peace, and economic justice, might directly participate in our democratic experiment in ways that could help our young republic achieve domestic social justice and regain our place among the nations as a collaborator for a world community that works for the whole human family.

[25] *The Prophetic Imagination*, 2nd ed. (Minneapolis: Fortress Press, 2001 [1978]), 3. The theme of this ground-breaking little book is further elaborated in the series of five lectures from the 1980s, published as *Hope within History* (Atlanta: John Knox, 1987).

[26] George A. Kennedy, trans. and ed., *Aristotle* On Rhetoric: *A Theory of Civic Discourse* (New York: Oxford Press, 1991), chap. 1, par. 1 (p. 36).

[27] At the same time, we need to be careful not to transfer to civil society or the whole human family biblical language that pertains to the church—such as "the body of Christ," or the covenant community. Biblically, only baptized Christians belong to the body of Christ, and "the covenant community" applies to the whole human race only if one has in mind the covenant of creation. There *is* a basis in scripture for speaking of the "covenant of creation" in a universal sense, but given that this is not part of common Christian parlance these days, that concept needs to be accompanied by explanation. Even the ready phrase "children of God," as in "every baby is a child of God," needs to be used with care; to apply the phrase universally vitiates the power of the image of adoption behind the prophets' use of "child, or son, of God" for Israel's election (Ex 4:23, Bar 3:37, Hos 11:1) and Paul's use of the idea for the effect of baptism and incorporation into Christ (Gal 4:1-7; Rom 8:15-16; and see Jn 1: 12). To say what most people mean by calling every human being a "child of God" (a beloved creature), one finds greater biblical warrant for saying everyone is created "in the image of God" (Gn 1:26-27; 5:1; 9:6).

Implementing Catholic Social Teaching

John Sniegocki

Catholic social teaching (CST) provides a very valuable set of principles for reflecting upon issues of public life. Its understandings of the common good, human rights, integral development, the universal purpose of created goods, and the importance of a preferential option for the poor, among other themes, contain much insight and set forth a positive and compelling social vision. A vexing question that has plagued CST, however, concerns the implementation of this vision. How can it be translated from the realm of teaching into the realm of practice? These questions have given rise to numerous debates concerning the nature of society, the proper relationship of church and state, and effective mechanisms of social change. In this essay I will explore some of these debates and will make some suggestions for the strengthening of CST. These suggestions will be derived in part through dialogue with the thought of Christian ethicist John Howard Yoder. In the latter part of the essay I will explore some of the implications of these suggested ideas for Catholic responses to the war in Iraq and to current forms of economic globalization. Finally, I will briefly bring my proposals into dialogue with the social teaching of Pope Benedict XVI.

Catholic Social Teaching and Social Change

Throughout most of the CST tradition the church has been understood to contribute to social change primarily through its ministries of moral formation. In particular, much emphasis has been placed on the moral formation of the political and economic leaders of society. These persons, influenced by church teaching, are expected in turn to implement just policies. Such an understanding of the role of the church in the moral formation of societal leaders can be clearly seen, for example, in the writings of Pope Leo XIII. In his 1891 encyclical *Rerum Novarum*, commonly regarded as the founding document of modern CST, Leo argued that the tensions between capital and labor would have no solution apart from the assistance of the Catholic Church. The main contribution of the church, says Leo, consists of "drawing rich and poor together, by reminding each class of its duties toward the other, and especially of the duties of justice."[1] Among the duties that the church teaches to the wealthy is the obligation to "duly and solicitously provide for the welfare and the comfort of the working people."[2] The primary role of the church in bringing about social reform is thus educational, the formation of conscience.

The model of social change that is envisioned by Pope Leo is largely top-down in nature. Leo was in fact rather fearful of the common people and their power to foment social instability. He warned, for example, against those who aim at "putting all government in the hands of the masses."[3] While Leo encouraged the formation of Catholic "workers' associations," he did not envision these groups as playing an activist role in demanding workers' rights. Rather, these associations were understood mainly as vehicles for mutual aid and for mutual encouragement in faith and morality.[4] Not only were these organizations not to foster social activism and the accompanying potential disruption of the social order, Leo in fact hoped that they would inhibit it. "It seems expedient," says Leo, "to encourage associations for handicraft workers and laborers, which, placed under the sheltering care of religion, may render the members content with their lot and resigned to toil, inducing them to lead a peaceful and tranquil life."[5] While Leo strongly encouraged the political and economic leaders of society to implement just policies (including a "just wage," limits on working hours, the prohibition of child labor, and so on), he did not encourage grassroots mobilization by the workers if these policies were not put into place. In such circumstances Leo instead counseled "tranquil resignation."[6]

The view of society that characterized Leo's thought is often described as "organic." The organic understanding of society, derived from the Middle Ages, emphasizes social harmony and the avoidance of conflict. It envisions society as an organism that functions harmoniously when each of its multiple, hierarchically structured parts contribute to the common good by carrying out the duties appropriate to its location in the social hierarchy. For Leo, one of the proper duties of the church is to provide spiritual guidance to the leaders of society, helping them to remain mindful of the common good.

Leo XIII's emphasis on the church's role in moral formation and moral appeal to the leaders of society, which can be termed a "chaplaincy model," has historically provided the dominant framework in CST for understanding how the church impacts economic and political life. Even when subsequent popes came to approve of a more activist role for workers' organizations in demanding workers' rights, the overall thrust of CST at the papal level remained primarily focused on moral appeal to political and economic elites to implement policy changes rather than encouraging grassroots mobilization as the vehicle of change.[7]

Many critics contend that this chaplaincy approach to social change, while well intentioned, is unrealistic. Mary Hobgood, for example, asserts with dismay that the agents of social change envisioned by CST tend to be "those very governments, international agencies, and business elites that the documents' own analysis has already located as a source and beneficiary of the existing economic system and the crisis it generates."[8] Because these persons benefiting from the existing order are more likely to seek to maintain this order rather than to change it, CST is then left with many fine ideas but no practical ways of implementing them. What is needed to strengthen CST, Hobgood argues, is greater emphasis on grassroots organization and activism. "The power of privileged elites," says Hobgood, "can only be limited by organized, imaginative counterpower. . . . The achieving of dignity and genuine social justice will not be the result of gifts bestowed by business elites and the states they control. Rather, social justice will occur when the marginalized mobilize to exercise their own self-empowerment."[9]

This alternative model of social change highlighted by Hobgood, stressing grassroots action and social struggle, stands in sharp contrast to the organic model with its emphasis on social harmony and top-down reforms. While the chaplaincy model of social change has been dominant in CST, it has not, however, been the only model of change in the tradition. Many Catholic bishops at the regional level, especially in Latin America and Asia, have emphasized a stronger and much more positive role for grassroots struggle in the quest for the common good. At the historic Medellín conference in 1968, for example, the Latin American bishops spoke positively of the work of a diverse array of grassroots organizations—base communities, small farmers' organizations, labor unions, and others—who were seeking to counteract the forces that supported unjust social structures. "Peasants' and workers' unions," the Latin American bishops state, "should acquire sufficient strength and power."[10] "It is necessary," they add, "that small basic communities be developed in order to establish a balance with . . . the groups in power. . . . The Church—the People of God—will lend its support to the downtrodden."[11] The bishops called upon the Latin American church "to encourage and favor the efforts of the people to create and develop their own grassroots organizations for the redress and consolidation of their rights and the search for true justice."[12] At later general conferences of Latin American bishops held at Puebla, Mexico, in 1979, Santo Domingo, Dominican Republic, in 1992, and Aparecida, Brazil, in 2007, these commitments to grassroots action for justice were broadly reaffirmed.[13]

The Asian bishops similarly have highlighted the importance of grassroots movements and of active social struggle. They have spoken positively of base communities, neighborhood groups, movements for "democracy, participation and human rights," "the women's movement," ecological movements, and similar organizations.[14] Acknowledging that the quest for justice will necessarily involve conflict, the Asian bishops stress that this conflict need not be viewed negatively. Rather, especially when carried out nonviolently and with respect for one's opponents, such conflict can be an integral part of the quest for the common good. "Social action work," the bishops state, "often faces the reality of conflict. We want to stress two points: conflict is not necessarily violence . . . , nor is it necessarily opposed to Christian charity. Secondly, conflict is often a necessary means to attain true dialogue with people in authority. The poor do not achieve this until they have shown that they are no longer servile and afraid. Dialogue of this type searches for the common good."[15]

While the Asian bishops assert the importance of endeavoring to maintain a constructive relationship with persons in positions of economic and political power, they also recognize that faithfulness to the gospel may at times require actions that risk breaking these ties. "The option for the poor," the bishops state, "may mean prophetically denouncing and opposing them [i.e. wealthy and powerful persons] if they refuse to share this concern [for the poor];

and this even at the cost of losing their aid and support. Thus, opting to be with the poor involves risk of conflict with vested interests or 'establishments,' religious, economic, social, political."[16]

These reflections of the Latin American and Asian bishops provide evidence of an alternative conception within CST as to how the church can best contribute to social change. The 1971 international Synod of Bishops' document *Justice in the World* contains similar themes, emphasizing for example the need for grassroots "social and political action" to overcome concentrations of wealth and power.[17] In the writings of Pope John Paul II, both the chaplaincy and the grassroots action perspectives are present. Most often John Paul continues to stress a rather non-conflictual model of social change, stating for example that poorer nations' efforts to improve the conditions of their people should be undertaken "without opposing anyone."[18] At the same time, however, John Paul does affirm more clearly than any previous pope the positive role that a certain type of social conflict, nonviolent in nature, can play in the quest for justice. In his final social encyclical, *Centesimus Annus*, John Paul states:

> The church is well aware that in the course of history conflicts of interest between different social groups inevitably arise, and that in the face of such conflicts Christians must often take a position, honestly and decisively. The encyclical *Laborem Exercens* moreover clearly recognized the positive role of conflict when it takes the form of a "struggle for social justice."[19]

What is to be condemned, says John Paul, is not conflict itself, but rather "the idea that conflict is not restrained by ethical or juridical considerations, or by respect for the dignity of others."[20]

This explicit recognition in papal teaching of the "positive role of conflict" as a tool for seeking justice is an important development in CST. John Paul's views on these issues seem to have been influenced especially by the experiences of the people of Eastern Europe in ending communist regimes through mass nonviolent action, as well as by experiences such as the nonviolent "people power" revolution in the Philippines that ended the Marcos dictatorship.[21]

It is my contention that through an increased willingness on the part of the papal magisterium to listen to the insights being expressed at the regional level in places like Latin America and Asia, CST could be further strengthened. A more thorough and consistent emphasis on the need for grassroots mobilization and nonviolent social struggle, and a deeper awareness of and willingness to name the powerful forces that oppose social change would strengthen CST. Rather than being viewed as in tension with the common good (as in the organic social model), nonviolent struggle can and should be seen as having an indispensable role to play in the quest for the common good. The challenge of Christians in a world of injustice is not to avoid struggle and conflict. Rather, it is to learn how to engage in active social struggle in loving and constructive ways.

Catholic Social Teaching and John Howard Yoder

In reflecting upon these issues of social change, social conflict, and the role of the Christian church, I would suggest that CST could also be further strengthened through dialogue with the thought of Christian ethicist John Howard Yoder. Yoder's thought complements the insights of the Latin American and Asian bishops, adding a more extensive discussion of the multiple ways that the church can contribute to social change without relying merely on moral appeal to political and economic leaders. In addition, Yoder's consistent emphasis on the centrality of nonviolence and efforts at reconciliation can serve as an important corrective to the tendency of some proponents of grassroots mobilization to occasionally lose sight of these values.

For Yoder, the social mission of the church has three main components: pioneering creativity, work for justice, and prophetic critique.[22] The first and primary social task of the church is that of "pioneering creativity" or what Yoder sometimes terms a "modeling mission." Relying on God's grace, the church seeks to incarnate gospel values in its own life and witness and thereby to be "salt" and "light" for the world. In many cases the example set by the church can provide inspiration for subsequent public policies, as will be discussed more below. Second, Yoder highlights the mission of direct action in pursuit of social justice, "the creative construction of loving, nonviolent ways to undermine unjust institutions and to build healthy ones."[23] This can take various forms, including lobbying and various forms of grassroots activism and mobilization. Closely connected with this is the third primary social mission of the church, that of prophetic critique, the willingness to "speak truth to power" publicly and boldly when harm is being caused.[24] All three of the social missions of the church—pioneering creativity, direct work for justice, and prophetic critique—are closely interrelated.

A fundamental component of Yoder's social thought is his questioning of the assumption that the primary persons shaping history are those at the top of the social ladder.[25] Here Yoder would agree with the proponents of grassroots mobilization discussed above. In the political realm, for example, Yoder argues that leaders are generally constrained from doing significant good by the many deals and compromises that they have had to make to attain and retain their current positions. While this is particularly true when politicians are highly dependent upon donations from corporations and other wealthy donors, as in the United States, the claim is applicable to most other political systems as well. In the context of such structural constraints, attempts at radical reform initiated from within the system by its formal leaders are unlikely. This is not to say, of course, that having sympathetic leaders is not important. Rather, the claim that is being made is that these leaders, in the absence of a broad social movement for change, will have limited ability to implement the needed reforms. The ruler, Yoder provocatively asserts, "is not at the place in society where the greatest contribution can be made."[26]

Yoder argues that the margins of society rather are the locus of creativity and the site of authentic, constructive social change. "The marginal," Yoder asserts, "is not irrelevant. The creativity provoked or enabled by that marginality is more relevant than is trying to fix the system on its own terms. It is on the margins that the search for alternatives prospers."[27] Yoder in his writings highlights the many ways that active, prophetic minorities have contributed throughout history to social change. These include initiatives such as the movement to abolish slavery, the civil rights movement, the labor movement, and the movement for women's rights.[28] In these cases it was grassroots action arising from the margins that reshaped the social and political context so that structural and legal reforms became possible that otherwise would have been impossible. "Progress in history," Yoder contends, "is borne by the underdogs."[29] A central social role of the church is to act in nonviolent solidarity with these marginalized "underdogs" and through its creative and prophetic actions to contribute to the broader social good.

In addition to influencing social transformation through support for grassroots movements of the poor and marginalized, another way of effecting social change is through the church's modeling mission. This modeling mission, Yoder emphasizes, involves much Spirit-led creativity. "It is the nature of the love of God," says Yoder, "not to let itself be limited by models or options or opportunities which are offered to it by a situation. . . . Jesus would ask, 'How in this situation will the life-giving power of the Spirit reach beyond available models and options to do a new thing whose very newness will be a witness to divine presence?' "[30] Yoder cites numerous instances of pioneering creativity on the part of the Christian churches and their impact on subsequent public policies. For example, Yoder contends that the practice of democratic decision-making embodied in New England town meetings drew its inspiration from the lived experience of democracy at work in "free church" movements such as the Puritans. The practice of religious liberty in the United States was significantly influenced by the Quaker experiment of Pennsylvania. The projects historically undertaken by the Catholic Church in the areas of education and health care, and the work of Quakers and other Christians in prison reform and international humanitarian assistance helped to provide an impetus for greater governmental commitment to these issues. These are but a few examples among many where pioneering action by the Christian churches (often by small, pacifist Christian churches such as the Quakers) paved the way for broader social change.[31]

The understanding of the social mission of the church put forth by Yoder is critical of the chaplaincy model of church-state relations, discussed above, which endeavors to affect social policy primarily by influencing persons in political and economic leadership positions. Yoder would characterize this approach as a form of "Constantinianism."[32] While Yoder has no inherent objection to seeking to influence these leaders (or even to Christians becoming these leaders), he does object when this would entail compromise of fundamental gospel values such as nonviolence or truthfulness. If Christians can be truthful and maintain their commitment to nonviolence and still be elected, for example, Yoder has no problem with this. He suggests, however, that such circumstances will likely be rare, as authentic gospel values tend not to be very popular. Moreover, as we have seen, Yoder suggests that moral appeals to leaders, in the absence of prophetic critique and pioneering creativity at the grassroots level, are not likely to be successful.

Views such as Yoder's, which emphasize nonviolence and principled pacifism, have often been criticized for their social implications. If the church as a whole were to adopt such views, critics say, it would become marginalized. It would therefore be unable to accomplish the good that could be accomplished by remaining in dialogue with and retaining the capacity to influence societal leaders who reject pacifist views. Yoder would see this as setting up a false choice. The church, Yoder would argue, can seek to model nonviolence in its own life and yet continue to engage in public dialogue with others who reject pacifist views. Yoder himself, while a pacifist, regularly engaged in respectful dialogue with just war proponents, encouraging them to be rigorously faithful to their own stated principles.[33] One need not, Yoder would argue, adopt another person's value system in order to try to hold them accountable to their own best values.

Persons such as Yoder who argue that the church should be normatively committed to nonviolence are often described as "sectarian." It is frequently claimed that these sectarians emphasize personal faithfulness at the expense of public effectiveness and social responsibility, in effect embracing a posture of withdrawal from the world. This sect model is generally contrasted with a "church" model that recognizes that apparent compromises of gospel values must be made in order to engage in social life in a "responsible" way.[34] I would argue that these church-sect typologies are generally not helpful, and often contribute to more confusion than clarity. Applied to Yoder, for example, the label of "sectarian" is simply mistaken if meant to imply a posture of withdrawal, lack of concern for social effectiveness, or lack of commitment to dialogue with persons outside the Christian community. Rather than forsaking effectiveness, Yoder argues that adherence to gospel values such as nonviolence will in fact tend to be the most efficacious approach (as seen, for example, in numerous cases of the ending of dictatorships through nonviolent action) since these values are most fully in accord with the nature of God's will and God's action in the world. "If Jesus Christ is Lord," Yoder asserts, "obedience to his rule cannot be dysfunctional."[35] While Yoder would reject any attempt to reduce arguments for pacifism or other Christian values to a calculus of effectiveness, he denies that faithfulness and effectiveness are necessarily in contradiction. Indeed, he argues that, properly understood, they generally will not be. "The cruciform life 'works,' " Yoder asserts, "because it goes with the grain of the cosmos."[36]

Yoder therefore clearly does not advocate withdrawal from social engagement. Rather, he believes that the church should be deeply engaged. What he does suggest, however, is that the primary form of the church's social engagement should not be the establishment of cozy relationships with persons in positions of political and economic power with the hope of influencing their decision-making. While moral appeals to such persons are valid and necessary, they are insufficient. Larry Rasmussen, a Christian ethicist influenced by John Yoder, makes a similar point. He is especially worried about the church losing the prophetic dimension of its witness, and thereby also undermining its effectiveness. Commenting on the U.S. Catholic bishops' pastoral letter on the economy, Rasmussen states: "Both on theological grounds—the understanding of church—and on strategic ones . . . it is doubtful [that] the bishops should favor a church/world model that prefers partnership with power."[37]

Efforts to effect change primarily by working within the prevailing options of given systems and by appeal to ruling elites, Rasmussen and Yoder suggest, serve both to undermine the radical nature of the Gospel and, pragmatically, will likely have a less constructive impact than would an approach that demonstrates and promotes more creative, far-reaching alternatives. Using the language of "pioneering creativity" employed by Yoder, Rasmussen asserts:

> Two parabolic actions are vital: unrelenting criticism and pioneering creativity. . . . Radical criticism would better expose and illumine the world of economic power. Pioneering experimentation would help shape Christian imagination and markedly aid public policy by demonstrating concrete possibilities. Both the wider world and the integrity of faith itself would be served.[38]

Implications for Responding to War and Economic Injustice

The model of social involvement outlined by persons such as John Yoder and Larry Rasmussen thus has three main components: 1) pioneering creativity, 2) action to seek reform of unjust public policies, and 3) prophetic criticism. They suggest that effectiveness in the second component—bringing about policy reforms—will depend significantly upon the presence of the other two components, pioneering creativity and prophetic critique. If any of these components is missing, the integrity of the whole will be undermined.

What implications would this Yoderian model of social involvement have for the response of the Christian churches (especially the Catholic Church) to concrete issues such as the current war in Iraq or current forms of economic globalization? It is to these questions that our attention now turns.

War in Iraq

The tradition of CST includes very strong statements challenging the practice of warfare. While affirming in principle the legitimacy for Catholics of both pacifist and just war positions, CST has increasingly questioned whether a just war is in reality any longer possible. Pope John Paul II in particular made many very bold and prophetic statements challenging the legitimacy of all modern wars. "Today," says John Paul, "the scale and horror of modern warfare—whether nuclear or not—makes it totally unacceptable as a way of settling differences between nations."[39] "Peace," he asserts, "never requires violence. . . . Especially those who come from countries whose soil is stained with blood know well that violence constantly generates violence. War throws open the door to the abyss of evil. . . . This is why war should always be considered a defeat: the defeat of reason and humanity. . . . War never again!"[40] "Violence is a lie," John Paul states, "for it goes against the truth of our faith, the truth of our humanity. . . . Do not believe in violence; do not support violence. It is not the Christian way. It is not the way of the Catholic Church."[41]

With regard specifically to the war in Iraq, John Paul II and other Vatican officials repeatedly made clear their opposition to the war.[42] In an interview on May 2, 2003, Cardinal Joseph Ratzinger (now Pope Benedict XVI) strongly reaffirmed John Paul II's negative judgment of the war and, like John Paul, also raised serious doubts that any modern war could be acceptable: "There were not," Cardinal Ratzinger stated, "sufficient reasons to unleash a war against Iraq. To say nothing of the fact that, given the new weapons that make possible destructions that go beyond the combatant groups, today we should be asking ourselves if it is still licit to admit the very existence of a 'just war.' "[43]

The U.S. Catholic bishops similarly issued statements prior to the start of the war in Iraq (most significantly a letter sent to President Bush) arguing that a decision to go to war would not satisfy just war conditions. They cited concerns that numerous criteria would not be met, including just cause, legitimate authority, last resort, proportionality, and others.[44] Since the war began, however, relatively little has been heard from church leaders. Virtually nothing has been said regarding the question of whether Catholics in the military should be fighting in a war that church teaching suggests does not meet just war criteria. Few Catholic bishops in the United States, for example, have publicly declared their support for those military personnel who refuse to fight in Iraq for reasons of conscience. To my knowledge, only one bishop has publicly taught that Catholic soldiers under his pastoral care *should* refuse to fight.[45] Only a handful of Catholics in the military have refused to serve in Iraq. Many Catholics in my experience are not even aware that church leaders have raised fundamental objections to the war.

If we analyze this response to the war in light of the principles highlighted above (calling for pioneering creativity, reform efforts, and prophetic critique), what conclusions might be drawn? Many of the CST statements on war can be viewed as very prophetic in nature, challenging the legitimacy of modern war and highlighting a variety of nonviolent alternatives. Yet these statements are largely unknown to many Catholics. The major focus of the institutional Catholic Church in the case of the war in Iraq seems to have been to attempt to prevent the war through appeal to political leaders. Thus, for example, Pope John Paul II sent an envoy to speak with President Bush and Saddam Hussein, and the U.S. bishops wrote a letter to President Bush. What seems particularly lacking in the church's response is a refusal to support an unjust war in practice, along with the necessary preparation to make that refusal a realistic possibility. In other words, the primary weakness is in the realm of "pioneering creativity." The failure to effectively educate Catholics about church teaching on warfare and the failure to actively encourage and give institutional support to those refusing to fight in the war clearly have limited the impact of the church's response to this war. In his book *When War Is Unjust: Being Honest in Just-*

War Thinking, John Yoder stresses that sincere adherence to just war principles can be claimed only if effective mechanisms are in place to foster and support refusal to participate in wars that don't meet those criteria.[46] On this account the Catholic Church in the United States has clearly fallen short.

What would an ecclesial response to the war in Iraq more fully shaped by a Yoderian perspective look like? It would certainly affirm the prophetic statements of CST that raise grave doubts about modern warfare and encourage nonviolent alternatives. At the same time, it would put major effort into making sure that these teachings are more widely known and acted upon. While appeals to political leaders would be seen as important and having their rightful place as one part of the church's response, this perspective would stress that the impact of these appeals, without the embodiment of these teachings in the actual lives of Christians, is likely to be very limited. This embodiment could take multiple forms, including refusal to participate in wars that do not meet just war criteria (or all wars) and public and sustained institutional support from the church for such conscientious nonparticipation in war. It could also include programs of training in the history and practice of nonviolent action, support for the strengthening of international institutions such as the United Nations, and support for grassroots anti-war and peacebuilding efforts, including innovative forms of Christian witness such as Christian Peacemaker Teams.[47] Also of crucial importance would be efforts to address some of the structural causes of war. This could include adoption of simpler lifestyles (and sharing of resources with those in need), reform of unjust economic policies, support for alternatives to oil and other fossil fuels as energy sources (to lessen the role of these resources in international conflict and the ecological damage caused by them), and various other actions on behalf of human rights.

Responding to Economic Globalization

As in the case of teachings about war and peace, CST contains many helpful and even prophetic teachings concerning current forms of economic globalization. In a 2003 speech to the Pontifical Academy of Social Sciences, for example, Pope John Paul II expressed grave concern that current forms of globalization were having negative effects on the poor and the environment and were fostering social conflict, even contributing to terrorism:

Special interests and the demands of the market frequently predominate over concern for the common good. This tends to leave the weaker members of society without adequate protection and can subject entire peoples and cultures to a formidable struggle for survival. Moreover, it is disturbing to witness a globalization that exacerbates the conditions of the needy, that does not sufficiently contribute to resolving situations of hunger, poverty, and social inequality, that fails to safeguard the natural environment. These aspects of globalization can give rise to extreme reactions, leading to excessive nationalism, religious fanaticism and even acts of terrorism.[48]

Many of the core principles of CST, such as the notions of "integral development" (which emphasizes concern for the total well-being of persons and the environment, rather than focusing solely on economic growth) and the "universal purpose of created goods" (which affirms that the goods of the earth are intended for all) can also make important contributions to the globalization debate. As in the case of church teachings on war and peace, however, these church teachings on economic issues are not widely known by Catholics. So a first step of an effective response must be to engage in widespread efforts to spread knowledge of and commitment to the core principles of CST, along with knowledge of the ways that current reality falls short of the CST vision. This knowledge, of course, must lead to action. Needed efforts would include moral appeals to policymakers with regard to issues such as trade policy, foreign aid, and Third World debt. As in the case of responses to war, however, what will be even more crucial is grassroots activism to strengthen the impact of these appeals and pioneering creativity in the task of constructing positive alternatives. This could take many forms, including:

- support for grassroots mobilizations such as the protests that have taken place at World Trade Organization (WTO), International Monetary Fund (IMF), and World Bank meetings. Such protests have played an important role in bringing issues of global economic policy into public consciousness.[49]
- support for the faith-based Jubilee movement for Third World debt relief.[50]
- support for campaigns to effectively address global poverty,

AIDS, global warming, and other issues that have detrimental impacts on people's lives throughout the world;[51]

- financial assistance to grassroots "alternative development" or "regeneration" projects, such as those funded by Oxfam America or the Small Planet Fund;[52]
- socially responsible purchasing, giving priority to the purchase of goods produced in ways that respect the rights of workers and the environment (such as fair trade goods, food produced by local family farms, organic food, and so on);[53]
- support for alternative forms of economic organization, such as worker- and consumer-owned cooperatives;[54]
- socially responsible investment, especially "community investment" (community investment refers to investing in organizations [including certain banks, credit unions, and community loan funds] whose central mission is to make loans to support cooperatives, small businesses, low income home ownership, environmentally sustainable business practices, the economic empowerment of women and minorities, and other projects that promote greater economic democracy and ecological sustainability);[55]
- reduction or elimination of meat consumption, given the major role that modern methods of meat production play in fostering world hunger and massive ecological damage.[56]

Some components of this proposed response to economic globalization have already been embraced by parts of the institutional church. The U.S. bishops' Catholic Campaign for Human Development, for example, helps to fund many inspiring grassroots organizations that work for greater economic democracy in the United States. Also, many Catholic religious orders have been in the forefront of the socially responsible investment and community investment movements. This has especially been true of orders of women religious. At the same time, however, most church investments, including Vatican investments, continue to be placed in conventional stocks and bonds, most churches have not integrated emphasis on socially responsible purchasing or investment or the importance of simple lifestyle into their educational efforts, and most Catholics have likely never heard of the Jubilee debt relief movement or even of the Bible passages on which it is based.[57] Nor, it is safe to say, would most Catholics know what the church teaches about trade policy. Many would even wonder why trade policy should be a concern of the church. So clearly there remains much important work to be done in developing a constructive and effective ecclesial response to the challenges of globalization.

The Institutional Church and Work for Justice

One final issue that it seems important to address at least briefly is the role of the institutional Catholic Church in pursuing the type of social engagement that this essay calls for. In his first encyclical, *Deus Caritas Est*, Pope Benedict XVI made a distinction between charity, which he believes to be a direct obligation of the church, and work for justice, which he understands to be a primary responsibility of the state and only an indirect responsibility of the church. "The Church," Benedict states, "cannot and must not take upon herself the political battle to bring about the most just society possible."[58] On the surface, these comments seem to contradict much post-Vatican II social teaching, such as the frequently quoted passage in *Justice in the World* that "action on behalf of justice and participation in the transformation of the world fully appear to us as a constitutive dimension of the preaching of the Gospel."[59] Yet Benedict himself goes on to assert that the church "cannot and must not remain on the sidelines in the fight for justice." Moreover, he stresses that the laity have "the direct duty to work for a just ordering of society."[60] How is the meaning (and apparent contradiction) of these comments to be understood? First, it is helpful to recognize that when Benedict speaks of the "Church" he often seems to mean, primarily, clerics. Thus, when he states that work for justice is not a direct duty of the church but is a direct duty of the laity, this for him is not a contradiction. Mainly what he seems to be saying is that priests (and the institutional church more broadly, such as persons employed by the church) should not be directly involved in politics in their role as representatives of the church. But what does being directly involved in politics mean? Speaking out on an issue such as abortion, for example, clearly has political implications, and in many contexts has clear partisan political implications. Is Benedict therefore implying that the church should not speak out on this or other politically contested issues? Clearly this is not the case. Benedict himself speaks out regularly on topics such as abortion, same-sex marriage, poverty, hunger, arms spending, war, Third World debt relief, the death penalty, and so on. What he wants to

assert and maintain, however, is the Catholic Church's independence from all political parties and political ideologies:

> If the Church were to start transforming herself into a directly
> political subject, she would do less, not more, for the poor and
> for justice, because she would lose her independence and her
> moral authority, identifying herself with a single political
> path and with debatable partisan positions. The Church is the
> advocate of justice and of the poor, precisely because she does
> not identify with politicians nor with partisan interests. Only
> by remaining independent can she teach the great criteria and
> inalienable values, guide consciences and offer a life choice
> that goes beyond the political sphere.[61]

Are Benedict's teachings in tension with the proposals made in
this paper, particularly with regard to the importance of Christian
support for grassroots mobilization in the quest for social justice?
In broad terms, I would argue that they are not. Benedict recognizes the centrality of concern for justice in the Christian life. While
he personally understands this calling to apply in different ways to
the laity (who are to be directly engaged in the necessary social
and political struggles) and the clergy (who are to focus primarily
on spiritual and moral formation, including formation of the laity
in the principles of Catholic social teaching), he nonetheless recognizes that "the pursuit of justice and the promotion of the civilization of love are essential aspects of her [the church's] mission
of proclaiming the Gospel of Jesus Christ."[62] "The poor," Benedict
affirms, "need to feel that the Church is close to them, providing
for their most urgent needs, defending their rights and working
together with them to build a society founded on justice and
peace."[63] Clearly this call to defend the rights of the poor and to
work together with them for justice and peace implies some involvement in grassroots social struggles. How to discern the appropriate role of the institutional church (including the clergy) in
relation to these grassroots movements for justice and peace is an
important and challenging issue. Should only lay people be directly involved? Benedict wisely cautions against the institutional
church becoming too identified with partisan politics. At the same
time, however, it seems important to recognize the significant roles
that have been played by the direct involvement of clergy and religious in social struggles of the past.[64] In the church's ongoing dis-

cernment concerning these issues, I believe that much can be gained from listening to the wisdom of those persons who have experience working for change in contexts of profound social injustice. This will include, among others, many of the Latin American and Asian bishops whose reflections on grassroots struggle and the importance of institutional church support for such struggle were highlighted earlier in this essay. Only through dialogue with these persons and with other clergy and laity who are deeply committed to the quest for justice will the proper role of the institutional church in these struggles be best discerned.

Notes

[1] Leo XIII, *Rerum Novarum*, no. 16, available in *Catholic Social Thought: The Documentary Heritage*, ed. David J. O'Brien and Thomas J. Shannon (Maryknoll, NY: Orbis Books, 1992).

[2] Ibid., no. 27.

[3] Leo XIII, *Graves de Communi Re*, no. 5; http://www.vatican.va/holy_father/leo_xiii/encyclicals/documents/hf_l-xiii_enc_18011901_graves-de-communi-re_en.html). For discussion of Leo's views on the importance of social order and his fears of social instability, see Donal Dorr, *Option for the Poor* (Maryknoll, NY: Orbis Books, 1992), chap. 2.

[4] Leo XIII, *Rerum Novarum*, nos. 36, 42.

[5] Cited in Dorr, *Option for the Poor*, 35.

[6] Leo XIII, *Rerum Novarum*, no. 20.

[7] For extensive discussion of top-down vs. grassroots models of social change in relation to each of the popes since Leo XIII, see Dorr, *Option for the Poor*.

[8] Mary Hobgood, *Catholic Social Teaching and Economic Theory: Paradigms in Conflict* (Philadelphia: Temple University Press, 1991), 235-36.

[9] Ibid., 242.

[10] "Justice" (one of the individually named documents issued by the bishops at the Medellín conference), no. 12. This document and the "Peace" document cited below can be found in Joseph Gremillion, ed., *The Gospel of Peace and Justice: Catholic Social Teaching Since Pope John* (Maryknoll, NY: Orbis Books, 1976).

[11] "Justice," no. 20.

[12] "Peace," no. 27.

[13] See the final document of the Puebla conference, in *Puebla and Beyond*, ed. Philip Scharper and John Eagleson (Maryknoll, NY: Orbis Books, 1979), esp. nos. 18 and 96; final document of the Santo Domingo conference, in *Santo Domingo and Beyond*, ed. Alfred Hennelly (Maryknoll, NY: Orbis Books, 1993), nos. 174-85. The final document of the Aparecida conference is available in Spanish at http://www.celam.info/download/Documento_Conclusivo_

Aparecida.pdf. At the Aparecida conference the Latin American church's preferential option for the poor and encouragement of grassroots efforts for social justice were again strongly reaffirmed. See Patricia Grogg, "Catholic Church Renews 'Option for the Poor,' " http://ipsnews.net/news.asp?idnews-38554.

[14]Federation of Asian Bishops' Conferences, "Journeying Together Toward the Third Millennium," in For All the Peoples of Asia, ed. Gaudencio Rosales and C. G. Arévalo (Maryknoll, NY: Orbis Books, 1992), 277-78. "We value the initiatives of people who organize themselves into self-reliant, participative, self-determining peoples' groups. These will enable the poor to become aware of their situation, realize their dignity and their human equality . . . and give them an instrument with which they can secure what is their due" ("Final Reflections of the 4th Bishops' Institute for Social Action," in ibid., 212-13).

[15]Ibid., 213.

[16]"Final Reflections of the 1st Bishops' Institute for Social Action," in For All the Peoples of Asia, 200.

[17]Synod of Bishops, Justice in the World, no. 9. The section numbers for this document (added by the editor) can be found in Gremillion, The Gospel of Peace and Justice.

[18]John Paul II, Sollicitudo Rei Socialis, no. 45; http://www.vatican.va/edocs/ENG0223/_INDEX.HTM.

[19]John Paul II, Centesimus Annus, no. 14; http://www.vatican.va/edocs/ENG0214/_INDEX.HTM.

[20]Ibid.

[21]See John Paul II's reflections on nonviolent action and the fall of communism in ibid., no. 23. For discussion of nonviolent action in the Philippines and the role of the Catholic Church, see Christina Astorga, "Culture, Religion, and Moral Vision: A Theological Discourse on the Filipino People Power Revolution of 1986," Theological Studies 67, no. 3 (2006): 567-601.

[22]This "threefold" social mission of the church is my summary of Yoder's views as expressed in his writings. It is not a categorization that he himself explicitly employed.

[23]John Howard Yoder and Michael Cartwright, The Royal Priesthood: Essays Ecclesiological and Ecumenical (Grand Rapids: Eerdmans, 1994), 212-13.

[24]"The Christian community is not only a model as community; it is a pastoral and prophetic resource to the person with responsibilities of office, precisely in order to keep the office from becoming autonomous as a source of moral guidance" (ibid., 186).

[25]Yoder rejects "the assumption that historical movement is mostly the work of powerful people" ("Ethics and Eschatology," Ex Auditu: An International Journal of Theological Interpretation of Scripture 6 [1990]: 125).

[26]John Howard Yoder, The Original Revolution: Essays on Christian Pacifism (Christian Peace Shelf Series) (Scottdale, PA: Herald Press, 1972), 177-78.

27John Howard Yoder, "Politics: Liberating Images of Christ," in *Imaging Christ: Politics, Art, Spirituality*, ed. Francis Eigo (Villanova, PA: Villanova University Press, 1991), 161.

28See "The Kingdom as Social Ethic," in *The Priestly Kingdom: Social Ethics as Gospel* (Notre Dame, IN: University of Notre Dame Press, 1984), "Christ, the Hope of the World," in *The Royal Priesthood*; "The New Humanity as Pulpit and Paradigm," in *For the Nations: Essays Evangelical and Public* (Grand Rapids: Eerdmans, 1997).

29Yoder, *The Royal Priesthood*, 137.

30Yoder, *The Original Revolution*, 50.

31For Yoder's discussion of the modeling mission of the church, see *Body Politics: Five Practices of the Christian Community before the Watching World* (Nashville: Discipleship Resources Press, 1992). Also see "Firstfruits: The Paradigmatic Public Role of God's People" and "The New Humanity as Pulpit and Paradigm," both in *For the Nations*; "The Kingdom as Social Ethic," in *The Priestly Kingdom*.

32For Yoder's reflections on Constantinianism, see "The Constantinian Sources of Western Social Ethics," in *The Royal Priesthood*, 135-47.

33Yoder wrote a book as part of this dialogue with just war theorists: *When War Is Unjust: Being Honest in Just-War Thinking*, 2nd ed. (Maryknoll, NY: Orbis Books, 1996).

34The church-sect typology is drawn from the work of Ernst Troeltsch, *The Social Teaching of the Christian Churches* (New York: Macmillan, 1931; published originally in German in 1912).

35Yoder, *The Priestly Kingdom*, 37.

36Speaking of the many historical successes of nonviolent action in bringing an end to dictatorial regimes (as in the Philippines, the former Soviet bloc countries, Chile, Serbia, South Africa, and so on), Yoder states: "Gene Sharp [author of many books on the history and strategy of nonviolent action] can distill [the power of nonviolence] out of the faith setting and translate it into Ivy League social science. It works even for people who have not studied it or who do not believe in it. How can that be? The reason is that what is known, when human life is conformed to the image of God in Jesus, is not a knowledge experiment, but a revelation of the way things really are. The cruciform life 'works' because it goes with the grain of the cosmos" (Yoder, "Politics," 164). Yoder is critical of those Christians who "will not risk the challenge of telling the world that servanthood, enemy love, and forgiveness would be a better way to run a university, a town, or a factory" (*For the Nations*, 40).

37Larry Rasmussen, "The Morality of Power and the Power of Morality," in *Prophetic Visions and Economic Realities: Protestants, Jews, and Catholics Confront the Bishops' Letter on the Economy*, ed. Charles Strain (Grand Rapids: Eerdmans, 1989), 142.

38Ibid., 145.

39John Paul II, "Homily at Bagington Airport," *Origins* 12 (1982): 55.

40John Paul II, Message for "Religions and Cultures" Meeting in Milan,

Italy (September 3, 2004), http://www.mercyoma.org/documents/Justice/kaspar.pdf.

[41]John Paul II, 1980 World Day of Peace Message, no. 10, http://www.vatican.va/holy_father/john_paul_ii/messages/peace/documents/hf_jp-ii_mes_19791208_xiii-world-day-for-peace_en.html. He cites the first part of this quote again in his 2005 World Day of Peace Message.

[42]For an overview of Vatican comments on the Iraq war, see Mark and Louise Zwick, "Pope John Paul II Calls War a Defeat for Humanity: Neoconservative Iraq Just War Theories Rejected," *Houston Catholic Worker* 23, no. 4 (July-August 2003), http://www.cjd.org/paper/jp2war.html.

[43]For a transcript of the interview in which Cardinal Ratzinger made these comments, see http://www.zenit.org/article-7161?l=english. For an overview of official Catholic teaching on war since Vatican II, see John Sniegocki, "Catholic Teaching on War, Peace, and Nonviolence Since Vatican II," in *Vatican II: Forty Years Later*, ed. William Madges, College Theology Society Annual Vol. 51 (Maryknoll, NY: Orbis Books, 2006), 224-44.

[44]The text of the U.S. bishops' letter to President Bush can be found at http://www.usccb.org/sdwp/international/bush902.shtml.

[45]The one bishop who has called upon those under his pastoral guidance to refuse to serve in the Iraq war is Bishop John Michael Botean of Canton, Ohio. Botean, who is head of the Romanian Catholic Eparchy of St. George (which is in communion with Rome and hence part of the Roman Catholic Church), has jurisdiction over all Byzantine-rite Romanian Catholics living in the United States. Bishop Botean warned his flock that "any direct participation and support of this war against the people of Iraq is objectively grave evil, a matter of mortal sin. Beyond a reasonable doubt this war is morally incompatible with the Person and Way of Jesus Christ. With moral certainty I say to you that it does not meet even the minimal standards of the Catholic just war theory." Bishop Botean instructed that this message be read during Mass at all of the parishes under his jurisdiction. He also had a copy mailed to every member of his church. For the full text of Bishop Botean's pastoral letter, see http://www.christusrex.org/www1/icons/botean.html.

[46]See Yoder, *When War Is Unjust*.

[47]To learn more about the inspiring work of Christian Peacemaker Teams, see http://www.cpt.org.

[48]Pope John Paul II, Address to the Pontifical Academy of Social Sciences (May 2, 2003), available at http://www.zenit.org/article-7151?l=english.

[49]For good discussions of the IMF, World Bank, and WTO, see Richard Peet, *Unholy Trinity: The IMF, World Bank and WTO* (London: Zed Books, 2003); Lori Wallach and Patrick Woodall, *Whose Trade Organization? A Comprehensive Guide to the WTO* (New York: Free Press, 2004); Bruce Rich, *Mortgaging the Earth: The World Bank, Environmental Impoverishment, and the Crisis of Development* (New York: Beacon Press, 1994).

[50]Information on the Jubilee debt relief movement can be found at http://www.jubileeusa.org.

[51]The Catholic Campaign Against Global Poverty (http://www.usccb.org/ sdwp/globalpoverty) is a helpful resource for pursuing some of these goals. Unfortunately, even Catholics who are active in social justice work are often unaware of the existence of this campaign co-sponsored by the U.S. Catholic bishops and Catholic Relief Services. More effective outreach and a greater prioritization of this campaign by the bishops are clearly needed.

[52]See http://www.oxfamamerica.org and http://www.smallplanetfund.org. For discussion of why some persons prefer to speak of "regeneration" or "reclaiming the commons" rather than "development" (which they view as implying Westernization and the inferiority of Third World peoples and cultures), see Wolfgang Sachs, ed., *The Development Dictionary: A Guide to Knowledge as Power* (London: Zed Books, 1992); The Ecologist, *Whose Common Future? Reclaiming the Commons* (Philadelphia: New Society Publishers, 1993).

[53]An excellent resource on socially responsible purchasing is the website of Coop America: http://www.coopamerica.org.

[54]For discussion of cooperatives, see the website of the International Cooperative Alliance: http://www.ica.coop.

[55]For information on socially responsible investment, see http:// www.socialinvest.org. For resources on community investment, see http:// www.communityinvest.org. A few especially good community investment institutions include the Self-Help Credit Union (http://www.self-help.org) and the Cooperative Fund of New England (http://www.cooperativefund.org).

[56]A recent United Nations Report, for example, concluded that livestock production is responsible for more greenhouse gases than all forms of transportation combined! The raising of animals for meat is also a major contributor to problems such as deforestation, desertification, groundwater depletion, and water pollution. See UN Food and Agriculture Organization (FAO), "Livestock a Major Threat to Environment," http://www.fao.org/ newsroom/en/news/2006/1000448/index.html; and Dan Brook, "Another Inconvenient Truth: Meat Is a Global Warming Issue," http://www.emagazine. com/view/?3312. With regard to the contribution of meat-based diets to world hunger, it takes on average about twelve pounds of protein from grains and beans to produce one pound of protein from feedlot beef. The remaining 90+ percent of the protein (along with similar proportions of many other nutrients) is lost to human consumption. The conversion ratios for other animals vary, but all are inefficient. Many Third World nations devote much of their land to growing animal feed crops to satisfy the demand for meat by the world's wealthy consumers while local people go hungry. While reducing meat consumption will not by itself bring about an end to world hunger (various unjust political-economic structures also need to be changed), it is nonetheless one essential component of the response that is needed. For discussion of these and other issues related to the impact of meat consumption, see John Robbins, *The Food Revolution: How Your Diet Can Help Save Your Life and the World* (Berkeley: Conari Press, 2001); Michael Jacobsen, *Six*

Arguments for a Greener Diet: How a More Plant-Based Diet Could Save Your Health and the Environment (Washington, DC: Center for Science in the Public Interest, 2006).

[57]For some discussion of Vatican investments, see Caroline Merrell, "Church Entrusts Its Talents to Top Bankers," *The Times*, July 12, 2005, http://business.timesonline.co.uk/tol/business/economics/article542933.ece.

[58]Benedict XVI, *Deus Caritas Est*, no. 28, http://www.vatican.va/holy_father/benedict_xvi/encyclicals/documents/hf_ben-xvi_enc_20051225_deus-caritas-est_en.html.

[59]Synod of Bishops, *Justice in the World*, no. 6.

[60]Benedict XVI, *Deus Caritas Est*, no. 29.

[61]Benedict XVI, Opening address at the 5th General Conference of the Episcopate of Latin America and the Caribbean (May 13, 2007), no. 4, http://www.zenit.org/article-19610?l=english.

[62]Benedict XVI, Message to the Pontifical Academy of Social Sciences (April 28, 2007), http://www.zenit.org/article-19517?l=english.

[63]Benedict XVI, Address to Brazilian Bishops (May 11, 2007), no. 3, http://zenit.org/article-19606?l=english.

[64]It is striking, for example, how important was the role played by the direct involvement of clergy in many of the cases discussed in *Living the Catholic Social Tradition: Cases and Commentary*, ed. Kathleen Maas Weigert and Alexia Kelley (Lanham, MD: Rowman & Littlefield, 2005).

Outside the Castle Walls

The Public Politics of Teresa's Vision

Elizabeth Newman

In this essay, I reflect on how Teresa of Avila has been received in my context (a Baptist seminary), why she has been received in this particular way, and how she can instruct us on the church as a political and public body, at once catholic and reformed. I focus specifically on *Interior Castle*, published toward the end of Teresa's life in 1577.

How Teresa Is Misread

For the past five years, I have read *Interior Castle* with my students (most of whom are preparing for ministry in a Baptist congregation). While they take exception to Teresa's self-deprecating remarks about women, they resonate with her emphasis, so they assume, on the spiritual life as an interior journey. Despite my own efforts to emphasize the communal aspects of Teresa's account, it is difficult to overcome their belief that *Interior Castle* is primarily the solitary journey of an individual soul.

More broadly speaking, from the perspective of our late modern context, it can easily seem that Teresa is a forerunner of the Christian individual who finds her identity primarily in an internal quest for God rather than in the public and sacramental practices of the church. After all, the journey she describes *appears* to be a journey inward; Teresa herself even refers to the "secrets" that will pass between the soul and God. The use of the word "interior" in the English translation of the title further underwrites this assumption; in the original, *las moradas* means simply "the mansions."

Some Baptists have emphasized, especially recently, something called "soul competency" as a Baptist distinctive. As one well-known figure in Baptist life defines it, soul competency (often used interchangeably with "the priesthood of the believer") "excludes human interference of any kind between the individual soul and God." Accordingly this theologian claims, "In its deepest sense, religion is a personal matter between the individual and God. . . . On the other hand, [however,] soul competency is inclusive. It includes salvation by grace through faith without the need of a human mediator or any institution, ecclesiastical or political."[1] For my students who are influenced by this kind of theology, it is not surprising that they would tend to read *Interior Castle* as the interior journey of a soul to God.

Likewise, Michel de Certeau, in *The Mystic Fable*, confirms the direction of this reading of Teresa. He describes *Interior Castle* as "the fiction of the soul." He argues that to the extent that "the world is no longer perceived as *spoken* by God," such that it becomes objectified and detached, then two orientations arise. One orientation takes up statements divorced from their value as spoken words, and orders them to "internal truth criteria." The other orientation "focuses on the speech act itself."[2] De Certeau claims that a mystic, like Teresa, takes up this second orientation. She substitutes her "speaking *I* for the inaccessible divine *I*," and so invents a space for an "other." But the mute ecstasies, the coincidental pleasure and pain (which one finds most fully in the Sixth Mansions), silence this "other." According to de Certeau: "The figure of the *I*, which always constructs a biographical novel, has become autonomized from what constituted it other than itself."[3] In other words, according to de Certeau, Teresa has authored an early modern "self," the figure of the autonomous "I." Such a reading, as Lawrence Cunningham notes, tries mistakenly to locate Teresa in "a social milieu in which confidence in the traditional structures of sacramentality, scriptural piety, and the ecclesial role of the contemplative (the older word for what we call a mystic) becomes attenuated."[4]

De Certeau's reading of Teresa is given some support, however, by Margaret Miles's insight that "devotional manuals have cumulatively formed modern consciousness to such an extent that the favorite character in fiction, 'autonomous Western man,' has come into being."[5] In discussing *The Pilgrim's Progress* (1678), for example, Miles notes that images in the natural world, cities and human beings are "externalizations of the pilgrim's inner struggles, temptations, comforts and assistance."[6] If we applied this reading to *Interior Castle*, then we would conclude that the real journey of the Christian life is an internal one, and the external images—such as most obviously the castle—merely illustrate the struggle within. Such a view seems especially appealing in light of the fact that the sisters to whom Teresa wrote were not able to travel far, if at all. Teresa herself acknowledges these restrictions in the final pages of her book. In her call to her sisters to imitate both Mary and Martha, she imagines her sisters objecting, "We would gladly lead souls to God, but, being unable to teach and preach like the Apostles, we do not know how." Among other things, Teresa tells the sisters that "The devil sometimes puts ambitious desires into our hearts."[7] Is this instance of pilgrimage, as Miles says about some pilgrimages of this time, adapting to the status quo rather than altering it?

Is *Interior Castle*, then, primarily about the wandering of the soul toward God (or an invented, silenced other, as de Certeau might state), a wandering made sadly poignant given the confined status of religious women in medieval Spain? Even more, is *Interior Castle* an early version of the autonomous self, one that ends up ultimately underwriting the dominant political and social order not only of Teresa's day, but also of ours?[8]

An Alternative Reading

As my title indicates, I think such readings miss the mark. To get a handle on an alternative understanding, I think we need to look more fully at the key question that drives Teresa's account. It's not the question that would come to dominate so many Protestants a century later, "Am I among God's elect?" Nor is it John Bunyan's more tormented existential question in *Grace Abounding to the Chief of Sinners*, "Can God be trusted?" Nor is Teresa's question, situated as she is at the beginning of the Reformation, "Where is the one true church?"

Rather, the key question driving her account is, as Teresa might put it, "How do we provide welcome to His Majesty?" This seems quaint, but in responding to this, Teresa is also addressing a related question: "What is God's *calling* to the church?" or stated somewhat differently, "*What does a faithful church, a faithful body, look like?*"[9] Such questions enable us to see that Teresa's vision is an ecclesial one, and therefore public and political.[10]

I make this claim in light of how Teresa reads scripture.[11] In fact, *Interior Castle* can and ought to be read as *commentary* on scripture. By calling Teresa a commentator on scripture, I do not mean that she necessarily understood herself in this light. Rather I mean that she *performed* or embodied a particular reading of scripture.[12] Finally, I wish to argue that her performance dramatizes the church as a political alternative both to medieval Constantinianism and to the apolitical self of late modernity.

Teresa's Performance of Scripture

So how does Teresa read or perform scripture? To respond to this, I want to turn to James McClendon and to what he refers to as the "baptist vision."[13] According to McClendon, this vision describes a logic or reading strategy of scripture in which "this is that" and "then is now." These two mottoes require some explanation. "This is that" comes from the King James Version of Acts 2:16 in which Peter, on the day of Pentecost, reads from the prophets, and says to his listeners, "This (what you see here today) is that." Peter is reading from the prophet Joel, "God declares . . . I will pour out my Spirit upon all flesh, and your sons and your daughters shall prophesy, and your young men shall see visions, and your old men shall dream dreams" (2:17). In other words, this outpouring is what you see here today. Prophecy is not only a record of the past, but is "a disclosure of the meaning and significance of the present."[14]

In a similar way, the phrase "then is now" refers to how talk about the "end times" is not just information about things to come in some remote time, but discloses the significance and reality of the present. Stated alternatively, McClendon notes that this vision can be expressed as a "shared awareness of the present Christian community as the primitive community and the eschatological community."[15] This is not intended as somehow a denial of history. Rather it is a claim "for the historical significance of this present time in the life of the church."[16] Thus McClendon can say that the "is" in "this is that" is "immediate and mystical." By "mystical," McClendon does not mean "subjective," but rather that God's word effects or brings about what it says. God is faithful so that the words of the prophet Joel are also words for the early Christians gathered in Jerusalem, words for Teresa's gathered hearers, as well as words for us.

While McClendon describes this as a baptist vision, he does not claim it as exclusively so. Under small "b" baptist, he includes, among others, Disciples of Christ, Mennonites, Church of the Brethren, perhaps some Methodists, assorted intentional communities, and others. Even more, in his Ethics, he includes Dorothy Day as someone who richly embodies this vision. I would also say that, for another example, Augustine, in his *Confessions*, uses this reading strategy when he classically retells the story of the fall, such that the adolescent Augustine stealing pears repeats Adam and Eve taking the forbidden fruit: this is that.

This reading strategy and performance are essentially what Teresa also uses. Toward the end of her book, Teresa states that "the words of the Lord are like acts wrought in us."[17] In other words, she understands that scripture is creative of a way of life. God's word feeds and nourishes such that those receiving it become the body of Christ. More specifically, *Interior Castle* follows the scriptural movement: creation, fall, and recreation.

Nowhere is this reading strategy more evident than in the key figure of her book: *moradas*, mansions, or dwellings. As is well known, Teresa describes these dwellings as set in a castle carved out of a single diamond. The castle has seven mansions, each with an abundance of expansive rooms through which souls can wander and move. At the center of the castle dwells "His Majesty." Teresa is in fact so struck by the beauty of this dwelling that she writes:

> I can find nothing with which to compare the great beauty of a soul and its great capacity. . . . There is no point in fatiguing ourselves by attempting to comprehend the beauty of this castle; for, though it is His creature, and there is therefore as much difference between it and God as between creature and Creator, the very fact that His Majesty says it is made in His image means that we can hardly form any conception of the soul's great dignity and beauty.[18]

This initial image, which emphasizes the soul and "His Majesty," might sound like a medieval version of one of the most popular gospel hymns in the twentieth century, "In the Garden": "I come to the garden alone, while the dew is still on the roses . . . [where Jesus] walks with me, And He talks with me. . . ." But Teresa's figure of dwelling, of God dwelling with us, is more rightly understood in light of the strategy, "then is now." In the opening lines of her book she writes, "I began to think of the soul as if it were a castle . . . just as in Heaven there are many mansions" ("In my Father's house, there are many dwellings; if it were not so, would I have told you that I go to prepare a place for you?" [Jn 14:2]). Her initial claim is that this future—heaven with many mansions—discloses who we are now.

To understand the richness of this figure of a God who dwells in our space, we need to consider how it appears elsewhere in scripture. In the Old Testament, Zion, the holy mountain in Jerusalem, is God's dwelling place. The psalmist, using language similar to Teresa's, describes it as "the perfection of beauty" (50:2). Zion is beautiful because it is identified with the City of David, the Israelites, and God's chosen ones with whom God dwells. Not only is Zion beautiful; it is also enduring. We read in Psalm 46, "There is a river whose streams make glad the city of God, the holy habitation (dwelling) of the Most High. God is in the midst of the city; it shall not be moved" (46:4-5). This is exactly what Teresa says in "the mansions": God is in the midst, the seventh dwelling, and will not be moved. According to Teresa, God dwells in the castle, in us, even if we don't know or see God. To use McClendon's scriptural reading strategy for Teresa, this is that: this castle is Zion, the abode of God.

In the Book of Revelation, there is again a holy city, made—like Teresa's castle—of jewels: jasper, gold, clear as glass (21:18). A voice from the throne repeats what was said about Zion, "See, the home (or tabernacle) of God is among mortals. He will dwell with them as their God; they will be his peoples, and God himself will be with them" (Rv 21:3-4). Though this dwelling appears to be about a future hope, Teresa assumes it is already a reality. Her point is not to jump into otherworldly future time but rather to emphasize that this reality is now. We are, through God's providential ordering of history, already a house with many dwellings where God resides. Contrary to de Certeau, then, Teresa is speaking not of an "indefinable reality"[19] but a cosmos first spoken by God to Israel and the church.

Finally, the figure of dwellings comes into focus most fully in Christ. According to the first chapter of John, God tabernacles among us in Jesus. This means that we are the dwelling of Christ. According to Teresa, the brilliance of the sun at the center of the dwellings cannot lose its splendor and beauty, though sin can cause the brightness to have "no effect upon the crystal."[20]

Now, Teresa's use of the indicative at this point might suggest a kind of collapsing of new creation or redemption into fallen creation. After all, does Christ already dwell in everyone? If the answer is "yes," this seems to short circuit human agency. Don't we need to have faith or take the sacraments or do good works to have Jesus inside us?

But here, I think we can emphasize that Teresa is reading scripture through the logic of "this is that" and "then is now." Since Christ was "tabernacled" in the flesh, Christ tabernacles in the flesh now. More classically put, what has not been assumed cannot be healed. This is not only a past fact, but discloses to us our own present condition with Christ. We are a new creation. In discussing this point, Douglas Harink cites 2 Corinthians 5: "For the love of Christ urges us on, because we are convinced that one has died for all; therefore all have died. . . . From now on, therefore, we regard no one from a human point of view. . . . So if anyone is in Christ, there is a new creation: everything old has passed away; see, everything has become new!" (5:14, 16, 17). These verses have often been interpreted as being about the individual who, through Christ, becomes a new creation. Harink argues, however, that

> The new creation being asserted here is not a claim about the state of the Christian; it is a claim about how the world and in particular the other human being, must be acknowledged as new creation by the Christian, who knows that the old creation has been invaded, challenged and judged, in the death of Christ. . . . The other who stands before me is already cosharer in that new creation; the task of the Christian in the face of this other is to call attention to that fact.[21]

In Teresa's depiction of persons as diamond castles, where Christ dwells, she is declaring that all persons are already sharers in Christ's new creation. This is not the same as saying that all are Christians. Rather, as Harink puts it, "In the apocalypse of Jesus Christ the world has changed."[22] Harink uses the language of apocalypse to refer to God's action, God's Word, and God's power in relation to the powers of this world. "God's power as the cross and resurrection of Jesus Christ exposes what the world names as power, wisdom, and riches as their opposite."[23] While Teresa does not use the word "apocalypse," she nonetheless understands that God's power in the cross and resurrection of Christ (new creation) exposes both the truth of who we are and the truth about the world and all other powers.[24]

I will return to Teresa's social-political context. To sum up, God dwelling with us is a present occurrence both of an Old Testament figure (Zion) and of an eschatological one (new creation in Christ). In continuity with scripture, then, Teresa's diamond castle or abode is therefore a providential figure. Ephraim Radner notes about such figures: "Protestant and Catholic together shared this sense that the outworking of the scriptural figures—prophecies, forms, images, events—of Christ contain, in some way, the truth of his teaching. It did not matter that people did not always get the truth . . . the history of the Church will, inevitably, share the same form as the life of Jesus."[25] How is the image of Zion, the City of God, or the resurrected Christ a "form" such that to fully share in this, we share in the life of Jesus? According to Radner, such figures order the life of the church, whether the church fully recognizes it or not. The form of the resurrected Christ means that Christ is no longer bound by the limitations of space and time. After the resurrection, Christ is enduringly present in the church and the world.

It is this cosmic vision that shapes Teresa's understanding of "the mansions," rather than an unmediated and solitary one that bypasses God's creation of Israel and the church.

Memory and Calling

Let us return now to the key question that I said Teresa is addressing, "What is God's calling to the church?" It is interesting to note that Teresa focuses early in her book on a loss of memory:

> It is no small pity, and should cause us no little shame, that, through our own fault, we do not understand ourselves, or know who we are. Would it not be a sign of great ignorance, my daughters, if a person were asked who he was, and could not say, and had no idea who his father or his mother was, or from what country he came? Though that is great stupidity, our own is incomparably greater if we make no attempt to discover what we are.[26]

Why, we might ask, has the memory of who we are faded? Why, in other words, has a truth so apparently vivid to Teresa become a "sign of ignorance" amongst her sisters, as well as her wider audience? I think, first, we have to say that it has to do with the fresh wounds of division in the church. Such division, according to John 17, makes it difficult to believe that the Father has sent the Son, and therefore that God dwells with us. Second, I think the memory has faded because the church has forgotten Israel. During this time, Christians treated the Jews terribly. They could either be expelled or convert. "There was no place for them in the kingdom of the 'Catholic Monarch' (a title bestowed on Ferdinand and Isabella by the Pope in 1492)."[27] Teresa's own grandfather was a Jew who was pressured into converting to Christianity (a *converso*); he continued Jewish practices in secret, was eventually forced by the Inquisition to confess apostasy, was required to do public penance, and suffered public shame and loss of honor. Third, memory has faded because, as political theorist Murray Jardine points out, while the late Middle Ages was a time of impressive technological innovation (the printing press, the clock, the compass, firearms), European culture was also in a state of decadence, the most obvious aspect being the corruption of the Catholic Church.[28] Jardine's broader and provocative thesis is that in the face of new technological powers, European culture failed to make theological sense of its new creative capacities. Further, he draws an analogy between that time and our own. For my purposes, we can say that the cultural shift taking place in Europe at this time resulted in disorientation and confusion such that how to carry forward the memory of the Christian drama became less clear.

While more could certainly be said about Teresa's social context, it is clear that the memory that brings together the figure of God's dwelling as a visible body—Israel, Sinai, the Torah, Christ and the *ekklesia* or assembly of God—has faded at this time. Thus, it could make sense to expel or cut off other parts of the body politic. Teresa's re-figuring of our lives as the dwelling place of God is also therefore a remembering of the church as a visible and public entity, one that is an alternative witness to the politics and powers of this world. To understand this alternative politics more fully, we need to turn to another key scriptural figure that shapes Teresa's performance: journey or exodus.

Journey

The castle has many mansions with many, many rooms; though God dwells in the inmost mansions (the seventh), God can be seen in all of them. Teresa further states:

You must not imagine these mansions as arranged in a row, one behind another, but fix your attention on the centre, the room or palace occupied by the King. Think of a palmito, which has many outer rinds surrounding the savoury part within, all of which must be taken away before the centre can be eaten. Just so around this central room are many more, as there also are above it. In speaking of the soul we must always think of it as spacious, ample and lofty; and this can be done without the least exaggeration, for the soul's capacity is much greater than we can realize, and this Sun, which is in the palace, reaches every part of it.[29]

Teresa's image captures the psalmist's description, "Whither shall I go from thy Spirit? Or whither shall I flee from thy presence? If I ascend to heaven, thou art there! If I make my bed in Sheol, thou art there" (Ps 139:7-8). For Teresa, it is the journey that enables us to see that we are already inside a relation with God, whether we accept this or not.

What kind of journey does Teresa describe? Again, as with the figure of dwelling, Teresa understands that the Exodus is also now; God is acting in history now to move us from slavery to freedom, and from captivity to salvation. This journey is now: there is an exodus (from the outer court). There is wandering in the wilderness or dry land; in the Third Mansions, Teresa tells her sisters to move through times of "aridity" and not "at a snail's pace."[30] There is a passing through waters and a raining down of manna; in the Fourth Mansions, Teresa discusses God's consolations as different kinds of fresh and refreshing waters. There is the giving of commandments; in the Fifth Mansions, Teresa refers particularly to love of God and neighbor.[31] There is entry into the Promised Land, yet this is not otherworldly; in the seventh and final mansions, Teresa discusses what life lived in communion with God and others looks like. Finally, Teresa herself is a Moses figure, encountering God in dramatic burning bush-like ways (through locutions and visions), and leading her hearers to the Promised Land. Teresa thus understands her time and place providentially and is interpreting these in biblical terms. The church at this time *is* the journey of the Israelites through which God creates a people. The most visible sign of this peoplehood is love of neighbor. As Teresa states, "The surest sign we are keeping the two commandments (love for His Majesty and love for our neighbor) is, I think, that we should really be loving our neighbour; for we cannot be sure if we are loving God, although we may have good reasons for believing that we are, but we can know quite well if we are loving our neighbour."[32]

Far then from being a journey into the invisible world of the interior soul, *Interior Castle*, read as commentary on scripture, helps us see that the journey is one that makes the body of Christ more visible for the world. In the Seventh Mansions, Teresa refers to John's gospel: "One day, when Jesus Christ was praying for His Apostles (I do not know where this occurs), He asked that they might become one with the Father and with Him, even as Jesus Christ our Lord is in the Father and the Father is in Him. I do not know what greater love there can be than this." And then she poignantly adds: "And we shall none of us fail to be included here, for His Majesty went on to say: 'Not for them alone (the Apostles!) do I pray, but also for all who believe in Me'; and again: 'I am in them.' "[33] Because of Christ's creative word, all who desire can share in this unity. This is not the creation of unity among Christians "where none presently exists," nor is it to re-create a unity that has been lost. Rather, as Brian Daley, S.J., notes about contemporary ecumenical efforts, it is "to allow the unity that already exists among us as God's gift, and is hindered or clouded by our sinfulness and 'slowness of heart' (Lk 24:25), to become more fully evident in the way Christians look upon each other, articulate their faith, carry out their worship, and act in the world."[34]

For Teresa, the beauty of this life together is seen not in the majestic castles that marked the Spanish countryside, but in an ecclesial way of life marked by humility, grace, and love capable of honoring and serving Christ. Teresa would thus agree with the way a contemporary theologian puts it: "God chooses to be present in the world not as a cosmic force or a transcendent principle but through a people. So it has always been with Israel."[35]

The Politics of Teresa's Vision

We are now in a better position to understand how Teresa, as scriptural commentator and performer, understands faith and public life. She certainly would not have been haunted by the modern question, "What role does theology have in the public realm?"[36] Such a question, as Stephen Long notes, assumes that "some discourse exists located in a social reality greater than that which, for

Christians, is the only truly catholic reality, the church. Whether the assumed broader social reality is called 'the public,' 'society,' 'civilization,' or 'the political,' to ask the question of theology's relevance to such a grand social reality inevitably subordinates the church to it."[37] Long's claim is not intended to shore up triumphalism but rather to challenge Christians not to be determined by "publics" and politics that domesticate the church.

As noted earlier, Teresa's key image of Christ dwelling with us is the fullest possible public. The world is changed—transformed into diamond dwellings for Christ—even if this goes unrecognized, or is violently rejected. The church is that body of people in continuity with Israel who participate in and witness to this new creation.[38] The church is not without sin and unfaithfulness, but the church knows the one thing that someday all the world will acknowledge. In Jesus, God has broken the walls of enmity that separate us one from another and from God.

Far from being a private spirituality, then, Teresa's scriptural performance is itself a politics. I use "politics" here to mean the formation and pattern of people around a common good, which in this case is God's gathering and calling of Israel and the church through Christ. In this political world, who is outside the castle walls? The barbarians? The Jews? The Iraqis? Teresa writes: "Many souls remain in the outer court of the castle, which is the place occupied by the guards; they are not interested in entering it, and have no idea what there is in that wonderful place, or who dwells in it, or even how many rooms it has."[39] Her claim implies that no one is outside the castle walls. Perhaps this sounds hegemonic; who are we to say that others are in the space of this castle? But by grounding her performance in the particularity of Israel and Christ's body, Teresa is actually challenging the triumphalistic political tyranny of her day (that expelled Jews and Muslims) as well as the political tyranny of our own day, which relegates faith to an apolitical sphere.

This challenge can best be seen in Teresa's understanding of honor. In Teresa's day, honor was tightly related to blood, wealth, and ancestry. As Archbishop Rowan Williams observes, honor was " 'objectified' as a matter of supreme public interest in such a way that an affront to one's public dignity or standing in the eyes of society becomes something worth killing for."[40] The Mafioso-style system of honor and revenge, Williams further notes, is repugnant to us today. Or more fully stated, it is simply incoherent.

Peter Berger argues in his essay "On the Obsolescence of the Concept of Honor" that the language of dignity and individual rights has replaced that of honor. "Honor is commonly understood as an aristocratic concept, or at least associated with a hierarchical order of society."[41] Even in Teresa's own day, Cervantes's *Don Quixote* debunks the illusions and follies of honor associated with chivalry. Yet, as Berger soberly states, "Modern man is Don Quixote on his deathbed, denuded of the multicoloured banners that previously enveloped the self and revealed to be *nothing but a man*: 'I was mad, but I am now in my senses. I was once Don Quixote de la Mancha' "[42] but am no longer. Don Quixote is disenchanted, to use Max Weber's phrase. Berger notes, "It is important to understand that it is precisely this solitary self that modern consciousness has perceived as the bearer of human dignity and of inalienable human rights."[43] Berger's point is that honor, associated with socially obliged roles or norms has been replaced by a self as such, the bearer of dignity and individual rights (regardless of his or her position in society). This latter view, of course, is deeply engrained in contemporary political thinking (at least in the United States). In going to war, for example, our country does not declare that it is protecting our honor; rather, we state that we are protecting, dying, and killing for freedom. Such freedom is the freedom that pertains to the individual and his or her rights. Berger does claim that concepts of honor have survived into the modern era, "in groups retaining a hierarchical view of society," such as traditional professions like law and medicine, and the military.[44] Even so, Berger notes that honor has become obsolete because the modern self experiences institutions (and institutional roles) as "oppressive realities that distort and estrange the self." "Institutions," he writes, "cease to be the 'home' of the self."[45]

Teresa has no desire to shore up the prevailing concept of honor in her day[46] and, by implication, the political institutions when they uphold such honor. But neither does she imagine the individual apart from the institution of the church. This can be seen in the fact that honor remains central to her understanding. She tells her sisters and her readers again and again not to offend "His Majesty," Christ. There is clearly in place a conviction that the honor of Christ can be offended. But how exactly does this happen?

For a clue, I think we can turn to a well-known scene in Teresa's own life when, during Lent of 1554 when she was thirty-nine years old, she comes upon a figure of Christ crucified. She is struck by the figure of Jesus in his moment of isolation, above all in Gethsemane. What further strikes her is that Christ, in his woundedness, *needs* her. As Williams discusses this scene, he notes that Teresa "had allowed herself to be hampered and controlled by anxiety about acceptability."[47] In her day, acceptability was related to honor: for women, it involved purity, attractiveness, wealth, social class, and so forth. Yet Teresa replaces this honor with an honor derived from Christ. "We must acknowledge," she states, "that, for all our natural poverty, we are enriched by God and are given favors in order to share them. . . . How can anyone benefit and share [her] gifts lavishly if [she] doesn't understand that [she] is rich?"[48] Such honor, such worth, is not dependent upon distorted social constructs, nor on an image of oneself as virtuous, but on God's freedom and love in Christ.[49] It is not a right but a gift.

The key way Christ is offended, according to Teresa, is when we reject His gifts: namely, communion with God and one another. To reject the offering of Christ is therefore to dishonor Christ. And yet can Christ really lose his honor? Can Christ be dishonored and humiliated? In Teresa's world, and in the Christian drama more broadly, the answer is surely "yes," because Christ does not force His gifts on us, nor does he defend his own honor. As Teresa discovered before the figure of Christ, He needs disciples who honor Him by receiving from Him, and thus acknowledging that we are not our own creators. Further, Christ's honor is defended not through violence but by tending to Christ's wounds (sacrifice) and by serving Christ. From the perspective of the dominant politics of Teresa's day, or ours, this might not sound like much of a politics. And yet Teresa is giving an alternative to the account of honor—based on purity of blood, lineage, social class, and so forth—that dominated the politics of her day and justified the use of violence to shore up the monarchy. At the same time, contrary to our politics of individual rights, which is also used to justify violence, Teresa maintains that the political good has to do with honoring Christ as a way of life.

Such honoring does not take place apart from the institution of the church, since it is through the church that one knows and honors Christ. If we understand that institutions are those places that "house practices,"[50] then Teresa's politics are sustained by the practices of the church. Teresa understands that God feeds us through such practices as hearing scripture, through prayer, worship and confession, and through friendship. Through these practices God creates us to be a people for the world. Teresa describes what this peoplehood looks like, in the Seventh Mansions, in her interpretation of the gospel scene when Jesus is visiting Mary and Martha, where Mary is lifted up as the one who is concerned with the "one thing needful." Teresa interprets the story differently: "Mary and Martha must work together when they offer the Lord lodging, and must have Him ever with them, and they must not entertain Him badly and give Him nothing to eat. And how can Mary give Him anything, seated as she is at His feet, unless her sister helps her? His food consists in our bringing Him souls."[51] We feed Christ not only by worshipping him but by practicing hospitality, both to Christ and to Christ in the other (Matthew 25).[52]

Teresa herself acknowledges, however, how limited her sisters seem to be: "The other thing you may say is that you are unable to lead souls to God, and have no means of doing so; that you would gladly do this, but, being unable to teach and preach like the Apostles, you do not know how."[53] Her advice is that "By doing things which you really can do, His Majesty will know that you would like to do many more, and thus He will reward you exactly as if you had won many souls for Him." To modern ears, this sounds politically inconsequential, particularly when we think of the dominant and powerful politics of Teresa's day.

I want, however, to return to McClendon's "this is that" reading of scripture and history, and claim that we are in the same position as Teresa's sisters and readers. We too easily imagine that we don't have the means to make things come out right. In the face of the overwhelming force of liberal political capitalism, and of the global market, we too might easily think that listening to scripture or practicing prayer or hospitality don't seem to be enough. Yet Teresa's counsel is ours as well: "The devil sometimes puts ambitious desires into our hearts, so that, instead of setting our hand to the work which lies nearest to us, and thus serving Our Lord in ways within our power, we may rest content with having desired the impossible."[54] As Teresa also knew, the politics of the church is not a system, much less an attempt to control power, but it is a people living in communion with God, willing to live a cruciform life out of love for God and the world. Teresa writes, "Do you know when people really become spiritual? It is when they become the slaves of God and are branded with His sign, which is the sign of the Cross, in token that they have given Him their freedom."[55]

Finally, there is a sense in which this life is hidden from the world. Teresa uses the image of a "silkworm," hidden in his cocoon, and relates this to Colossians 3:3: "For you have died, and your life is hidden with Christ in God." Like the silkworm, patiently and slowly spinning its silk, Teresa states, God takes whatever we can offer and unites it with His offering to the Father, "so it may have the value won for it by our will, even though our actions in themselves may be trivial."[56] Our lives are hidden in Christ because the world sees prayer, confession, corporate worship, and the works of mercy as politically insignificant. And yet, as Teresa indicates, worship transforms the body of Christ into a visible and public entity as Christ unites our meager offerings to his own. This last image is clearly a eucharistic one, which means that Teresa understands Word and Table as recreating the church in her own time, just as God recreates it in ours, to be an alternative for the world.[57]

Notes

[1] Herschel H. Hobbs, *You Are Chosen: The Priesthood of All Believers* (San Francisco: Harper & Row, 1990), 3. Hobbs also calls soul competency the "distinctive contribution of Baptists to the Christian world." While Hobbs is on the more moderate, liberal side of Baptist life, conservative Baptists invoke "soul competency" as well. For example, Adrian Rogers, conservative Southern Baptist Convention president in 1979, 1986, and 1987, gives a similar endorsement of the priesthood: "Because I believe so much in the priesthood of the believer and our accountability to God alone, I would never, I hope till I die, compromise conviction on the altar of cooperation" (quoted by Bill Leonard, *God's Last and Only Hope* [Grand Rapids: Eerdmans, 1990], 149).

[2] Michel de Certeau, *The Mystic Fable, Volume 1: The Sixteenth and Seventeenth Centuries*, trans. Michael B. Smith (Chicago: University of Chicago Press, 1992), 188.

[3] Ibid., 200.

[4] Lawrence S. Cunningham, "The Mystic Fable, Vol. 1: The Sixteenth and Seventeenth Centuries," (book reviews), *Commonweal*, May 7, 1993; http://findarticles.com/p/articles/mi_m1252/is_n9_v120/ai_13869303.

[5] Margaret Miles, *Practicing Christianity: Critical Perspectives for an Embodied Spirituality* (New York: Crossroad, 1988), 59.

[6] Ibid., 51.

[7] Teresa of Avila, *Interior Castle*, trans. E. Allison Peers (New York: Doubleday Image, 1961), 237. See p. 76 above, text at note 54.

[8]There is no doubt that Teresa did not challenge some stereotypical social roles, particularly regarding women. My own concern, however, is to challenge the reading of *Interior Castle* that interprets it as primarily the interior journey of a soul.

[9]We find a clue as to why this question would have been the upmost in her mind if we look at her life's work: namely, the reformation of the Carmelite order. Such work displays her concern to shore up the Body of Christ so that the church could be more faithful. My own interest in Teresa's life and work is that I think if we can move beyond a thoroughly modern reading of *Interior Castle*, we can find insights about how to be a more faithful church in our own context. For asking similar kinds of questions in our contemporary context, see Ephraim Radner, *Hope among the Fragments* (Grand Rapids: Brazos, 2004), esp. chap. 11, "Enduring the Church, How to Be a Fool," 199-214.

[10]My thesis is not that Teresa systematically sets out to give an ecclesiology. She is rather notoriously disorganized in her writing, often repeating herself or losing where she was when she left off. Even so, my emphasis is that her vision is an ecclesial one.

[11]This might sound odd, since Teresa apparently did not practice the reading of scripture as we do today—in the sense of having a Bible before her on which she could meditate and reflect. Further, while Teresa quotes from scripture, she does so sporadically and sometimes with a poor memory of a particular verse. She was, though, immersed in a particular kind of scriptural piety through her formation, prayer, and the liturgy. As Keith Egan helpfully reminded me in personal correspondence, Teresa "is in a way a reader and performer of scripture within a community. She did not have access to the whole Bible in Spanish—big chunks in anthologies but not the complete Bible. She heard the Bible in community—in sermons, and in whatever reading she could do—an avid reader. She is an ecclesial reader. Is not the religious community an ecclesial community? Teresa wanted the solitude to hear God's Word."

[12]I gleaned this way of putting the matter from Jacob Goodson, "Pragmatism and the Baptist Theology of Martin Luther King, Jr.," unpublished. One way to say this is that Teresa uses scripture to understand her time and place. As Goodson notes, "The scriptural tradition being the norm is not a Romantic return to scripture but is a recognition that to live in the time and place God puts you is to live in that time and place in biblical terms" (8). Teresa rightly understood that to speak faithfully of God requires training by the gospel: "Theology is thinking what to say to be saying the gospel" (Robert Jenson, as quoted by Stanley Hauerwas, *A Better Hope, Resources for a Church Confronting Capitalism, Democracy, and Postmodernity* [Grand Rapids: Brazos, 2000], 121).

[13]James Wm. McClendon, Jr., *Ethics: Systematic Theology, Vol. 1* (Nashville: Abingdon Press, 1986), 31-35.

[14]James McClendon, "Embodying the 'Great Story': An Interview with James McClendon," by Ched Myers. Available at http://thewitness.org/archive/dec2000/mcclendon.html, 3.

[15]McClendon, *Ethics*, 31.

[16]Ibid.

[17]Teresa, *Interior Castle*, 218. Teresa says earlier that, "The soul begins to live and nourishes itself on this food [confession, sermons, good books]" (91).

[18]Ibid., 4.

[19]De Certeau, *The Mystic Fable*, 12-13.

[20]Teresa, *Interior Castle*, 11.

[21]Douglas Harink, *Paul among the Postliberals: Pauline Theology beyond Christendom and Modernity* (Grand Rapids: Brazos, 2003), 252-53.

[22]Ibid., 252.

[23]Ibid., 257. Harink adds, "Conversely, the truth about God's power and wisdom is revealed in the gospel story of the self-giving vulnerability of Jesus' crucifixion at the hands of the rulers of this age."

[24]Thus Teresa writes, "Fix your eyes on the crucified and nothing else will be of much importance to you" (*Interior Castle*, 233).

[25]Radner, *Hope among the Fragments*, 126. Radner further states that "a figure is a form that God actually makes historical experience fit, like some providential mold."

[26]Teresa, *Interior Castle*, 4.

[27]Archbishop Rowan Williams, *Teresa of Avila* (New York: Continuum, 1991), 17. As Williams further notes, Castile, in the first half of the sixteenth century was "marked by social restlessness and hostility on a large scale. . . . The expulsion of the remaining Muslims had been accompanied by comparable pressure on Jews."

[28]Murray Jardine, *The Making and Unmaking of Technological Society: How Christianity Can Save Modernity from Itself* (Grand Rapids: Brazos, 2004), 130.

[29]Teresa, *Interior Castle*, 13.

[30]Ibid., 39 and 45.

[31]Ibid., 103.

[32]Ibid.

[33]Ibid., 219. Teresa is quoting John 17:20, 23.

[34]Brian Daley, "Rebuilding the Structure of Love: The Quest for Visible Unity among the Churches," in *The Ecumenical Future*, ed. Carl E. Braaten and Robert W. Jenson (Grand Rapids: Eerdmans, 2004), 74.

[35]Scott Bader-Saye, *Church and Israel after Christendom* (Boulder: Westview, 1999), 109.

[36]D. Stephen Long, *John Wesley's Moral Theology: The Quest for God and Goodness* (Nashville: Kingswood Books, 2005), 210.

[37]Ibid. In a similar vein, Frederick Bauerschmidt notes the difficulty of reading Julian of Norwich as "political" in the face of modern Western political orders that presume "theology and politics are or should be something distinct. Theology is concerned with either private realms of religious inwardness or the semiprivate realm of the church as a voluntary association, whereas politics is concerned with the state and the exercise of public authority. To mix the two is to put modern pluralistic society at risk" (*Julian*

of Norwich and the Mystical Body Politics of Christ [Notre Dame: University of Notre Dame Press, 1999], 3).

[38] As Bader-Saye puts it, "God is resolved to work through the risky means of calling and forming a people for obedience so that the world will know God and God's ways" (*Church and Israel after Christendom*, 110). This is both the witness of Israel (Ez 36:22-26) and the church.

[39] Teresa, *Interior Castle*, 6.

[40] Williams, *Teresa of Avila*, 25. For a fuller discussion of honor, see 24-34.

[41] Peter Berger, "On the Obsolescence of the Concept of Honor," in *Liberalism and Its Critics*, ed. Michael Sandel (New York: New York University Press, 1984), 150.

[42] Ibid., 152.

[43] Ibid., 153.

[44] Ibid., 151.

[45] Ibid., 156. As Berger describes it, "Dignity, as against honor, always relates to the intrinsic humanity divested of all socially imposed roles or norms. It pertains to the self as such, to the individual regardless of his position in society" (153).

[46] As Teresa notes in the First Mansions, the person absorbed in possessions, honors, and business is prevented from "gazing at the castle and enjoying its beauty" (*Interior Castle*, 17).

[47] Williams, *Teresa of Avila*, 70.

[48] Teresa, as cited by Williams, 69.

[49] Ibid., 32 and 69.

[50] McClendon, *Ethics*, 193.

[51] Teresa, *Interior Castle*, 236.

[52] Along similar lines, Keith Egan has suggested that the Seventh Mansions can be read as a re-statement of the Beatitudes. In addition, the concept of honor that Teresa endorses is perhaps most fully described in 1 Corinthians 12. My thanks to Sharon K. Perkins for this latter connection.

[53] Teresa, *Interior Castle*, 237.

[54] Ibid.

[55] Ibid., 234.

[56] Ibid., 238. According to Teresa, "The silkworm is like the soul which takes life when, through the heat which comes from the Holy Spirit, it begins to utilize the general help which God gives to us all, and to make use of the remedies which He left in His Church–such as frequent confessions, good books and sermons. . . . And, before we have finished doing all that we can in that respect, God will take this tiny achievement of ours, which is nothing at all, unite it with His greatness and give it such worth that its reward will be the Lord Himself" (92).

[57] I wish to thank Keith J. Egan and Jacob L. Goodson for reading an earlier draft of this essay and offering helpful comments.

Religious Liberty and the Common Good

A Baptist Engagement
with the Catholic Americanist Tradition

Coleman Fannin

The idea of the common good has been revived in recent years by the political and religious left to illustrate citizens' shared responsibility for social justice. Meanwhile the right sometimes employs common-good language to support the role of capitalism in the creation of wealth or to call for legislation restricting certain behaviors. But what *is* the common good? Where is it located? The philosophers and theologians who conceived and refined the idea of the common good agreed that it presupposes agreement about specific moral ends and the practices necessary to pursue them. In contrast, those on the right and left (and center) privatize such ends and/or conflate a civic common good with that of Christianity and other faith traditions, thereby dissociating the common good from its communal contexts and elevating the nation-state as its primary caretaker and defender.

Contemporary notions of the common good rest on the modern presumption that some form of moral reasoning must be available to all rational persons.[1] Among Protestant ethicists wary of relativism, the quest for objectivity typically falls into biblicism or, as in divine command or Christian realism, leaves substantive Christian claims behind. Recognition of these weaknesses has led some Protestants to turn to Catholicism, but Catholic theologians often elevate a reductionist form of natural law as a universal basis for morality and/or Catholic social teaching as a blueprint for civic duty. Indeed, Catholics in the United States have proven vulnerable to the same confusion regarding the common good. In this essay I will investigate what Donald Pelotte has named the "Americanist tradition," the history of Catholic accommodation to the condition of religious liberty that my Baptist forbears helped create.[2] I will explain how John Courtney Murray, the foremost representative of the Americanist tradition, was able to negotiate this condition better than Baptists and other Protestants due to his ecclesial location, but was ultimately unable to craft a satisfactory notion of the common good. I will then argue that his failure can be overcome only through a radical theology that locates the common good (and politics itself) not in the nation-state but in diverse and overlapping communities with shared commitments. If the common good requires a moral framework that can be neither naturally perceived nor coerced, and if some conceptions of what is good are better than others, then Baptists and other Christians must reconsider our approach to moral formation in light of our sociopolitical location.

The Common Good as Theopolitical Concept

The notion of a common good originated with Greek and Roman philosophers, who held definite convictions about the nature of the good and assumed the context of a *polis* or republic that shared them. Likewise, theologians from Augustine to Aquinas and on to Luther and Calvin engaged this notion from the standpoint of a union of church and society and of Christian and citizen. In short, these thinkers insisted that civic activity presupposes a web of tacit agreements; that is, economics and politics *as such* do not govern themselves but stand under the judgment of a moral framework. As Aristotle understood, such a framework enables discussion of the relationship between the interests of individuals and those of their families and community. It also includes agreement about the ultimate end (the highest good or *summum bonum*) for human beings, which shapes their character through participation in concrete practices.[3]

Enlightenment philosophy and liberal political theory undermined this presupposition. Early liberals generally agreed that the classical concept of the common good could not be sustained and insisted that modern states be organized instead around the protection of the natural rights of the individual to pursue his or her own good, albeit with virtue and in accordance with moral (natural) law. For this purpose individuals enter into a social contract bound by reason and the rule of law. Thus the founders of the

United States declared in the Declaration of Independence that the purpose of government is to secure "self-evident" rights, a purpose derived "from the consent of the governed." However, a different group of leaders expressed a lingering concern for the common good in the preamble to the Constitution, which ascribes a set of goals to the nation's people: "to form a more perfect Union, establish Justice, insure domestic Tranquility, provide for the common defence, promote the general Welfare, and secure the Blessings of Liberty to ourselves and our Posterity."

The precise nature of the relationship between human rights and the common good has been a matter of debate ever since. "Conservative" or libertarian (or classical) liberals have insisted that the preamble refers not to government but to the Constitution itself. The above objectives are merely descriptions of what the people must work for in order to preserve the rights granted them by the state; thus human rights are first principles, for if they are infringed upon, the common good suffers and the nation is threatened by totalitarianism. Further, the protection of business and free enterprise leads to prosperity and advancement of the common good, an argument supposedly vindicated by the failure of communism. "Liberal" (or social) liberals, however, posit a role for the state in fostering a morality based on agreement not about a *telos* but about respect for a broader spectrum of rights. Particular moral frameworks contribute to the common good insofar as they foster such respect and are regulated by a neutral conception of justice that prevents the distortions they inevitably bring to public life.

Despite this diversity, political liberalism remains the dominant philosophy in American public life. Its preeminent example is John Rawls, who, in distinguishing between the good and the just, defined the common good as "certain general conditions that are . . . equally to everyone's advantage" and conceived of the organization of diverse conceptions of the good in terms of "overlapping consensus."[4] Here political authority derives its legitimacy from agreement on the part of individuals and groups, religious and otherwise, to refrain from contesting and directing public morality in exchange for the freedom to privately pursue their various ends. However, a host of theorists known as communitarians have contended that this form of liberalism produces individualism that actually harms the common good. Some have also called into question the self-evidence of rights and explained that any political order favors the interests of certain groups. Further, a radical minority denies that a substantive conception of the common good can be inserted into the liberal order through procedural means and instead contends that it can be found only in groups that share deep moral agreements. Still, the vast majority of liberals *and* communitarians accept that "society" requires something like the nation-state. In other words, the common good subsists in institutions and systems that operate in a manner benefiting everyone and is advanced or hindered to the degree that they function properly. Not all institutions and systems are directly related to government, but many are (and increasingly so), and although they often operate across them, the boundaries of the society they serve are defined and defended by the nation-state.[5]

This presents a number of practical problems. For example, the sheer number of different ideas makes reaching agreement difficult, increasing the likelihood that efforts to promote the common good will require coercion. Also, individuals or groups may refuse to sacrifice some of their freedom for the sake of others or choose to receive the benefits of the common good without contributing to it. It is not difficult to see consequences in areas such as education, the environment, health care, and poverty. Yet liberals and communitarians largely agree that the social possibilities of democratic capitalism are worth the risks; therefore the debate is usually framed in terms of tensions among competing interests, and the state must primarily protect either individual rights or social values. As Brian Stiltner explains, "It is often assumed that this is a zero-sum game; for instance, to ensure more political freedom means further to privatize and stigmatize citizens' religious beliefs, while a political accommodation of some citizens' beliefs entails a greater burden on those citizens who do not participate in the favored religion(s)."[6]

The Other Side of Religious Liberty

Their fear of absolute claims in the wake of the "Wars of Religion" has been exaggerated, but the framers of the Constitution did recognize the necessity of handling religion with special care.[7] Therefore they placed freedom of religion at the beginning of the Bill of Rights as the condition by which other freedoms could flourish. If anything about the founding was providential, it was the First Amendment, which prohibited religious establishment but, unlike disestablishment in much of Europe, allowed for religious expression and (theoretically, at least) assumed its role in fostering the common good.

Many Baptists claim that religious liberty is our "trophy," our unique contribution to history, and the work of Roger Williams, John Leland, Isaac Backus, and others in prying the sword out of the hand of the church can scarcely be overvalued.[8] Yet Baptists have not proven adept at negotiating the situation produced by their advocacy. No longer in a position of dissent, we were the first to apply the democratic spirit of the early republic to our congregations. In a culture infused by Protestant morality, Baptists saw no need for an articulated ecclesiology; in fact, we saw that culture's existence as a vindication of Baptist principles. However, the Civil War and industrialization ended its hegemony in the North and, later, the fundamentalist-modernist controversy marked the beginning of the end in the South, where Baptists were "the center of gravity."[9] Much of the conflict in the Southern Baptist Convention (SBC) in the last century was caused by differing reactions to this breakdown, as Baptists became vulnerable to modernism *and* fundamentalism. The response of "moderate" Baptists to subsequent division has been to emphasize "soul liberty" (or "soul competency"), a concept closely related to religious liberty that refers to each individual's accountability before God and his or her right to choose to have (or not have) faith and to interpret the Bible for him or herself. A classic formulation was given by Southern Baptist leader Herschel Hobbs when, echoing his predecessor E. Y. Mullins, he wrote that "religion is a personal matter between the individual and God" and that soul liberty "includes salvation by grace through faith without the need of a human mediator or any institution, ecclesiastical or political."[10]

A closer examination of Mullins is helpful for two reasons. First, he argued that the Catholic view of sacraments is the antithesis of soul liberty. As Elizabeth Newman explains, for Mullins "the seven sacraments illustrate in a 'striking way' that priestly mediation is necessary, thus implying the soul's incompetency." Second, he claimed that democracy is inherent to the state *and* the church as an "inevitable corollary" of soul liberty.[11] Contemporary scholars such as Glenn Hinson and Walter Shurden have promulgated a similar ecclesiology, and Newman argues that while Shurden is careful to affirm the role of the community in the Baptist vision, he makes two false assumptions. First, the church is important but *not necessary*; instead it is "subsequent to the faith of the individual that he or she brings to the larger body." Second, the church and the individual "need to be kept in tension."[12]

Shurden's position reflects a legitimate fear of coercion, and Newman approvingly quotes James McClendon's claim that soul liberty implies "the rejection of violence as the basis of community."[13] Yet Shurden sets up an inevitable trade-off that ultimately places the individual over the community, which finally becomes optional. He and other Baptists are also right to emphasize the integrity of the human person. However, no person exists outside communal bonds, and even those Christians not born into believing families or congregations learn of the faith from others and engage in practices carried through time by the church. We do not "choose" to be part of these narratives; we simply *are* part of them and they part of us.[14] Here Newman offers three accurate criticisms: first, freedom does not reside in the individual as a right but comes as a gift at God's initiative; second, private interpretation places the authority of the individual *above* that of scripture; and third, soul competency reflects a conception of "religion" as, in William Cavanaugh's words, "a set of beliefs which is defined as personal conviction and which can exist separately from one's public loyalty to the State." In the early modern period the common understanding of religious faith shifted from one inseparable from community and tradition to one defined by a criterion of independent propositions or individual experience. With this development, "Religion is no longer a matter of certain bodily practices within the Body of Christ, but is limited to the realm of the 'soul,' and the body is handed over to the State."[15]

Cavanaugh's conclusion reaches the heart of my argument. In short, soul liberty has become problematic for Baptists in two ways. First, it has not provided us with an identity that is sustainable over time. If the freedom of the individual soul is the heart of the Baptist vision, then it is difficult, if not impossible, for this vision to serve a normative function. That is, we have no basis for claiming that we or any other groups are "real Baptists." Further, without proper notions of the church, tradition, and authority we are open to perversions of them (for example, fundamentalism). Second, this lack of identity makes it difficult to discern the dangers that accompany the nation-state and its culture.

Like their fellow citizens, moderate Baptists accept that the nation-state is the keeper of the common good. One source will have to suffice as evidence. The common good appears regularly in the publications of the Baptist Center for Ethics. For example, in "A Baptist Pastoral Letter Supporting Public Education," the Center identifies churches as one of many types of organizations that contribute to the common good. Children "deserve the nurture of a good society" advanced by public schools that are committed to separation of church and state and therefore "free from coercive pressure to promote sectarian faith." In other words, churches are necessarily *divisive* but American society is a "just society" and its institutions are *unifying*. The letter closes with this statement: "We call on Baptists to recommit themselves to the nation's founding principle of 'E Pluribus Unum.' A society based on unity out of diversity will embrace every child and recognize the vital role public schools play in achieving national unity."[16]

The problem is not that it is wrong to support public education or that such education should include state-sponsored prayer. Rather, the problem is that while state institutions are *public,* churches are *private* (at least in regard to their deepest convictions) and incapable of producing unity or justice without the state. Similarly, James Evans says that while "honoring the Scriptures and following a covenant ethic is certainly good, it must be seen as a particular good—that is, a good that is not self-evident to everyone." Therefore faith is best kept private except when it can contribute to a universal ideal (such as "caring for the poor and disadvantaged") that "transcends religious belief" and promotes the common good.[17] Again, the problem is not that Baptists should abandon working with other groups for common goals; it is the assumption that the state's principles *are* self-evident and the implicit denial of the possibility that Christian ideals are at times more correct than a public (or American) amalgam of perspectives. Yet the Center sees no obstacle to expecting accountability to biblical norms. After the 2006 election Robert Parham called on the Democratic majority to demonstrate faith not through prayer—Jesus "spoke for prayer in private"—but through public service because "the nation hungers for a politics of humility that pursues the common good." He also claimed that "both faithful and secular Democrats" share "a commitment to do justice," but he defined justice in biblical, not secular (Rawlsian), terms.[18] It is unclear how one can expect a state separated from the church by a "high wall" to operate according to biblical standards, but the Center applies such standards *without translation* to a wide range of institutions, including the IRS.[19]

These Baptists identify particular failures of the state in pursuing the common good but do not consider that it might simply be incapable of doing so. Although they recognize the presence of "selfish individualism," they fail to see that democratic capitalism fosters it. To be clear, questioning soul liberty does not mean questioning religious liberty or institutional separation of church and state; it means recognizing that these developments come with a responsibility. Those who resist community because it threatens the individual conscience and who resist ecclesial structures because they limit options for association fail to recognize that the challenge facing Baptists is not the loss of individuality, for Martin Marty was correct in claiming that the United States has undergone "baptistification."[20] Rather, the challenge is that we have lost our sense of what McClendon terms "a shared and lived story."[21]

Many Christians no longer see themselves as first part of the church. For example, a recent survey reported that when asked, "Do you think of yourself first as an American or first as a Christian?" 48 percent of American Christians answered "American first" while only 42 percent answered "Christian first."[22] This is not a new problem, but it does have new significance. Early Baptists formed our tradition out of dissent from established churches in Europe, and their heirs in America shaped it in the midst of a Protestant culture. In these contexts much about Christian living could be taken for granted, allowing Baptists to stress soul liberty and the priesthood of all believers in order to differentiate themselves. Today, however, these principles are not enough to sustain identity. Many Baptists remain dedicated to local churches, but most are more influenced by generic evangelical or liberal teaching (and personalities) than by the Baptist tradition. More important, divided and optional Baptist organizations are no match for the formation of the state and market. The point is not that Baptists must decide to stand wholly for or against the nation or culture; it is that we must develop the ability to discern what we can embrace and what we must reject. This will require a re-envisioning of our ecclesiology, one engaging the Great Tradition found in its most robust form in the Catholic Church. Baptists have a long history of anti-Catholicism—see George Truett's speech on the steps of the U.S. Capitol in 1920—that still reappears.[23] However, it is worth asking what we might learn from Catholicism, especially considering that Catholic political theory almost single-handedly kept the notion of the common good alive through the twentieth century. First, however, it is important to know the history of how Catholics came to see themselves as contributors to the *nation's* common good.

Americanism and the Common Good

Catholics have been assessing their place in the United States since the mid-eighteenth century, but back then their starting point was a theoretical (though not always practical) rejection of religious liberty. "Americanists" such as John Ireland, John Keane, and Denis O'Connell challenged this position, only to be rebuked by Leo XIII in *Testem Benevolentiae Nostrae* (1899). Not until the adoption of the Declaration on Religious Freedom (*Dignitatis Humanae*, 1965) by the Second Vatican Council did the church's teaching shift definitively. Central to this story is John Courtney Murray, the Jesuit once silenced yet "vindicated" by the declaration, which he helped compose.[24] After the Council, conservative and liberal Catholic moral theologians began a struggle over who would lay authentic claim to its vision, and Murray has functioned as a "totem" for both factions and a target for radical critics who question whether the Catholic Church can indeed be reconciled with the American state.[25]

Murray's consideration of religious liberty in the 1950s and early 1960s was consistent with his prior treatment of intercredal cooperation.[26] Pelotte notes that by the early 1940s Murray was already crafting his church-state theory. "It mattered little to Murray whether one spoke of the relation between Church and State or of religious liberty or of cooperation. All three represented various ways of speaking about the same issue." Indeed, it was intercredal cooperation that first drew the ire of two professors at Catholic University, Francis Connell and Joseph Fenton, who would challenge Murray on religious liberty. Murray's subsequent work on education continued this trajectory, and the "school question" offers a good entry point into the Americanist narrative.[27]

Catholics lived almost without incident in the colonies and early republic, but immigration in the mid-nineteenth century added to their numbers and heightened their sense of being outsiders. With Protestant America at its zenith, it was difficult for Catholic immigrants to be perceived as anything but a threat to that way of life. They responded in roughly two ways: those of French and German origin cultivated the practices of devotionalism and the theology of ultramontanism, while those of Irish descent embraced a more Americanized conception of "church." Yet *both* imbibed the national ethos; as Jay Dolan notes, papal infallibility and certainty about the church "gave Catholic outsiders a confidence that they were the ones on whom the future of America rested."[28] Catholicism welcomed an impressive stream of converts—including Orestes Brownson, forerunner of the Americanists—and a question presented itself: would ultimate success come by converting the nation or by joining its project?

Meanwhile Protestants, thriving after the Second Great Awakening, turned their attention to social problems, especially among urban immigrant populations, and came to see education as the key to inculcating morality *and* republicanism. Agreement on theological points that separated denominations was thought to be impossible, and civil liberty and religious liberty were inseparable in the popular mind. Still, a strong sense of national unity endured even after the Civil War, and Protestants "recaptured the vision of John Winthrop's 'city on a hill,' to which all nations would look for guidance and inspiration." While the education movement was nonsectarian and varied according to region, it was also highly organized and focused on its goal. "Once this movement took hold, its supporters promoted it with a crusader's zeal, and before long the schoolhouse became the established church of the American republic."[29] Catholic leaders were troubled because they could not assent to the ideology of public education, and their equally thorough response generated heated opposition.[30] "Catholics could not understand the fuss," Dolan says. "They claimed to be loyal Americans, but because they challenged the Protestant culture of the public schools they were labeled 'un-American' and enemies of the republic."[31] All parties recognized that education is neither religiously nor politically neutral. Today, however, many Christians join secularists in arguing the opposite. Others call for injecting "values" into public education, still others advocate withdrawal to private or home schools, but all understand the goal of education as *serving the common good of the nation.*

By Murray's day, loyalty to America was no longer a question for Catholics. The Americanists' spirit of conversion had vanished, replaced by the consensus of the postwar era. How do we explain this turn of events? According to John Tracy Ellis, at the end of the nineteenth century "children born to the rough and tumble crowd of Catholic immigrants" were already "second to none in their true American character and spirit." Yet the body politic remained leery, inducing in them "an eagerness to 'belong.' "[32] Thus Catholic mobilization (or institutional buildup) in the first half of the twentieth century was not solely inward-looking; it included what Philip Gleason calls the "evangelical, outward-directed impulse" systematized by Pius XI in the program of Catholic Action and reflecting the European intellectual and cultural revival closely linked to neo-scholastic philosophy and theology. The Catholic Worker movement was one facet of this "apostolic ferment," but it was the formation of the National Catholic War Council during the First World War and the belated embrace of the social gospel spirit by its successor, the National Catholic Welfare Conference, that began to cement a sense of belonging confirmed by World War II.[33]

As Philip Gleason points out, "Set against the monstrous contrast of Naziism, with its heavy overtones of romantic antimodernism, the American version of modernity—which was, of course, nothing other than the American way of life—looked very good indeed."[34] The Catholic Church was also a longtime opponent of communism, giving it the credibility to stand proudly with the nation as the Cold War began.[35] Further, economic recovery propelled the descendants of immigrants into the same spheres of wealth as other citizens; historians such as Ellis and Thomas MacAvoy recovered Americanism on the intellectual front; and the election of John F. Kennedy signaled political arrival. Still, these "halcyon days" included a drift toward privatism.[36] Catholics had not yet become indifferent, only uninterested in converting their fellow Americans. In David J. O'Brien's words, Will Herberg's *Protestant, Catholic, Jew* argued that "Catholicism had become a way of being American, of finding identity and belonging while worshiping not the God of the Scriptures but America itself."[37] Thus it is not surprising that many saw the church's teaching on religious liberty as an embarrassment.

The rise of a "new nativism" only heightened the tension. Murray saw that this nativism "was not so much Protestant as it was naturalist, operating on the premise that democracy demanded a naturalist, secularist philosophy."[38] The same certainty that had once comforted Catholics now called their loyalty to the United States into question. The loudest critic was journalist Paul Blanshard, who fit the secularist profile despite being an ordained minister. Yet suspicion also came from the National Council of Churches; Baptists such as J. M. Dawson, who helped found Protestants and Other Americans United for Separation of Church and State (POAU) to prevent funding of religious education; and theologians such as Reinhold Niebuhr, who argued that separation of religion and education "represents a gain for our public life, since organized religion is bound to be divisive, and it is a divisiveness we simply cannot afford."[39] Blanshard distinguished the Roman hierarchy from the Catholic people who "fight and die for the same concept of freedom as do other true Americans." More important, he prefaced his only direct reference to Murray as follows: "It is an understatement to say that the Roman Catholic Church is *in* politics. It *is* political."[40] That claim, of course, was what Kennedy took great pains to deny in front of a group of mostly Baptist Houston ministers when he claimed that he only "happened" to be a Catholic, that the church did not speak for him, and that he supported the "absolute" separation of church and state.[41]

Despite the nativist interruption, theologians were laying the groundwork for the engagement with the modern world that would come to fruition at Vatican II. A key area of inquiry was the common good, and its first great synthesizer was French Thomist Jacques Maritain. Maritain argued from the basis of human freedom and distinguished between the human being as an individual that relates to a social order and as a person with an ultimate, spiritual end. However, he argued that humans participate in a common good in *both* orders; therefore they have social obligations but cannot be subordinated to them. He positioned his personalism (or "integral humanism") as a middle way between individualism and socialism. Maritain sought to bring the dimensions of the human person together by distinguishing the private good, which is subordinate to the community's temporal good, from the superior spiritual good, and he grounded the rights that form the basis of the state in the natural law and the common good.[42] He influenced a diverse group of thinkers, including Dorothy Day and Peter Maurin and Pope Paul VI, in addition to Murray, who recognized that applying Maritain's insights to the American context required an updated consideration of religious liberty.

The Case of John Courtney Murray

Murray's theology was the culmination of more than a century of struggle. To immigrants fleeing persecution and famine the United States was a welcome alternative, as it was after two world wars and in the face of communism, and Catholics co-existed rather well with their Protestant neighbors. The nation was changing, however, and Murray sensed the implications. He agreed with Niebuhr that democracy demands a basis that cannot be achieved through "organized religion" but rejected secularism in mild or strict forms.[43] He also did not share the elite self-criticism regarding Catholic anti-intellectualism that led to "acceptance of modern secular standards in the realm of ideas and culture."[44] Murray challenged the presentation of Catholic positions by priests such as Connell and Fenton, as he was convinced that anti-Catholicism was due primarily to the official preference for establishment. In short, popes from Pius IX to Pius XII had theorized the ideal (or "thesis") to be a harmony of church and state and accepted toleration (the "hypothesis") only for the sake of the common good. They initially opposed state churches but in response to continental liberalism began to see them as a means of defense.[45]

Murray's initial statements met with resistance from traditionalists, much of it citing Leo XIII against him. He responded with a series of articles affirming Leo's critiques of continental liberalism but stating that the pope's defense of the confessional state was contingent.[46] He also applied a hermeneutic distinguishing between permanent and historically (and polemically) conditioned teachings to church and state, where traditionalists had set up particular embodiments as universal ideals.[47] Further, Murray argued that the "genius" of the First Amendment rightly separated the temporal and spiritual orders and that the West had developed a new truth about human dignity: *freedom,* the responsibility of each citizen for his or her own religious beliefs grounded in natural law philosophy and enshrined in constitutional democracy.[48] This importing of a truth from outside the church upset Alfredo Cardinal Ottaviani, who by 1955 had convinced the Vatican to silence Murray on the church-state issue. The silencing was lifted in time for the publication of We Hold These Truths in 1960 and for Murray to attend the council's second session at the request of the American bishops.

Keith Pavlischek describes the dilemma of religious liberty as that of "justifying political neutrality toward particular conceptions of the good." Liberalism attempts to do so via one of two approaches, which Pavlischek calls "horns." One is prudential and seeks a *modus vivendi* or "a possible convergence of rational support for certain institutions, laws, and public policy" among divergent groups; it is associated with progressives. The other is foundationalist and expects that rational persons can reach a common set of convictions; it is characteristic of neo-conservatives.[49] Although both groups have claimed Murray, his goal was to create a space between the horns for a strictly juridical notion of religious liberty. He recognized that the foundationalist position could not hold and that the thesis-hypothesis doctrine, a version of the *modus vivendi* argument, was inadequate. However, is Pavlischek correct in concluding that Murray still ends up with something close to the latter?

Murray began his analysis of nature in *We Hold These Truths* with a distinction between the temporal and spiritual orders. Nature has its own form of reasoning that can be instantiated in public discourse, the purpose of which is to deliberate over means for achieving limited ends for all persons—the common good. Constitutionalism is beneficial because it is premised on decentralization of government through separation of powers, allowing for deliberation. In this context the Catholic Church confronts the natural order only *indirectly* through its member-citizens; its primary importance lies in the realm of grace, where it can direct people to their true and ultimate end. This distinction guards against a "monism" in which the political becomes primary; rather, grace is primary because it perfects nature. According to Murray, "There is indeed a radical discontinuity between nature and grace, but nature does not therefore become irrelevant to grace." He distinguished this "incarnational humanism" from an "eschatological humanism" descended from Augustine and Luther to neo-orthodoxy that emphasizes the permanence of sin, God's judgment, and the cross (173-80).[50]

Murray was convinced that the Reformation left no ground for social polity, but he connected the Catholic conception of natural law to the self-evident truths outlined in the Declaration of Independence. A realist epistemology does not require that truth be universally available, nor does denying the universal availability of truth imply that truth is a matter of opinion. Yet Murray believed the self-evidence of ethical truth to be the foundation of the American proposition and the consensus regarding its viability, a consensus sustained by public argument balancing the individual freedom and civic order found in the First Amendment. Unlike secularism or theocracy and contra Baptists who appeal to Roger Williams, the establishment and free exercise clauses of the First

Amendment are not "articles of faith" but "articles of peace." That is, they are political, not theological, and therefore do not imply a free-church ecclesiology (68-74).[51] Religious liberty is a right because it is inseparable from human dignity—it *allows* the person to act according to conscience and *prevents* the state from coercing him or her. Murray explained this move via the history of Western constitutionalism culminating in the "public philosophy" of the United States. In short, both nation and church have flourished, vindicating the philosophy. "Catholic participation in the American consensus has been full and free, unreserved and unembarrassed, because the contents of this consensus—the ethical and political principles drawn from the tradition of natural law—approve themselves to the Catholic conscience" (55). Still, Murray sensed that the philosophy was increasingly on "the brink of barbarism" and that civic unity was endangered by the transition from *religious* to *moral* pluralism (29-30, 37-39).[52]

At the end of *We Hold These Truths,* Murray described the demise of the "older American morality" that "believed in a direct transference of personal values into social life." This idealist version of foundationalism, whose "naïve biblical perfectionism" Murray implicitly associated with the social gospel, was unable to deal with modern society because it did not recognize the autonomy of the political order. Equally troubling was the "ambiguous" pragmatism of neo-orthodoxy (in other words, Niebuhrian realism), as it was vulnerable to Realpolitik, especially in foreign policy.[53] Contra the latter *modus vivendi* approach and Locke's law of nature, Murray hoped to retrieve the classical natural law tradition and "its equation of morality with right reason" (249-52). "To the early American theorists and politicians the tradition of natural law was an inheritance. This was its strength; this was at the same time its weakness." Because this inheritance was not understood, voluntarism, a consequence of Protestantism, eroded the consensus. Murray solemnly explained what "widespread dissent" from the philosophy would entail: "The guardianship of the original American consensus . . . would have passed to the Catholic community" (55-57).[54]

The Church, the State, and the Pursuit of the Common Good

Pavlischek admits that while Murray "grappled with the issue of religious liberty better than any twentieth-century Christian ethicist," his interest "has little to do with [Murray's] Catholicism."[55] However, Murray's theology cannot be separated from his location. Raised in the Catholic subculture and educated and employed by its institutions, he was, like his immigrant forebears, able to assume much about the public and political integrity of a church that resists the claims of states simply because it is a transnational body. Further, the robust natural law tradition enabled him to argue that the church ought not attempt to transform the nation into the City of God but ought to present its vision on the basis of reason and lay witness. Murray was not a Rawlsian proceduralist; he expected more than a minimum of morality in society. Still, he recognized limits to what could be infused by a juridical state and instead saw the church as the primary actor for the common good in the space created by the state (186-90).

In his early articles Murray criticized the Protestant view that the right of religious liberty resides in the individual conscience and is therefore a *sui generis* category. He reasoned that such a definition was meant in part "to further, not simply respect for human rights in the political order, but the institutional interests of organized Protestantism in the religious order." That is, Protestants wanted absolute freedom to organize and propagandize, but Murray argued that such rights "are subject to the same general standard of social control as the general rights of free association and free speech—the interests of the common good, as reasonably conceived by the collective conscience of the community, and as implemented by the authority of the state."[56] However, in the social ontology Aquinas inherited from Aristotle, violations of the natural (moral) law violate the common good; thus traditionalists claimed that the many Americans who did not accept Catholic moral premises undermined Murray's appeal to that good. This debate showed Murray that "the state's responsibility for the materially and spiritually good society could be used to override any right claimed in favor of the 'free exercise of religion' if the larger society were Catholic."[57] Thus, his mature argument limited legal coercion to the secular and civil common good and placed religious unity beyond its grasp. He clarified this idea by making a crucial distinction between the common good, which includes all social goods (spiritual, moral, and material), and the "public order," which includes three goods achieved by "the power inherent in the coercive discipline of public law": public peace, public morality, and justice.[58]

Recent thinkers have followed the vision of Murray and Maritain while further integrating it with Catholic social teaching. For example, David Hollenbach hails Murray's public philosophy but re-frames the common good in terms of *solidarity* in order to respond to the challenges of urbanization and globalization. Hollenbach attempts to synthesize the Augustinian view that temporal goods are partly the church's responsibility with the Thomistic emphasis on the necessary completion of those goods by the eternal good of the human *telos*. Further, he challenges mere tolerance in the public square, arguing instead for an "intellectual solidarity" that is neither neutral nor secular and accommodates the convictions of all parties in dialogue.[59] Similarly, Stiltner argues that Maritain's combination of natural law and personalism and its contrast between universal and particular can be described as "communal liberalism," which "aims to create room in society for substantive discussion about ethical issues and to guide cooperative political action for just and good solutions."[60]

These appeals to the best of liberalism and communitarianism reflect Murray's attempt to insert natural law between the horns of religious liberty. As Pavlischek shows, however, Murray's counter to liberal Protestants and secularists that the religion clauses are mere "articles of peace"—that is, political and not theological—left him with a concept of justice very close to the *modus vivendi* approach he wanted to reject. By deliberately separating nature from grace in regard to the common good, he could only hope that consensus would be achieved via the operation of natural law. Further, his concern for accommodation by the state undermined any traction his "principled" justification of religious liberty had for traditionalist Catholics.[61] Although he sought the opposite, Murray's theory left little distinctive or substantive public role for the Church, especially if pluralism and bureaucracy continued to grow. Although they wisely advocate seeking solutions to social problems through dialogue among local and global communities, Hollenbach and Stiltner tend to default to government institutions for the assessment and implementation of such solutions.[62]

There is much Baptists can affirm in Murray's Americanism. We can hail his work on religious liberty, for today the Catholic Church has joined most Protestants in renouncing coercion. We can also look to Catholic social teaching for guidance and embrace a notion of the common good that takes social justice seriously. Other elements are more difficult to appreciate. Murray recognized the necessity of a moral consensus to support the political arrangement of the First Amendment. Wary of foundationalism, moderate Baptists typically describe religious liberty as an individual right and neutral means of accommodation. As noted above, however, we also advocate an active state that pursues the common good. With Murray we imagine a necessary and public role for Christianity, but our ecclesiology works against it as much as secularism does. Like Alasdair MacIntyre and Jeffrey Stout, Murray engaged liberal democracy *as a tradition*.[63] He did not share Stout's pragmatism and, like MacIntyre, believed that if democracy became secular it would have to be rejected. Still, unlike MacIntyre, he did not think that it had done so or that it was a rival to the Christian tradition. Finally, he argued that while religious pluralism is "the native condition of American society," it is also "against the will of God" (37-39). A compelling question, then, is whether secularism has advanced to the point that religious pluralism has become moral pluralism.

The experience of U.S. Catholicism supports an affirmative answer. Although he praised *Dignitatis Humanae*, Murray later advocated other reforms, including a reassessment of the hierarchy.[64] In fact, many Catholics saw Vatican II as the culmination of a movement that had much in common with early Americanism. "What this meant was that Catholics tried to solve the riddle of religion and modernity overnight," Dolan says. "It proved to be quite difficult."[65] While the church's sluggishness was partly to blame for the post-council confusion, that confusion indicated that many Catholics were already so much like their neighbors that they were more than willing to accept the shifts Murray lamented. The subculture, along with distinct views on issues such as abortion or marriage, now made little sense. Soon the rush toward all things secular encountered a society in the throes of conflict over civil rights and Vietnam (and, later, Watergate). "For American Catholics, what happened next was surely one of history's most ironic twists," Gleason explains. "Before they had time to get used to being partisans of modernity, the modern world in its most advanced American embodiment became an object of loathing."[66] Yet this caused little questioning of Americanism, which instead became the ground on which discussions of other issues took place. Is it possible to both support the nation-state as such and fervently oppose much of its culture and/or policy? To answer this question, Catholics of the left and right have embraced what George Weigel terms the "Murray Project" and offered narrations of its decline, but each has ignored key aspects of Murray's thought.[67]

The presence of formerly Protestant characteristics in Catholicism indicates something about their shared environment. Although neo-scholasticism, the church's response to modernism after the First Vatican Council, maintained the supernatural virtue of faith, it also asserted that natural reason discloses essential truths about God and humanity. "From this it followed that the application of faith to virtually every sphere of life could be determined in some detail," Gleason says. "Catholicism came to be viewed as a culture, a total way of life." Unfortunately, this way of life was so closely identified with neo-scholasticism that when the latter was abandoned the former was also largely lost.[68] This mirrors the experience of Protestants, who no longer generate moral consensus among themselves, let alone the public. Today many Catholics join them in seeing only the nation, not any form of church, as necessary to maintain whatever vision emerges from moral pluralism.

We must also consider whether the state actually functions in the way Murray thought. He has been rightly critiqued for his description of natural law and for overestimating its influence on the American founding, and David Schindler shows that Murray did not fully take into account the work of Henri de Lubac and *nouvelle théologie* on the supernatural.[69] If the civic common good needs only perfection by the church, Christians have little theological recourse when the will of the majority contradicts what natural law requires. Michael Baxter adds that Murray's distinction between temporal and spiritual orders—a civic and spiritual common good—leads inevitably to dualism. Murray was right about the political arrangement of the United States, but by "excluding final ends" this arrangement "relegate[s] matters of theological truth to a separate sphere, and therefore is not, in Augustinian terms, genuine politics at all."[70] The state does not fully accommodate the church's freedom; in fact, some religious claims (such as selective conscientious objection) threaten its conception of the common good. Further, if soul liberty implies "the rejection of violence as the basis of community," Baptists and Catholics must ask whether the common good can be maintained by a militarist state.

Despite his disdain for foundationalisms, Murray's natural law methodology reflects the modern pursuit of universal morality I described earlier, in part because it rests on a deficient reading of Aquinas, who was not concerned with those who doubt basic moral commitments. Aquinas assumed an ecclesial location and explained the relationship of action, reason, and will in light of creation and providence. The treatise on law reflects his understanding of human agency as shaped by the ends it pursues and governed by law as a dictate of practical reason. We participate in God's law by knowing its demands through nature and habit, and what makes us rational creatures is our ability to deliberate over the means for achieving our good ends and exercise judgment in choosing among them. Thus every human action participates in the natural law in a minimal sense, and we can observe many similar commitments among persons. However, natural law does not provide or account for substantive moral guidance; that comes from participating in communities with shared ends that provide the preconditions for employing concepts such as "good" and "justice."[71]

An important task for Baptists who cherish religious liberty is to imagine workable alternatives that take politics seriously without accepting the natural occurrence of the state, its definition of "public," or its necessity for pursuing the common good. According to Cavanaugh, the state not only created violence "and then charged citizens for its reduction" but also precipitated "a shift from 'complex space'—varied communal contexts with overlapping jurisdictions and levels of authority—to a 'simple space' characterized by a duality of individual and state."[72] One way to counter this development is to renew congregations and associations— Baptist strengths that bear witness to overly determined (meaning, centralized and hierarchical) ecclesiologies. Yet we have much to (re)learn about the necessity of the church and its Great Tradition for carrying the gospel across the centuries. If William Portier is right in claiming that *Dignitatis Humanae* should be interpreted not as an endorsement of pluralism but as "a formal rejection of Christendom, ushering in a new 'post-Constantinian' age in the Church's history," then perhaps we too can hear "the Johannine incarnational imperative to make the word flesh" and join Catholicism in "[crying] out to be embodied in a culture at the center of which is the church."[73] Such a culture requires only the recognition that the common good is more than spiritual and is properly explored and expressed among ecclesiastical communities and in their relationships with other groups from which they regularly learn and borrow. When agreements cannot be reached, however, the Christian response is not coercion but faithfulness and obedience to the rule of Christ.[74]

Portier has an ally in Benedict XVI, who calls for "creative minorities" that "reach other people and offer them a different way of seeing things." These minorities live not independently but "naturally from the fact that the Church as a whole remains and that it lives in and stands by the faith in its divine origins."[75] In other words, they endure only because they are part of a visible body connected to the Great Tradition; from that location they are able to critique the culture and, when necessary, the church. One model is the Catholic Worker movement. Through the personalism of Maritain and Emmanuel Mounier, Dorothy Day and Peter Maurin came to see the common good as an antidote to individualism when pursued in community. In the words of Mark and Louise Zwick, "Peter and Dorothy were driven by the gospel and believed in striving together with others toward the common good—rather than by the invisible hand of the market or by imposing one's views by violence."[76] Congregations and Catholic Worker houses should not be idealized, and identifying primarily with them does not entail withdrawing from public life. However, doing so redefines our conceptions of "public" through the practices of prayer, worship, the sacraments, and the works of mercy. These communities enable us to negotiate the politics in which we find ourselves, challenge us to recover Jesus' radical love for all persons—our friends, our enemies, and the poor—and give us the strength to bear witness to the gospel.

Notes

[1]This presumption has often been accompanied by the further claim that authentic moral reasoning stands above the particular claims of any one group. For example, the Center for American Progress identifies the common good with progessivism and claims that securing it means, among other things, "putting the public interest above narrow self-interest and group demands." The center discusses the common good almost exclusively in terms of individuals and government, the goal of which is "to protect public goods that promote the national interest" and "to ensure every American has a real shot at his or her dreams." Further, to achieve this on an international scale, "common good progressivism focuses on new and revitalized global leadership grounded in the integrated use of military, economic and diplomatic power" (John Halpin and Ruy Teixeira, "Common Good Progressivism," Center for American Progress, http://www.americanprogress.org/events/special_events/commongoodprogressivism.html [accessed May 30, 2007]).

[2]Donald E. Pelotte, *John Courtney Murray: Theologian in Conflict* (New York: Paulist Press, 1976), 145-46. For an analysis of the transition from Leo XIII's condemnation of Americanism to Pelotte's matter-of-fact claim, see William L. Portier, "Americanism and Inculturation: 1899-1999," *Communio* 27, no. 1 (2000): 139-60.

[3]Thomas W. Smith, "Aristotle on the Conditions for and Limits of the Common Good," *American Political Science Review* 93, no. 3 (1999): 625-36. Still, Smith thinks Aristotle is helpful precisely because he is not concerned with "contested religious doctrines."

[4]John Rawls, *A Theory of Justice* (Cambridge: Harvard University Press, 1971), 246. The idea of overlapping consensus is not inherently inconsistent with a communal, non-state view of the common good. However, Rawls errs in taking this consensus to imply the presence of a "public reason" that is held by all rational citizens and specifically excludes conceptions of the good. See Rawls, *Political Liberalism* (New York: Columbia University Press, 1993).

[5]Globalization and the rise of international government necessitate additional analysis of these realities. However, to the extent that these factors add additional, ever-higher levels of economic, political, and moral authority, my conclusions still apply.

[6]Brian Stiltner, *Religion and the Common Good: Catholic Contributions to Building Community in a Liberal Society* (Lanham, MD: Rowman & Littlefield, 1999), 4-8.

[7]For a different view of the impact of the Wars of Religion, see William T. Cavanaugh, " 'A Fire Strong Enough to Consume the House': The Wars of Religion and the Rise of the State," *Modern Theology* 11, no. 4 (1995): 397-420; and Cavanaugh, *Theopolitical Imagination: Discovering the Liturgy as a Political Act in an Age of Global Consumerism* (New York: T&T Clark, 2002).

[8]For a "moderate" Baptist perspective, see J. Brent Walker, ed., *The Trophy of Baptists: Words to Celebrate Religious Liberty* (Macon, GA: Smyth & Helwys, 2003).

[9]Edward L. Queen II, *In the South the Baptists Are the Center of Gravity: Southern Baptists and Social Change, 1930-1980* (Brooklyn: Carlson, 1991), 16. Queen took his title from a comment in Victor I. Masters, "Baptists and the Christianizing of America in the New Order," *Review and Expositor* 17 (July 1920): 297.

[10]Herschel Hobbs, *You Are Chosen: The Priesthood of All Believers* (San Francisco: Harper & Row, 1990), 3, quoted in Elizabeth Newman, "The Priesthood of All Believers and the Necessity of the Church," in *Recycling the Past or Researching History: Studies in Baptist Historiography and Myths*, ed. Anthony R. Cross and Philip E. Thompson (Waynesboro, GA: Paternoster, 2005), 51. Hobbs added that soul liberty is "the distinctive contribution of Baptists to the Christian world." He chaired the 1963 committee that revised the SBC's statement of faith ("The Baptist Faith and Message") originally crafted by Mullins's 1925 committee. Barry Hankins notes that disagreement with this conception of soul liberty and a strict-separation view of church and

state motivated the conservative cause in the SBC split. Hankins, *Uneasy in Babylon: Southern Baptist Conservatives and American Culture* (Tuscaloosa: University of Alabama Press, 2002), 15-17, 107-38.

[11]Newman, "The Priesthood of All Believers," 52; E. Y. Mullins, *The Axioms of Religion* (Philadelphia: Judson Press, 1908), 55, 60-61. For a different view, see Philip E. Thompson, "Sacraments and Religious Liberty: From Critical Practice to Rejected Infringement," in *Baptist Sacramentalism*, ed. Anthony R. Cross and Philip E. Thompson (Waynesboro, GA: Paternoster, 2003): 36-54.

[12]Newman, "The Priesthood of All Believers," 53; Walter B. Shurden, "The Baptist Identity and the Baptist *Manifesto*," *Perspectives in Religious Studies* 25, no. 4 (1998): 321-40.

[13]James Wm. McClendon Jr., *Systematic Theology*, vol. 1, *Ethics* (Nashville: Abingdon Press, 1986), 30, quoted in Newman, "The Priesthood of All Believers," 54.

[14]As Newman points out, Ludwig Wittgenstein's philosophy of language is a helpful tool in this regard. See note 71 below.

[15]Cavanaugh, "A Fire Strong Enough to Consume the House," 403-5.

[16]Baptist Center for Ethics, "A Baptist Pastoral Letter Supporting Public Education," http://www.ethicsdaily.com/static.cfm?mode=public_education_letter (accessed April 13, 2007). In a related article, executive director Robert Parham implies that Baptists who support the common good must support public education (Bob Allen, "201 Baptist Ministers Sign Letter Supporting Public Education," http://www.ethicsdaily.com/article_detail.cfm?AID=7351 [dated May 12, 2006; accessed April 13, 2007]).

[17]James L. Evans, "The Voice of Faith Necessary in Social Issues," http://www.ethicsdaily.com/article_detail.cfm?AID=7651 (dated July 21, 2006; accessed April 13, 2007).

[18]Robert Parham, "A Bible Verse for Victors," http://www.ethicsdaily.com/article_detail.cfm?AID=8143 (dated November 13, 2006; accessed April 13, 2007).

[19]Susan Pace Hamill, "Taxation and Justice," http://ethicsdaily.com/article_detail.cfm?AID=7792 (dated August 22, 2006; accessed April 13, 2007). Hamill notes that "instead of embodying justice and working for the common good, our system of taxation reflects the values of selfish individualism." She describes tax justice in terms of secular standards such as "fair burden" and "adequate revenue" but contends that taxation is a "moral conversation" into which Jesus' admonition "from everyone to whom much has been given, much will be required" ought to be inserted.

[20]Martin E. Marty, "Baptistification Takes Over," *Christianity Today,* September 2, 1983, 33-36. For a recent example of this type of rhetoric, see John Pierce, "A Conversation with Bill Leonard," *Baptists Today*, January 2007, 4-5, 14-17.

[21]McClendon, *Systematic Theology*, 332. The task of ethics is "the discovery, understanding, and creative transformation of a shared and lived story, one whose focus is Jesus of Nazareth and the kingdom he proclaims—a story

that on its moral side requires such discovery, such understanding, such transformation to be true to itself."

[22]Pew Research Center Publications, "Muslim Americans: Middle Class and Mostly Mainstream," Pew Research Center, May 22, 2007; http://pewresearch.org/pubs/483/muslim-americans (accessed May 30, 2007). In contrast, when asked, "Do you think of yourself first as an American or first as a Muslim?" 47 percent of American Muslims answered "Muslim first" but only 28 percent answered "American first."

[23]Truett argued that the Baptist faith is the "exact opposite of Catholicism." "The Catholic doctrine of baptismal regeneration and transubstantiation is to the Baptist mind fundamentally subversive of the spiritual realities of the gospel of Christ. Likewise, the Catholic conception of the church, thrusting all its complex and cumbrous machinery between the soul and God, prescribing beliefs, claiming to exercise the power of the keys, and to control the channels of grace—all such lording it over the consciences of men is to the Baptist mind a ghastly tyranny in the realm of the soul and tends to frustrate the grace of God, to destroy freedom of conscience, and to hinder terribly the coming of the Kingdom of God" (George W. Truett, "Baptists and Religious Liberty," *Christian Ethics Today* 7, no. 1 [February 2001], http://www.christianethicstoday.com/issue/032/Baptists and Religious Liberty By George W Truett, May 16 1920_032_22_.htm [accessed May 30, 2007]).

[24]Contrary to what was long claimed, Murray was not the principal architect of *Dignitatis Humanae*. Instead his argument for human dignity and juridical freedom was a later addition to the French revision of his fourth draft (J. Leon Hooper, introduction to John Courtney Murray, *Religious Liberty: Catholic Struggles with Pluralism* [Louisville: Westminster John Knox, 1993], 36-37).

[25]"Totem" is coined by William L. Portier in "Theology of Manners as Theology of Containment: John Courtney Murray and *Dignitatis Humanae* Forty Years After," *U.S. Catholic Historian* 24, no. 1 (2006): 83-85.

[26]John Courtney Murray, "Current Theology: Christian Co-operation," *Theological Studies* 3 (September 1942): 413-31; Murray, "Current Theology: Co-operation: Some Further Views," *Theological Studies* 4 (March 1943): 100-11; Murray, "Current Theology: Intercredal Co-operation: Its Theory and Its Organization," *Theological Studies* 4 (June 1943): 257-68.

[27]Pelotte, *John Courtney Murray*, 14-16. Pelotte shows that Murray was involved in the school question by the late 1940s, when he helped the American bishops with their written opposition to the Supreme Court's *Everson* and *McCollum* decisions. In the early 1950s he participated in an influential assessment of academic freedom that supported giving tax money to private (and parochial) schools and religious education in public schools. His mature thought on the issue is found in chapter six of *We Hold These Truths*.

[28]Jay P. Dolan, *The American Catholic Experience: A History from Colonial Times to the Present* (Notre Dame: University of Notre Dame Press, 1992), 238-39.

[29]Ibid., 266-67. Winthrop was an English Puritan and the first governor of the Massachusetts Bay Colony. He made his famous remark in a speech given en route to the New World.

[30]David O'Brien, *Public Catholicism*, 2nd ed. (Maryknoll, NY: Orbis Books, 1996), 36. "People had to be persuaded to join a church, to support its minister and its works, and to make its teachings a part of their daily lives. To resist the evangelical project and insure the survival of Catholicism, bishops, priests, and lay leaders had to do the same."

[31]Dolan, *The American Catholic Experience*, 269.

[32]John Tracy Ellis, *American Catholicism*, 2nd ed. (Chicago: University of Chicago Press, 1969), 123, 157, 190. Ellis claimed that "the fundamental principle of separation of Church and State has always been accepted by the American hierarchy from the time of Archbishop [John] Carroll to our own day" and that Americanists from Carroll to Ireland to Francis Cardinal Spellman erred only in occasional excess. He and Murray had a close relationship. See Pelotte, *John Courtney Murray*, 36-50.

[33]Philip Gleason, *Keeping the Faith: American Catholicism, Past and Present* (Notre Dame: University of Notre Dame Press, 1987), 184. William M. Halsey analyzes this period in *The Survival of American Innocence: Catholicism in an Era of Disillusionment, 1920-1940* (Notre Dame: University of Notre Dame Press, 1980).

[34]Gleason, *Keeping the Faith*, 30-31.

[35]Thomas W. O'Brien examines the influence of the Cold War on Murray's thought in *John Courtney Murray in a Cold War Context* (Lanham, MD: University Press of America, 2004).

[36]James Hennesey, *American Catholics: A History of the Roman Catholic Community in the United States* (New York: Oxford University Press, 1981), 287-88.

[37]David J. O'Brien, *Public Catholicism*, 204. See Will Herberg, *Protestant, Catholic, Jew: An Essay in American Religious Sociology*, rev. ed. (Garden City, NY: Anchor Books, 1960).

[38]Hennesey, *American Catholics*, 295. See also Pelotte, *John Courtney Murray in a Cold War Context*, 17-18; and John Courtney Murray, "Paul Blanshard and the New Nativism," *Month* 5 (April 1951): 214-25.

[39]Reinhold Niebuhr, "A Note on Pluralism," in *Religion in America: Original Essays on Religion in a Free Society*, ed. John Cogley (New York: Meridian Books, 1958), 49, quoted in O'Brien, *John Courtney Murray in a Cold War Context*, 207.

[40]Paul Blanshard, *American Freedom and Catholic Power* (Boston: Beacon Press, 1949), 4-5, 43. Blanshard concluded that "if [the people] controlled their own Church, the Catholic problem would soon disappear because, in the atmosphere of American freedom, they would adjust their Church's policies to American realities." For more on the conflict between Blanshard and Murray, see Mark Massa, "Catholic-Protestant Tensions in Post-War America: Paul Blanshard, John Courtney Murray, and the 'Religious Imagination,' " *Harvard Theological Review* 95, 3 (2002): 319-39.

⁴¹John F. Kennedy, "Address to the Greater Houston Ministerial Association," American Rhetoric, http://www.americanrhetoric.com/speeches/jfkhoustonministers.html (accessed May 30, 2007). Audio and video of Kennedy's address are also available at this site.

⁴²Jacques Maritain, *The Person and the Common Good* (New York: Charles Scribner's Sons, 1947); Maritain, *Man and the State* (Chicago: University of Chicago Press, 1951).

⁴³Murray lamented the metaphorical "wall of separation between church and state" that first appeared in an 1802 letter from Thomas Jefferson to the Danbury (Conn.) Baptist Association and was solidified by the 1947 Supreme Court case *Everson v. Board of Education* (John Courtney Murray, "Separation of Church and State," *America*, December 7, 1946, 261-63; Murray, "Separation of Church and State: True and False Concepts," *America*, February 15, 1947, 541-45).

⁴⁴Gleason, *Keeping the Faith*, 32. "The main thrust of Catholic liberalism in the fifties was unquestionably that Catholics should abandon separatism, outgrow their siege mentality, and break out of their Catholic ghetto" (Gleason, 186). Ellis was among those who pressed this point in regard to education.

⁴⁵John Courtney Murray, "Contemporary Orientations of Catholic Thought on Church and State in the Light of History," *Theological Studies* 10 (September 1949): 177-234; Murray, "The Problem of State Religion," *Theological Studies* 12 (June 1951): 155-78. Even the social reformer John Ryan, who utilized a natural law methodology similar to that of Murray, employed the thesis-hypothesis doctrine. See John A. Ryan and Moorhouse F. Miller, eds., *The State and the Church* (New York: Macmillan, 1922).

⁴⁶John Courtney Murray, "The Church and Totalitarian Democracy," *Theological Studies* 13 (December 1952): 525-63; Murray, "Leo XIII on Church and State: The General Structure of the Controversy," *Theological Studies* 14 (March 1953): 1-30; Murray, "Leo XIII: Separation of Church and State," *Theological Studies* 14 (June 1953): 145-214; Murray, "Leo XIII: Two Concepts of Government," *Theological Studies* 14 (December 1953): 551-67; Murray, "Leo XIII: Two Concepts of Government: Government and the Order of Culture," *Theological Studies* 15 (March 1954): 1-33. A sixth article was near publication when Murray was silenced.

⁴⁷John Courtney Murray, "The Declaration on Religious Freedom," *Concilium* 15 (May 1966): 6-16. Murray described this in Lonerganian terms as a shift from classicism to historical consciousness: in the former, truth is objective and exists in timeless propositions, while in the latter, truth progresses both through history and in being grasped by the subject, yet retains objectivity. On Murray's indebtedness to Bernard Lonergan, see J. Leon Hooper, *The Ethics of Discourse: The Social Philosophy of John Courtney Murray* (Washington: Georgetown University Press, 1986), 121-56.

⁴⁸John Courtney Murray, *We Hold These Truths: Catholic Reflections on the American Proposition* (Lanham, MD: Sheed & Ward, 2005 [1960]), 79-

81, 186-90. Subsequent references to this volume will be made parenthetically in the text.

[49]Keith J. Pavlischek, *John Courtney Murray and the Dilemma of Religious Toleration* (Kirksville, MO: Thomas Jefferson University Press, 1994), 6, 9-10.

[50]In the Augustinian view, Murray said, "the divine promise is not of peace but of the sword," and he claimed it "would fix a great gulf of separation between orders that are only distinct." Thomas Ferguson contrasts Murray's Thomism with Reinhold Niebuhr's Augustinianism in *Catholic and American: The Political Theology of John Courtney Murray* (Kansas City: Sheed & Ward, 1993), 149-51. See also Thomas C. Berg, "John Courtney Murray and Reinhold Niebuhr: Natural Law and Christian Realism," *Journal of Catholic Social Thought* 4, 1 (2007): 3-27.

[51]However, Murray did use Williams to fortify his appeals to social peace and the distinction between state and society. "Murray's main point is that the First Amendment is a law written by lawyers rather than a dogma written by theologians" (Portier, "Theology of Manners as Theology of Containment," 93-94).

[52]"Today the barbarian is the man who makes open and explicit rejection of the traditional role of reason and logic in human affairs. He is the man who reduces all spiritual and moral questions to the test of practical results or to an analysis of language or to decision in terms of individual subjective feeling" (Murray, *We Hold These Truths*, 29-30).

[53]Some concluded that the nation was founded on pragmatism. "On the contrary, [the fathers] thought, the life of man in society is founded on truths, on a certain body of objective truth, universal in its import, accessible to the reason of man, definable, defensible. If this assertion is denied, the American Proposition is, I think, eviscerated at one stroke" (Murray, *We Hold These Truths*, ix).

[54]Murray quoted the Third Plenary Council of Baltimore's (1884) description of the fathers as "building better than they knew" (Murray, *We Hold These Truths*, 46). The line is from a poem by Ralph Waldo Emerson describing the dome of St. Peter's Cathedral. Orestes Brownson first employed it to celebrate the American founding; his connection to the Third Plenary Council, if any, is unclear.

[55]Pavlischek, *John Courtney Murray and the Dilemma of Religious Toleration*, 4.

[56]John Courtney Murray, "Current Theology: Freedom of Religion," *Theological Studies* 6 (March 1945): 96-98. "The old individualist argument . . . does not work. As soon as one begins to spread ideas, one moves in a new ethical dimension—that of the social good; and one comes under a new ethical principle of control—the interests of the common good" (98).

[57]Pavlischek, *John Courtney Murray and the Dilemma of Religious Toleration*, 186. See Thomas Aquinas, *Summa Theologica*, I-II.92.

[58]Murray, *The Problem of Religious Freedom* (Westminster, MD: Newman,

1965), 29-30. "Let there be as much freedom, personal and social, as is possible; let there be only as much restraint and constraint, personal and social, as may be necessary for the public order" (31).

[59]David Hollenbach, *The Common Good and Christian Ethics* (New York: Cambridge University Press, 2002), 22-34, 137-38. "There are many indications in the United States today that tolerance of diversity occupies the place held by the common good in the thought of Aristotle, Thomas Aquinas, and Ignatius Loyola. Tolerance of difference, not the common good, has become the highest social aspiration in American culture" (24).

[60]Stiltner, *Religion and the Common Good*, 163.

[61]Pavlischek, *John Courtney Murray and the Dilemma of Religious Toleration*, 103-4.

[62]Even Benedict XVI's first encyclical grants the state that guarantees religious liberty a degree of autonomy and the responsibility to achieve justice through politics. Here faith and social doctrine, though oriented to God, serve as a "purifying force" for political reason on the basis of natural law. Thus "political life" is given over to the state while the church offers a "contribution" to the common good. Still, the pope is critical of the "mere bureaucracy" of a state without love and instead advocates one that "generously acknowledges and supports initiatives arising from the different social forces" (Pope Benedict XVI, *Deus Caritas Est*, December 25, 2005, sec. 28-29). Elsewhere there are clues that Benedict is thinking of the United States, which he describes as "little more than a free space for different religious communities to congregate" (Joseph Ratzinger, "Letter to Marcelo Pera," in Joseph Ratzinger and Marcello Pera, *Without Roots: The West, Relativism, Christianity, Islam* [New York: Basic Books, 2006], 109-13).

[63]Alasdair MacIntyre, *Whose Justice? Which Rationality?* (Notre Dame: University of Notre Dame Press, 1988); MacIntyre, *Three Rival Versions of Moral Enquiry: Encyclopaedia, Genealogy, and Tradition* (Notre Dame: University of Notre Dame Press, 1990); Jeffrey Stout, *Democracy and Tradition* (Princeton: Princeton University Press, 2004).

[64]David J. O'Brien, *Public Catholicism*, 235. While the Council enabled American Catholics "to abandon equivocation in speaking about the First Amendment," it also "opened the door to the possibility that individual Catholics might apply its principles to their own relationship to ecclesiastical authority."

[65]Dolan, *The American Catholic Experience*, 425-28.

[66]Gleason, *Keeping the Faith*, 32.

[67]Pavlischek, *John Courtney Murray and the Dilemma of Religious Toleration*, 191-96. Perhaps the greatest inconsistency is that these dueling parties advocate an expansive state in some areas and a limited one in others. Their claims are reflected in two volumes of essays: Robert P. Hunt and Kenneth L. Grasso, eds., *John Courtney Murray and the American Civil Conversation* (Grand Rapids: Eerdmans, 1992); and J. Leon Hooper and Todd David Whitmore, eds., *John Courtney Murray and the Growth of Tradition* (Kansas City: Sheed & Ward, 1996).

[68]Gleason, *Keeping the Faith*, 169-71, 174.

[69]David L. Schindler, *Heart of the World, Center of the Church: Communio Ecclesiology, Liberalism, and Liberation* (Grand Rapids: Eerdmans, 1996).

[70]Michael J. Baxter, "Writing History in a World without Ends: An Evangelical Catholic Critique of United States Catholic History," *Pro Ecclesia* 5, no. 4 (1996): 447. "A genuine politics, by contrast, is grounded in the service of 'true religion' from which flow 'true justice' and 'true peace' as embodied by the citizenry, not of any earthly city but of the pilgrim City of God." Baxter critiques Ellis, Dolan, and O'Brien as representatives of "Americanist historiography."

[71]As John Bowlin explains, Wittgenstein argued that one masters a moral concept only as one comes to grasp how it contributes to the pursuit of certain ends and as one learns "to see the point of certain activities and concedes the truth of certain moral and empirical judgments." Some activities and judgments arise from custom or convention, but others stem from *nature* and are given and trusted prior to any choice; to not accept them is to be unable to act with the rationality necessary for ordinary conversation. Thus they function not as knowledge in the usual sense but as *rules* for linguistic usage, as the boundaries of what Wittgenstein called our "language-game." That is, in a way resembling the first precepts of the natural law, they delineate the "form of life" all humans share as rational creatures (John R. Bowlin, "Nature's Grace: Aquinas and Wittgenstein on Natural Law and Moral Knowledge," in *Grammar and Grace: Reformulations of Aquinas and Wittgenstein*, ed. Jeffrey L. Stout and Robert MacSwain [London: SCM Press, 2004], 161-62. See Ludwig Wittgenstein, *Philosophical Investigations*, 3rd ed. [New York: Macmillan, 1968; reprint, Upper Saddle River, NJ: Prentice-Hall, 1999], sec. 251; and Wittgenstein, *On Certainty*, ed. G. E. M. Anscombe and G. H. von Wright [Oxford: Basil Blackwell, 1969; reprint, New York: Harper & Row, 1972], sec. 124, 136, 356-60, 505, 558).

[72]William T. Cavanaugh, "Killing for the Telephone Company: Why the Nation-State Is Not the Keeper of the Common Good," *Modern Theology* 20, no. 2 (2004): 249-52.

[73]Portier, "Theology of Manners as Theology of Containment," 103-4.

[74]I am grateful to Paul Fiddes for reminding me that English Baptist theologians of the seventeenth and eighteenth centuries insisted that the local congregation has liberty only because it stands under the rule of Christ who is present among them. They understood that liberty can never be created or enforced from outside. Further, the congregation cannot make responsible decisions without attending to the rule of Christ manifested in other places. That is, there can be no common good without fellowship with other persons, Christian and non-Christian.

[75]Joseph Ratzinger, "Letter to Marcelo Pera," 121-23.

[76]Mark Zwick and Louise Zwick, *The Catholic Worker Movement: Intellectual and Spiritual Origins* (New York: Paulist Press, 2005), 298.

The "Princeton Statement" on Church-State Relations

Reflections on a Little-Known Text

Patrick Hayes

In February 1948, the Catholic Commission on Intellectual and Cultural Affairs (CCICA)—a small but important collective of leading American Catholic intellectuals—approved an arrangement of informal conferences that would take place between members of different scholarly disciplines on the question of church-state relations.[1] The conferences were not organized in a vacuum, but were a concrete response of high-minded Catholics to contemporary cultural movements and critics, mainly Protestant, who believed that Catholics ought to make their position known to the nation once and for all. These discussions brought some of America's foremost Catholic thinkers together to address the peculiar ecclesiological issues attendant on the problem as manifest in the American context. They also helped to clarify and counter those charges erroneously leveled against American Catholics as they themselves grew in political might and economic and social standing. The legacy left by the participants in these and similar conferences has prompted some in our own day to look back upon this era as offering some of American history's most probing explorations of the Catholic Church's relationship to the state.[2]

It must be admitted that Catholics' contributions to this post-World War II discourse were delayed and reactive. Already, Protestant America had issued a number of challenges. The CCICA's response helped to address specific concerns raised by such groups as Protestants and Other Americans United for the Separation of

Church and State, a nativist organization founded by Joseph Martin Dawson in 1947. Dawson had been resurrecting some of the old canards about Catholic loyalties to the papacy, which he believed to be the singular most imposing threat to American democratic institutions.[3] His most immediate gripe was with the appointment of Myron Taylor as the United States representative to the Vatican, which he took as a constitutional violation of the separation clause. But other charges were also levied against American Catholics, not least of which was that the Catholic Church was such a formidable voting bloc that it ultimately could, given its members' deference to clergy, make drastic alterations to the body politic based upon the dictates of Rome.

Quite independently from this movement, the poster child for the new nativism was author and columnist Paul Blanshard.[4] His series of anti-Catholic screeds, serialized first in *The Nation* in 1946 and 1947 and later collected as *American Freedom and Catholic Power*, placed American Catholics on the defensive.[5] Blanshard was joined by other critics in the pages of Protestant periodicals such as *The Christian Century*, *The Protestant*, and *The Converted Catholic*.[6] Harold Fey, the editor of *The Christian Century*, had already wondered whether Catholics could "win America" in a book-length broadside in 1946.[7] The pressure placed upon Catholics by these controversialists forced them to express themselves in the clearest terms as to where their loyalties lay.

Clarification was needed, but Catholics were challenged by their own attitudes toward those who would subjugate them. Who were these Protestants and secularists to make claims upon those faithful of the one, true church? Those outside the true religion, it was felt, were in error—and error had no legitimate claims to rights. If a nation such as the United States was to impose sanctions on a Catholic population that dared to assume its political role, as Blanshard and others hoped, such sanctions could not be considered by Catholics as anything but illegitimate. The divide created by the nativism at mid-century was to be bridged, not by equally negative attacks upon Blanshard and his partisans, but through the more positive strategy of cogent, rational discourse. The risk for Catholics was to suggest that Protestants and others had valid claims, the recognition of which would somehow signal capitulation. In 1948, members of the CCICA hoped to seek a resolution to this conundrum.

A prevailing sense of confusion over the role of the Catholic

Church in American society, both by Catholics and Protestants, was the immediate occasion for the CCICA conferences. In early 1948, Jesuit Father John Courtney Murray, a founding member of the CCICA, began to organize a group of historians, philosophers, political scientists, and others in anticipation of the CCICA's annual meeting, which took place on May 16, 1948, at the College of New Rochelle. The expectation was that the membership would discuss this as a central theme the following year in St. Louis.[8]

Murray felt that he needed to drum up support to put the subject on the agenda of the wider membership, and lobbied the Commission's executive director, Father Edward Stanford, O.S.A., to solicit the expertise of its membership.[9] Church-state questions had already been a preoccupation with Murray.[10] With Stanford's approval, Murray obtained the services of natural law theorist Heinrich Rommen, who later prepared a philosophically oriented paper on church-state relations.[11] Thomas Mahony, a Boston attorney and former president of the Catholic Association for International Peace, was assigned a paper summarizing recent Supreme Court decisions.[12] The medievalist Gerhart Ladner, then of the University of Notre Dame, and theologian Gustave Weigel, S.J., of Woodstock College, also contributed papers. Ladner's text dealt with the church's position from its historical beginnings in the New Testament to Boniface VIII, while Weigel's treated the question of church-state relations in Latin America.[13] All told, some fifteen members were asked to submit work on various aspects of the problem, eventually generating over 116 single-spaced pages by November 1948.[14] All would prepare their papers for circulation among the membership, which was then about two hundred strong. The problem of church-state relations was suggested as a topic of discussion at local CCICA meetings, too, and the membership was encouraged to submit reflections and summaries of these meetings to Stanford's office. One such local meeting took place in Princeton on January 16, 1949, between a small group of academics affiliated with the university and nearby industries.[15] The Princeton gathering would prove vital to the direction of the whole Commission on this and other subjects, and may be considered an integral moment in the protracted conflict over the writings of John Courtney Murray on this topic.[16] Murray himself used the discussions in his own thinking on church-state questions, both in his intra-church writings as well as his responses to secular or Protestant counterparts.[17] The Princeton group also helped frame an emerging Catholic position on church-state relations in America for years to come.

The Princeton Statement on Church and State

In the days leading up to the Princeton meeting, an outline of the main problems—historical, philosophical, and theological—was prepared by Murray and his confrère, Wilfrid Parsons, S.J., to stimulate discussions at the regional level. It served to spark the tinder of disagreement that characterized future exchanges between members, some of whom vociferously dissented from the majority of their colleagues. While they were aware of the potential contretemps, the Princeton members felt free to express their concerns. Many of those gathered had a personal fondness for one another and felt at ease in expressing themselves, even though a guest, the Dominican chaplain at Princeton, Father Hugh Halton, was present. Halton carried on some rather personal attacks against some Catholics on the Princeton faculty, including several who had assembled in the CCICA meeting, though no one appeared to be deterred.

Fortunately, there exists a report of the meeting written by the economist David McCabe, and two accompanying documents—both unsigned—that can be found in the CCICA archive at The Catholic University of America.[18] These two memoranda served to give substantive form to what was hoped would be the "essential Catholic position" on church-state relations. In attendance were Joseph Becker (Bell Telephone Laboratories), Jacques Maritain (Philosophy), McCabe (Economics), Marston Morse (Mathematics and the Institute of Advanced Study), and Hugh Taylor (Dean of the Graduate School), as well as three guests that included wives and Halton.

One of the commentators was the mathematician Marston Morse, the colleague of Albert Einstein at the Institute for Advanced Study, but by far the most important contribution came from the second commentator.[19] A letter from McCabe to Stanford reveals the identity of the author of this longer document. It was written by Jacques Maritain.[20] His nine-page memorandum on the church-state problem, reproduced as an appendix to this essay, is a little-known text in Maritain scholarship. It would be labeled "The Princeton Statement" by the CCICA membership. Before turning to this text, a short examination of the McCabe report is warranted because it supplies a general picture of the proceedings on that day. It is in light of those discussions that Maritain offered to draft his own memorandum.

McCabe's report is brief, but three main points are discernable, with the first two pertaining to understanding the church's position along the twin axes of time and space. First, everyone at the meeting agreed that the situation that prevailed in Western Europe in the Middle Ages, namely, the privileged standing the church had with respect to civil affairs, could not necessarily be taken as optimal for or determinative of future epochs. Indeed, it was regrettable that this attitude perdured in the church where those accepted departures from that ideal were seen as simply a matter of expediency (as in the case of the United States). "Expediency" was to be distinguished from a "recognition that changes in the pattern of civilization alter what must be considered right in the application of unchangeable principles to the conditions of the particular time. Adjustment of the rights of the Church to the political, social, and moral climate for the common good of mankind is a matter of justice, not of expediency."[21]

Second, apart from the possibility of constructing a theory to "fit modern society," there is the difficulty of adapting it to a variety of geo-political contexts. "Justice forbids the denial of any rights to any individual anywhere that we assert for ourselves as a matter of natural right in this country."

Third, with respect to

> freedom of worship and of religious teaching, a distinction was suggested between recognizing the rights of individuals and admitting that an organized religious body as such has a natural right to propagate a false religion; error has not the same natural right to propagation as truth. On the other hand, it was suggested that as an individual has a natural right to search for truth, individuals have a right to search for truth collectively and publicly.

In addition to the McCabe report, Marston Morse offered his own commentary, which attempted to answer the question: "Which spiritual laws are relevant to the problem of Church and State?" It is included in the appendix to this essay. Morse took note that one aspect of the church-state problem concerned the right or duty of the State to put constraints upon the practice and teaching of untrue religions. In the idealized historic past certain basic spiritual or temporal laws were applied in the resolution of this problem. The question arises as to which of the authoritative laws and commands of the Church are most relevant to the problem of Church and State in the setting of the present age.

Morse was not seeking to qualify or otherwise legitimate certain demands the church might place upon a modern state. Rather, his concern was to square the practical ability of states to realize the ideal in a pluralistic society with the demands of justice imbedded within the church's own tradition. Justice required an authentic freedom, ensured by a state that upholds "the right of men to seek God without constraint." For the Princeton group, the key issue was the new situation respecting pluralism faced by the Catholic Church in the American context.

This is confirmed and clarified in Maritain's own commentary, about which a short preliminary word is in order. According to McCabe, Maritain did not intend his statement for publication outside the membership. McCabe had contacted Maritain about attaching his name to the statement and he apparently declined, further stipulating that if he had intended it for publication, the commentary would have been phrased differently.[22] Even seen in this context, Maritain's text offers a remarkable glimpse into his thought on the subject of church-state relations. It is a tightly argued memorandum, but one that is less circumspect and more open than his other writings on this subject. Because it has never before appeared, I reproduce it in full as an appendix to this essay, followed by Morse's statement.

The memorandum is broken into eight brief sections, each dealing with a fundamental issue. First, Maritain was concerned to take account of the prevailing political winds then blowing across America, a reading perhaps quickened by the enormous growth in the Catholic population in America, both by natural increase and by immigration.[23] His remarks also came on the heels of two important Supreme Court opinions, namely the *Everson* and *McCollum* decisions, which attempted to shore up the "wall" that stood between the church and the state.[24] Many non-Catholic Americans became deeply suspicious of their Catholic neighbors who had expressed deep regret over the results of these cases. A latent but pervasive distrust of Catholics was also in the background, especially around the fear of the cabal of Catholic domination.[25]

Maritain sought to address their concerns by pointing out how Europeans had viewed similar worries. Recalling the famous lines of Montalembert on religious minority-majority relations, Maritain viewed the current American chill toward Catholics as emerging from the idea that if Catholics were ever to gain political control through the sheer power of their numbers, there would be no hesitation in stamping out other religions through the coercive powers of the state.[26] Maritain countered with a reference to Henry Cardinal Manning's response to Gladstone: "If Catholics were in power tomorrow in England, not a penal law would be proposed, not the shadow of a constraint put upon the faith of any man. We would that all men fully believed in the truth; but a forced faith is a hypocrisy hateful to God and man."[27]

A second point concerned certain condemned propositions of liberalism. Maritain was quick to note how the idea of absolute freedoms or rights is rightly condemned as potentially threatening to the truth or to the common good, yet to disregard these freedoms' or rights' underlying principles is to deny justice. Thus, Maritain claimed, the principles themselves are fixed and enduring, but their historical conditioning is relative and flexible insofar as they continue to apply changing criteria of justice.[28] In the American context, the church necessarily had to abandon the medieval ideal in favor of a more adaptable program—not because of expediency or equivocality on the principles, but because any concrete application of the church's influence in the body politic rose or fell with its own peculiar reading of "a typical, specific structure or pattern of civilization." This guaranteed both the acknowledgment of immutable principles from the past (the so-called "thesis" or ideal) together with the justifying reasons by which they are employed in contemporary situations (various "hypotheses" or, better, sites of application). In this way, the church places before the civil order assertions that are rooted within a long-standing tradition, yet ones that remain fresh despite changes in epochs and societies. Throughout Maritain's memorandum, one cannot help being impressed by a realism that is born of a keen observation of the American proposition.

Maritain was also aware of the spiritual implications of his perspective. He hoped to give a certain philosophical priority to the church's evangelical mission, no doubt because he had such confidence in it, especially in view of distinctly "secular" and pluralistic societies like America. The very best way to preserve the freedoms enjoyed by the church, he argued, was not to enjoin the state to use its coercive powers against heresy, nor even to promote a privileged juridic status for itself. Rather, the church simply had to be herself through "the virtue of the apostolate and [its] God-given radiance" and in the "fecundity of her works and of the power of the word of God." By virtue of the great good this would contribute to the common welfare of society, the church's superiority would assume its natural place.

One could argue that Maritain's belief in the reasoning power of human beings to adjudicate the truthfulness of the church's position is somewhat naive, almost childlike. But the import of his position is clear and, I think, realistic. While the faith one has in the moral capacities of one's fellow citizens is often tested, it must be granted that the fundamental ability to reason through civic problems, many of which are inordinately complex, seems a necessary and sure component of life in the social order. That means that there is a tremendous responsibility laid at the feet of all Catholics to do their best to render their church's moral claims in the public square as intelligibly as possible. Only then can non-Catholics be convicted by the arguments of the Catholic Church or, at the very best, will they avoid the temptation toward philippics.

Impact of the Princeton Statement

Other points raised by the memorandum could be discussed, but in the remainder of this paper, I would like to indicate briefly how it affected the Catholic intellectual community of the day. First, it was not easy to sell this to the membership. Some of the most vocal on the whole question were utterly opposed to Maritain's argument. For instance, Louis Mercier of Georgetown University—a Frenchman who taught previously at Harvard—was an intransigent who had a formidable ally in Father Paul Hanley Furfey, the noted sociologist from the Catholic University of America. Mercier believed that, as the *Syllabus of Errors* of 1864 had condemned liberalism and Leo XIII's *Longinqua Oceani* of 1895 had condemned Americanism, taken together they settled the question about the separation of the Catholic Church from the state.[29] For Mercier, the relation should be seamless: the Catholic Church ought to have a juridic status above all other groups and the state ought to impose restrictions on these other groups, even to the point of suppression.

Mercier was interested in protecting the long-understood principle of the Catholic Church that "error has no rights" and that any true exercise of "rights" could be found only in the free and faithful observance of the natural and divine law. In an eight-page reply of his own, Mercier wrote, quoting the Princeton statement, that

> the recognition as a moral obligation of equal rights and liberties to all goes without saying, if they are genuine rights and liberties. But there can be no rights or liberties to act against the immutable principles of the natural law and the revealed law any place, any time, no matter what the historical conditions or "climate" may be. In fact, the historical conditions or climate may themselves be due to violations of the natural and revealed law.[30]

Mercier believed it was misleading for the Princeton statement to assert the impossibility of formulating principles of action at any given time that "would permit automatic and universal application of basic laws under all possible future conditions." For Mercier, "under all possible future conditions, it will always be right to worship God, and to live according to God's physical and moral laws, [and it will always be wrong not to do so]."

It was not in the "historical climate" of a given period that Mercier found the key to clarifying church-state relations. Rather, the Catholic Church's encyclicals and constant tradition, especially the natural-law tradition, were the measure. "According to our manuals of ethics and the Encyclicals," he wrote, "even according to the mere natural law, the following tenets of modern liberalism are false: Absolute freedom of thought, of reading, of conscience, of the press, of teaching, of worship. Moreover, according to natural ethics, there should be a private and a public worship of God. The precepts of natural religion and of the natural law are the minimum of morality needed by the state." From this one could not conclude otherwise: "separation of Church and State is not natural. The union of Church and State is natural and desirable, understanding that the state is independent in purely civic matters, the Church in purely religious matters, and that in mixed affairs there may be positive agreement."

At first blush, these positions display a certain disconnection from the reality of the situation of contemporary American Catholicism. But Mercier's remarks were meant to be unsettling and even incompatible with the widely accepted foundations of democratic pluralism.[31] His conclusions were blunt:

> To Catholics in the United States, especially to those living in non-Catholic centers, these are "hard sayings," in spite of the recognition that there should be no coercion in matters of religion. It would be so much more comfortable to say: "We Catholics are as liberal as you are. We place your right to believe what you please on the same footing as the right we claim to believe what the Catholic Church teaches." But Catholics could only speak thus hypocritically.[32]

Mercier's reply to the Princeton Statement seemed to polarize the CCICA on what members called "the essential Catholic doctrine" on the relation of the Catholic Church to the state. Hugh Taylor, the Princeton dean and a chemist by training, later confided to Stanford, "If I have to choose between two Frenchmen on the subject of the Catholic position in this matter I shall vote for Jacques Maritain."[33] He was not alone. Maritain's memorandum planted the seeds for the philosophical grounding of much subsequent Catholic scholarship. Vestiges can be detected in the work of John Courtney Murray, especially in his later reading of the Leonine literature.[34] For example, Murray goes into great detail over the "spoliation" of the temporal powers of the popes through the encroachments of civil rulers.[35] He also affirms, with considerable nuance, that this is a genuine development of doctrine. Additionally, Jerome Kerwin, a political scientist at the University of Chicago, looked to Maritain's paper in the construction of his own volume on the Catholic viewpoint on church and state.[36] It would be profitable, I suspect, to do a comparative analysis of Maritain's January 1949 memorandum and *Man and the State*, his Walgreen Lectures for later that year.[37] In both, Maritain's realism helped create a distinctly Catholic position on the American experiment, the product of a sensitive thinker for which the Church in America remains indebted, even as it continues to contribute to an evolving public philosophy.

APPENDIX

Memorandum of Jacques Maritain Drafted as a Result of the Princeton Regional Meeting of the CCICA, January 16, 1949, on the Church-State Problem*

I. Many non-Catholics are afraid that—at least as regards "mixed matters" (concerning both the spiritual and the temporal order)— we are now invoking freedom for ourselves only in order to deprive them of it on the day when we gain political power. The manner in which some Catholics express themselves (as Montalembert observed in France almost a century ago)** seems to be of a nature to confirm these people in their error.

It is therefore an essential task to get rid of such misunderstanding and make clear that for the Catholics of contemporary democratic nations, especially for the Catholics of this country, the recognition of equal rights and liberties for all citizens is conceived of not as a matter of expediency, but of moral obligation.

In other terms it is necessary both to maintain the immutable principles by virtue of which the Church has condemned theological liberalism, and to establish intrinsic validity of statements like Cardinal Manning's declaration to Gladstone: "If Catholics were in power tomorrow in England, not a penal law would be proposed, not the shadow of a constraint put upon the faith of any man. We would that all men fully believed the truth; but a forced faith is a hypocrisy hateful to God and man. . . . If the Catholics were tomorrow the 'Imperial race' in these Kingdoms they would not use political power to molest the divided and hereditary religious state of the people. We would not shut one of their Churches, or Colleges, or Schools. They would have the same liberties we enjoy as a minority."

---

*The documents of Jacques Maritain and Marston Morse are reprinted with the permission of The American Catholic History Research Center and University Archives of The Catholic University of America.

**" 'When I am the weaker, I claim freedom from you since it is your principle; when I am the stronger, I take it from you, since that is my principle.' Such was the formula ascribed by Montalembert to his opponents."

II. What are the meaning and implications of the "liberal" theses condemned by the Church? According to liberalism: 1) the "modern freedoms" (freedom of conscience, freedom of the press, etc.) are absolute, unconditional and limitless rights, to such an extent that man's obligations toward truth or common good are to be simply disregarded; 2) systems which are founded upon these freedoms and rights and which put them into force are the only just ones; for the acknowledgment of those freedoms and rights is in itself a matter of absolute moral necessity; 3) as a result many things that the Church did or claimed in the past with regard to civil society are to be considered as unacceptable in justice or at least as founded on principles rendered definitely outworn by the evolution of ideas and societies.

On the contrary, if said freedoms and rights are understood in a relative sense, and as required by virtue of historical conditions—not of absolute necessity by right—in such a way that their recognition does not entail any condemnation of the juridical structure of past regimes, there is no shadow of theological liberalism in upholding them. Even the Church herself puts forward today such freedoms as freedom of teaching, freedom of conscience, etc.

III. Many difficulties in present controversies stem from an insufficiently elaborate use and interpretation of the classical distinction between the "thesis" and the "hypothesis." Too often this distinction is understood in a univocal sense. Then it happens that the "thesis" confuses a universal, immutable principle with a particular application of it exemplified in a more or less idealized past, as if at any epoch whatever in human history a perfect or ideal state of affairs might be found in actual existence; and the "hypothesis" means only empirical circumstances which prevent the realization of such thesis by virtue of mere reasons of expediency.

Things being understood in this way, the conclusion that the Catholics should like to have now or in the future, if only this were possible, a body politic which would forbid the teaching of untrue religions or philosophies and make Protestants, Jews, Moslems or unbelievers second-rate citizens—in other terms, a body politic which would oppose the basic tenets of the American Constitution, by practicing religious discrimination and granting state privileges to a given Church—seems hardly avoidable.

IV. We would get an intellectual equipment more fit to deal with the problem if we considered on the one hand the universal, immutable principles that transcend history, on the other hand the particular, concrete applications that are called for by the various typical climates which replace each other in human history. In such a view, there is analogy, not univocity, in the manner in which the immutable principles are to be applied in such typically diverse ways. The notion of historical climate does not mean a mere set of empirical circumstances considered from the point of view of expediency, but a typical, specific structure or pattern of civilization, the intelligible features of which it is imperative to recognize as peculiar to a given historical age.

Things being thus understood, it is obvious that the same immutable principles (for instance the superiority of the spiritual order over the temporal one, or man's obligations toward truth) have to apply in the historical climate of the middle ages or of the "baroque age" and in the historical climate of modern times in typically diverse ways, and that both the manner of realization used in the past, and the manner of realization we have now to promote (not according to the false philosophy of liberalism, but to the concrete conditions of our historical climate) can be genuinely justified, however different they may be.

V. The historical climate of modern civilization, in contradistinction to medieval civilization, is characterized by the fact that it is a "secular," not a "sacral" civilization. The unity of religion is not a prerequisite for political unity, and men subscribing to diverse religious or non-religious creeds have to share in and work for the same political or temporal common good. The State is not the temporal arm of the Church; more perfectly differentiated than in the middle ages (according to the root distinction stated by Christ between the things that are God's and those that are Caesar's), it is autonomous and independent within its own sphere. The equality of all members of the city has been recognized as a basic political tenet. The importance of the inner forces at work in the human person, in contradistinction to the external forces of coercion; the freedom of individual conscience with regard to the state; the truth—always taught by the Catholic Church, but disregarded as a rule by the princes and kings in the past—that faith cannot be imposed by constraint, have become, more explicitly than before, crucial assets to civilization, and are to be especially emphasized to escape the worst dangers of perversion of the social body and of state totalitarianism.

In proportion as peoples become both more perfectly rid of individualistic liberalism and more explicitly aware of the historical climate of modern civilization, the immutable principle of the superiority of the spiritual order will have to apply, not in putting the state at the service of the Church or in asking Kings to expel heretics, but in recognizing for all citizens (I do not say for all religions) equal rights—without any juridical or political privilege to those professing a given creed—and not only in securing full freedom for the Catholic Church, but in positively facilitating, even in evoking, the religious, social and educational work by means of which she, as well as the other spiritual or cultural groups recognized by the State, cooperates in the common welfare.

So, by means of freedom and free cooperation with the state, not of state coercion or of any privileged juridical status, the superiority of the entirely true religion over the other creeds would be able to assert itself, by virtue of the apostolate and God-given radiance of the Catholic Church, of the fecundity of her works and of the power of the word of God. Moreover, given such a regime, in proportion as the number of Catholics increases in a nation the import of the institutions of the Church would increase in actual fact, without any infringement upon the liberties of other citizens.

On the other hand, such a conception of both distinction and cooperation between Church and State is of a nature to give full assurance to the non-Catholics with regard to the attachment of the Catholics to freedom not as a matter of expediency, but of moral obligation, and with regard to the unquestionable truth of Cardinal Manning's statement quoted above.

One has good reason to believe that the conception outlined here makes explicit the real meaning of the principles set forth by the fathers of the American Constitution, and finds a symbol in the oath taken by the President of the United States on the Bible, as well as in the three prayers pronounced by a priest, a minister, and a rabbi on his inauguration. Nevertheless the eighteenth century philosophical lexicon made the position of the authors of the Constitution somewhat ambiguous, so that the genuinely modern conception, fully acceptable to the Church, with which the tradition of this country is pregnant, has not yet been explicitly stated nor fully realized in actual fact. As a result the American sense of the expression "separation between Church and State" (which means in reality distinction and cooperation in mutual freedom and without any privilege for any particular spiritual or cultural group) runs the risk of veering toward the European sense of the same expression (no contact whatever between Church and State). The most efficacious way for American Catholics to prevent such a deviation seems to be first to establish their own conception of and devotion to freedom and equal rights on clear-cut and unquestionable principles, and thus to provide Christendom with the new pattern of realization of the Catholic principles on Church-State relations that is needed today.

VI. It seems that another point of doctrine, the distinction between the possession of a right and its exercise, can also be helpful in the matter. I can possess a right, for instance to personal freedom, and be prevented in justice from claiming its actual exercise, if my country is waging a just war and assigns me to be drafted.

The Church does not lose any of the rights she has claimed or exercised in the past. Nevertheless she can renounce the exercise of certain of them, not because she is forced to do so, but voluntarily and by virtue of the consideration of the common good, the historical context having changed. She exercised in the past the right of making subjects exempt from obeying excommunicated kings and emperors, or the right of delivering heretics to the secular arm to be burned to death. She always possesses those rights in their roots. If she made them emerge in actual exercise in the historical climate of today, this very exercise would harm the common good both of the Church and the souls and of civil society [sic]. So by reason of justice (justice toward the common good both of civilization and the Kingdom of God) does the Church give up the exercise of such rights.

VII. The Concordat concluded between the Holy See and Portugese State in 1940 (*Acta Apostolicae Sedis*, Ser. II, 7:7 [June 1, 1940]) is a particularly interesting example of arrangements adapted to the requirements of the present age. See the important address (November 18, 1941, *A Situacão da Igreia no regime da Concordata*, partially translated in *The Commonweal*, February 5, 1943) in which the Cardinal Patriarch of Lisbon comments upon this concordat.

VIII. According to the principles put forward in this paper, the legislation enforced in certain States which both make use of and grant privileges to the Church should not be described as objectionable by right, but as peculiar to less evolved areas (and perhaps, in some cases, as harmful to the general welfare of our present civilization taken as a whole).

•

(In addition to Maritain's remarks, Marston Morse contributed the following)

Which spiritual laws are relevant to the problem of Church and State?

I shall comment on one phase of this problem.

A particular aspect of the problem of Church and State concerns the right or duty of the State to put constraints upon the practice and teaching of untrue religions. In the idealized historic past certain basic spiritual or temporal laws were applied in the resolution of this problem. The question arises as to which of the authoritative laws and commands of the Church are most relevant to the problem of Church and State in the setting of the present age. A statement of superiority of the spiritual power over the temporal order is no less valid than formerly, but in addition other laws of the Church may have a new and increased relevance. Religious constraint in a land such as America would condition the right of men to seek God by the light of reason, would affect Catholics in the exercise of Christian love towards their neighbors, and would seriously modify the problem of the promulgation of the Faith.

Basic spiritual laws are infinite in meaning although necessarily finite in statement. The circumstances to which such laws apply may admit infinite variety as the future unfolds. It is clearly impossible at any one time to formulate principles of action that would permit automatic and univocal application of basic laws under all possible future conditions, or even to enumerate all the possible historic conditions to which a given law should apply to the exclusion of all others. What is meant here can be made clear by describing an analogous situation in natural science.

When a law of fundamental natural science is applied to a difficult new problem it is necessary to make an a priori study of the conditions defining the problem. This in no sense implies the lack of truth of the basic law; it does indicate the need of a more extensive formulation of the consequences of the basic law. Frequently it is found that other basic laws must be invoked to solve the problem. This again implies no limitation on the truth of the law first proposed as containing a solution; it does indicate that the problem is more complex than originally supposed. There is no question of expediency; one seeks the composite implication of all the basic laws which bear on the problem. It is as much an error to omit a relevant law as to draw a false implication from the totality of relevant laws. In neither case is the true solution obtained.

The difficulties in a concrete situation of determining the joint consequences of several commands of the Church are illustrated by the problem of loving one's enemy (a country) and at the same time upholding truth and justice.

To pass from the general to the particular it might be illuminating to consider one sector of American life, namely the older Protestant rural community. How would the lives of Catholics or Protestants be affected by any understanding that Catholics might at some future time exercise a constraint upon the Protestant faith? Those who know such Protestant communities recognize their emphasis upon simple Christian virtues, their naïve theology, their self-contained social and cultural life, and (from the point of view of America) their long tradition. The ordinary individual in such a community is insulated from all Catholic influences; his ethical and moral standards advance or regress with the community. The religious community is for him an extension of the family and his search for truth ordinarily collective. To affect a change in such a community in the direction of understanding the Catholic faith, opening up the possibility of conversion of individuals, requires patient preparation based on education and Christian love. To crystallize an understanding that religious restraints are to be part of Catholic policy in case Catholics control the State in America would shock such a community into an uncomprehending intolerance of everything Catholic.

The problem of an approach to a unified Christian State demands education of all, including Catholics, to reduce the social, intellectual and cultural barriers and to remove misunderstandings based on ignorance. If men could first become brothers they would be more likely to speak in terms of love than in terms of force. They might then speak of all the verities and not merely those which separate. Non-Catholics who are striving in good faith to find a more perfect life have a right to receive Christian treatment and help. The existence of such a right is inconsistent with an expectation of future religious constraint.

In sum, the spiritual laws and commands of the Church which appear to bear upon the problem of freedom of religious practice in the setting of the present age are not one but many, and include laws which are at the heart of the Faith. Their total implication points to the moral duty of Catholics of opposing restraints upon faith and religious practice as injurious to the true cause of the promulgation of the Faith; the exercise of Christian love; and the right of men to seek God without constraint.

Notes

¹On the CCICA, see Patrick J. Hayes, *The Catholic Commission on Intellectual and Cultural Affairs, 1945-1965* (Ph.D. diss., Washington, DC: The Catholic University of America, 2003).

²For instance, Thomas Charles Berg, "Anti-Catholicism and Modern Church-State Relations," *Loyola University Chicago Law Journal*, 33 (Fall 2001): 121-72; Philip Hamburger, *Separation of Church and State* (Cambridge: Harvard University Press, 2004); Richard John Neuhaus, *The Naked Public Square: Religion and Democracy in America* (Grand Rapids: Eerdmans, 1984); John McGreevy, *Catholicism and American Freedom: A History* (New York: W. W. Norton, 2003); John Noonan, *The Lustre of Our Country: The American Experience of Religious Freedom* (Berkeley: University of California Press, 1998).

³See Joseph Martin Dawson, *Separate Church and State Now* (New York: Richard R. Smith, 1948).

⁴For commentary on the rise of this "new nativism," see Donald Pelotte, *John Courtney Murray: Theologian in Conflict* (New York: Paulist Press, 1976), 17-21.

⁵Paul Blanshard, *American Freedom and Catholic Power* (Boston: Beacon Press, 1949).

⁶On these latter two journals, see Ralph Lord Roy, *Apostles of Discord: A Study of Organized Bigotry and Disruption on the Fringes of Protestantism* (Boston: Beacon Press, 1953), 156-65, 254-59.

⁷See Harold E. Fey, *Can Catholicism Win America?* (New York: The Christian Century, 1946), and, among others, Harold R. Rafton, *The Roman Catholic Church and Democracy—The Teachings of Pope Leo XIII* (Boston: Beacon Press, 1951); Harold R. Rafton, *What Do Roman Catholic Colleges Teach? A Review of Ryan and Boland's Book,* Catholic Principles of Politics (Boston: Beacon Press, 1953). This latter volume challenged the arguments of John Ryan and Francis Boland's book, *Catholic Principles of Politics,* rev. ed. (New York: Macmillan, 1948).

[8]"Minutes of the Executive Committee Meeting, Augustinian College, Washington, D.C., February 21-22, 1948," in Archives of the Catholic University of America (hereafter ACUA), CCICA Collection. The archive of the CCICA is presently uncatalogued. I thank David J. O'Brien, then CCICA chairperson, for permission to consult these materials when they were housed at the College of the Holy Cross. Copies may be found in a number of other repositories, including the Archives of Georgetown University (hereafter AGU). The reference to the minutes noted above can be found also in AGU, Wilfrid Parsons, S.J., Papers, CCICA, Box 7:16.

[9]Murray to Stanford, January 17, 1948, in ACUA, CCICA, Annual Meetings: Julian Huxley and UNESCO.

[10]In fact, he was about to deliver a major address on the subject for the second annual meeting of the Catholic Theological Society of America in June 1948, less than a month after the New Rochelle meeting. Murray was not able to deliver the paper the previous year due to illness. During the 1947 CTSA convention, Joseph Clifford Fenton of The Catholic University of America gave a paper in Murray's stead, later published as "The Theology of the Church and the State," *Proceedings of the Second Annual Meeting of the Catholic Theological Society of America* (Boston: Catholic Theological Society of America, 1947): 7-42. Murray's June 1948 paper was a long treatise that was published as "Governmental Repression of Heresy," *Proceedings of the Third Annual Meeting of the Catholic Theological Society of America* (Chicago: CTSA, 1948): 26-98, with response by Francis J. Connell, "Discussion of Governmental Repression of Heresy," ibid., 98-101.

[11]Rommen's brief paper, with refinements suggested by the St. Louis meeting, would serve as the basis for a longer article that he published as "Church and State," *Review of Politics* 12, no. 3 (1950): 321-40. See Heinrich Rommen, *The State in Catholic Thought: A Treatise in Political Philosophy* (New York: Herder, 1945).

[12]Thomas H. Mahony, "A Legal Inquiry on the Church-State Problem in the U.S.A.," in AGU, Varia Collection, Box 7:138. The text was later reprinted under the same title in *Catholic Educational Review* 48, no. 2 (February 1950): 75-95.

[13]Ladner's contribution to the CCICA gathering contains the rudiments of an expanded article later published as "The Concepts of *ecclesia* and *christianitas* and the Relation to the Idea of Papal *plenitudo potestatis* from Gregory VII to Boniface VIII," *Miscellanea historicae pontificae* 18 (1954): 49-77. Weigel's text, so far as I know, remained unpublished.

[14]Edward Stanford, "The Catholic Commission on Intellectual and Cultural Affairs," *Catholic Educational Review* 47, no. 6 (1949): 398-99.

[15]David McCabe, "Report of the Princeton Area Group," n.d., ACUA, CCICA, Inactive Files: Father Stanford, Box 1 (hereinafter "Report"). The report is given by McCabe in typescript with additional marginalia. Stanford later retyped and excerpted portions of the text for distribution among the members.

[16]On Murray's writing on church-state questions, see Victor Yanitelli, "A

Church-State Anthology: The Work of Father Murray," *Thought* 27 (1952): 6-42. Father Yanitelli also provided a review of the drama that resulted between Murray and his chief theological interlocutors, Fathers Francis Connell and Joseph C. Fenton, encompassing the early moments of the controversy brought on by Murray's CCICA paper. Yanitelli, "Chronicle: A Church-State Controversy," *Thought* 26 (1951): 443-51. A fuller account is given by Joseph A. Komonchak, "The Silencing of John Courtney Murray," in *Cristianismo nella storia: Saggi in onore di Giuseppe Alberigo*, ed. A. Melloni et al. (Bologna: Il Mulino, 1996), 657-702.

[17]For example, among Murray's Catholic interlocutors, see Father Joseph Clifford Fenton, "The Theology of the Church and the State," *Proceedings of the Second Annual Meeting of the Catholic Theological Society of America*, 7-42. Fenton gave a paper at the CTSA convention in Murray's stead with the assurance that Murray would present at the following year's convention. He did so and the respondent was Fenton's ally, Redemptorist Father Francis Connell, who would continue to hammer out his position in subsequent articles. See John Courtney Murray, "Governmental Repression of Heresy," *Proceedings of the Catholic Theological Society of America* 3 (1948): 26-98; Francis J. Connell, "Discussion of 'Governmental Repression of Heresy,' " ibid., 98-101; Connell, "Christ the King of Civil Rulers," *American Ecclesiastical Review* 119 (October 1948): 244-53. Murray had been writing on church-state issues for several years before the 1948 CCICA gathering. See John Courtney Murray, "Current Theology: Freedom of Religion," *Theological Studies* 6 (March 1945): 85-113; Murray, "Freedom of Religion I: The Ethical Problem," *Theological Studies* 6 (June 1945): 229-86; Murray, review of *Religious Liberty: An Inquiry* by M. Searle Bates, *Theological Studies* 7 (March 1946): 151-63; Murray, "Separation of Church and State," *America* 76 (December 1946): 261-63; Murray, "Separation of Church and State: True and False Concepts," *America* 76 (February 1947): 628-30; Murray, "Religious Liberty: The Concern of All," *America* 77 (February 1948): 513-16; Murray, "Robert Bellarmine and the Indirect Power," *Theological Studies* 9 (December 1948): 491-535.

[18]David McCabe, "Report of the Princeton Area Group." Unless otherwise indicated, all subsequent quotations are from these texts.

[19]Marston Morse was a convert to Catholicism. Born on March 24, 1892, in Waterville, Maine, he graduated summa cum laude from Colby College and completed his doctorate at Harvard in 1917. After teaching at Cornell, Brown, and Harvard, he settled at the Institute for Advanced Study in 1935, and remained there for the rest of his career. It was at the Institute that he worked on the calculus of variations in the large, contributing a novel technique of differential topology known as Morse theory, an important contribution to string theory. For his work, he received the prestigious Bôcher Memorial Prize and was elected to the American Academy of Arts and Sciences and the National Academy of Sciences. Morse received many awards for his work. These include the Presidential Certificate of Merit for his war work (1947), the National Medal for Science from the United States for his mathematical

contributions, the Legion d'honneur and the Croix de Guerre from France, and twenty honorary degrees from universities throughout the world. He died in 1977.

[20]David McCabe later confirmed the authorship of both Morse's and Maritain's commentaries in a letter to Edward Stanford, OSA. McCabe to Stanford, February 27, 1949, in ACUA, CCICA, Inactive Files: Father Stanford, Box 1.

[21]McCabe, "Report of the Princeton Area Group." In his letter, McCabe also urged that the discussion continue, if only to counter the charge of "expediency" against Catholics in the United States, where others saw Catholics using the separation doctrine to further the church's missionary or educational objectives in America while simultaneously denying those same rights in European countries like Spain. "I need not stress," McCabe wrote frankly, "that Spain is a terrible albatross around our necks."

[22]McCabe to Stanford, February 27, 1949, in ACUA, CCICA, Inactive Files: Father Stanford, Box 1.

[23]In the period from 1900 to 1950 the Catholic population of the United States grew by 166 percent. In the second half of the twentieth century the American Catholic population again more than doubled, so that current figures suggest about 27 percent of the total population of the United States self-identifies as Catholic. See Bryan T. Froehle and Mary Gautier, *Catholicism USA: A Portrait of the Catholic Church in the United States* (Maryknoll, NY: Orbis Books, 2000), 3-4.

[24]*Everson v. Board of Education*, 330 U.S. 1 (1947); *McCollum v. Board of Education*, 333 U.S. 421 (1948).

[25]For example, William Warren Sweet, *The American Churches: An Interpretation* (New York: Abingdon-Cokesbury, 1948), 67: "Wherever Roman Catholicism secures dominance there you will have at least the threat of religious intolerance; wherever the Roman Catholics are a minority there— and there only—do they give even lip service to complete religious liberty. Here is a valid justification for seeing to it that the Roman Catholics be kept in a minority, not only in the United States but throughout the world, if the great principle of complete religious liberty is to be maintained."

[26]" 'When I am the weaker, I claim freedom from you since it is your principle; when I am the stronger, I take it from you, since that is my principle.' Such was the formula ascribed by Montalembert to his opponents." Compare the dictum of Louis Veuillot cited by Heinrich Rommen: "When you are the majority, we demand our liberty on the basis of your principles (the so-called principle of indifferentism). When we are in the majority, we will refuse your liberty on the basis of our principles" (Rommen, "A Philosophical Inquiry on the Church State Problem," in AGU, Varia Collection, Box 7:138).

[27]Henry Edward Manning, *The Vatican Decrees and Their Bearing on Civil Allegiance* (London: Catholic Publication Society, 1875), 93-96.

[28]Several earlier texts on this theme have been collected in Maritain's *Natural Law: Reflections on Theory and Practice*, ed. William Sweet (South Bend: St. Augustine's Press, 2001).

[29]Attention may be drawn to the following passage in Leo's encyclical: The Church amongst you, unopposed by the Constitution and government of your nation, fettered by no hostile legislator, protected against violence by the common laws and the impartiality of the tribunals, is free to live and act without hindrance. Yet, though all this is true, it would be very erroneous to draw the conclusion that in America is to be sought the type of the most desirable status of the Church, or that it would be universally lawful or expedient for State and Church to be, as in America, dissevered and divorced. The fact that Catholicity with you is in good condition, nay, is even enjoying a prosperous growth, is by all means to be attributed to the fecundity with which God has endowed His Church, in virtue of which unless men or circumstances interfere, she spontaneously expands and propagates herself; but she would bring forth more abundant fruits if, in addition to liberty, she enjoyed the favor of the laws and the patronage of the public authority. (Pope Leo XIII, "Catholicity in the United States: Encyclical Letter *Longiqua oceani*" [January 6, 1895], in *The Great Encyclical Letters of Pope Leo XIII* [New York: Benziger Brothers, 1903], 320-35, here at 323-24)

[30]Louis J. A. Mercier, "A Discussion of the Princeton Statement on the Relations of Church and State," ms., ACUA, CCICA, Inactive Files: Father Stanford, Box 2, here at page 1. Mercier's text was edited and retyped by Stanford for distribution to the membership. Subsequent references are to this text unless indicated otherwise.

[31]An example is Mercier's vehemence in response to a proposition found in the Princeton Statement: "The historical climate of modern civilization is characterized by the fact that it is 'secular.' " Mercier's terse reply: "Too bad for the climate and modern civilization. The duty of Catholics is precisely to oppose secularism" (ibid., 3).

[32]Ibid., 6.

[33]Taylor to Stanford, April 19, 1949, in ACUA, CCICA, Inactive Files: Father Stanford, Box 1.

[34]John Courtney Murray, "Leo XIII on Church and State: The General Structure of the Controversy," *Theological Studies* 14 (March 1953): 1-30; "Leo XIII: Separation of Church and State," *Theological Studies* 14 (June 1953): 145-214; "Leo XIII: Government and the Order of Culture," *Theological Studies* 15 (March 1954): 1-33.

[35]Murray, "Leo XIII on Church and State," 5, n.21.

[36]Jerome Kerwin, *Catholic Viewpoint on Church and State* (New York: Hanover House, 1960).

[37]Such a comparison would be supplemental to the edited collection of Timothy Fuller and John Hittinger, *Reassessing the Liberal State: Reading Maritain's Man and the State* (Washington, DC: The Catholic University of America Press, 2001).

Part II

EXPLORING THE CONTEMPORARY AMERICAN CONTEXT

Does Systematic Theology Have a Future?

A Response to Lieven Boeve

William L. Portier

If contemporary Catholic systematic theologians in the United States find themselves in the doldrums, Lieven Boeve's *God Interrupts History* brings a refreshing breeze from Leuven. The subtitle, *Theology in a Time of Upheaval*, alludes to the title of a 2005 talk by then Cardinal Joseph Ratzinger and locates Boeve in the discussion of European culture to which Ratzinger's talk contributed.[1] A time of upheaval indeed, and Boeve identifies the neuralgic point in contemporary Catholic systematic theology: the "resolutely modern" form of theologizing named by Paul Tillich as "correlation theology," the approach of the majority of modern theologies (32), "no longer appears to function today" (34).

Students of George Lindbeck and proponents of the so-called "Yale School" have been claiming this for years. Boeve groups them together with John Milbank's "Radical Orthodoxy" and those identified with the journal *Communio* as "anti-moderns." Anti-moderns share with correlationists the presupposition that their primary contemporary potential dialogue partner is secular modernity. But Boeve is not about to sign up for the Yale School. Correlation is stalled rather than fundamentally flawed, and he wants to reconceive it. First, he deconstructs the context of correlation theology's putative dialogue partner which, in his reading, also turns out to be the context rejected by the anti-moderns as radically discontinuous with Christian tradition.

Then, as an alternative to secularization, Boeve describes what he calls the "de-traditionalization" of both Christian and Enlightenment traditions. The result is a plurality of worldviews and approaches to life. Contemporary Western plurality includes variants of both Christianity and the Enlightenment, but neither is clearly dominant. This de-traditionalization and pluralization is the recontextualization that Boeve proposes. Contemporary theology (in the West?) finds itself in dialogue with a de-stabilized context. With this re-defined context, a pluralized Christian tradition is neither clearly continuous, as with correlationist theology, nor clearly discontinuous, as with theologians Boeve calls "anti-modern" or "counter-cultural."

Interruption is the category that Boeve uses to support this methodological recontextualization. Located in the space between a correlationist bridge and an anti-modern rupture, interruption structures the mediation between tradition and context. For Boeve it promises to hold both correlationist continuity and anti-modern discontinuity together in one recontextualized theology. God interrupts history. As paradigm for interruption as a theological category, Boeve takes "the resurrection of the Jesus who died on the cross" (46).

Boeve's own account is much richer than my necessarily limited summary suggests. The comments to follow are confined mostly to the methodological considerations of the second chapter, "A New Method." My comments cluster around three questions. First, who are the anti-moderns? Second, what would recontextualized theology really look like? Third, what was the context for correlation theology? Why was it plausible? In pursuing these questions, I am looking to clarify our understanding of *context* and *particularity*.

Anti-Modern in Principle or in Fact?

Can thoroughgoing theological intrinsicists really be anti-modern in principle? Is it more likely that they are "anti-modern" on the basis of contingent judgments about contextual particularities? Boeve frames his project of recontexualizing the "stalled correlation" of post-Vatican II theology against those he calls "anti-moderns." The anti-moderns cluster around Radical Orthodoxy, *Communio*, and Yale postliberalism. They presuppose "a principle of rigid discontinuity" (37) between context and tradition. In the following brief comments, I want to interrogate the designation "anti-modern" and propose other ways of thinking about the differences between these two loosely defined groups, the correlationists and the anti-moderns.

The first point to note is that neither *Communio* nor Radical Orthodoxy is a theological movement in any strict sense. Second, the deep differences among those Boeve designates as anti-moderns make it hard to imagine them as a single group. The theology of nature and grace can serve as one example. To the extent that there is a common project going forward at *Communio*, at least in the English-language group, its roots are deep in Henri de Lubac's theology of nature and grace with its rejection of the modern pure nature hypothesis as contributing to Christianity's contemporary "exile" from modern culture. David Schindler's Introduction to the 1998 Crossroad Herder edition of de Lubac's *The Mystery of the Supernatural*[2] articulates this position in a programmatic way. Though he studiously avoids reference to Schindler, Milbank's *The Suspended Middle*[3] might be read as a refutation, or at least an alternative, to Schindler's interpretation of de Lubac.

Milbank's "intrinsicism" is even more radical than Schindler's. But despite this key difference, it is precisely their intrinsicism on the question of nature and grace that makes it difficult to imagine either Schindler or Milbank wanting to jettison every intrinsic connection between context and Christian belief. One has only to read Hans Urs von Balthasar's 1972 "Communio-A Programme," which appeared in the first number of the journal, or scan the first page of the Introduction to *Radical Orthodoxy*[4] to see that dialogue with culture or engagement with the world is central to both projects.

So, in another sense, despite their differences, Boeve is correct to group them together. But they do not belong together because they are anti-modern, if that means denying any intrinsic connection between context and Christian belief. What they have in common is a refusal to dialogue with culture on non-theological terms. This is the point both of Milbank's critique of secular reason (Boeve, 31) and of Schindler's critique, in his book *Heart of the World, Center of the Church*,[5] of Murray's politics. To the extent that *context* is such a non-theological term, both Schindler and Milbank would no doubt want to question and qualify it.

What they have in common—and here we could add the Yale School and its numerous Hauerwasian descendants in the United States—is a desire to "re-theologize theology." Negatively stated, this is a postliberal impulse in the sense that it rejects the liberal project of translating Christian theology into categories that seem to come from a neutral place, such as religion, experience, or, in questions about Christianity's relation to world religions, the near canonical troika of inclusivism, exclusivism, and pluralism. A similar impulse seems to move Boeve at key points. As he points out, such talk in terms of universal structures can only be *a posteriori* (39). Content and method are always the "closest partners" (8). He follows Edward Schillebeeckx's understanding of experience as always interpreted. He insists that interruption is not a formal and empty category but is narratively charged with Christian specificity (48, 205). As Karl Barth, Balthasar, Stanley Hauerwas, Schindler, Lindbeck, and Milbank would all agree, "It is not in the first instance as human beings that Christians are Christians but it is as Christians that they are human, irreducibly determined by their particular Christian narrativity" (39).

Unless context were to have much more material specificity than Boeve gives it, I am hard put to see where the force of "anti-modern" as a "rigid discontinuity" (37) with context comes from. My sense is that this has something to do with the work that Boeve wants the formal-sounding word *context* to do. Like those he names anti-modern, Boeve seems to want to draw his deep resources from the theological tradition rather than from some set of theoretical observer categories that can round on theology. And yet like *practice*, *narrative*, and other staples of the postliberal lexicon, *context* is obviously not a theological term. Shouldn't *context* be further particularized? Whose context? In what sorts of categories would theologians talk about it and fill it with content?

Is the force of *anti-modern*, then, primarily polemical? Is what divides Boeve's recontextualized correlationism from those he calls anti-modern a function of different positions on issues of inner-church reform that "anti-moderns" might see as driven primarily by such seemingly secular standards as "equality" and "inclusivity"? This question points to a deeper concern that might help us get at what, if any, substantive theological differences there are between Boeve and those he calls "anti-moderns." How might such seemingly secular standards as "equality" and "inclusivity" be thought theologically?

Both "correlationists" and "anti-moderns" would affirm the graced character of our world. Clearly, both groups do not understand this affirmation in precisely the same way. What is the difference? This goes to the question of how Boeve understands *context* and the work he wants it to do. When Boeve attributes to "anti-moderns" a presupposition of "rigid discontinuity" between context and Christian tradition, is he suggesting that Ratzinger, Schindler, Milbank, et al.—all theological children of de Lubac and his intrinsicism—deny the graced character of our world?[6] If not, it would seem that we must then talk about particular contexts, such as the European Union or the United States in their pluriformity, and specify with all the attending ambivalence their connections to the faith or tradition in question.

Context is key here. In order to "conceptualize the relationship between theology and context" (3), the two terms, it would seem, would have to be always already related. At least this would be the case in a world of theological intrinsicism. But the precise sense that Boeve wants to give *context* eludes me. Sometimes *context* sounds like a rough equivalent for *world* as in "church and world." In its normative theological sense, recontextualization "calls for a theological program in which insight into the *intrinsic link between faith and context* [italics added] inspires theologians to take contextual challenges seriously, in order to come to a contemporary theological discourse that can claim both theological validity and contextual plausibility" (3, n. 4). Boeve posits an "intrinsic link" between "the significance of revelation, faith, Church, and tradition, and the context in which they are given form" (7). Thus faith and Church do not stand externally opposed to the world. They help to constitute it and are in turn partly constituted by it. This "intrinsic link" is such that "history ultimately becomes co-constitutive of the truth of faith" (7).

Here one can recognize a familiar thread that runs through Schillebeeckx's theology from its beginning—from development of doctrine to hermeneutics to ideology critique and mysticism and politics. Boeve calls it "reflection on the development of tradition and tradition hermeneutics" (87). As Newman put it at the end of the first Section of chapter 1 of *An Essay on the Development of Christian Doctrine*, it is the concern for how the Christian "idea" changes with new forms "in order to remain the same."[7] Boeve thinks this is Christianity's strength. He describes the "intrinsic bond" between faith and context theologically as "the incarnational driving force of the Christian faith" (30). Part of the work that Boeve wants *context* to do is to drive development, to help the tradition change in order to stay alive. Context *inter-*

rupts tradition and impels it to grow or recontextualize (87).[8]

The problem with "anti-moderns," then, seems to be that they continually "point to the need to hark back to pre-modern conceptual patterns in order to reflect on the cause of the Christian faith in today's literally post-modern context." They tend to see the appeal to the "intrinsic link" between faith and context as obscuring the "strangeness" or newness of Jesus, his Gospel, and the Church (31). Boeve's anti-moderns, then, are inclined to stand in the way of the faith changing contextually in order to remain the same. They are temperamentally, or perhaps even contextually, disposed to stress the present identity of the faith.

But this issue with the "anti-moderns" does not strike me as a matter of theological principle. It has to do with judgments about what de Lubac wisely called the "ebb and flow in theology"[9] or what Boeve, invoking J.-B. Metz, calls *Korrektivtheologie* (4). Questions about continuity and discontinuity between tradition and context are not primarily questions of theological principle. They are inevitably tied to historical questions having to do with such issues as the genealogy of modernity. Not only must contemporary theologians affirm in principle the kind of theological intrinsicism they might learn from de Lubac, but they must also try to sort through these tradition-transmission kinds of questions about modernity's origins. As a wise historian of philosophy once put it, Europe is Christian in origin but not in consequence. Within each individual theologian, modernity/postmodernity dwells together in often confused or uneasy relationship with Christianity.

I cannot imagine a more radical theological intrinsicist than John Milbank. In his esoteric reading of de Lubac, one cannot even distinguish the order of redemption from the order of creation. But this is not just a question of theological principle. From Jaime Balmes to Charles Taylor, from Felicité de Lamennais to Johann-Baptist Metz, Catholic scholars have tried to sort through the tangles of Catholicism's relation to modernity. Theology has an ebb and flow of generations. Theologians read history differently and, most importantly, they read the signs of the times differently. What, for example, am I as an American to make of the intrinsic connection between tradition and context if my context is an empire that makes war without end?[10] Continuity/discontinuity questions about tradition and context do not admit of theoretical theological resolution. They have to do with multiplicities of judgments about contingencies. I don't see how any of Boeve's "anti-modern" theologians could be in principle theologically opposed to his key notion of an intrinsic connection between tradition and context. But they have different sensibilities about particular contexts, different judgments about the recent history of theology, and different readings of the signs of the times. Rather than as matters of principle, continuity/discontinuity questions are more likely to be worked out in the doing of theology.

What Would Recontextualized Theology Really Look Like?

The irreducible plurality of narratives that characterizes the contemporary de-traditionalized context for theology in the West drives Boeve's recontextualization proposal in the direction of Christian particularity and the need "to develop conceptual patterns that recognize and account for the irreducible significance of the particular." He identifies this concern with the significance of the particular as precisely the point at which "dialogue with the contemporary context has the potential to be productive" (39). In a section entitled "From Correlation to Recontextualization," Boeve goes on to urge theologians to a "determination to take the radical historicity and contextuality of Christian faith and of theology seriously" (40). This is nothing less than *the* task, bequeathed by history, if you will, to present generations of Catholic theologians in the West. It is a generational commitment that I have been trying to carry out for a long time. As a graduate student in systematic theology, the seemingly formal exhortations of our professors to thematize historicity sent me off in the direction of American Catholic history.[11] In thinking about how to train future theologians, I have become convinced that really turning to the particular, really trying to take "the radical historicity and contextuality of the Christian faith and theology seriously" will mean that theologians of the future will look more like historians, anthropologists, practitioners of cultural studies, and art and film critics than like authors we now recognize as systematic theologians.

At various points in chapters 2 and 4, Boeve alludes to the Yale-Chicago split of the last decades of the twentieth century as instantiating his continuity/discontinuity question (for example, 62, 76). I am tempted to say that the battle is over and Yale has won. But even in the more robust forms of postliberalism we find in Stanley Hauerwas and his students, categories such as *narra-*

tive, practice, form of life, particularity, and even *church* are expected to do heavy theological lifting, and yet they remain almost completely formal and unlocated.

In chapter 4, following his discussion of Vergote's critique of Schillebeeckx, Boeve cites David Tracy's 1989 reply to George Lindbeck in *Theological Studies,* entitled "The Uneasy Alliance Reconceived."[12] Beginning from Lindbeck's *The Nature of Doctrine,*[13] and Tracy's reply five years later, I want to sketch what a theology that really took the particular and historicity seriously might look like. Though they do so in very formal and non-particular ways, both Tracy and Lindbeck seem to converge in advocating something like a Geertzian approach to contemporary questions of theological method. Such an approach would demand that Catholic theologians in the United States begin to develop skills in the area of cultural studies generally and more particularly in the constellation of fields known as American Catholic studies. If they did, they might look a lot like Vince Miller.

In the final chapter of *The Nature of Doctrine,* Lindbeck lays out the methodological implications of the "cultural-linguistic" approach to doctrine that the book proposes. One of the tasks of the kind of descriptive theology he envisions is to give "a normative explication of the meaning a religion has for its adherents." Lindbeck calls such description "intra-textual" and compares the task of cultural-linguistic or postliberal theologians to that of ethnographers. Ethnographers approach broad interpretations and abstractions such as culture or context "from the direction of exceedingly extended acquaintances with extremely small matters."[14]

But, according to Lindbeck, neither ethnographers nor cultural-linguistic theologians have a merely descriptive task. He goes on to argue that this task of describing what he calls a "religion" from within (displaying the informal logic of its actual life) is a "highly constructive enterprise." A well-trained theologian will inevitably face questions about how to live this embodied life in "new domains of thought, reality and action." It is at this point that Lindbeck speaks of "redescribing" the world in terms of the biblical story.[15] In such a conception of theology as Lindbeck's, the skill sets involved in cultural studies, anthropology, and history become *theologically* important in a way that recalls Boeve's "intrinsic link" between tradition and context. If history is constitutive of the truth of faith, then theologians need the skills to talk about particular histories.

David Tracy's reply to Lindbeck's project makes remarkably similar arguments. He begins by invoking Friedrich von Hügel's threefold typology of the mystical, institutional, and intellectual elements of a "great religion." It is in addressing our access to the "mystical" or religious element (forms of devotional practice, liturgy, symbols, and practices of both popular and elite cultures) that Tracy turns to the ethnographic. He is talking specifically about Catholicism and Catholic theology. We must have, he argues, more than the familiar theological, social scientific, philosophical, and historical approaches to the religious lives of Catholics. In addition to these familiar approaches, he urges especially anthropology and what at Chicago is called "history of religions" as helping to "discern the forms, the interrelationships, the history of the entire symbolic religious life of Catholic Christianity."

We still await, says Tracy,

> the Clifford Geertz to write *Catholicism Observed* in different cultures, or the Wendy Doniger [his colleague at Chicago] to illuminate the great myths and symbols of Mexican, Polish, Italian, and Irish forms of Catholic life. . . . Above all, we need not only philosophers and theologians but historians of religion and anthropologists to study the myths, rituals, symbols, and symbolic forms of this amazing, pluralistic and rich Catholic tradition.[16]

"Such historical, social-scientific, anthropological, and history of religions perspectives," he concludes, "in my judgment, are what are most needed to challenge, enrich, and change, the familiar forms of Catholic studies, including Catholic theological method." Tracy wrote these words almost twenty years ago. The kind of work he was describing was just beginning in the academy. In the intervening years, it has taken off. No student of von Hügel's third element, the "intellectual/theological," Tracy warned, "can afford to neglect that work."[17] Indeed, it is difficult to imagine how a student could excel in the practice of doing theology without having the kinds of ethnographic/cultural tools needed to describe and re-describe the actual life of a particular Christian community.

Were we really to make this turn to the particular, really to take historicity seriously, we would have to ask what the future will be for "systematic theology" and bibliographically exhaustive, meta-discourse-sounding books such as *The Analogical Imagination*. David Tracy seems to have decided that even he cannot read everything. The word *fragment* and its plural appear frequently in his titles since the early 1990s. This leaves us with the unsettling but potentially exciting question of what might lie in systematic theology's future.

What Was the Context for Correlation? Why Was It Plausible?

Boeve notes at the outset that his immediate dialogue partner in *God Interrupts History* will be "the modern theology with which countless post-conciliar students of theology were raised." Karl Rahner, J.-B. Metz, Hans Küng, David Tracy, and Edward Schillebeeckx represent this theological orientation. They sought to build bridges between culture and faith. They saw a basic continuity between the modern project of emancipation and Christian faith (4). It is this theological orientation that Boeve seeks to rejuvenate and renew through his proposal for recontextualization.

Boeve himself draws attention to the centrality of context. In this section, I want to ask about the context for correlation theology. What made it plausible? Considering these questions might help to clarify the notion of context by example and it might also shed light on a contemporary context in the West, a context shared by both Boeve and his project of recontextualization as well as by those he calls "anti-modern."

With the exception of David Tracy who is a bit younger, the Catholic theologians who represent the correlation orientation all came to adulthood around mid-twentieth century. As the Great Depression was for their parents, World War II was the formative experience of their generations. It was after World War II in 1951 that Paul Tillich, a German writing in the United States, put correlation at the thematic center of his *Systematic Theology*.[18] Tillich stood in a long liberal Protestant tradition going back to Friedrich Schleiermacher. After Vatican II, both Tracy, who probably borrowed it directly from Tillich, and Schillebeeckx used *correlation*, usually with the modifiers *mutual* and *critical*, to describe what they were doing.

How did the term *correlation* make its way into Catholic theology? The stock answer would be the Second Vatican Council. But what were the plausibility structures through which the Holy Spirit worked the dramatic interruption—some have called it a rupture—

that was the council? What was the key non-theological, contextual factor that made it possible for the seeds of *ressourcement* in patristics, scripture, and liturgy to bear fruit at the council? My short answer would be World War II.

In the century between the revolutions of 1848 and World War II, Catholicism built up a robust international subculture. With its lay associations, Latin language and liturgy, the pope as a transnational figure, and its counter-revolutionary mysticism, Ultramontane Catholicism presented a formidable and, we should emphasize, popular cultural alternative to secular modernity in its political and intellectual forms. Joseph Komonchak provides a brilliant description of this cultural ensemble, which he calls "Modern Roman Catholicism." As Komonchak's designation rightly suggests, much about Ultramontane antimodernism, neo-scholastic theology, for example, was thoroughly modern. It was Modern Roman Catholicism, Komonchak argues, that collapsed at Vatican II.[19]

The phrase *modern world* came easily to Catholic theologians in the years after Vatican II. But it is a phrase that tends to mystify and obscure the deeply political nature of Modern Roman Catholicism's conflicts with modernity, or better, modern states. The phrase conjures a scenario in which the Church at Vatican II turns suddenly and inexplicably to face something called the "modern world" just as suddenly and inexplicably as it had turned its back on the same "modern world" a hundred years before. This story tends to baffle students who have their minds in gear. How could the Church have been so blind? Thank God and Karl Rahner and Hans Küng, Edward Schillebeeckx and John Courtney Murray for Vatican II.

Theology cannot be reduced to politics. But the more we emphasize the political nature of the conflict between a transnational church and various liberal secular states in Europe, the more important World War II becomes in understanding what happened in Catholic theology in the second half of the twentieth century. As American Catholic thinkers from Orestes Brownson to John Courtney Murray could testify, neither Ultramontane Catholicism nor its secular political opponents accepted religious liberty in any sense that a citizen of the United States would have recognized. World War II changed all that. It left something called liberal democracy, no longer identified with open anti-clericalism, occupying the moral high ground. The war utterly discredited conservative alternatives to "republican" politics. "Christian democracy" became a serious possibility for European Catholics. Eventually the Declaration on Religious Liberty reconciled the church to modern politics. The text of the decree is less than clear on whose terms that reconciliation takes place. It performs Boeve's continuity/discontinuity dilemma and leaves readers wondering whether it implies a dualist or an integral theology of nature and grace.[20]

Komonchak's thesis that it was the broad antimodern subculture of Modern Roman Catholicism that collapsed after Vatican II has wide application. In 1978 John Coleman told the story of *decolumnization* in the Netherlands. This "breaking through" the three columns that made up Dutch society—the Calvinist, the Catholic, and the secular—spelled the end of Dutch Catholicism as a subculture and provided the deep context for Schillebeeckx's theology.[21] In the essays Rahner wrote on the eve of the council, we can see him grappling with the dissolution of German Catholicism as a subculture. This struggle is clearly the context for his early thoughts on the "anonymous Christian."[22] That Rahner and Schillebeeckx were two of the most popular post-conciliar writers in the United States should come as no surprise. With its more immigrant cast and the demographics of upward mobility, the American Catholic subculture was dissolving at the same time.[23] Whether we call it a collapse or a dissolution, the passing into history of the modern/anti-modern Catholic subculture is a turning point in twentieth-century Catholic thought and clearly the context for the Catholic embrace of correlation in the years after Vatican II.

In the ebb and flow of theology, Rahner, Küng, Schillebeeckx, and their colleagues found themselves in a new current. As the subculture collapsed, they were in a position to step out into the "modern world" as fully formed adults. Lord knows, we have heard enough horror stories about formation in the subculture. No doubt our conciliar heroes had such stories of their own. Nevertheless, they all appear to have emerged from their formation with an identity as Catholics that was robust and secure. Touched by temperament and in their educations by the various intellectual openings to the age that punctuated a century of anti-modern Catholicism, they were ready to stand in two worlds. We might say that correlation came naturally to them.

Without reducing theology to psychology, we might safely guess that many theologians formed as Catholics in a de-traditionalized and pluralized context will be more concerned with issues of identity and formation than the generation of Rahner and Schillebeeckx. This is not necessarily to retreat into one's own identity and become totalitarian and oppressive (85).

A healthy and plausible concern for identity and formation, more than an antimodern animus, drives the younger theologians I know who are associated with various forms of postliberal theology. Though it deserves a much fuller and more careful reading than I can give here, I am wondering if Boeve's treatment of identity and formation in chapter 4 (50-53, 82-88) is sufficiently robust and stable to sustain the kind of interrupters he wants contemporary theologians to be. Interrupting in a rhetorically effective manner requires no little confidence.

For Catholic theologians in the United States, it is the times rather than any principled theological anti-modernism that require a more radical critique of our nation and our culture than even a recontextualized correlationism is likely to produce. It is difficult to push positively on the intrinsic link between faith and context when the context is an empire. Without denying in principle the intrinsic link between faith and context, Christian theological interruptions of the U.S. contextual conversation need to be strong and sustained, coming right up to the edge of rupture. However clumsy they might be, efforts to make imperial citizenship thematic for theology cannot simply be dismissed as anti-modern posturing or a denial of the graced character of our world. Rather they are attempts to read the signs and make contingent judgments in a time of upheaval. In this I have long been inspired by Schillebeeckx's essay on "Christian Conscience and Nuclear Deterrent."[24] He wrote it in 1982 when he was sixty-eight years old. It was during the early Reagan years when the United States and its NATO allies were deploying on Dutch soil medium-range nuclear missiles pointed at the Soviet Union. That is the kind of contextual particularity to which theologians are called to attend.

While my own sensibility and inclination lean in what Professor Boeve might call an anti-modern direction, I find much to affirm in his analysis and methodological proposals. I do not think we disagree on matters of theological principle. If we do disagree, it is more likely on judgments about the particularities of our present time of upheaval. We are probably inclined to weigh differently, for example, the importance of identity and formation in contemporary contexts. I am grateful to Lieven Boeve for his company at the 2007 annual meeting of the College Theology Society and for the enjoyment and stimulation I derived from reading *God Interrupts History*. In many parts of it, I rejoiced to recognize the voice and project of Edward Schillebeeckx going forward in a new generation.

Notes

[1] Lieven Boeve, *God Interrupts History: Theology in a Time of Upheaval* (New York: Continuum, 2007), 16, n.6. Hereafter, page references will be given parenthetically in the text. All references in the text are to this book. An earlier version of this paper was my contribution to a June 1, 2007, panel on the book organized by Anthony Godzieba for the annual meeting of the College Theology Society. Kathleen McManus and Vincent Miller were the other panelists. Professor Boeve responded.

[2] Henri de Lubac, *The Mystery of the Supernatural*, trans. Rosemary Sheed (New York: Crossroad, 1998 [1965]).

[3] John Milbank, *The Suspended Middle: Henri de Lubac and the Debate Concerning the Supernatural* (Grand Rapids: Eerdmans, 2005).

[4] John Milbank, Catherine Pickstock, and Graham Ward, eds., *Radical Orthodoxy: A New Theology* (New York: Routledge, 1999).

[5] David L. Schindler, *Heart of the World, Center of the Church: Communio Ecclesiology, Liberalism, and Liberation* (Grand Rapids: Eerdmans, 1996).

[6] On the question of how we might understand the world as graced, see Frederick Christian Bauerschmidt, "Confessions of an Evangelical Catholic: Five Theses Related to Theological Anthropology," *Communio* 31, no. 1 (Spring 2004): 67-84. Bauerschmidt's first thesis is: "Rejecting a two-tiered theology of nature and grace and the ethic that goes with it does not mean that grace is everywhere in the same way" (70). His exposition of the two approaches we might take to understanding nature and grace in an integral way strikes me as relevant to discussion of the sense in which we can say that there is an "intrinsic connection" between faith and context. Compare Boeve on Vergote's critique of Schillebeeckx (see Boeve, 72-73).

[7] John Henry Newman, *An Essay on the Development of Christian Doctrine*, 6th ed., with a foreword by Ian Ker (Notre Dame: University of Notre Dame Press, 1989), 40.

[8] "Christian faith experience is both the experience of the interruption by tradition and context and interrupts tradition and context" (87). Or, with reference to an important 1994 article in which Schillebeeckx thematizes the notion of break or rupture: "The focus on the intrinsic relationship between tradition and context, and the need for recontextualization at each shift in context, is Schillebeeckx's strong point here: new experiences of faith in a changed context serve to place old forms of the tradition under scrutiny and thereby press for a development of the tradition" (81).

[9]"Ebb and Flow in Theology" is the title of chap. 1 of *The Mystery of the Supernatural*. Here de Lubac defends *ressourcement* against the charge of "archaism." "Furthermore, neither St. Augustine, nor St. Thomas, nor many others could consider all the problems which arise and will always arise in the human mind as it studies the datum of dogma, in the same terms as we must, without unthinkingly adding any personal factors, consider them today. In this sense it is true to say that we never retrace our steps. We never return to the past. Our faith is not old, is not something of the past: it is eternal, and always new" (18).

[10]Use of the term "empire" with reference to the United States can no longer be limited to the hyperbole of aging leftists. See Wes Avram, ed., *Anxious about Empire: Theological Essays on the New Global Realities* (Grand Rapids: Brazos Press, 2004), particularly the essay by Robert Bellah, 21-26.

[11]William L. Portier, "From Historicity to History: One Theologian's Intergenerational American Catholic Narrative," *U.S. Catholic Historian* 23, no. 2 (Spring 2005): 65-72; "Confessions of a Fractured Catholic Theologian," *Horizons* 32 (2005): 117-22.

[12]David Tracy, "The Uneasy Alliance Reconceived: Catholic Theological Method, Modernity, and Postmodernity," *Theological Studies* 50 (1989): 548-70.

[13]George A. Lindbeck, *The Nature of Doctrine: Religion and Theology in a Postliberal Age* (Louisville/London: Westminster John Knox Press, 1984).

[14]Here Lindbeck quotes Clifford Geertz, *The Interpretation of Cultures* (New York: Basic Books, 1973), 21.

[15]All the phrases in quotation marks in this paragraph are taken from Lindbeck, *The Nature of Doctrine*, 113-15.

[16]Tracy, "The Uneasy Alliance Reconceived," 548-49.

[17]Ibid. The pages dealing with the convergence between Lindbeck and Tracy were put in their final written form in dialogue with my colleague Brad Kallenberg, to whom I am grateful for our collaboration.

[18]See the opening pages of *Systematic Theology*, vol. 1 (Chicago: University of Chicago Press, 1951).

[19]Joseph Komonchak, "The Enlightenment and the Construction of Modern Roman Catholicism," *Catholic Commission on Intellectual and Cultural Affairs Annual* (1985): 31-59. "My thesis," Komonchak writes, "is that it was the social and political consequences of the Enlightenment that principally engaged the Church's attention during the modern era and that it was to combat these that the Church chose to deal with the intellectual issues as it did. The larger issue was cultural, political, and social" (34).

[20]William L. Portier, "Theology of Manners as Theology of Containment: John Courtney Murray and *Dignitatis Humanae* Forty Years After," *U.S. Catholic Historian* 24, no. 1 (Winter 2006): 83-106. This entire issue is devoted to *Dignitatis Humanae* on its fortieth anniversary.

[21]John A. Coleman, *The Evolution of Dutch Catholicism, 1958-1974* (Berkeley and Los Angeles: University of California Press, 1978).

[22]See Karl Rahner, *The Christian Commitment: Essays in Pastoral Theol-*

ogy, trans. Cecily Hastings (New York: Sheed & Ward, 1963) and "Anonymous Christians," in *Theological Investigations*, vol. 6, *Concerning Vatican Council II*, trans. Karl-H. and Boniface Kruger (New York: Crossroad, 1982), 390-98.

[23]On the key role of the dissolution of the subculture and the centrality of questions about identity in understanding contemporary Catholicism in the United States, see William L. Portier, "Here Come the Evangelical Catholics," *Communio* 31, no. 1 (Spring 2004): 35-66.

[24]*Doctrine and Life* 32 (1982): 98-112.

Religion as a Basis of Lawmaking under the Nonestablishment Norm[*]

Michael J. Perry

The question whether in a liberal democracy religion—religious rationales—may serve as a basis of lawmaking must be disaggregated into two distinct questions. First, is religion a *morally* legitimate basis of lawmaking in a liberal democracy? Second, is religion a *constitutionally* legitimate basis of lawmaking in the United States? I have addressed the first question elsewhere[1]—as have many others.[2] In my judgment, the answer is yes, and, again in my judgment, the most powerful defense of that answer is philosopher Christopher Eberle's important book *Religious Conviction in Liberal Politics* (2002).[3] This essay addresses the second question. This question, which is about constitutional legitimacy, should not be confused with the first question, which is about moral legitimacy.

Like other liberal democracies, the United States is committed to the right to freedom of religious practice. Unlike most other liberal democracies, however, the United States is also committed to the nonestablishment of religion.[4] According to the constitutional law of the United States, government—that is, lawmakers and other government officials—may neither prohibit the "free exercise" of religion nor "establish" religion.[5] Does the nonestablishment norm (as I like to call it) ban religion as a basis of lawmaking? More precisely, should the nonestablishment norm be understood to ban laws (and policies) for which the only discernible rationale—or, at least, the only discernible rationale other than an *implausible* secular rationale—is religious? (In the United States an implausible secular rationale—by which I mean a secular ratio-

---

[*]© Michael J. Perry, 2007.

nale that rational, well-informed, and thoughtful fellow citizens could not affirm—is constitutionally inadequate.[6]) R is the only discernible rationale for a law if but for R—if in the absence of R—the law would not have been enacted.

It is a good thing that government in the United States is constitutionally forbidden to establish religion. So far as I can tell, there is a virtual consensus among us citizens of the United States, *including those who are religious believers*, that, all things considered, it is good both for religions and for social harmony that our lawmakers may not establish religion. The serious question among us, therefore, is not whether the constitutional law of the United States should include the nonestablishment norm but *what the nonestablishment norm should be understood to mean—to forbid—in one or another context.*[7] In this essay I ask what the nonestablishment norm should be understood to forbid in the context of lawmaking. I conclude that the answer to the question whether the nonestablishment norm should be understood to ban laws for which the only discernible rationale is religious, depends: yes with respect to some religious rationales, no with respect to others. I also conclude, however, that insofar as the nonestablishment norm is concerned, lawmakers are free to support laws—to vote to enact laws—on the basis of any religious rationale whatsoever. Those two conclusions may seem to pull in opposite directions; I explain in this essay why they do not.

The Central Meaning of the Nonestablishment Norm

The idea of an "established" church is familiar.[8] For Americans, the best known and most relevant example is the Church of England, which from before the time of the American founding to the present has been the established church in England[9] (though the Church of England was much more strongly established in the past than it is today[10]). In the United States, however, unlike in England, there may be no established church. The nonestablishment norm forbids government to treat any church as the official church of the political community. (When I say "any church," I mean to include any range of theologically kindred churches—for example, Christian churches, which, though denominationally diverse, are sometimes referred to in the singular, as "the Christian church.") More precisely, to say that government may not establish religion is to say that government may not privilege any church in relation to any other church on the basis of the view that the favored church is, as a church, as a community of faith, better along one or another dimension of value—truer, for example, or more efficacious spiritually or politically,[11] or more authentically American.[12] In particular, government may not privilege, in law or policy, membership in any church—in the Fifth Avenue Baptist Church, for example, or in the Roman Catholic Church, or in the Christian church generally;[13] nor may it privilege a worship practice—a prayer, liturgical rite, or religious observance[14]—or a theological doctrine peculiar to any church.

There is no serious controversy among constitutional scholars, jurists, or lawyers in the United States today about the central meaning of the nonestablishment norm: The norm centrally means—it centrally forbids—what the preceding paragraph says it forbids.[15] There *are* serious controversies, however, about what the nonestablishment norm forbids—that is, about what the norm should be understood to forbid—beyond what it centrally forbids.[16]

Does the Nonestablishment Norm Forbid Government to Affirm Religious Premises?

Let's turn to one such controversy: *Given its uncontested central meaning, should the nonestablishment norm be understood to forbid government to affirm religious (theological) premises?*

There are many different ways in which government in the United States affirms, or has affirmed, one or more religious premises. Here are some prominent examples: In 1954, the Congress of the United States added the words "under God" to the Pledge of Allegiance ("one nation under God").[17] Also in 1954, "Congress requested that all U.S. coins and paper currency bear the slogan, 'In God We Trust.' On July 11, 1955, President Eisenhower made this slogan mandatory on all currency. In 1956 the national motto was changed from 'E Pluribus Unum' to 'In God We Trust. ' "[18] The proceedings of many courts in the United States, including the United States Supreme Court, begin with a court official intoning "God save the United States and this Honorable Court."[19] Some states provided that their public schools should begin the day with Bible reading or prayer.[20] Some state officials, including some state judges, posted the Ten Commandments on government property, such as a public school classroom or hallway, a courtroom wall, or a courthouse lawn.[21] In at least some such instances, government was affirming one or more religious premises. Is the non-establishment norm best understood to forbid government to affirm any religious premise whatsoever, no matter what the premise?

I am about to sketch two different understandings of what the nonestablishment norm forbids. But it bears emphasis that no sensible understanding of what the norm forbids denies either of these two propositions:

> First, the nonestablishment norm forbids government to affirm any religious premise whose affirmation by government would violate the central meaning of the norm. For example, government may not affirm—explicitly or implicitly, directly or indirectly—that Jesus is Lord, or that the Roman Catholic Church is the one true church.

> Second, *if* there are one or more religious premises that government may affirm—one or more premises, that is, whose affirmation by government would not violate the central meaning of the nonestablishment norm—government, in affirming such a premise, may not coerce anyone to affirm the premise or disadvantage anyone who refuses to do so.[22]

Given the central meaning of the nonestablishment norm, the first proposition follows as night follows day. We don't need the nonestablishment norm to warrant the second proposition; the free-exercise norm—the right to the free exercise of religion—is sufficient. As a moment's reflection will confirm, the free-exercise norm protects not only one's freedom to practice one's own religion, but also one's freedom *not* to practice, *not* to participate in, someone else's religion or indeed any religion at all. That "negative" freedom—that freedom not to practice a religion one does not accept—includes the freedom not to affirm a religious premise one does not accept.

Now, imagine two different understandings of what, in the context at hand, the nonestablishment norm forbids. According to the first, and more restrictive, understanding, government may not affirm any religious premise whatsoever. According to the second, and less restrictive, understanding, government may affirm any religious premise whatsoever whose affirmation by government would not violate the central meaning of the norm.[23] The more restrictive understanding would make sense only if there were *no* religious premise whose affirmation by government would not violate the central meaning of the nonestablishment norm. But there are *some* religious premises whose affirmation by government does not violate the central meaning of the norm. A single example will suffice. Since 1954, the Pledge of Allegiance has echoed Abraham Lincoln's Gettysburg Address in declaring that we are "one nation under God." (At Gettysburg, Lincoln resolved that "this nation, under God, shall have a new birth of freedom. . . .") In affirming, with Lincoln, that ours is a nation that stands under the judgment of a righteous God,[24] government is not treating any church—including the denominationally diverse Christian church—as the official church of the political community; government is not favoring any church in relation to any other church on the basis of the view that the favored church is, as a church, as a community of faith, better along one or another dimension of value; government is not privileging membership in, a worship practice of, or a theological doctrine peculiar to any church. The less restrictive understanding of what the nonestablishment norm forbids in this context makes more sense than the more restrictive understanding, because there are *some* religious premises whose affirmation by government does not, or would not, violate the central meaning of the nonestablishment norm.[25]

Let's look more closely at the less restrictive understanding, according to which, again, having "under God" in the Pledge, or the like, does not violate the nonestablishment norm. Would it violate the nonestablishment norm, according to the less restrictive understanding, to have "under Christ" in the Pledge ("one nation under Christ") or "In Christ We Trust" (or "Jesus Is Lord") as the national motto, or to begin a session of court with "Christ save the United States and this Honorable Court"? To arrive at the right answer, we must inquire: In adding "under Christ" to the Pledge, is government treating any church as the official church of the political community? Is it favoring any church in relation to any other church on the basis of the view that the favored church is, as a church, as a community of faith, better along one or another dimension of value? It seems undeniable that in adding "under Christ" to the Pledge, government *is* treating the Christian church—the Christian church *as a whole,* though not any particular denomination of it—as the official church of the political community; government *is* favoring the Christian church in relation to other churches and communities of faith on the basis of the view that the Christian church is, as a church, as a community of faith, better along one or another dimension of value. So, according to the less restrictive understanding of what the nonestablishment norm forbids, having "under Christ" in the Pledge *would* violate the norm.[26] For government to affirm any religious premise (or premises) that is ecumenical (nonsectarian) as among the great monotheistic faiths—Judaism, Christianity, and Islam—would not be for it to violate the nonestablishment norm.[27] By contrast, for government to affirm any religious premise that is sectarian as among the monotheistic faiths would be for it to violate the norm. In affirming any religious premise that is not ecumenical as among Christians, religious Jews, and Muslims—for example, the premise that Jesus is Lord—government is violating the nonestablishment norm, even according to the less restrictive understanding of what the norm forbids.

Why shouldn't we go further and embrace an understanding of the nonestablishment norm according to which government may not affirm any religious premise whatsoever? Again, the central meaning of the nonestablishment norm does not require such an understanding. Moreover, no historically grounded reading of the norm—no reading grounded in *American* history—supports that understanding, and it is, after all, the *American* Constitution we are expounding. "[The establishment clause] was not . . . understood to be a prohibition against employing generalized religious language in official discourse. The notion that the First Amendment was designed to impose a secular political culture on the nation would have struck most 19th Century judges as absurd."[28] I can discern no good reason either for expecting the Supreme Court to accept and enforce an understanding of the nonestablishment norm that is not historically grounded or for thinking that the Court should accept and enforce such an understanding.[29] It is surely at least a minor virtue of the understanding of the nonestablishment norm I am defending here—the less restrictive understanding—that it does not entail a conclusion—namely, that having "under God" in the Pledge or "In God We Trust" as the national motto, or beginning a session of court with "God save the United States and this Honorable Court," violates the constitutional imperative that government not establish religion—most citizens of the United States would greet as ridiculously extreme.[30]

True, having "under God" in the Pledge, "In God We Trust" as the national motto, and the like, offends some citizens of the United

States.[31] But so long as government fully respects one's right to the free exercise of religion, government's affirmation of one or more religious premises does not violate anyone's human rights. For example, that the Constitution of the Republic of Ireland makes a number of theological affirmations—while also vigorously protecting every Irish citizen's right to freedom of religious practice—does not violate anyone's human rights.[32] More generally, the international law of human rights features the right to freedom of religious practice but does not include anything like a nonestablishment norm; in particular, the Declaration on the Elimination of All Forms of Intolerance and of Discrimination Based on Religion or Belief, which is the principal international document concerning religious freedom, includes nothing like a nonestablishment requirement.[33]

Is it really the case that the more restrictive understanding of what the nonestablishment norm forbids in this context yields the conclusion that having "under God" in the Pledge or "In God We Trust" as the national motto, or beginning a session of court with "God save the United States and this Honorable Court," is unconstitutional? Is there a way for one who accepts the more restrictive understanding to avoid that conclusion—a conclusion that, as I said, most citizens of the United States would greet as ridiculously extreme?

Consider the suggestion that having "under God" in the Pledge or "In God We Trust" as the national motto (or the like) is not unconstitutional because such statements do not really constitute an affirmation by government of a religious premise; instead, such statements are merely patriotic or ceremonial utterances devoid of authentically religious content.[34] In 1983, Supreme Court Justice William Brennan, joined by Justice Thurgood Marshall, wrote:

> I frankly do not know what should be the proper disposition of features of our public life such as "God save the United States and this Honorable Court," "In God We Trust," "One Nation Under God," and the like. I might well adhere to the view . . . that such mottoes are consistent with the Establishment Clause . . . because they have lost any true religious significance.[35]

In 2004, Chief Justice William Rehnquist, joined by Justice Sandra Day O'Connor, said something similar: "The phrase 'under God' is in no sense a prayer, nor an endorsement of any religion. . . . Reciting the Pledge, or listening to others recite it, is a patriotic exercise, not a religious one; participants promise fidelity to our flag and our Nation, not to any particular God, faith, or church."[36]

Asserting that "one nation under God" or "In God We Trust" are merely patriotic or ceremonial utterances devoid of authentically religious content is obviously a convenient strategy for avoiding the conclusion that under the more restrictive understanding of the nonestablishment norm, having "under God" in the Pledge or "In God We Trust" as our national motto is unconstitutional. It is also a palpably disingenuous strategy.[37] There are *some* citizens, no doubt, for whom the statements are merely ceremonial, religiously empty utterances; it is simply mistaken, however, to think that the statements are religiously empty for most, or even for many, citizens of the United States—or that they were religiously empty for the members of Congress who, in 1954, added "under God" to the Pledge.[38] For most Americans, the statements resonate, as indeed they were meant to, with a rich and authentically theological content: that there is a God; that God created us and sustains us; that every human being has a God-given dignity and inviolability; and that, as Lincoln proclaimed in his Second Inaugural, we stand under the judgment of that righteous God.[39]

There is no intellectually honest way for one who accepts the more restrictive understanding of the nonestablishment norm to avoid the conclusion that having "under God" in the Pledge or "In God We Trust" as the national motto, or beginning a session of court with "God save the United States and this Honorable Court," is unconstitutional. For one who is intellectually honest, to accept the more restrictive understanding is to accept that conclusion.[40]

Does the Nonestablishment Norm, Properly Understood, Ban Religion as a Basis of Lawmaking?

Now, the question-in-chief: Is religion a legitimate—a *constitutionally* legitimate—basis of lawmaking in the United States? More precisely, should the nonestablishment norm be understood to ban laws (and policies) for which the only discernible rationale (at least, other than an implausible secular rationale) is religious?[41]

Two clarifications are essential. First, the principal laws at issue are those that are coercive, because coercive laws for which the only discernible rationale is religious seem to some to be a kind of religious imposition on those they coerce.[42] Kent Greenawalt, for example, has written of laws "that enforce a purely religious morality," that "they unacceptably impose religion on others." He gives, as an example, "laws against homosexual relations based on the view that the Bible considers such relations sinful."[43] Second, by a "religious" rationale I mean a rationale that depends, at least in part, on a religious premise; a "secular" rationale, by contrast, does not depend on any religious premise. By a "religious" premise I mean, in this essay, a premise—a claim—about the existence,[44] nature, activity, or will of God, such as the premise that same-sex unions are contrary to the will of God.[45]

I argued in the preceding section that according to the most balanced understanding of what it forbids, the nonestablishment norm forbids government to affirm some religious premises—but that it also leaves room for government to affirm some religious premises, namely, premises whose affirmation by government does not, or would not, violate the central meaning of the nonestablishment norm.[46] It follows from that argument that the nonestablishment norm should *not* be understood to ban laws for which the only discernible rationale is a religious rationale that depends on a premise (or premises) that government *may* affirm (because its doing so does not, or would not, violate the central meaning of the nonestablishment norm), such as the premise that every human being has a God-given dignity and inviolability.[47] It also follows, however, that the nonestablishment norm *should be* understood to ban laws for which the only discernible rationale is a religious rationale that depends on—and in that sense affirms—a religious premise that government may *not* affirm.

A lawmaker supports a law—she votes to enact a law—"on the basis of" a religious rationale if but for the religious rationale—if in the absence of the religious rationale—she would not vote to enact the law; put another way, a lawmaker votes to enact a law "on the basis of" a religious rationale if there is no secular rationale that by itself would move her to enact the law.[48] However, the nonestablishment ban I am articulating here is indifferent to whether a lawmaker who voted to enact a law *actually* did so, either wholly or partly, on the basis of an "offending" religious rationale—a rationale that depends on a religious premise government may not affirm. There are several good reasons for that indifference:

- It is unrealistic to expect most lawmakers to have a confident answer to the question whether they would have voted to enact a law but for an offending religious rationale.
- The ban, qua legal, is meant to be judicially enforceable. If most lawmakers themselves don't have a confident answer to the question whether they would have voted to enact a law but for an offending religious rationale, how is a court supposed to know whether they would have done so?
- Moreover, if courts were in the business of speculating about whether the lawmakers would have voted to enact a law but for an offending religious rationale, some lawmakers would respond by engaging in strategic behavior aimed at making it appear that they would have voted to enact the law on the basis of a plausible secular rationale and/or a non-offending religious rationale.
- Finally, consider this scenario: A court speculates that the lawmakers in State A would have voted to enact law L on the basis of a plausible secular rationale and therefore concludes that L is not unconstitutional, while a different court speculates that the lawmakers in State B would not have voted to enact the very same law on the basis of any plausible secular rationale and therefore concludes that L *is* unconstitutional. In State A, L is constitutional; in State B, L *is* unconstitutional. What an unseemly state of affairs that would be!

So the nonestablishment norm is better understood not to forbid a lawmaker to support a law on the basis of an offending religious rationale, but only to ban laws for which the only discernible rationale is an offending religious rationale.

As a practical matter, how significant is a ban on such laws? In the United States today there are, and in the foreseeable future there will be, almost no actual or proposed laws—at least, almost no proposed laws that have a realistic chance of becoming actual laws—that fit the profile "laws for which the only discernible rationale is an offending religious rationale." For example, a plausible secular rationale—a secular rationale that rational, well-informed, and thoughtful fellow citizens could affirm—is discernible for laws banning most abortions.[49] There is one policy, however, with respect to which the ban may have bite: Many states refuse to recognize—they refuse to extend the benefit of law to—same-sex unions. If no plausible secular rationale can account for that policy—if the rationale that accounts for the policy depends on

the premise that same-sex unions are contrary to the will of God—
this becomes the determinative question: May government affirm
the premise that same-sex unions are contrary to the will of God?
I address this question elsewhere.[50]

As I said at the beginning of this essay, the principal question at
issue here—whether religion (religious rationales) is *a constitutionally* legitimate basis of lawmaking *in the United States*—should
not be confused with a different question that has been contested
in the United States (and elsewhere) for the last thirty years or so:
Is religion a *morally* legitimate basis of lawmaking *in a liberal
democracy;* more precisely, is it morally legitimate for lawmakers
in a liberal democracy to enact laws on the basis of a religious
rationale? Again, the answer to that question, in my judgment, is
yes.[51]

Some who give that answer may be inclined to think that the
nonestablishment ban articulated and defended here—the ban on
laws for which the only discernible rationale is an offending religious rationale—is unduly restrictive of religious believers. So let
me explain why they should resist that thought. First, laws for
which the only discernible rationale depends on a religious premise
government *may* affirm, *including the premise that every human
being has a God-given dignity and inviolability,* are *not* subject to
the ban. Second, although laws for which the only discernible rationale is an offending religious rationale are subject to the ban, in
the United States today there are, and in the foreseeable future
there will be, as I just remarked, few if indeed any actual or proposed laws that fit that profile. The serious question, then, is not
whether the nonestablishment ban on laws for which the only discernible rationale is an offending religious rationale is unduly restrictive, but whether as a practical matter the ban has much if any
bite at all.

Moreover, insofar as the nonestablishment norm is concerned,
a lawmaker is free to support a law on the basis of any religious
rationale whatsoever, even an offending religious rationale[52]; she
is free to support a law that but for an offending religious rationale—a rationale that depends on a religious premise that under
the nonestablishment norm government may not affirm—she would
not vote to enact.[53] As it happens, however, the vast majority of
religious believers in the United States offer nonreligious rationales for their political positions on controversial moral issues. Even
"Most religious conservatives do, frequently and loudly, make ar-

guments for their positions *on nontheological grounds.* . . . The evils of abortion, the value of heterosexual monogamy, the costs of promiscuity and pornography—all these issues are constantly being raised by social conservatives without appeals to the divine inspiration of the Bible."[54] So, again, the serious question is not whether the nonestablishment ban on laws for which the only discernible rationale is an offending religious rationale is unduly restrictive, but whether as a practical matter the ban has much if any bite at all.[55]

The right to freedom of religious practice, which I discuss elsewhere,[56] is widely regarded as a human right to which every government should be committed and to which liberal democracy, as such, is committed. I have not argued in this essay that every nation, or even every liberal democracy, should be committed to the nonestablishment of religion. Whether it is a good thing, on balance, that in the United States government is constitutionally forbidden to establish religion and whether it would be a good thing for government in, say, the United Kingdom to be forbidden to establish religion are separate questions; an affirmative answer to the former question does not entail an affirmative answer to the latter (although an affirmative answer to the latter question may well be correct). It is often the case that, as Kent Greenawalt has written, "What principles of restraint, if any, are appropriate . . . depend on time and place, on a sense of the present makeup of a society, of its history, and of its likely evolution."[57]

It is an important question, but not one I address here, whether it would be a good thing for government in some or even all liberal democracies to be forbidden to establish religion. As a citizen of the United States, my concern is whether it is a good thing that government in the United States is constitutionally forbidden to establish religion. As I said at the beginning of this essay, there is, so far as I can tell, a virtual consensus among us citizens of the United States, *including those of us who are religious believers*, that, all things considered, it is good both for religions and for social harmony that our lawmakers, state as well as federal, may not establish religion. The serious question among us, therefore, is not whether the constitutional law of the United States should include the nonestablishment norm *but what the nonestablishment norm should be understood to mean—to forbid—in one or another context.* In this essay I asked what the nonestablishment norm, given its central meaning, should be understood to forbid in the context of lawmaking: Should it be understood to ban laws for which the only discernible rationale is religious? My answer: Yes, but only if the rationale depends on a religious premise that under the nonestablishment norm government may not affirm.

Notes

[1] I have changed my mind over the years. See Michael J. Perry, *Love and Power: The Role of Religion and Morality in American Politics* (New York: Oxford University Press, 1991); Michael J. Perry, *Religion in Politics: Constitutional and Moral Perspectives* (New York: Oxford University Press, 1997); Michael J. Perry, *Under God? Religious Faith and Liberal Democracy* (Cambridge: Cambridge University Press, 2003).

[2] See, for example, Richard John Neuhaus, *The Naked Public Square: Religion and Politics in America*, 2nd ed. (Grand Rapids: Eerdmans, 1986); Kent Greenawalt, *Religious Convictions and Political Choice* (New York: Oxford University Press, 1987); Stephen L. Carter, *The Culture of Disbelief: How American Law and Politics Trivialize Religious Devotion* (New York: Basic Books, 1993); Robert Audi and Nicholas Wolterstorff, *Religion in the Public Square: The Place of Religious Convictions in Political Debate* (Lanham, MD: Rowman and Littlefield, 1997); Kent Greenawalt, *Private Consciences and Public Reasons* (New York: Oxford University Press, 1995); Paul J. Weithman, ed., *Religion and Contemporary Liberalism* (Notre Dame: University of Notre Dame Press, 1997); Robert Audi, *Religious Commitment and Secular Reason* (Cambridge: Cambridge University Press, 2000); Symposium, "Religiously Based Morality: Its Proper Place in American Law and Public Policy?" 36 *Wake Forest Law Review* (2001), 217-570; Christopher J. Eberle, *Religious Convictions in Liberal Politics* (Cambridge: Cambridge University Press, 2002); Terence Cuneo, ed., *Religion in the Liberal Polity* (Notre Dame: University of Notre Dame Press, 2005) ; Eduardo M. Penalver, "Is Public Reason Counterproductive?" *West Virginia Law Review* 110 (2007).

[3] See also Christopher J. Eberle, "Religious Reasons in Public: Let a Thousand Flowers Bloom, But Be Prepared to Prune" (unpublished ms., 2007). Indeed, given a recent paper by Gerald Gaus, in which he agrees with Eberle that citizens and their elected representatives may rely solely on religious reasons in making political choices, I am inclined to think that the debate is largely over. See Gerald F. Gaus, "The Place of Religious Belief in Public Reason Liberalism" (unpublished ms., 2007). See also Jürgen Habermas, "Religion in the Public Sphere," 14 *European Journal of Philosophy* 1 (2006); Virgil Nemoianu, "The Church and the Secular Establishment: A Philosophical Dialog between Joseph Ratzinger and Jürgen Habermas," 9 *Logos* 17 (2006): "In a clear and unmistakable manner Habermas condemns all those who keep trying to sentence the religious discourse in the public square to

silence, to eliminate and liquidate it all together. 'It is in the best interest of the constitutional state to act considerately (*schonend*) toward all those cultural sources out of which civil solidarity and norm consciousness are nourished.' Communicativeness implies necessarily and by its very definition the effort of mutual understanding."

In his book, Eberle persuasively defends what he calls "the ideal of conscientious engagement." It is an ideal that speaks to all lawmakers in a liberal democracy but that nonetheless has a special importance for lawmakers inclined to support laws on a religious basis. According to the ideal, a lawmaker should not vote to enact a law unless:

> o The rationale on the basis of which the lawmaker supports the law does not deny that every citizen—indeed, every human being—has inherent dignity and is inviolable. (Again, one of the things that makes a democracy *a liberal* democracy is the democracy's commitment to the proposition that every human being has inherent dignity and is inviolable.)
>
> o The lawmaker (or someone with whom she is allied) has publicly presented the rationale on the basis of which she (they) supports the law.
>
> o Moreover, she has tried to discern and, if successful, has publicly presented one or more other rationales for the law, in an effort to persuade as many of those who reject her rationale as possible that they too have reason to support the law—or at least that they have less reason than they might have thought to oppose the law.
>
> o Finally, the lawmaker has been open- rather than close-minded, in this sense: She has publicly and sincerely considered the (principal) arguments against the law, including the arguments against the rationale on the basis of which she supports the law.

For a more elaborate statement of the ideal of conscientious engagement, see Eberle, *Religious Conviction in Liberal Politics* (above, note 2), 104-5.

As I have articulated it here, the ideal of conscientious engagement speaks directly to lawmakers. (Ordinary citizens sometimes function as lawmakers—for example, when they vote in a referendum on a proposed amendment to the state constitution.) So it bears mention that the ideal also speaks, albeit indirectly, to all citizens: Citizens should encourage their elected representatives to act in accord with the ideal—and should hold them to account when they fail to do so.

[4]Like the United States, France is constitutionally committed to the nonestablishment of religion, which in France is called "laïcité." See Cecile Laborde, "Secular Philosophy and Muslim Headscarves in Schools," *Journal of Political Philosophy* 13 (2005):

> On 11 December 1905, republicans in power [in France] abolished the *Concordat* which, since 1801, had regulated the relationships between the French state and "recognized religions" and had, in practice, entrenched the political and social power of the dominant Catholic Church. The first two articles of the 1905 Law of Separation between Church and State read:

Article 1. The Republic ensures freedom of conscience. It guarantees the free exercise of religions.

Article 2. It neither recognises nor subsidises any religion.

The principle of separation between church and state has since been recognized as a quasi-constitutional principle, and is implicitly referred to in Article 1 of the 1946 Constitution, according to which "France is an indivisible, *laique,* democratic and social republic." (308)

[5]The First Amendment to the United States Constitution states: "Congress shall make no law respecting an establishment of religion, or prohibiting the free exercise thereof . . . ." I concur in Kent Greenawalt's judgment that "By far the most plausible reading of the original religion clauses—based on their text, the history leading up to their enactment, and legislation enacted by Congress—is that Congress could protect but not impair free exercise in carrying out its delegated powers for the entire country and within exclusively federal domains, that Congress could neither establish a religion within the states nor interfere with state establishments [of religion], and that Congress could not establish religion within exclusively federal domains" (Kent Greenawalt, "Common Sense about Original and Subsequent Understandings of the Religion Clauses," 8 *Journal of Constitutional Law* 479, 511 [2005]; see also p. 491).

The religion clauses have long been held to apply—it is constitutional bedrock that they apply—not just to Congress but to the entire national government, and not just to the national government but to state government as well. In effect, then, the clauses provide that government may neither establish religion nor prohibit the free exercise thereof. See Michael W. McConnell, "Accommodation of Religion: An Update and Response to the Critics," 60 *George Washington Law Review,* 685, 690 (1992): "The government may not 'establish' religion and it may not 'prohibit' religion." McConnell explains, in a footnote attached to the word "establish" that "the text [of the First Amendment] states the 'Congress' may make no law 'respecting an establishment' of religion, which meant that Congress could neither establish a national church nor interfere with the establishment of state churches as they then existed in the various states. After the last disestablishment in 1833 and the incorporation of the First Amendment against the states through the Fourteenth Amendment, this 'federalism' aspect of the Amendment has lost its significance, and the Clause can be read as forbidding the government to establish religion" (ibid., 690, n. 19). (As I have explained elsewhere, a constitutional doctrine is constitutional bedrock if the doctrine is well-settled and there is no significant support—in particular, among the political elites—for abandoning the doctrine. See Michael J. Perry, *We the People: The Fourteenth Amendment and the Supreme Court* [New York: Oxford University Press, 1999].)

[6]See Michael J. Perry, *Constitutional Rights, Moral Controversy, and the Supreme Court: A (Partial) Theory of Judicial Review* (Cambridge: Cambridge University Press, 2009 [forthcoming]).

[7]However, "One current Justice on the Supreme Court [Clarence Thomas] . . . twice has asserted that the states should be bound by Free Exercise Clause norms, but should not be bound by Establishment Clause norms" (Ira C. Lupu and Robert W. Tuttle, "Federalism and Faith," 56 *Emory Law Journal* 19, 49 [2006], 49-51).

[8]If the idea is insufficiently familiar, see Michael W. McConnell, "Establishment and Disestablishment at the Founding, Part I: The Establishment of Religion," 44 *William & Mary Law Review* 2105 (2003). According to McConnell: "An establishment is the promotion and inculcation of a common set of beliefs through governmental authority. An establishment may be narrow (focused on a particular set of beliefs) or broad (encompassing a certain range of opinion); it may be more or less coercive; and it may be tolerant or intolerant of other views. During the period between initial settlement and ultimate disestablishment, American religious establishments moved from being narrow, coercive, and intolerant to being broad, relatively noncoercive, and tolerant. Although the laws constituting the establishment were ad hoc and unsystematic, they can be summarized in six categories: 1) control over doctrine, governance, and personnel of the church; 2) compulsory church attendance; 3) financial support; 4) prohibitions on worship in dissenting churches; 5) use of church institutions for public functions; and 6) restriction of political participation to members of the established church" (2131).

For a sketch of different kinds of religious establishment, from strong to weak, see W. Cole Durham, Jr., "Perspectives on Religious Liberty: A Comparative Framework," in *Religious Human Rights in Global Perspective: Legal Perspectives*, ed. Johan D. van der Vyver and John Witte, Jr. (The Hague: Kluwer, 1996), 19ff.

[9]See Akhil Reed Amar, "Foreword: The Document and the Doctrine," 114 *Harvard Law Review* 26, 119 (2000): "Let us recall the world the Founders aimed to repudiate, a world where a powerful church hierarchy was anointed as the official government religion, where clerics ex officio held offices in the government, and where members of other religions were often barred from holding government posts."

[10]How established is the Church of England today? See Cheryl Saunders, "Comment: Religion and the State," 21 *Cardozo Law Review* 1295, 1295 (2000): "The special status of the Church of England manifests through legal links with the British crown. Under legislation, the reigning queen or king is 'supreme governor' of the church and swears a coronation oath to maintain it. As such, the monarch may not be a Catholic, or marry a Catholic, and must declare on accession to the throne that he or she is a Protestant.

This is surprising enough in a western liberal democracy at the end of the twentieth century. But there is more. The monarch also appoints the archbishops and other reigning church dignitaries. Twenty-six of these 'Lords Spiritual' sit in the upper house of the legislature, the House of Lords. The British Parliament can legislate for the church and can prescribe modes of worship, doctrine, and discipline. And the church has delegated legislative authority in relation to church affairs. Measures initiated by the church may be accepted or rejected, but not amended, by the Parliament and override earlier inconsistent law."

Professor Saunders then states: "As usual with the British system of government, however, what you see is not exactly what you get. In advising the crown on appointments to church positions, the prime minister draws names from a list provided by church authorities. As a practical matter, Parliament is unlikely to veto legislative measures initiated by the church, or to act unilaterally in relation to other church affairs. Vernon Bogdanor draws attention to a House of Commons debate on the ordination of women priests in 1993, in which several Members expressed the view that the House should not be discussing the view at all" (1295-96).

Clearly, and happily, that England has an established church does not mean all that it once meant. Nonetheless, that England *still* has an established church remains controversial. See, for example, Kenneth Leech, ed., *Setting the Church of England Free: The Case for Disestablishment* (Croydon, England: Jubilee Group, 2001); Clifford Longley, "Establishment—It's Got to Go," *The Tablet* (London), May 11, 2002, 2; Paul Weller, *Time for a Change: Reconfiguring Religion, State, and Society* (New York: T & T Clark, 2005). See "The Act of Settlement Debate," *The Tablet* (London), August 11, 2007, 4; Tim Hames, " 'would have been more honest to have called it the Dangerous Catholics Act,' " *The Tablet* (London), August 11, 2007, 5 (the "it" in the title is the 1701 Act of Settlement).

[11]More efficacious politically? Imagine: A Machiavellian advisor counsels the powers-that-be—who, let us assume, are atheists—that it would be better for social harmony if there were an established church, and that because the vast majority of the citizens are members of Church A, it makes more sense to establish Church A than Church B or Church C (etc.).

[12]As Justice William Brennan once put it: "It may be true that individuals cannot be 'neutral' on the question of religion. But the judgment of the Establishment Clause is that neutrality by the organs of *government* on questions of religion is both possible and imperative" (*Marsh v. Chambers*, 463 U.S. 783, 821 [1983] [Brennan, J., joined by Marshall, J., dissenting]).

[13]For an example of a position that privileges the Christian church generally, see "Other Faiths Are Deficient, Pope Says," *The Tablet* (London), February 5, 2000, 157: "The revelation of Christ is 'definitive and complete', Pope John Paul affirmed to the Congregation for the Doctrine of the Faith, on 28 January. He repeated the phrase twice in an address which went on to say that non-Christians live in 'a deficient situation, compared to those who have the fullness of salvific means in the Church.' " "Nonetheless, [Pope John Paul II] recognised, following the Second Vatican Council, that non-Christians can reach eternal life if they seek God with a sincere heart. But in that 'sincere search' they are in fact 'ordered' towards Christ and his Church" (ibid.).

[14]See Douglas Laycock, "Freedom of Speech That Is Both Religious and Political," 29 *University of California, Davis Law Review*, 793, 812-13

(1996), arguing that "at the core of the Establishment Clause should be the principle that government cannot engage in a religious observance or compel or persuade citizens to do so."

[15]See, for example, Carl H. Esbeck, "The 60th Anniversary of the *Everson* Decision and America's Church-State Proposition," 23 *Journal of Law and Religion* (2007-08, forthcoming): "While Americans robustly debate religious beliefs and doctrine, it is the promise that our government will not throw its weight behind one side or the other of these debates. . . . The government, rather, is to maintain a form of 'neutrality.' "

[16]I have addressed one such controversy elsewhere. See Perry, *Under God?* (above, n. 1), 3-19. I don't discuss here the nonestablishment caselaw fashioned by the justices of the Supreme Court of the United States. It bears mention, however, that if Justice Clarence Thomas is right, that caselaw "is in hopeless disarray" (*Rosenberger v. Rector and Visitors of University of Virginia*, 515 U.S. 819, 861 [1995] [Thomas, J., concurring]). Many constitutional scholars have said much the same thing. See, for example, Jesse H. Choper, *Securing Religious Liberty: Principles for Judicial Interpretation of the Religion Clauses* (Chicago: University of Chicago Press, 1995), 174-76; William Van Alstyne, "Ten Commandments, Nine Justices, and Five Versions of One Amendment—The First *('Now What?')*," 14 *William and Mary Bill of Rights Journal* 17 (2005). Akhil Amar has referred to "the many outlandish (and contradictory) things that have been said about [the nonestablishment norm] in the *United States Reports*" (Amar [above, n. 9], 119).

[17]For a history of the Pledge of Allegiance, which makes its first appearance in 1892, see John W. Baer, *The Pledge of Allegiance: A Centennial History, 1892-1992* (Annapolis, MD: John W. Baer, 1992). The story of adding "under God" to the Pledge involves both the Knights of Columbus (a Roman Catholic organization) and post-World War II anti-communism. See ibid, 62-63.

[18]Ibid.

[19]See *Marsh v. Chambers*, 463 U.S. 783, 786 (1983): "In the very courtrooms in which the United States District Judge and later three Circuit Judges heard and decided this case, the proceedings opened with an announcement that concluded, 'God save the United States and this Honorable Court.' The same invocation occurs at all sessions of this Court."

[20]See, for example, *Engel v. Vitale*, 370 U.S. 421 (1962); *School District of Abington Township v. Schempp* and *Murray v. Curlett*, 374 U.S. 203 (1963).

[21]See, for example, *Stone v. Graham*, 449 U.S. 39 (1980); *McCreary County v. American Civil Liberties Union of Kentucky*, 125 S.Ct. 2722 (2005); *Van Orden v. Perry*, 125 S.Ct. 2854 (2004).

[22]Sharp disagreement about whether government is in fact coercing anyone—or, more generally, about what, at the margin, "coerce" should be understood to mean—is not uncommon. See, for example, *Lee v. Weisman*, 505 U.S. 577 (1992).

[23]William Marshall has written that "First Amendment law is relatively settled on the theoretical position that explicit state sponsorship of religion is

impermissible." It is clear from his article that by "state sponsorship of religion" Marshall means to include the kind of state affirmation of religious premises entailed by state sponsorship of prayer. Marshall cites two cases in support of his statement of what is "relatively settled": *Santa Fe Independent School District v. Doe*, 530 U.S. 290, 309 (3000); *Lee v. Weisman*, 505 U.S. 577, 587 (1992). See William P. Marshall, "The Limits of Secularism: Public Religious Expression in Moments of National Crisis and Tragedy," 78 *Notre Dame Law Review* 11, 21 and n. 57 (2002). Now, I don't mean to deny that the Supreme Court's nonestablishment rhetoric lends much support, direct and indirect, to the proposition that "state sponsorship of religion is impermissible." (But see *Marsh v. Chambers*, 463 U.S. 783 [1983].) Nonetheless, the decision in each of the two cases Marshall cites can readily be understood on the basis of the rule—a rule most naturally assimilated to the free exercise norm—that *if* there are one or more religious premises that government may affirm—one or more premises, that is, whose affirmation by government would not violate the central meaning of the nonestablishment norm—government, in affirming such a premise, may not coerce anyone to affirm the premise.

Still, I am undoubtedly swimming against the tide of much scholarly opinion in arguing for the less restrictive understanding of the nonestablishment norm. For a sampling of that opinion, see Kent Greenawalt, "Five Questions about Religion Judges Are Afraid to Ask," in *Obligations of Citizenship and Demands of Faith*, ed. Nancy L. Rosenblum (Princeton: Princeton University Press, 2000), declaring that "the core idea that government may not make determinations of religious truth is firmly entrenched" (196, 197); Andrew Koppelman, "Secular Purpose," 88 *Virginia Law Review* 87, 108 (2002), stating that it is an "axiom" that the "Establishment Clause forbids the state from declaring religious truth"; Douglas Laycock, "Equal Access and Moments of Silence: The Equal Status of Religious Speech by Private Speakers," 81 *Northwestern University Law Review* 1, 7 (1986) ("In my view, the establishment clause absolutely disables the government from taking a position for or against religion. . . . The government must have no opinion because it is not the government's role to have an opinion.") But see Steven H. Shiffrin, "The Pluralistic Foundations of the Religion Clauses," 90 *Cornell Law Review* 9, 72 (2004): "The United States Constitution is best interpreted to be consistent with monotheistic ceremonial prayers that do not involve coercion."

[24]The Declaration of Independence, which marks the first formative moment in the emergence of the United States of America, famously relies—explicitly so—on belief in God: "We hold these truths to be self-evident, that all men are *created* equal, that they are endowed *by their Creator* with certain inalienable rights . . ." (emphasis added). If the Declaration marks a formative moment in the birth of the United States, two texts of Abraham Lincoln mark formative moments in the nation's rebirth: the Gettysburg Address and the Second Inaugural Address, which is surely one of the most theologically intense political speeches in American history. "The Almighty," said Lincoln

in his Second Inaugural, "has his own purposes. 'Woe unto the world because of offences! for it must needs be that offences come; but woe to that man by whom the offence cometh!' " Lincoln continued: "If we shall suppose that American Slavery is one of those offenses which, in the providence of God, must needs come, but which, having continued through his appointed time, He now wills to remove, and that He gives to both North and South, this terrible war, as the woe due to those by whom the offence came, shall we discern there any departure from those divine attributes which the believers in a Living God always ascribe to Him? Fondly do we hope—fervently do we pray—that this mighty scourge of war may speedily pass away. Yet, if God wills that it continue, until all the wealth piled by the bond-man's two hundred and fifty years of unrequited toil shall be sunk, and until every drop of blood drawn with the lash, shall be paid by another drawn by the sword, as was said three thousand years ago, so still it must be said 'the judgments of the Lord, are true and righteous altogether.' With malice toward none; with charity for all; with firmness in the right, as God gives us to see the right, let us strive on to finish the work we are in."

Although we citizens of the United States of America don't recite the Declaration, the Gettysburg Address, or Lincoln's Second Inaugural, we *do* recite, frequently, the Pledge of Allegiance. According to the Pledge, the United States of America is a nation "under God": a nation that, as Lincoln insisted in his Second Inaugural, stands under the judgment of a righteous God. Politicians and others are fond of asking God to "bless" America. Lincoln understood that the God who can, in judgment, bless America can also, in judgment, damn her: "He gives to both North and South, this terrible war, as the woe due to those by whom the offence came . . . As was said three thousand years ago, so still it must be said 'the judgments of the Lord, are true and righteous altogether.' "

[25]See *ACLU of Ohio v. Capitol Square Review & Advisory Board*, 243 F.3d 289, 293 (6th Cir. 2001): "For most of our history as an independent nation, the words of the constitutional prohibition against enactment of a law 'respecting an establishment of religion' were commonly assumed to mean what they literally said. The provision was not understood as prohibiting the state from merely giving voice, in general terms, to religious sentiments widely shared by those of its citizens who profess a belief in God. . . . The principal thrust of the prohibition was to prevent any establishment by the national government of an official religion, including an established church such as that which existed in England at the time the American colonies won their independence from the Crown."

[26]According to the less restrictive understanding of what the nonestablishment norm forbids, affirming one or another version of the Decalogue also violates the norm. See Paul Finkelman, "The Ten Commandments on the Courthouse Lawn and Elsewhere," 73 *Fordham Law Review* 1477, 1480-98 (2005). See Frederick Mark Gedicks and Roger Hendrix, "Uncivil Religion: 'Judeo-Christianity' and the Ten Commandments," *West Virginia Law Review* 110 (2007).

²⁷Ibid. In the recent *Decalogue Cases* [*Van Orden v. Perry*, 125 S.Ct. 2854 (2005); *McCreary County v. ACLU*, 125 S.Ct. 2722 (2005)], Justice Scalia conceded that government cannot invoke the blessings of "God," or even say his name, "without contradicting the beliefs of some people that there are many gods, or that God pays no attention to human affairs." Nevertheless, Justice Scalia declares that the contradiction is of no constitutional moment, because the historical understanding of the Establishment Clause permits government wholly to ignore those who do not subscribe to monotheism. Noting that more than 97 percent of American believers are either Christians, Jews, or Muslims, Justice Scalia concludes that the government invocation or endorsement of belief in a monotheistic God does not violate the Establishment Clause.

²⁸*ACLU of Ohio v. Capitol Square Review & Advisory Board*, 243 F.3d 289, 297 (6th Cir. 2001). Earlier in its opinion, the court quoted the following passage from an article by Steven Smith: "In approving the establishment clause, the framers had adopted a principle of institutional separation, but they had undertaken neither to impose a secular political culture on the nation nor consented to abandon their own religious values or culture when serving as public officials. Indeed, any such undertaking would have required a seemingly impossible intellectual and psychological surgery. Proclaiming a national day of thanksgiving, or inviting a chaplain to offer a prayer before congressional sessions, were actions of undeniable religious import. But through these actions the government did not intrude into the internal affairs of any church. Nor did these actions confer governmental authority upon churches; Congress did not endow the chaplain with authority to debate, vote, or directly influence governmental decisions. Hence thanksgiving proclamations and legislative prayers were simply not inconsistent with the decision reflected in the establishment clause" (ibid., quoting Steven D. Smith, "Separation and the 'Secular': Reconstructing the Disestablishment Decision," 67 *Texas Law Review* 955, 973 [1989]).

²⁹I began the paragraph accompanying this note by asking why shouldn't we go further and embrace an understanding of the nonestablishment norm according to which government may not affirm any religious premise whatsoever. However, someone may want to ask a question that pushes in the opposite direction: Why shouldn't we embrace an understanding according to which government may affirm a specifically Christian premise if the premise is nonsectarian as among Christians? The simplest answer: It is constitutional bedrock that government may not affirm such a premise.

A bit of American history is interesting here. The National Association to Secure the Religious Amendment to the Constitution was formed in 1864 "to propose the following change to the preamble to the Constitution (in brackets): 'We, the People of the United States, [recognizing the being and attributes of Almighty God, the Divine Authority of the Holy Scriptures, the Law of God as the paramount rule, and Jesus, the Messiah, the Savior and Lord of all,] in order to form a more perfect union, establish justice, ensure domestic tranquility, provide for the common defense, promote the general welfare, and secure the blessings of liberty to ourselves and our posterity, do ordain and establish this Constitution for the United States of America' " (Jay Alan Sekulow, *Witnessing Their Faith: Religious Influence on Supreme Court Justices and Their Opinions* [Lanham, MD: Rowman and Littlefield, 2005], 125). The Christian Amendment, as it was called, "was considered twice by Congress: once in 1874 and again in 1894. The House Judiciary Committee rejected the amendment on both occasions" (ibid., 126).

[30]As even those who reject the less restrictive understanding of the nonestablishment norm will likely agree, the Supreme Court will not, in any remotely foreseeable future, rule that having "under God" in the Pledge (or "In God We Trust" as the national motto, or the like) is unconstitutional. If the Supreme Court, in a science-fiction scenario, were to so rule, the citizenry of the United States would rush to amend the Constitution to overrule the Court. See Steven G. Gey, ' "Under God,' the Pledge of Allegiance, and Other Constitutional Trivia," 81 *North Carolina Law Review* 1865, 1866-69 (2003) (reporting on the virtually unanimous negative response to the federal court's [subsequently amended] decision in *Newdow v. U.S. Congress*, 292 F.3d 597 [9th Cir. 2002]); Evelyn Nieves, "Judges Ban Pledge of Allegiance from Schools, Citing 'Under God,' " *The New York Times*, June 27, 2002; Howard Fineman, "One Nation, Under . . . Who?" *Newsweek*, July 8, 2002, 20. Religious liberty scholar Steven Shiffrin has argued that the United States has evolved from a country that is historically Christian into a country that is "officially monotheistic." See Steven H. Shiffrin, "Liberalism and the Establishment Clause," 78 *Chicago-Kent Law Review* 717, 727 (2003). See also Shiffrin, "The Pluralistic Foundations of the Religion Clauses" (above, n. 23), 70-73: "Proponents of a high wall between church and state, who would remove 'under God' from the Pledge of Allegiance, are wishing for a country that does not exist and probably never will. Our Constitution must be interpreted in the light of our evolving traditions—like it or not. So we make compromises and today government can say 'In God we trust' on its coins but not 'In Christ we trust.' "

[31]See Steven D. Smith, *Foreordained Failure: The Quest for a Constitutional Principle of Religious Freedom* (New York: Oxford University Press, 1995), 164-65, n. 66: "The very concept of 'alienation,' or symbolic exclusion, is difficult to grasp. How, if at all, does 'alienation' differ from 'anger,' 'annoyance,' 'frustration,' or 'disappointment' that every person who finds himself in a political minority is likely to feel? 'Alienation' might refer to nothing more than an awareness by an individual that she belongs to a religious minority, accompanied by a realization that at least on some issues she is unlikely to be able to prevail in the political process. . . . That awareness may be discomforting. But is it the sort of phenomenon for which constitutional law can provide an efficacious remedy? Constitutional doctrine that stifles the message will not likely alter the reality—or a minority's awareness of that reality."

[32]In its Preamble, the Irish Constitution affirms a nonsectarian Christianity: "In the name of the Most Holy Trinity, from Whom is all authority and to

Whom, as our final end, all actions both of men and States must be referred, we, the people of Eire, humbly acknowledging all our obligations to our Divine Lord, Jesus Christ, Who sustained our fathers through centuries of trial, . . . do hereby adopt, enact, and give to ourselves this Constitution." Moreover, Article 6 states, in relevant part: "All powers of government, legislative, executive, and judicial, derive, *under God,* from the people, whose right it is to designate the rulers of the State and, in the final appeal, to decide all questions of national policy, according to the requirements of the common good" (emphasis added). And Article 44 of the Constitution states, in relevant part: "The State acknowledges that the homage of public worship is due to Almighty God. It shall hold His Name in reverence, and shall respect and honor religion." On "religion in the Preamble," see, J. M. Kelly, *The Irish Constitution,* 3rd ed., ed. Gerard Hogan and G. F. Whyte (Dublin: Butterworths, 1994), 6-7. (Although it affirms Christianity, the Irish Constitution explicitly disallows the "endowing" of any religion. Article 44.2.1 states: "The State guarantees not to endow any religion.")

Given the religious commitments of the vast majority of the people of Ireland, it is not at all surprising that the Irish Constitution affirms Christianity. In so doing, the Irish Constitution violates no human right. Three things are significant here. First, the religious convictions implicit in the Irish Constitution's affirmation of Christianity in no way deny—indeed, they affirm—the idea that *every* human being, *Christian or not, is* inviolable; they affirm, that is, the idea of human rights. Second, the Irish Constitution's affirmation of Christianity is not meant to insult or demean anyone; it is meant only to express the most fundamental convictions of the vast majority of the people of Ireland. Third, and most importantly, the Irish Constitution protects the right, which is a human right, to freedom of religious practice; moreover, it protects this right not just for Christians, who are the vast majority in Ireland, but for all citizens. Article 44 states, in relevant part: "Freedom of conscience and the free profession and practice of religion are . . . guaranteed to every citizen. . . . The State shall not impose any disabilities or make any discrimination on the ground of religious profession, belief or status." Article 44 also states that "legislation providing State aid for schools shall not discriminate between schools under the management of different religious denominations, *nor be such as to affect prejudicially the right of any child to attend a school receiving public money without attending religious instruction at that school"* (emphasis added). Therefore, the conclusion that in affirming Christianity the Irish Constitution violates a human right—or that in consequence of the affirmation Ireland falls short of being a full fledged liberal democracy—is, in a word, extreme. For an excellent essay on religious liberty in Ireland, see G. F. Whyte, "The Frontiers of Religious Liberty: A Commonwealth Celebration of the 25th Anniversary of the U.N. Declaration on Religious Tolerance—Ireland," 21 *Emory International Law Review* 43 (2007).

If what Brian Barry says in the following passage is true with respect to England, which has an established church, then it is even more true—it is true in spades—with respect to the United States, which has no established church but only such comparatively minor things as "under God" in the Pledge and "In God We Trust" as the national motto: "We must, of course, keep a sense of proportion. The advantages of establishment enjoyed by the Church of England or by the Lutheran Church in Sweden are scarcely on a scale to lead anyone to feel seriously discriminated against. In contrast, denying the vote to Roman Catholics or requiring subscription to the Church of England as a condition of entry to Oxford or Cambridge did constitute a serious source of grievance. Strict adherence to justice as impartiality would, no doubt, be incompatible with the existence of an established church at all. But departures from it are venial so long as nobody is put at a significant disadvantage, either by having barriers put in the way of worshipping according to the tenets of his faith or by having his rights and opportunities in other matters (politics, education, occupation, for example) materially limited on the basis of his religious beliefs" (Brian Barry, *Justice as Impartiality* [New York: Oxford University Press, 1995], 165 n. c).

[33]In chap. 2 of *Religious Faith, Liberal Democracy, and Moral Controversy* (forthcoming) I explain why liberal democracies, given their commitment to the morality of human rights—to the inherent dignity and inviolability of every human being—should and do protect, as a legal right, the right to freedom of religious practice. It is not the case, however, that given their commitment to morality of human rights, liberal democracies should refrain from establishing religion. From the perspective of the morality of human rights, it is a matter of indifference whether liberal democracies establish religion—so long as they comply fully with the right to freedom of religious practice. See also John Finnis, "Religion and State: Some Main Issues and Sources," http://ssrn.com/abstract=943420 (2006), 30 (arguing that so long as they comply fully with the right to freedom of religious practice, "in establishing their constitutional arrangements a people might without injustice or political impropriety record their solemn belief abut the identity and name of the true religious faith and community"). As a practical matter, then, a liberal democracy may establish religion only in a weak sense of "establish." A liberal democracy may not, for example, discriminate against any of its citizens because they are not members of the established church. As the bishops of the Catholic Church stated at Vatican II: "If, in view of particular circumstances, obtaining among peoples, special civil recognition is given to one religious community in the constitutional order of society, it is at the same time imperative that the right of all citizens and religious communities to religious freedom should be recognized and made effective in practice.

Finally, government is to see to it that the equality of citizens before the law, which is itself an element of the common good, is never violated, whether openly or covertly, for religious reasons. Nor is there to be discrimination among citizens" (*Dignitatis Humanae*, 6).

[34]See Marshall (above, note 23), 23 (discussing "ceremonial deism").

[35]*Marsh v. Chambers*, 463 U.S. 783, 818 (1983) (dissenting).

[36]*Elk Grove Unified School District v. Newdow*, 542 U.S. 1, 31 (2004)

(concurring in judgment). *Newdow* is the case in which it was claimed that just as having public school children recite a prayer violates the nonestablishment norm, so too having them recite the Pledge of Allegiance violates the nonestablishment norm, because the Pledge states that the United States is a nation "under God" and recitation of the Pledge is therefore a religious exercise. The U.S. Court of Appeals for the Ninth Circuit agreed, and the case ended up in the U.S. Supreme Court, where "Six Justices reversed on a procedural ground, arguing that Newdow did not have standing to bring the action. Three justices, however, namely, Chief Justice Rehnquist and Justices O'Connor and Thomas, disagreed with [the Ninth Circuit] on the merits.

Analyzing [the Ninth Circuit's] opinion requires separation of two issues: First, is the Pledge *a religious* exercise, and, second, can a government actor constitutionally require that the Pledge be part of the official public school day? Chief Justice Rehnquist and Justice O'Connor both denied that the Pledge was a religious exercise and, therefore, concluded that it could be a part of the official public school day. Justice Thomas conceded that the Pledge was religious but . . . argued it was constitutional nonetheless" (Shiffrin, "The Pluralistic Foundations of the Religion Clauses" [above, note 23], 65-66).

Shiffrin argues "that the Pledge is religious and that it is constitutional for Congress to encourage its use, but that it should not be considered constitutionally permissible to use the Pledge in public school classrooms" (ibid., 66).

[37]See Richard John Neuhaus, "Nasty and Nice in Politics and Religion in the Public Square: A Survey of Religion and Public Life," *First Things*, March 2004, 69, 70.

[38]No one with any doubt on this score should fail to read Steven Gey's article. See Gey (above, note 30), 1873-80.

[39]See note 24 above. See Douglas Laycock, "Theology Scholarships, the Pledge of Allegiance, and Religious Liberty: Avoiding the Extremes, Missing the Liberty," 118 *Harvard Law Review* 155, 225-26 (2004) (arguing that recitation of the Pledge of Allegiance is a profession of faith); ibid., 226-27 and n. 458 (noting others who argue that recitation of the Pledge is a profession of faith).

[40]See Shiffrin, "The Pluralistic Foundations of the Religion Clauses" (above, note 23), 66-70 (explaining why the positions of Rehnquist and O'Connor in the *Newdow* case [see above, note 36] are untenable).

[41]Steve Shiffrin has addressed much the same question and, unless I misunderstand him, has given much the same answer I give here. See Steven Shiffrin, "Religion and Democracy," 74 *Notre Dame Law Review* 1631, 1652-56 (1999).

[42]See Robert Audi, "Liberal Democracy and the Place of Religion in Politics," 32: "Non-religious people often tend to be highly and stubbornly passionate about not being coerced to [act in accordance with religious reasons]. . . . Many who are not religious are incensed at the thought of manipulation in the name of someone else's non-existent deity."

[43]Kent Greenawalt, "History as Ideology: Philip Hamburger's *Separation of Church and State*," 93 *California Law Review* 367, 390-91 (2005). See

Stephen Macedo, "Transformative Constitutionalism and the Case of Religion: Defending the Moderate Hegemony of Liberalism," *Political Theory* 26 (1998), 71: "The liberal claim is that it is wrong to seek to coerce people on grounds that they cannot share without converting to one's faith"; Robert Audi, "The Place of Religious Argument in a Free and Democratic Society," 30 *San Diego Law Review* 677, 701 (1993): "If you are fully rational and I cannot convince you of my view by arguments framed in the concepts we share as rational beings, then even if mine is the majority view I should not coerce you."

[44]On nonexistence. Atheism is a religious position—a position on a religious question—for purposes of the nonestablishment norm. See Derek H. Davis, "Is Atheism a Religion? Recent Judicial Perspectives on the Constitutional Meaning of 'Religion,' " 47 *Journal of Church and State* 707 (2005).

[45]See Eberle, *Religious Conviction in Liberal Politics* (above, note 2), 71: "I shall understand a religious ground . . . as any ground that has *theistic content*. Paradigmatic religious grounds are, for example, a putative experience of God as affirming racial harmony, the claim that God has revealed in the Bible that homosexual relations are morally forbidden, the testimony of a religious authority that God abhors despoliation of the environment."

[46]Although under the nonestablishment norm there are some religious premises government may not affirm—for example, the premise that God created the universe not 6,000 years ago, as some "young-earth creationists" claim, but many billions of years ago—government may nonetheless affirm a premise that is consistent with a religious premise it may not affirm, so long as government's rationale for affirming the nonreligious premise does not rely on a religious premise government may not affirm. So government may affirm the premise that the universe is many billions of years old.

[47]See *Edwards v. Aguillard*, 482 U.S. 578, 615 (1987) (Scalia, J., dissenting): "Our cases in no way imply that the Establishment Clause forbids legislators merely to act upon their religious convictions. We surely would not strike down a law providing money to feed the hungry or shelter the homeless if it could be demonstrated that, but for the religious beliefs of the legislators, the funds would not have been approved. . . . Political activism by the religiously motivated is part of our heritage."

[48]See Eberle, *Religious Conviction in Liberal Politics*, 73: "Whether [one] supports a given law on the basis of his religious convictions alone depends on the answer to a counterfactual question: would [he] continue to regard moral claim C (on the basis of which he supports a proposed law) as sufficient reason for that law if he didn't believe that theistic claim T constitutes adequate reason for C?"

[49]See Perry, *Religious Faith, Liberal Democracy, and Moral Controversy* (note 33 above), chap. 5.

[50]Ibid., chap. 6.

[51]See above, notes 1, 2, and 3.

[52]This is not to deny that a religious rationale may be inconsistent with the morality of liberal democracy or with one or more constitutional norms other

than the nonestablishment norm or with both. Consider, for example, the religious claim that in God's created order, some human beings do *not* have inherent dignity.

[53]See Audi and Wolterstorff (above, note 2), 105 (Wolterstorff writing; emphasis in original): "It belongs to the *religious convictions* of a good many religious people in our society that *they ought to base* their decisions concerning fundamental issues of justice on their religious convictions. They do not view it as an option whether or not to do so. It is their conviction that they ought to strive for wholeness, integrity, integration, in their lives: that they ought to allow the Word of God, the teachings of the Torah, the command and example of Jesus, or whatever, to shape their existence as a whole, including, then, their social and political existence. Their religion is not, for them, *something other* than their social and political existence; it is *also* about their social and political existence."

It is sometimes suggested that in liberal democracies—or at least in religiously pluralistic liberal democracies like the United States—it is inappropriate to bring religious arguments about contested political issues into the public square; one should leave one's religious arguments at home and bring only secular arguments into the public square. However, if one concludes—as Chris Eberle and I both do—that religious rationales are a morally legitimate basis of lawmaking in a liberal democracy, then presumably one also concludes that religious rationales may be brought into the public square—that is, that religious arguments are a morally legitimate subject of public political argument. But even if one were to reject the conclusion that religious rationales are a morally legitimate basis of lawmaking in a liberal democracy, one should still conclude that religious rationales are a morally legitimate subject of public political argument: It would make little if any sense to discourage lawmakers and other citizens from presenting religious rationales in public political argument, because, like it or not, in some liberal democracies it is inevitable—certainly in the United States it is inevitable—that from time to time some lawmakers and other citizens will support a contested law on the basis of a religious rationale. It is obviously better that the rationale (unless it is politically quite marginal) be critically engaged in public political argument than that it be ignored. See Perry, *Under God?* (above, note 1), 38-44.

It bears repeating that as a political-moral matter—though not as a constitutional matter—lawmakers should abide by the ideal of conscientious engagement. See above, note 3.

[54]Ross Douthat, "Theocracy, Theocracy, Theocracy," *First Things*, August/September 2006, 23, 28 (emphasis added).

[55]John Finnis represents the Roman Catholic Church's view of the relationship among morality, reason, and religion when he writes: "Individual voters and legislators can rightly and should take into account the firm moral teachings of a religion if it is the true religion, so far as its teachings are relevant to issues of law and government. . . . In saying that voters and other bearers of public authority have this liberty, I assume that the true religion itself holds

out its moral teaching as a matter of public reason, i.e., as accessible and acceptable by a purely philosophical enquiry and only *clarified* and/or made *more* certain by divine revelation or the theological-doctrinal appropriation of that revelation" (Finnis, "Religion and State" [above, note 33], 29).

So for Roman Catholic bishops pronouncing on controversial political issues, the nonestablishment norm has no bite.

[56]See Perry, *Religious Faith, Liberal Democracy, and Moral Controversy*, chap. 2.

[57]Kent Greenawalt, *Private Consciences and Public Reasons* (above, note 2), 130.

How to "Vote Catholic"

Dueling Catholic Voter Guides in the 2006 Midterm Elections

Harold E. Ernst

While the appearance of voter guides targeted toward American Catholics during election seasons is not a new phenomenon, such guides do seem to have received enhanced notoriety in recent national election cycles. In part this has been due to the suspicion of many that some such guides, under the guise of offering unbiased guidance as to how Catholic doctrine bears on particular political issues, may in fact express a hidden partisan agenda. Thus the dissemination of one guide engenders the publication of another to diminish its allegedly pernicious effects, or to emphasize a supposedly neglected point of view, or to correct the perceived errors of another publication—and so the multiplication of competing guides continues. In this article I consider just two of the voter guides circulating in the period leading up to the 2006 midterm elections, those issued by groups calling themselves Catholic Answers Action and Catholics in Alliance for the Common Good. I have selected these two guides in particular because they were among those appearing most prominently nationwide, and also because they present such contrasting approaches to "how to vote Catholic." Indeed, the appearance of the second of these two guides was quite explicitly motivated by a desire to counter the perceived distortions of the first. Both guides claim to represent authentic Catholic teaching concerning the moral duty of Catholic voters, and yet they present wildly divergent visions of what constitutes the proper approach to Catholic moral discernment in the voting decision. After examining in turn the content and character of each of these dueling voter guides, I provide a brief theological assessment of their relative adequacy, and offer some concluding suggestions concerning the perils and possibilities of Catholic advocacy in the political realm.[1]

The "Catholic Answers Action" Voter Guide

Catholic Answers Action of San Diego titled its 2006 voter guide, "Voter's Guide for Serious Catholics."[2] As its opening words explain, "If you take your Catholic faith seriously then this voter's guide is for you," for it will "help you cast your vote in an informed manner consistent with Catholic moral teaching and fundamental human rights."[3] It is perhaps worth noting at the outset that this introductory comment detailing the purpose of the guide is ambiguous in important respects, and these elements of ambiguity are central to the evaluation of the guide's appropriateness. The suggestion that its position is grounded in "Catholic moral teaching" is certainly unsurprising in a voter guide aimed at Catholics, and the text will attempt to establish this claim through repeated references to the *Catechism of the Catholic Church*, as well as to two papal statements and a number of documents issued by Vatican congregations. But how is one to interpret the statement that the guide will "help you cast your vote in an informed manner consistent with" that Catholic teaching?

Is the claim made here *merely* consistency, in a non-exclusive sense, such that alternative and even substantially divergent construals might also be deemed "consistent?" If so, then some additional justification will be necessary to warrant the assertion that "serious Catholics" will want to adopt the approach detailed here, rather than some alternative that may be no less (or even more) "consistent" with Catholic teaching. And even if an exclusive consistency is claimed, there remains the interpretation of the character of the "help" that the guide provides in casting a vote "in an informed manner." Is the nature of this "help" simply to collect and summarize the relevant teaching itself, such that any objective reader who considered that teaching directly could be expected to be "informed" in the same "manner" as one who only read the voter guide? Or is the implication that the Catholic teaching in question does not itself provide sufficient guidance for its proper application to the context of the American elections, and so some added and extraneous "help" is necessary to translate or apply that teaching to this situation? If so, it will be necessary to distinguish this "help" from the Catholic teaching itself, and to question whether the extraneous paradigm employed is binding in some respect or should be judged on its own merits. Furthermore, under this latter interpretation one might be puzzled as to why no documents of the United States Conference of Catholic Bishops (USCCB) are cited in the guide, since many of these have been purposed precisely toward providing some "help" to assist American Catholics in voting "in an informed manner consistent with Catholic moral teaching."[4]

The guide immediately goes on to specify further the particular nature of the "help" it provides.

> This guide will help you tell the difference between candidates' positions that are morally acceptable and ones that are so contrary to fundamental moral principle that they are inconsistent with public service.
>
> On most issues that come before voters or legislators, the task is selecting the most effective policy to implement or apply a moral principle. Good Catholics must embrace the principles, but most of the time there isn't a specifically "Catholic position" on the best way to implement that principle.
>
> But some issues concern "non-negotiable" moral principles that do not admit of exception or compromise. One's position either accords with those principles or does not. No one endorsing the wrong side of these issues can be said to act in accord with the Church's moral norms. . . .
>
> This voter's guide identifies five issues involving non-negotiable moral values in current politics and helps you narrow down the list of acceptable candidates, whether they are running for national, state, or local offices.[5]

This lengthy quote signals the principal thrust of the voter guide's argument, which begins from the familiar principle/application distinction. With regard to most political issues, there is no single "Catholic position" that can be identified, because a universal moral principle may admit of various and disparate approaches to its particular application, and so "good Catholics" may legitimately disagree as to which competing policy proposal is most appropriate in a contingent historical situation, without thereby disregarding the binding character of the principle itself. But some political issues, the guide reasons, because they relate to "non-negotiable" moral principles, are effectively limited to only a single possible policy position that is consistent with moral norms. In such cases, because there is an identifiably "Catholic position," any politician on the "wrong side" of that issue is effectively disqualified from consideration by his or her identifiable violation of a universally binding moral principle.

There seem to be multiple instances of conceptual confusion embedded in this general outlook. The first is a sometime conflation of the principle/application distinction in the document as a whole, despite expressly relying on that construct as a foundational element in its argument. Inconsistency in applying the "non-negotiable" tag, sometimes at the level of principles or values while other times at the level of applications or issues, appears as both a contributor to and evidence of this conceptual conflation. The result is that the guide effectively adopts the position that some moral principles prescribe one and only one policy option, and politicians who fail to adopt this position thereby disqualify themselves as acceptable candidates, for such positions are "inconsistent with public service." The existence of moral principles that "do not admit of exception or compromise" does not mean that particular policy proposals are similarly constrained. Given that politics may be characterized as "the art of the possible," a policy position reliant on exceptions and compromise may well be the best available application of the "non-negotiable" principle in a particular political context.[6] To endorse such a policy position, even though it does not wholly satisfy the requirements of the moral principle, can thus be "to act in accord with the Church's moral norms," despite the guide's assertion to the contrary.

A second element of conceptual confusion in the guide rests in its apparently unreflective identification of "non-negotiability" with an absolute priority of significance or importance. The five "non-negotiable issues" it names are abortion, euthanasia, embryonic stem cell research, human cloning, and homosexual "marriage." According to the guide, "These were selected because they involve principles that never admit of exceptions and because they are currently being debated in U.S. politics. . . . If an issue does not meet the tests of non-negotiability and being 'in play' politically, then the guide does not focus on it."[7] In a section titled, "How to Vote," the guide instructs voters to choose the candidate who most closely conforms to "the Catholic position" on these five issues alone. Only in an instance where several candidates appear "equal" in this evaluation should the voter go on to consider "their views on other, lesser issues."[8]

But surely this decision paradigm suggests an arbitrariness[9] that is difficult to defend in the broader moral complexity of the voting decision. For example, one might wonder about the exclusion of torture from the list of "non-negotiable issues," for this too involves an exceptionless moral principle and is "in play" politically, and so would seem to meet the guide's self-proclaimed "tests."[10] But, more generally, the difficulty lies in the guide's perspective, which is not argumentatively established but merely asserts that there are five "key moral issues" upon which a voting decision should be exclusively determined.[11] That a given issue may be "non-negotiable," in the guide's sense that the moral principle involved only admits of a single policy option,[12] is not by itself sufficient for establishing that that issue be granted a priority of importance in the voter's decision-making process. Nor is it the case that simply because other issues are *not* "non-negotiable" (in the guide's sense that one cannot determine a single "Catholic position" on the issue), that therefore any possible position on these issues must be deemed acceptable, or that a candidate's position on such an issue could not supply the basis of a voter's legitimate moral objection to voting for that candidate.

In short, the guide mistakes isolating those issues where a clearly defined "Catholic position" might be identified with isolating the relevant issues for faithful Catholics to consider in exercising their voting responsibilities. Indeed, the primacy the guide gives to the five "non-negotiable issues" is not finally based on an assertion of their inherent importance in promoting the common good, but rather that on these debated issues there is some *identifiable certainty* with regard to what constitutes "the Catholic position."[13] A quotation from the Frequently Asked Questions section accompanying the guide on the Catholic Answers Action website is instructive in this regard. Question 7 is, "By selecting these five issues, are you saying that other issues aren't important?" The response reads in part: "No. Issues such as education, health care, the environment, jobs, trade, and taxes are very important—but on them Catholics are permitted a wide liberty. On the five non-negotiables, there is only one possible position for a conscientious Catholic to take: complete opposition. The Church mandates no such uniformity on these other issues. . . . There is no Catholic party line."[14]

Notice that this outlook effectively renders the evaluation of political issues to a zero-one dichotomy: either the church has mandated strict uniformity or it has permitted wide liberty; either an issue is such that only a single position is permissible or virtually any position is defensible; either Catholic voters are able to be absolutely sure of the "right" political position or they are unable to make any determination as to whether a given position comports more or less with Catholic moral teaching. In defaulting to a recommendation to consider only those issues about which some moral certainty may be passively provided, rather than encouraging the active consideration of all the "very important" issues involved in the election, the guide appears to be premised upon a relatively dim view of individual Catholic voters' capacities for making responsible prudential judgments[15] in conscience.[16] Thus "serious Catholics" should decide their votes based upon those issues about which church teaching has supplied certain guidance, rather than risk getting bogged down in complex (and perhaps even irresolvable) moral discernments concerning those issues for which no fixed position has been provided. "A well-formed conscience will never contradict Catholic moral teaching. For that reason, if you are unsure where your conscience is leading you when at the ballot box, place your trust in the unwavering moral teachings of the Church."[17]

The "Catholics in Alliance for the Common Good" Voter Guide

Catholics in Alliance for the Common Good of Washington, D.C., titled its 2006 voter guide, "Voting for the Common Good: A Practical Guide for Conscientious Catholics."[18] As before, I find it instructive to begin to consider the text by attending to its own statement of purpose: "This voting guide was created to inform Catholics about the fullness of our Church's teachings and to help us make choices in the voting booth that reflect the fullness of those values."[19] Even an only moderately attentive reader will have recognized that the key word in this statement of purpose is "fullness," and so will have already sensed there an implicit rejection of any partial or limited selection of relevant Catholic values in the voting decision. But just in case such a reader might fail to recognize that this guide is quite explicitly intended as a response and counter to the approach of the Catholic Answers Action guide, the text goes on to make this character abundantly clear. In the first section, titled "How Should Catholics Vote?" one reads: "In recent years some have suggested that we can answer this question by applying a simple 'litmus test' of a few selected issues. But common sense tells us that deciding who to vote for is much more complicated."[20] And as part of its response to the question, "Are all Catholic issues equally important?" the guide declares: "Some have argued that because some issues are never morally acceptable, these alone must determine our vote. This point of view [is] not supported by Church teaching. Our challenge is to embrace the fullness of Catholic issues and make an informed and balanced decision that will best provide for the common good of all humanity."[21]

As these passages indicate, one should well expect that the "help" offered here for "conscientious Catholics" will be quite different from the "help" we have seen offered to "serious Catholics." What is the nature of the "help" offered by this guide? It begins with the counsel that Catholics are obliged to take account of the full scope of those themes encompassed in Catholic social teaching. "Most importantly, . . . we need to understand that our Church's social teachings call us to consider a broad range of important issues—on everything from poverty to war, human rights, abortion, and the environment. *There is no Catholic voting formula, and there is rarely, if ever, a perfect candidate for Catholic voters.*"[22] The guide then goes on to name three principles that "can help you make a sound and faithful decision" when voting:

1. Inform your Conscience—on Church teaching and the candidates' positions.
2. Apply Prudence—when deciding how to apply Catholic values to voting.
3. Vote for the Common Good—by focusing on what's best or everyone, especially the poor and vulnerable.[23]

On the surface, the first of these principles might seem only to duplicate the guidance provided by the Catholic Answers Action guide, for it too called for Catholics to inform their consciences about church teaching and to investigate the stated positions of the candidates. But in fact the instructions provided by this guide are substantively distinct from the prior example in three important respects. First, the conception of conscience countenanced here is significantly broader than in the Catholic Answers Action guide, where it was described as "like an alarm" that "warns you when you are about to do something you know is wrong."[24] The Catholics in Alliance guide, in contrast, portrays conscience not merely as a negative limit but as a positive capacity in "the quest for truth," which enables us "to act prudently in accord with the law written in all our hearts."[25] This outlook obviously grants greater importance to the subjective dimension in the voting decision, and so relativizes the adequacy of any strictly defined rule-based approach: "Listening to one's conscience is necessary to make any moral decision."[26]

The second and third differences relate to the way in which this guide counsels voters to go about informing their consciences. For the task of "learning about the Church's positions on important issues," the guide states, "We recommend starting with the U.S. Conference of Catholic Bishops' *Faithful Citizenship* document. . . ."[27] In a starkly different approach from focusing attention on only five "non-negotiable" issues, this guide recommends *Faithful Citizenship* for "a list of all the important Catholic issues," and notes that this list "contains some 50 different issues."[28] And for the task of researching the candidates' positions on these important issues, this guide recommends not only the standard advice to consult their websites and monitor media coverage of the campaign, but also adds this instruction: "It's important to look at a candidate's actions . . . in addition to what he or she is saying about the issue today—in order to understand how he or she may act in the future."[29] Each of these three differences militates against a more formulaic approach to the voting decision, where Catholics might be compelled to prefer a candidate whose stated positions on a select number of political issues better comport with church teaching. These differences also serve to provide the theoretical license for Catholics to choose a candidate whose stated positions stand in direct contrast with church teaching on specific issues.

The same impulse is evident in the guide's treatment of its second principle, "Apply Prudence," which emphasizes the importance of the principle/application distinction, here highlighted as a distinction between knowing and doing. "*While an informed conscience is essential for knowing right from wrong, actually doing the right thing requires the virtue of prudence. . . . It is like* a 'moral common sense,' and it requires us to ask the practical question, *which candidate will actually deliver more tangible progress for the Common Good?*[30] Thus prudential judgments will be especially important in voting decisions, since "Seldom does a single candidate or party offer a consistently Catholic set of positions."[31] This means that "we often must vote for candidates who may hold the 'wrong' Catholic positions on some issues in order to maximize the good our vote achieves in other areas."[32] "For example, a candidate may not entirely share the Church's principles on an issue, but still do much through his or her actions to promote Catholic Social Teaching."[33] This outlook attempts to recognize the inherent complexity in applying moral principles to concrete situations, such that even though "Our Church's social teaching is clear," still "Catholics must thoughtfully and prayerfully consider and debate what is most pressing and possible in our time."[34] Finally, in its commentary on the third principle, "Vote for the Common Good," the guide simply notes that "A culture of the common good provides for the health, welfare, and dignity of all people, and promotes the best interests of everyone, not just the few. It also focuses on helping those who need it most—the poor and vulnerable."[35]

In addition to elaborating on these three general principles for Catholic voting, this guide includes a Frequently Asked Questions section. To the question, "Are all Catholic issues equally important?" it provides the following response. "No. While we ought to consider the full range of Catholic issues when we go to the voting booth, this does not mean that all these issues are equally important. Issues that bear directly on the life and dignity of human beings, such as abortion, poverty, torture, and war, demand our most urgent attention."[36] No reference to Catholic social teaching is provided to justify naming these four issues, rather than some others, so one is not immediately able to discern whether this primacy is extracted from church teaching itself or is an extraneous "help" supplied by the guide's authors. Nevertheless, this gesture at a kind of inherent priority for some issues may come as welcome practical guidance to many readers of the guide, who might otherwise be understandably overwhelmed by the instruction to consider each candidate's stand on "some 50 different issues." After all, how many of us create decision matrices to determine how we arrive at our voting decisions for each elected office? More to the point, in order to arrive at a final preference for a single candidate, would not the consideration of such an extended list of issues simply *require* some perception of their relative importance?

But upon more careful examination this guidance is seen to communicate less of a distinguishing priority than might have at first appeared. Note that the issues that "demand our *most* urgent attention" are those that "bear directly on the life and dignity of human beings, *such as* abortion, poverty, torture, and war."[37] Not only is there no suggestion of a priority among these four issues, but because the list is expressly conveyed as non-exclusive, we cannot even conclude that these four issues should take precedence over others. Rather, we are left to consider as demanding our "most urgent attention" *all* those issues that "bear directly on the life and dignity of human beings." This criterion would certainly seem to also include issues such as euthanasia, embryonic stem-cell research, human cloning, and the death penalty. But might we not judge that it further includes genocide, the global arms trade, nuclear weapons, and terrorism? What about discrimination, immigration, health care, employment, human rights, marriage, and environmental protection?[38] The difficulty is apparent: *every* issue of concern in Catholic social teaching bears at least indirectly on "the life and dignity of human beings," and a particularly integrated sense of the human person as an inherently social being could well lead one to claim that all of these issues relate directly to human life and dignity. When every issue is "most" urgent, none is. And even if we were to construe the term "directly" more narrowly, and so come to only ten (or twenty? or thirty?) "most important" issues, we are still faced with questions of how to evaluate the *relative* importance underlying that prioritization, both among the "most important" issues themselves and in relation to those other issues that are also of real, but lesser, importance.

This absence of any tangible perception of how some issues might take priority over others shows itself most vividly in the guide's answer to another question, "Is it okay to vote for a 'pro-choice' candidate?" The response begins as follows: "When confronted with this question in 2004, Cardinal Ratzinger (now Pope Benedict XVI) responded that it could be acceptable for a Catholic to vote for a 'pro-choice' candidate if 'proportionate reasons' exist, and if the voter is voting based on those reasons and not the candidate's 'pro-choice' beliefs."[39] Now, for this response to constitute a "yes" answer, which the guide's authors clearly intend as evidenced by the subsequent discussion they provide, it must expressly require some defensible perception of the relative importance of the candidate's various positions in the context of the current election. For how else could the voter credibly judge that his or her reasons for preferring the "pro-choice" candidate, in spite of that candidate's "pro-choice" position, were *proportionate* reasons?

Comparative Analysis of the Two Voter Guides

The two voter guides considered here are not just radically different, but even competitive and contradictory, in their instructions. And yet, in a more general sense, these two very different guides also share much in common. Both begin from the perspective that Catholics have a moral duty to participate in the life of our nation, and that taking seriously the opportunity to cast a vote in democratic elections is an essential part of this obligation. Both situate their respective instructions concerning how to properly exercise one's right to vote in the context of a broader obligation for Catholics to promote the common good of human society. Both acknowledge (at least ostensibly) that there are many civic issues of importance to Catholics in this regard, and yet hold (at least ostensibly) that some issues should receive relatively more attention in the voting decision. Both assert that the guidance they provide is grounded in the authentic moral teaching of the Catholic Church, and regularly cite selected authorities to bolster this claim. Both deny that they are intended to endorse specific candidates or parties, and both originate from organizations purporting to be non-partisan. Both maintain that there are identifiably "Catholic positions" on at least some political issues, and thus designate these as "Catholic issues." Both contend that "good," "faithful," "serious," or "conscientious" Catholics will want to adhere to these positions in their voting decisions. And, as this accumulation of modifying appellations might suggest, both are willing, at least implicitly, to anathematize those Catholics who reject the distinctive voting approach each prescribes.

What accounts, then, for the remarkable differences in their respective recommendations to Catholic citizens who wish to allow church teaching to inform their voting decisions? Important elements contributing to the divergence of these two guides lie hidden behind almost all of the aforementioned points of apparent commonality. Each interprets the obligation of Catholic voters quite differently, with the first emphasizing the need to vote according to those issues where church teaching is most unequivocal, while the second emphasizes the obligation to attend to the whole range of issues addressed in Catholic social teaching in the light of conscience. Each implicitly entails a different conception of which issues are most pressing for promoting the common good, with the first limiting itself to those issues where it finds moral clarity, while the second explicitly denies such limitation and the privileging of that narrow selection of issues.[40] Each has a distinct perspective on the character of "Catholic issues" in contemporary politics, with the first holding that there are only a handful with a clearly fixed "Catholic party line," while the second argues that there are "Catholic positions" on many issues and balancing these multiple interests depends upon subjective prudential judgments. Each exercises a distinctive selection of authoritative sources (and even of passages within a given source)[41] to justify its respective position, with the first favoring citations that seem to limit individual discretion, while the second highlights texts that relativize or deny such limitation.

Finally, however, it must be acknowledged that a significant source of the disparity in these two Catholic voting guides is the differing partisan preferences of their authors or sponsoring organizations. Ultimately, one cannot escape the sense that these documents reflect as much the mind of a political operative as a religious educator.[42] No matter how well-intentioned, the authors of each guide seem in some respects to have mistaken their own political preferences or agenda for the preferences or agenda of the church itself. In that sense these two Catholic voter guides often appear as ugly mirror images of each other. Where the first may be seen as effectively giving self-declared "pro-life" candidates a free pass on almost every other social issue, the second may be seen as effectively giving political cover or absolution to "pro-choice" candidates. Where the first appears to improperly limit a Catholic voter's moral obligation to merely avoiding indirect material cooperation with evil (to use the traditional term), the second appears to improperly ignore that obligation by highlighting the benefits of attending to other important social issues without adverting to the countervailing "costs." While the sponsoring organizations of these two guides may qualify as "non-partisan" under the technical requirements of Section 501(c)(4) of the Internal Revenue Code, I submit that a well-informed and reasonably objective reader of either would view that claim with considerable suspicion (and whatever doubt remained would be quickly eliminated by even a cursory review of their respective websites).

Rather than concluding merely by "cursing the darkness," however, I would like to offer three final suggestions that might at least point the way toward "lighting a candle," in the sense of providing for a more effective and coherent approach to characterizing Catholic advocacy in the political realm. For notwithstanding the respective demerits of each of these two voter guides (and on my reading they are many), I think we can learn something from each of them, and still more from considering them in tandem. First, I think these two guides highlight the very great (indeed, perhaps almost inescapable) risk that any such attempt to "help" Catholic voters might ultimately succumb to a tendency to advocate for particular partisan political preferences.[43] If the character of the prescribed rule or voting paradigm is extraneous to church teaching itself, if it functions at the level of application rather than principle, then it must itself be subject to criticism as a contingent construct rather than authoritatively promoted as "the" Catholic approach to the voting decision, to which "serious" or "conscientious" Catholics must faithfully adhere. Given the ubiquitous propensity to validate one's subjective preferences (even unconsciously) as more consistent with or even mandated by some objective norm, it seems to me that, on strictly theological grounds, we should be very cautious in accepting or endorsing voter guides of this kind.

Second, I propose we consider whether it would not be better to wholly discard the language of "Catholic issues" and "Catholic positions." In the Catholic understanding of the human person as ontologically relational, as imaging the Triune God, as the being which only fully finds itself through the sincere self-offer of itself to others, and who therefore requires a communitarian existence for its flourishing, *every* social or political issue is in some respect a "Catholic issue." Use of this term, which connotes a false distinctiveness, may facilitate the inappropriate tendency to attend only to a select number of issues while ignoring all others. The broad use of the term "Catholic positions" (as well as its bolder cousin, "the Catholic party line") seems to me similarly ill-advised, for it too easily suggests that the Catholic Church is merely

another special interest group, advocating specific policy proposals on political issues to suit its own peculiarly partisan ends. Too
often this language problematically flattens the critical distinction
between universal moral principles and their application in particular circumstances,[44] an application that is necessarily conditioned by a contingent set of empirical discernments and prudential judgments.[45] What is more, the language of "Catholic
positions" on political issues may even be enervating to the mission of the church, which has the duty of enlightening consciences
and fostering justice while also respecting the legitimate autonomy
of the political sphere.[46]

My third suggestion is somewhat more tentative, and has to do
with the difficult matter of the prioritization of certain issues in
the voting decision. As we have seen, these two guides take very
different approaches on this question, with the first granting a
kind of absolute priority to specific issues over all others, while
the second eschews virtually any tangible basis for recognizing a
meaningful priority of select issues.[47] Ultimately, it is precisely this
question of prioritization, of what kind and how characterized,
that is crucially at issue. The following assessment from political
scientists Clarke E. Cochran and David Carroll Cochran, concerning the policy positions of each political party on "life issues,"
is instructive:

> The mainstream liberalism of the Democratic party and the
> mainstream conservativism of the Republican party both
> reject the church's position on key life issues, even while
> embracing it on others. Indeed, this area is perhaps the most
> important reason many Catholics feel as though they lack a
> political home in the contemporary United States. Moreover,
> life issues offer those Catholics who are strong partisans for
> one party or the other the material for attacks on each other,
> further weakening Catholic witness. Although debates con-
> tinue over what issues to include under the church's teaching
> on the dignity of human life, and especially over what priority
> each should have, it is clear that a Catholic understanding of
> these issues, their relationship, and the proper policy re-
> sponses offer[s] a radical alternative to both left and right.[48]

It seems clear that these two guides exemplify just this potential for "life issues" to offer "strong partisans for one party or the

other material for attacks on each other, further weakening Catholic witness. " The Catholic Answers Action guide insists that any candidate taking the "wrong" position on its five "non-negotiable" issues[49] must be regarded as a threat to the common good: "It is a serious sin to deliberately endorse or promote any of these actions, and no candidate who really wants to advance the common good will support any action contrary to the non-negotiable principles involved in these issues."[50] The Catholics in Alliance for the Common Good guide counters by challenging the sufficiency of those select issues for identifying an authentically "pro-life" candidate as part of its case for the legitimacy of voting for a "pro-choice" politician: "Can one really claim to be 'pro-life' and yet support the death penalty, turn a blind eye to poverty, and not take steps to avoid war? Our Church teaches that the answer to this question is 'no.' "[51] Thus the question of "what issues to include under the church's teaching on the dignity of human life, and especially of what priority each should have," is an essential aspect of the dispute. A Catholic voter who recognizes both candidates (or parties) as seriously deficient with regard to some elements of the "life issues" is still presented with the task of assessing their degrees of *relative* deficiency, if he or she is to come to a prudential judgment of preferring one over the other. And this challenge of prioritization also extends to all the other political issues to be considered in a given election.

I want to suggest that the teaching of the U.S. bishops might actually indicate something of a middle course between these two voting guides, one that does insist upon the emphasis of the second guide in attending to a broad range of social issues, and yet that recognizes something of the implicit instinct in the first guide that some issues really are distinctive in a way that merits a legitimate primacy of importance. Consider the character of the following three quotations, each of which conveys the idea that the unity and integrity of the church's social vision can come into coherence only if certain foundational values are first solidly established in the political order. First, there is this comment by Joseph Bernardin in a 1976 homily he delivered as the archbishop of Cincinnati: "Life before and after birth is like a seamless garment. . . . If we become insensitive to the beginning of life and condone abortion or if we become careless about the end of life and justify euthanasia, we have no reason to believe that there will be much respect for life in between."[52]

Second, there is this statement from the USCCB's *Living the Gospel of Life*, insisting on the necessary priority of opposition to abortion and euthanasia, notwithstanding the importance of a broad spectrum of related issues in a consistent ethic of life (such as war, capital punishment, poverty, racism, hunger, employment, education, housing, health care, and protection of the environment):

> But being *"right"* in such matters can never excuse a wrong choice regarding direct attacks on innocent human life. Indeed, the failure to protect and defend life in its most vulnerable stages renders suspect any claims to the "rightness" of positions in other matters affecting the poorest and least powerful of the human community. If we understand the human person as the "temple of the Holy Spirit"—the living house of God—then these latter issues fall logically into place as the crossbeams and walls of that house. *All direct attacks on innocent human life, such as abortion and euthanasia, strike at the house's foundation.* These directly and immediately violate the human person's most fundamental right—the right to life. Neglect of these issues is the equivalent of building our house on sand. Such attacks cannot help but lull the social conscience in ways ultimately destructive of other human rights.[53]

Third, there is *Faithful Citizenship* itself. Section VII of the document is titled, "Moral Priorities for Public Life," and of the four categories named there, the first is "Protecting Human Life."[54] Certainly a broad spectrum of "life issues" is specified here, for in addition to abortion and euthanasia the document addresses cloning, the intentional targeting of civilians, biotechnology, war, the preemptive or preventive use of force, nuclear weapons, landmines, the global arms trade, and the death penalty. But in this same section the bishops also quote themselves in *Living the Gospel of Life*, declaring that certain issues are of prime significance in preserving the common good: "Abortion and euthanasia have become *preeminent* threats to human life and dignity because they directly attack life itself, the *most fundamental good and the condition for all others.* They are committed against those who are weakest and most defenseless, those who are truly 'the poorest of the poor.' "[55]

What is essential to note about each of these three texts is that here the primacy of select issues is not regarded as coming at the expense of those that are less central, but rather brings the importance of those other issues into clearer relief, by highlighting the interconnections between what is most central and what is more peripheral. That is to say, the primacy here is at the level of principle, in the sense that concerns that are more foundational or basic to the inviolable dignity of the human person illustrate and illumine the importance of those additional concerns that are seen to be extensions of that same foundation.[56] In this way, "voting Catholic" neither should be construed as a single-issue "litmus test," nor should it devolve into an undifferentiated and idiosyncratically applied attention to the full spectrum of social issues.[57] Rather, "voting Catholic" should give witness to the "both/and" sensibility of the Catholic tradition, recognizing both the *plurality* of social issues that must concern us, and the *order* of their individual significance, which varies according to the relationship of each to the foundational principles underlying Catholic social teaching.[58] How else can we come to a defensible judgment as to "which candidate will actually deliver *more* tangible progress for the Common Good?"[59]

Notes

[1]A version of this paper was delivered at the June 2007 meeting of the College Theology Society at the University of Dayton. I am grateful to members of the audience there for their questions and observations.

[2]Catholic Answers Action, *Voter's Guide for Serious Catholics* (hereafter, CAA), available at http://www.caaction.com (accessed June 8, 2007).

[3]CAA, 3.

[4]While I am thinking here primarily of *Faithful Citizenship*, the quadrennial statement the U.S. bishops issue prior to each presidential election season, the USCCB has also published any number of additional documents providing moral guidance on particular topics (e.g., *Strangers No Longer, A Place at the Table, Living the Gospel of Life, The Harvest of Justice Is Sown in Peace, Economic Justice for All*, and so on).

[5]CAA, 3.

[6]The guide itself will later cite Pope John Paul II as acknowledging the legitimacy of just this sort of "exception" in *Evangelium vitae*, 73: "An elected official whose absolute personal opposition to procured abortion was well known could licitly support proposals aimed at limiting the harm done by such a law and at lessening negative consequences at the level of general opinion and public morality." The guide employs this quotation in a section

titled, "When There Is No 'Acceptable' Candidate," as support for the view that voting for the least objectionable among a slate of objectionable candidates is not to "promote intrinsic evils," but rather "is an action aimed at limiting the evil, and an action that limits evil is good" (CAA, *Voter's Guide for Serious Catholics*, 12).

[7]Ibid., 14-15.

[8]Ibid., 11.

[9]Notwithstanding the fact that this is precisely what the guide is at pains to avoid—"But voting cannot be arbitrary"—in its insistence that individual decisions of conscience in voting must be properly bound by what the candidate might do in office, "since morality requires that we avoid doing evil to the greatest extent possible, even indirectly" (ibid., 5).

[10]Perhaps the response would be that it is exceedingly rare for a politician to adopt an explicitly "pro-torture" position, and so in this sense the issue is not "in play." But many candidates do advocate interrogation practices variously described as "enhanced techniques" or "rough tactics," and the political debate is in part over whether these practices actually constitute torture, euphemistically described.

[11]CAA, 10-11.

[12]Ibid., 16.

[13]This perhaps explains why the guide offers no guidance on how a voter might decide between two candidates who were each "wrong" on one of the five issues. Since each of the "non-negotiable" issues is regarded as a kind of absolute, there would be no explicit justification for taking the view, for example, that voting for a candidate who favored homosexual marriage would be preferable to voting for the alternative candidate who was "pro-choice." Without any paradigm for construing relative importance among the five issues, these two candidates must be regarded as "equal."

[14]Catholic Answers Action, *Voter Guide FAQ*, http://www.caaction.com/index.php?option=com_content&task=category& sectionid=3&id=7&Itemid=66 (accessed June 8, 2007).

[15]While the Catholic Answers Action guide does call for prudential judgments to be exercised (though not in those terms), these are generally limited to the (admittedly complex) task of evaluating how to do the least harm when there is no perfectly acceptable candidate across the five non-negotiable issues. For example: "In some political races, each candidate takes a wrong position on one or more issues involving non-negotiable moral principles. In such cases you may vote for the candidate who takes the fewest such positions or who seems least likely to be able to advance immoral legislation, or you may choose to vote for no one" (CAA, 12). That is to say, the judgments involved are carefully prescribed by the decision paradigm supplied in the guide, and do not extend beyond that paradigm.

[16]In a section titled "The Role of Your Conscience," the guide reveals a rather crude conception of this moral faculty, which appears less as an active capacity for discerning truth than a blank slate for recording and recalling moral dictates. "Conscience is like an alarm. It warns you when you are about

to do something that you know is wrong. It does not itself determine what is right or wrong. For your conscience to work properly, it must be properly informed—that is, you must inform yourself about what is right and what is wrong. Only then will your conscience be a trusted guide" (CAA, 13).

[17]Ibid., 13.

[18]Catholics in Alliance for the Common Good, *Voting for the Common Good: A Practical Guide for Conscientious Catholics* (hereafter, CACG), available at http://www.thecatholicalliance.org (accessed June 8, 2007).

[19]CACG, 3.

[20]Ibid., 2.

[21]Ibid., 8.

[22]Ibid., 2 (emphasis in original by bold type).

[23]Ibid., 4.

[24]CAA, 13.

[25]CACG, 4.

[26]Ibid.

[27]CACG, 5. In addition to its references to *Faithful Citizenship*, the guide also includes quotations from the *Catechism of the Catholic Church*, documents of the Congregation for the Doctrine of the Faith, and remarks of Pope John Paul II.

[28]CACG, 8. While the Catholic Answers Action guide may seem to supply Catholic voters with all it contends they need to know regarding church teaching for the purpose of making their voting decisions, the Catholics in Alliance for the Common Good guide implicitly requires its readers to consult *Faithful Citizenship* in order to come to a fully informed decision, since the guide only names 19 of the "some 50 different issues" upon which it contends Catholics' voting decisions should be based.

[29]CACG, 5.

[30]Ibid., 5 (emphasis in original by bold type).

[31]Ibid., 5.

[32]Ibid., 6.

[33]Ibid., 5-6.

[34]Ibid., 6.

[35]Ibid.

[36]Ibid., 8.

[37]Ibid., 8 (emphasis mine).

[38]The "Election Day Checklist" included as part of the guide would seem to license just such a broad inclusion of issues under the category of "human life and dignity": "What will the candidate do to address affronts to human life and dignity such as poverty, torture, abortion, war, the death penalty, *and a lack of freedom and opportunity?*" (ibid., 12, emphasis mine).

[39]Ibid., 8.

[40]In fact, however, Catholics in Alliance for the Common Good may signal its own favored set of issues, and a selection no less limited than the one it criticizes. A "bulletin insert" available for download from the organization's web site begins with the headline, "Voting Catholic Means . . . Voting for the

Common Good." After a quotation from *Faithful Citizenship* and some bullet points regarding difficulties in contemporary American society, it reads: "This November, Help Restore America's Commitment to the Common Good." What follows is a checklist naming exactly five issues: "Vote For: A living wage for working families; Health care for all; Retirement security; Care for God's creation; Security through diplomacy" (Catholics in Alliance for the Common Good, *Voting for the Common Good Insert*, http:// www.catholicsinalliance.org/resources/voting-for-the-common-good-insert.html [accessed June 8, 2007]).

[41]For example, both documents cite the 2004 memo from Cardinal Joseph Ratzinger, "Worthiness to Receive Holy Communion: General Principles," supplied by the then-prefect of the Congregation for the Doctrine of the Faith at the request of Cardinal Theodore McCarrick in the latter's capacity as head of the USCCB's Task Force on Catholic Bishops and Catholic Politicians. The Catholic Answers Action guide quotes this document as support for its distinction between "non-negotiable" and "negotiable issues": "Not all moral issues have the same moral weight as abortion and euthanasia. . . . There may be a legitimate diversity of opinion even among Catholics about waging war and applying the death penalty, but not however with regard to abortion and euthanasia" (CAA, 15-16). The Catholics in Alliance guide draws upon this same source, but to a quite different effect, citing it as indicating that "it could be acceptable for a Catholic to vote for a 'pro-choice' candidate if 'proportionate reasons' exist . . ." (CACG, 8). Note that attending to the import of both of these citations, rather than merely selecting the one most agreeable to its basic line of reasoning, would necessarily complicate the argument of each voter guide.

[42]This line from *Faithful Citizenship* might qualify as a useful test in judging the "help" a Catholic voter guide provides: "A Catholic moral framework does not easily fit the ideologies of 'right' or 'left,' nor the platforms of any party." Both a guide that may appear to force a voter lockstep toward unreserved support for one party, and a guide that may appear to serve as an enthusiastic apologist for another party (while undermining the credibility of the first), would seem to fail this test (United States Conference of Catholic Bishops, *Faithful Citizenship: A Catholic Call to Political Responsibility* [issued 2003; cited 8 June 2007]; http://www.usccb.org/faithfulcitizenship).

[43]As the U.S. bishops cautioned amidst the Catholic politicians/communion controversy during the 2004 presidential election season, "The polarizing tendencies of election-year politics can lead to circumstances in which Catholic teaching and sacramental practice can be misused for political ends" (United States Conference of Catholic Bishops, *Catholics in Political Life* [June 2004]; http://www.usccb.org/bishops/catholicsinpoliticallife.shtml).

[44]There are instances where the Catholics in Alliance for the Common Good guide, despite its substantially greater theological sophistication in general, also slips into eliding this distinction. Consider this line from the guide's "Election Day Checklist": "Does this candidate support an economic system that demands opportunity and human dignity for all—a living wage,

health care, affordable education, and human rights?" (CACG, 12). While all these elements are clearly *desiderata* at the level of principle in Catholic social teaching, the use of "demands" here would seem to have surreptitiously moved to the level of application (implicitly excluding the validity of preferences for incentive-based programs, for example, which some Catholic voters may prudently judge to be better means to achieve these same ends).

⁴⁵A clear perception of this distinction is perhaps no more prevalent among Catholics than non-Catholics today. We would do well to emphasize more carefully the implications of the caution the U.S. bishops issued in *The Challenge of Peace*, 9-10: "We stress here at the beginning that not every statement in this letter has the same moral authority. At times we reassert universally binding moral principles. . . . At still other times we reaffirm statements of recent popes and the teaching of Vatican II. Again, at other times we apply principles to specific cases. When making applications of these principles, we realize—and we wish readers to recognize—that prudential judgments are involved based on specific circumstances which can change or which can be interpreted differently by people of good will . . ." (United States Catholic Bishops, *The Challenge of Peace: God's Promise and Our Response*, in *Catholic Social Thought: The Documentary Heritage*, ed. David J. O'Brien and Thomas A. Shannon [Maryknoll, NY: Orbis Books, 1992], 494).

⁴⁶Pope Benedict XVI seems to have a similar concern in mind in *Deus caritas est*, 28: "Faith enables reason to do its work more effectively and to see its proper object more clearly. This is where Catholic social doctrine has its place: it has no intention of giving the Church power over the State. Even less is it an attempt to impose on those who do not share the faith ways of thinking and modes of conduct proper to faith. Its aim is simply to help purify reason and to contribute, here and now, to the acknowledgement and attainment of what is just" (*God Is Love* [San Francisco: Ignatius Press, 2006]).

⁴⁷In this respect, as in others, the Catholics in Alliance guide shows the marks of its founding motivation in a reaction against, and intentional counter to, the Catholic Answers Action guide. As is characteristic of reactions against, it is so intent on disallowing the voting approach it (rightly) criticizes as inadequate that it is loath to sanction *any* substantive prioritization of certain issues, lest it seem to give some quarter to the enemy. The result is that it not only deconstructs a decision paradigm that it perceives as a partisan subterfuge, but also imposes its own conceptual paradigm that seems vulnerable to the same charge (as conveyed in the rhetoric surrounding and applying its three core principles, which in themselves are unimpeachable in theological terms). It may well be that the extreme character of the prioritization adopted by the Catholic Answers Action guide also stems from a kind of reaction against, in this case a reaction against the approach of the U.S. bishops in *Faithful Citizenship*, which is perceived as insufficiently attentive to the question of priority (and so that document is ignored, as are statements of the USCCB in general).

⁴⁸Clarke E. Cochran and David Carroll Cochran, *Catholics, Politics, and*

Public Policy: Beyond Left and Right (Maryknoll, NY: Orbis Books, 2003), 182.

[49]It is worth repeating that the specification of these five issues in the guide is grounded not in their inherent importance, or even in the assertion that they are constitutive of a "pro-life" position, but rather simply in the judgment that those are the issues in the contemporary political debate where Church teaching is unequivocal (since an intrinsic evil is involved). Of the five issues (abortion, euthanasia, embryonic stem cell research, cloning, and homosexual "marriage"), only the first four would typically be accounted among the "life issues."

[50]CAA, 6.

[51]CACG, 9. Note that I am not challenging the bare accuracy of the guide's claim here, but rather suggesting that it is tendentiously stated and so provides no real guidance to a Catholic voter who already acknowledges the importance of a broad range of "life issues." Partisans of the opposite persuasion could with equal justification ask, "Can one really claim to advance the common good and yet support an unlimited 'right' to abortion, turn a blind eye to euthanasia, and not take steps to end embryonic stem cell research? Our Church teaches that the answer to this question is 'no.' "

[52]Cited in Richard M. Doerflinger, "The Pro-Life Message and Catholic Social Teaching: Problems of Reception," in *American Catholics, American Culture: Tradition and Resistance*, ed. Margaret O'Brien Steinfels (Lanham, MD: Sheed and Ward, 2004), 53.

[53]United States Conference of Catholic Bishops. *Living the Gospel of Life: A Challenge to American Catholics* (1998), 23 (emphasis in original); http://www.usccb.org/prolife/gospel.shtml.

[54]The other three are "Promoting Family Life," "Promoting Social Justice," and "Practicing Global Solidarity."

[55]*Faithful Citizenship*; *Living the Gospel of Life*, 5 (emphasis mine).

[56]This perspective should overcome the conceptual or tactical "either/or" political scientists Kenneth D. Wald and Allison Calhoun-Brown describe as having developed in the Catholic community: "The church leadership has long been deeply divided over tactics in the antiabortion campaign. For some bishops, abortion is the paramount moral issue of the day and a candidate's position on that single issue remains a litmus test of acceptability. . . . Another camp, stimulated by the late Joseph Cardinal Bernardin of Chicago, has taken the position that abortion should be part of a 'seamless garment' of issues—including nuclear war, human rights, capital punishment, doctor-assisted suicide, and poverty—all involving threats to human life. Candidates should be judged on the full range of their beliefs, not just abortion" (*Religion and Politics in the United States*, 5th ed. [Lanham, MD: Rowman & Littlefield, 2007], 265-66).

[57]Notice that neither of these approaches seems to fulfill the judgment of Cochran and Cochran that "a Catholic understanding of these issues, their relationship, and the proper policy responses offer[s] a radical alternative to both left and right." Indeed, the two voter guides considered here seem more

to validate or legitimize the respective tendencies of the right and left than to portray the Catholic understanding as offering a radical alternative to them.

[58]Elsewhere I have attempted to defend this point more systematically, by suggesting the way in which this outlook expresses an extension of the Vatican II concept of a "hierarchy of truths" into Catholic social teaching. See my "The Hierarchy of Truths Forty Years Later: The Expansive Evolution of a Vatican II Theme," *Josephinum Journal of Theology*, forthcoming.

[59]CACG, 5 (emphasis mine). By "defensible" here I mean a judgment that could be defended on more than mere *de gustibus* grounds, and so avoids the omnipresent tendency toward selectively reading Catholic teaching in a way that too conveniently validates one's subjective political preferences absent any consideration of that teaching.

Table Fellowship in a Land
of Gated Communities

Virgilio Elizondo as Public Theologian

Mary Doak

Virgilio Elizondo has never to my knowledge identified himself as a "public theologian." Yet his theological work directly engages church and society with an inspiring and prophetic vision of the better world that God is calling us to bring into reality. While most theologians have retreated to the relative safety of inner-academic debates, including debates over whether it is possible to develop a public theology, Elizondo has been doing precisely what so many have argued cannot be done in a secular society: he has articulated a thoroughly theological vision in civic space and with impact on the broader community.[1]

The term "public theology" was originally coined by Martin E. Marty as a call for a critical theological engagement with U.S. society, culture, and politics.[2] While liberation and political theologies developed in Latin America and Europe, and black liberation and feminist theologies arose in the United States, some theologians also began to take up Marty's idea of a "public theology" that would be a critical, contextual theology for the United States. The proponents of public theology largely agreed that this public theology should do at least two things: 1) it must address issues of society, politics, and culture theologically, and 2) it ought to articulate this theology in a manner accessible to the wider population.[3] In other words, theologians should no longer confine themselves to a "trickle down" public impact, trusting that their academic critiques will eventually have an effect on the wider society by first transforming the conversations taking place in universities and colleges. Instead, advocates of public theology have argued that theologians ought to address society and culture directly and in a clear yet explicitly theological manner.[4] Some theologians have suggested adding a third requirement for public theology: this theology must grapple with the American commitment to the separation of church and state, so that the publicly engaged theology is consistent with the demands of religious freedom in a pluralistic democracy.[5]

I will argue here that Elizondo not only fulfills these requirements of public theology, but also expands our conception of what such a theology might be and do. Though he is rightly classified as a Latino theologian, Elizondo's work develops as a critical but hopeful vision for the United States. He achieves new insights into the meaning of Christian faith, while providing a perspective on the problems and the possibilities of our society for *all* of its members. Perhaps of special interest given our debates today, Elizondo develops a theology that is public in its topic and manner, yet remains thoroughly rooted in his particular ecclesial tradition. Sharing the concerns of the correlational theologies of Marty and others who advocate a public theology, Elizondo addresses issues of American life in a manner respectful of those who do not share his tradition and with appreciation for as well as criticism of the American project.[6] At the same time, Elizondo's theology satisfies the requirements of the non-correlationalists in that his position is developed out of the substance of his particular theological tradition, remains deeply rooted in that tradition, and provides a vision and practice of community that is counter-cultural in its challenge to widespread American practices and values.[7] Elizondo thus demonstrates that theology can be public and particular, open and traditional, at the same time. He shows that it is possible (even for Christian theologians!) to claim one's proper place in the public conversation while allowing others an equal place.

My analysis below of Elizondo's contributions to public theology will be structured according to the three characteristics of public theology listed above. Most of the following discussion will focus on the manner in which Elizondo fulfills the first criterion by providing a critical theological perspective on U.S. culture and society. I will then more briefly discuss Elizondo's success in fulfilling the second criterion by articulating his ideas in a publicly accessible style and in public forums. Finally, I will defend Elizondo's contributions to public life as consistent with religious freedom, since the socio-political (and perhaps even legislative) implications of his theology do not require or encourage explicit governmental support for religious beliefs.

Elizondo's Theology *of* the Public: *Mestizaje* as Theological Vision

Elizondo's theology is deeply and explicitly rooted in the socio-cultural and devotional experiences of Mexican-Americans, especially those in the southwestern United States. Indeed, Mexican-American culture is a major source for Elizondo's theology, as he works to uncover and to celebrate the theological insights that this community has to offer to the larger society and to the universal church. Yet Elizondo also attends carefully to the Bible (especially the gospels) and to the wider Christian tradition as theological sources that inform, corroborate, and critique aspects of Mexican-American Christianity. He maintains that the religiosity of this people "still must be judged by the word of the gospel," even while he insists that "if the gospel is not reinterpreted through the expressions, language, and symbols of the faith community, it will appear as a foreign, lifeless, or even destructive doctrine, not an incarnated, life-giving power."[8]

Elizondo develops this mutually illuminating correlation between the Gospels and Mexican-American experience especially in his *Galilean Journey: The Mexican-American Promise*. In this book, he argues that the Mexican-American experience of *mestizaje*, of mixture both racially (indigenous and European) and culturally (Mexican and American), reveals an important aspect of the gospel story. Elizondo finds theological significance in the belief that God became incarnate in the border area of Galilee, the inhabitants of which were devalued by the rest of the country for their lack of cultural and religious purity. From this location of *mestizaje* and as one of those dismissed for being from an insignificant and not fully Jewish region, Jesus initiated the reign of God with a ministry of table fellowship that united people who could be expected to reject such intimate contact with each other. Social outcasts and sinners were especially welcome in this table fellowship, but so were the rich and the powerful, provided they could accept the de-centering of themselves this table fellowship required.[9] In Elizondo's reading of the gospels, *mestizaje*, understood as people coming together in their differences to create a new reality, thus emerges as integral to the redemptive work of Jesus Christ.

This theology of *mestizaje* is further developed in Elizondo's interpretation of the devotion to Our Lady of Guadalupe. As he argues especially in his *Guadalupe: Mother of the New Creation*, the Virgin of Guadalupe appeared after the Spanish Conquest as one of the devalued, indigenous women in order to unite the Europeans and the indigenous, the Christian and the Aztec, in a new community. In Elizondo's interpretation, Our Lady of Guadalupe was not only an affirmation of the dignity of the Mexican people to whom and as one of whom the Virgin appeared. Through an apparition that combines Aztec and Christian religious symbols, she united the seemingly irreconcilable. Further, she sent the poor and socially insignificant native, Juan Diego, to ask the Spanish bishop to build her a new home on the outskirts (rather than the center) of town. She thus invited all to relinquish relations of domination and exclusion and instead to build a new community through the coming together of peoples and cultures in the Americas. The Virgin of Guadalupe proclaimed herself "the mother of all of the nations," so that all might see themselves as brothers and sisters (in a Marian echo of Jesus' invitation to join a new family that calls God "our Father").[10]

Theologically, then, *mestizaje*, or the intimate communion of peoples, is intended by God to be an experience of community in which our differences enrich our common life. Unfortunately, as Elizondo notes, the new life and possibilities that emerge from our coming together are frequently rejected rather than celebrated: mestizo people are often treated as marginal by both parent groups, not fully included or allowed to feel at home anywhere. As Elizondo reminds us, when the U.S. conquered the large area of Mexico that has become the southwestern United States, "the dominant society quickly labeled us [Mexicans] as inferior and good only for cheap labor."[11] Under the conditions of a sinful and divided humanity, this new life of *mestizaje* thus emerges in a painful struggle to survive. The opportunity for a greater realization of community too often becomes further evidence of our divisions. In his own experience growing up as a Mexican-American, Elizondo remembers that "in Mexico I was considered too Anglo to fit in, while in the USA, I was too Mexican to be fully accepted."[12]

In Elizondo's work, the theological celebration of *mestizaje* becomes an inspiring and prophetic vision of and for the American experience of the (as yet incomplete) formation of a new community from the diverse peoples on this continent and in this country. The inclusive community Elizondo envisions is not best described either as a melting pot wherein all become a new uniformity, or as a salad or mosaic wherein we remain largely unaffected by the juxtaposition of our differences. Instead, Elizondo suggests that the challenge and possibility of life in the Americas is more appropriately imagined in terms of the cooking of a rich stew.[13] We can and should retain much of the difference that makes us distinct from one another (individually and, for Elizondo especially, as various peoples), but we must also be changed by one another as we create together a new common reality. Accepting Jesus' table fellowship has never been easy, Elizondo contends, since the powerful have to embrace their own decentering, the powerless have to overcome a sense of inferiority and fear of humiliation, and all have to risk being changed by these new relationships.[14] The enriching possibilities that emerge in the new community do not, then, come without a cost: everyone has to be willing to give something up, and even to experience the friction and discomfort that Elizondo compares to the heat that produces a good stew.

A final characteristic of Elizondo's theological vision of public life that must be mentioned, even in this brief discussion of his work, is Elizondo's emphasis on uniting the prophetic and the festive. While challenging us to denounce current injustices and the various cultural practices and societal structures that exclude and demean some yet privilege others, Elizondo also invites us to celebrate life as we know it and the communities we experience, however flawed they may be. The prophetic and the festive are, of course, both evident in Jesus' ministry insofar as the one who challenged the Sadducees is also described as "a glutton and a drunkard."[15] Elizondo's contribution here is to draw our attention to the necessary mutual coherence of the prophetic and the festive rather than to treat them as separate attitudes. As he astutely observes, "The prophetic without the festive turns into cynicism and bitterness. . . . The festive without the prophetic can easily turn into empty rituals or even degenerate into drunken brawls. It is the prophetic-festive that keeps the spirit alive and nourishes the life of the group as a group."[16]

Before ending this overview of the content of Elizondo's theology of public life and turning to the remaining two criteria of public theology, a few comments on the contribution of Elizondo's vision are in order. Given the ongoing academic debate over the correlational approach to theology, which is often accused of losing the specificity of the Christian gospel, it is especially noteworthy that Elizondo's engagement with Mexican-American experience results in a theology with important insights into the meaning of Christian faith. Indeed, Elizondo's celebration of *mestizaje* has considerable theological richness as a development of the evangelical basis as well as the socio-political implications of the Second Vatican Council's definition of the mission of the church to be "a sign and instrument" of union with God and unity among humanity.[17] Informed by Henri de Lubac's ecclesiology, this conciliar expression of the hope of the church for unity is deeply rooted in biblical and patristic views of sin as separation, such that redemption is the overcoming of this separation from God along with the restoration of a unity-amid-diversity in the human community. Elizondo's attention to the significance of Jesus' Galilean background enables us to see more clearly that the church's eucharistic celebration of the unity that will be fully achieved at the end of history ought to be an intentional practice of *mestizaje*, continuing the table fellowship of Jesus Christ as a foretaste of the eschatological fulfillment of our unity.[18] In this world of alienation and oppression, as Elizondo's theology clarifies, the mission of the church to be an instrument of human community in God requires that Christians learn not merely to overcome exclusion, but also to welcome the new life that emerges (usually painfully and as a threat to established identities) when we encounter one another in our diversity. The church cannot, then, be the church by itself or by clinging to a static identity: only through actively pursuing a common and mutually enriching life with non-Christians can we fulfill our mission to be a sacrament of human unity-amid-diversity.

Elizondo's vision of joyful *mestizaje* is offered as a challenge not only to the church but also to society, as this ideal provides a critical perspective on the reality of U.S. history and our ongoing failure to realize the national project of becoming one out of many (*e pluribus unum*). As Elizondo points out, racism, classism, cultural elitism, and, perhaps especially, capitalism's focus on individual success all oppose or militate against the development of a radically inclusive community that respects the dignity of all.[19] The difficulty, we should further note, is not only that we fall short in our efforts to embody our expressed ideals, but also that many of our contemporary values conflict with the ideal of an inclusive, harmonious society. Gated communities, for example, are a growing trend in urban and suburban life, and are advertised as a positive feature of real estate. Yet this withdrawal into homogenous groups protected against outsiders is surely the antithesis of the inclusive table fellowship Elizondo envisions. How can we foster *mestizaje* when we are retreating into gated communities? Indeed, the privatization of so much of American society, the loss of common spaces, and the devaluation of public institutions where we encounter others from across the social spectrum result in greater barriers to coming together in our differences. One wonders if the United States is becoming a huge gated community, erecting barriers to secure itself against the threat of outsiders. Both nationally and locally, we are constructing exclusive, homogeneous communities in which we are protected from those whose differences threaten us. Elizondo's recovery of the profoundly human (as well as theological) significance of *mestizaje* recalls us to our earlier North American hope to become a new people enriched by diversity and able to govern ourselves better by listening to one another. Whether we are inspired by the desire to continue Jesus' redemptive ministry of table fellowship or by the American hope that *mestizaje* will enrich our national life (or by both), Elizondo enables us to see more clearly how problematic is the restructuring of public space as a shopping mall, open to all only insofar as we come together for individual consumption before retreating to the private space of families and to our selective, homogenous neighborhoods and communities.

Even while this critical perspective is essential, a public theology that is only a prophetic jeremiad (particularly one that opposes society in the name of a pure, homogenous church) will not have the resources to support the desired resistance through countercultural practices of joyful *mestizaje*. We need not only to identify the sins and the effects of sin in our society, but also to articulate an inspiring vision and to develop a celebratory practice that fosters real human encounters in public space. Elizondo's insistence on combining the prophetic and the festive is thus crucial: the beauty of the reign of God as it is partially present among us is a key theme in Elizondo's theology and is the basis for the celebration that he believes is necessary to sustain resistance to injustice and exclusion.[20]

Elizondo's Theology *in* Public: Theology as Table Fellowship

As indicated above, a theology that intends to be truly public in its implications for society must be public in its form and not merely in its content. To restate this point in the terms we have been using here: theology cannot foster inclusive practices of table fellowship while remaining within the gated community of academic discourse. Instead, a public theology must risk (and enjoy) the challenges of engagement with a wider community of people who may not share the presuppositions of university theology, a risk Elizondo has consistently undertaken. His theology is unusually accessible to the general public, due not only to his remarkably clear and jargon free style of communication, but also to the venues he chooses for publicizing his thought. Elizondo has, of course, published in standard academic presses such as Orbis Books and Liturgical Press, as well as in *Concilium*, but his ideas often appear first in such places as *Our Sunday Visitor, St. Anthony Messenger*, and the Mexican American Cultural Center Press. More importantly, Elizondo does not limit himself to print media, but has developed and communicated his theology in countless sermons and lectures to parish and civic groups, in his many years with the Mexican American Cultural Center, and through his work as rector of San Fernando Cathedral, where his theology was embodied and communicated in liturgy and ritual within and beyond the cathedral walls.[21] While many academic theologians occasionally preach or give parish talks, Elizondo's theology is more truly public in that it was not developed primarily in the academy but in and through his involvement with civic and parish life, especially in San Antonio, Texas.

Elizondo has also developed a public voice through his work in visual media. In addition to having a cathedral mass televised so that this liturgical theology might reach a wider audience, Elizondo has produced or collaborated in the production of at least fifteen videos and television series that have appeared on PBS as well as on Catholic television. These video projects include "Meditation Time" (a thirteen-part series of meditations on the psalms), "Touching God" (a television series on the richness of sacramentals), "Soul of the City" (about San Fernando Cathedral), and "Nuestra Señora de Guadalupe, Madre de las Americas."[22] Through these and his other videos, as well as his embodiment of theology in liturgy and ritual, Elizondo has creatively developed new forms of public communication for theology. He thus implicitly challenges theologians to move beyond the usual academic audiences and to take seriously the various forms of visual and aural media that are essential means of cultural communication today.

A further and perhaps more radical development in the public manner of doing theology is provided by Elizondo's insistence on listening to and theologizing with people, rather than lecturing at them. His aim is not merely to provide his insights to others, but to embody a theological table fellowship that includes all voices in the conversation, as he assists others in articulating their own theological insights. This communal approach to theology, in which Elizondo allows his thought to be enriched by ideas and experiences that academic theology seldom encounters, is especially evident in Elizondo's pastoral work and teaching. This theological method can, however, also be detected in the frequent appeal throughout his theological corpus to the stories and theological insights of parishioners, family members, and friends.[23] Perhaps the frequently lamented difficulty so many of us have in finding a public audience for our theology is that we merely want to lecture larger groups of people, and such groups of people interested in being lectured at are frequently not forthcoming.

Since Christian faith is not only a belief but also a practice, it is significant that Elizondo's theology includes public practices of a hospitable table fellowship. In his work at San Fernando Cathedral, Elizondo encouraged the development of public rituals and fiestas that share the joy of *mestizaje* and table fellowship with the wider civic community, especially (but not only) in the role of the cathedral in the civic celebration of the birth of modern-day Texas, and in the multireligious celebration of Thanksgiving Day at the cathedral.[24] The goal of these and other public fiestas and rituals, according to Elizondo, was not to deny the particularity of the cathedral's Catholic and Mexican roots, nor to promote one religion over others, but rather to reach out to others in a celebratory welcome of all in their distinctness.[25] As Elizondo describes the vision behind these public rituals, "because we had suffered segregation, we would work and struggle so that no one in the future would have to suffer as we had in the past."[26]

In fostering a spirit of welcome and inclusion at San Fernando Cathedral, and through fiestas that publicly celebrate the religious, cultural, and racial diversity of the city of San Antonio, Elizondo has shown what new ecclesial practices forming Christians in a spirituality of human community might look like. The church, Elizondo maintains, must be a site of the public practice of the reign of God, challenging the socio-economic, racial, and ethnic divisions that currently separate us even within our church communities. His practice of public hospitality demonstrates that the church is most faithful to its own identity, and perhaps even most likely to flourish, when it has an outward rather than an inward focus and is willing to risk its established identity to welcome others.

Elizondo's Theology *as* Public: Religious Freedom and Public Action

Given the thoroughly public character of Elizondo's theological work, and especially his expressed desire to celebrate the richness of Mexican-American Catholicism without denigrating other religions and ethnicities, it is appropriate to consider the manner in which Elizondo's public practice of theology is consistent with a pluralistic, secular society. To my knowledge, Elizondo has never written on religious freedom or proffered an interpretation of the First Amendment, yet he is keenly aware of the challenges of developing a public religiosity that does not stifle religious differences. Further, amid so much contemporary debate over the proper public and political role (if any) of religion in a secular society, we cannot responsibly neglect at least a brief consideration of this issue.

In contrast to the current trends to disparage religious disestablishment as an incoherent concept that cannot be practiced consistently, I contend that John Courtney Murray in the 1960s and Franklin I. Gamwell in the 1980s have shown that religious freedom requires the observance of a few basic rules in order to ensure that a politically active religious faith does not result in the legislative establishment of that religion.[27] Though a thorough defense of this understanding of religious freedom is beyond the scope of my comments here, I submit that three principles need to be clearly acknowledged: 1) all laws embody values, so that religion appropriately enters public life in the discussion of the values at stake in legislation; 2) legislation is concerned with governing behavior, and should not explicitly teach or require the acceptance of the values implicit in the legislation; and 3) the behavior that legislation properly governs is limited to that behavior that affects the common good of society and the public order.[28] Simply put, all laws should be moral, but not all morality should be legislated, or else, as John Courtney Murray warned, we imperil morality as well as religious freedom.[29] It is simply not the case, as we hear so frequently asserted these days, that it is inconsistent to believe a certain behavior is wrong and yet not seek legislation against it. To the contrary, a public exercise of religion that is consistent with religious freedom (and, as Vatican II noted, consistent also with God's respect for the dignity of the person) must seek only legislation governing behavior necessary to the public order and the common good (however defined), and should not attempt to legislate adherence to particular beliefs or personal morality.[30]

A more adequate discussion would defend these rules against the criticism that they are insufficient to allow religion's proper concern for its place in society as well as society's need for religion, but our conversation here must be limited to discussing Elizondo's theology in relation to these criteria for protecting religious freedom. We should first acknowledge that Elizondo has been more directly engaged as a cultural activist than as a political activist. Most of his work has been concerned with the thoroughly public task of reinforcing Mexican-Americans' pride and self-confidence in the value of their *mestizo* cultural identity, and with confronting the exclusion and cultural elitism that are often reinforced through social and cultural practices even when the law formally guarantees equality.[31] Through his work with the Mexican American Cultural Center and with Communities Organized for Public Service in San Antonio, Elizondo has also been involved in empowering Latinos and the poor both politically and economically. These aspects of Elizondo's form of public theology thus remind us that much can and ought to be done in our public life that does not require a change in legislation. Indeed, the quality of our public life deteriorates (along with religious freedom) when all efforts at social and cultural change become reduced to efforts to pass new laws.

Nevertheless, Elizondo's vision of an inclusive society respecting the dignity and equality of all is indeed a religiously based ideal that concerns the public order, so that all legislation should be consistent with this ideal; at times legislative changes will be necessary to enable society to more closely approximate this goal. Elizondo's own awareness that his ideal for society impinges on legislative agendas is especially evident in his support for Cesar Chavez's efforts to extend legal protection to farm workers and in Elizondo's concern about current immigration laws.[32] Since few, regardless of their position on the issues, deny that these matters pertain to the common good and the public order, Elizondo's approach exemplifies how a religiously informed set of values can inform public life and even at times influence legislation without seeking to legislate adherence to the religious values themselves.

Perhaps more importantly, Elizondo's corpus embodies a logic that is contrary to the current presumption (especially articulated by John Milbank) that Christians and Christian theologians should oppose secular society on the grounds that Christian discourse must either "master or be mastered by" all other forms of discourse.[33] Instead, Elizondo seeks to celebrate his Mexican-American identity in a way that strengthens others in their own religious and ethnic identities. He argues for practices of inclusion that refuse to react to the experience of having been dominated by seeking to dominate others, intellectually, religiously, or in any other way. In fact, Elizondo believes "it would be a disaster" if religion were to become a force of societal division in the United States.[34] Further, he has been clear that his vision of a hospitality that welcomes others is deeply rooted in a commitment to the truth of the gospel and is based on the story of Jesus, even while non-Christians might endorse this goal for other—perhaps secular—reasons. Insisting that it is through our particularity that we achieve universality, Elizondo espouses an openness to others that comes not from insecurity about the religious truth he has embraced, but rather from his thoroughly Catholic confidence that all are children of God with something to share.

Conclusion

Elizondo has developed a form of the accessible, socially concerned public theology that many theologians in the last thirty years have sought, and he has done so with a theology of table fellowship that challenges the various forms of gated communities to which we are currently inclined. The practice of mutual hospitality and engagement that he demonstrates is obviously opposed to our current tendencies to withdraw into socio-economically and culturally homogenous communities. Instead, Elizondo seeks to inspire people to revive public spaces and festivals and to be open to the enrichment we will find in unscripted encounters with people who differ from us in class, race, ethnicity, education, and country of origin. Perhaps even more radically (given current trends), Elizondo's vision of table fellowship challenges also our theological withdrawal into an academic gated community, admitting only those with doctoral degrees to the conversation, and he resists current ecclesial tendencies to recreate the church as a gated community retreating into a religious identity protected against the insights of others. His work, especially at San Fernando Cathedral, suggests that the church will thrive not by focusing on recreating a separate Catholic subculture, but by looking outward to explore how we might better serve the larger community and help others be more fully who they are. In his recovery of an ideal deeply rooted in Christianity but also in U.S. history, Elizondo calls into question all our various efforts to find security and a meaningful identity by defining more sharply our national, ecclesial, and intellectual borders.

As we face an increasingly interconnected world, the challenge of mutual encounter will surely become more prevalent in all aspects of our lives. It seems reasonable to assume that people will continue to be tempted to respond either by clinging to a secure particular identity and community or by embracing a rootless universality that allows neither identity nor community. In this context, Elizondo's interpretation of the meaning of the gospel for our times will continue to provide an important alternative, one in which particularity is celebrated, shared, and welcomed as the basis for new life and unimagined possibilities for all. This theology helps us to see that, in a world of oppression, alienation, and exclusion, the mission of the church to be a sign and instrument of human community is no trite enactment of the obvious. Rather, this mission demands a creative and committed discipleship, and provides the basis for a profound critique of current social and ecclesial structures and practices.

Notes

[1] I am grateful to the "Mysticism and Politics" and the "Contemporary Theologies" sections of the College Theology Society for allowing me to present an earlier version of this analysis at their joint session during the 2007 annual meeting and for the insights shared in that session. Our common conversation helped me to grasp the extent to which Elizondo's christology is oriented by the image of the Second Coming, or the eschatological fulfillment. I am also grateful

to William Collinge and to two anonymous reviewers, whose suggestions have made this article much better than it would otherwise have been.

[2]Martin E. Marty, "Two Kinds of Two Kinds of Civil Religion," in *American Civil Religion*, ed. Russell E. Richey and Donald G. Jones (New York: Harper and Row, 1974), 139-157.

[3]See especially Linell Elizabeth Cady, *Religion, Theology, and American Public Life* (Albany, NY: SUNY Press, 1993); Mary Doak, *Reclaiming Narrative for Public Theology* (Albany, NY: SUNY Press, 2004); Michael J. Himes and Kenneth R. Himes, *Fullness of Faith: The Public Significance of Theology*, Isaac Hecker Studies in American Religion and Culture (New York: Paulist Press, 1993); Parker Palmer, *The Company of Strangers: Christians and the Renewal of America's Public Life* (New York: Crossroad, 1983); Max Stackhouse, *Public Theology and Political Economy* (Grand Rapids: Eerdmans, 1987); and Ronald F. Thiemann, *Constructing a Public Theology: The Church in a Pluralistic Culture* (Louisville: Westminster, 1991). In addition, David Tracy, William Dean, and Richard John Neuhaus have written important methodological works that have significantly influenced the conversation about public theology.

[4]There is also considerable debate among those who want clearly theological contributions to public life over whether explicitly Christian or biblical language should be used, but this is a separate conversation and one that I will not directly engage here. For further discussion, see especially David Hollenbach, S.J., "Public Theology in America: Some Questions for Catholicism after John Courtney Murray," in *Theological Studies* 37 (1976): 290-303, and the discussions in David Hollenbach, S.J., ed., "Theology and Philosophy in Public: A Symposium on John Courtney Murray's Unfinished Agenda," in *Theological Studies* 40 (1979): 700-15.

[5]See especially Doak, *Reclaiming Narrative for Public Theology*; Franklin I. Gamwell, "Religion and Reason in American Politics," in *Religion and American Public Life: Interpretations and Explorations*, ed. Robin W. Lovin (New York: Paulist Press, 1986), 90, 92; Franklin I. Gamwell, *The Meaning of Religious Freedom* (Albany: SUNY Press, 1995); and John Courtney Murray, S.J., *We Hold These Truths: Catholic Reflections on the American Proposition* (Kansas City: Sheed and Ward, 1960).

[6]I am here following David Tracy's understanding of a mutually critical correlational approach to theology. See especially David Tracy, *Blessed Rage for Order: The New Pluralism in Theology* (New York: Paulist Press, 1978).

[7]See especially Stanley Hauerwas, *A Community of Character: Toward a Constructive Christian Social Ethic* (Notre Dame: University of Notre Dame Press, 1981).

[8]Virgilio Elizondo, *Galilean Journey: The Mexican-American Promise*, rev. ed. (Maryknoll, NY: Orbis Books, 2000 [1983]), 47.

[9]Ibid., esp. chaps. 4 and 5.

[10]Virgilio Elizondo, *Guadalupe: Mother of the New Creation* (Maryknoll, NY: Orbis Books, 1997), 62-73, esp. 68. See also Elizondo, *Galilean Journey*, 9-13.

[11]Virgilio Elizondo, "*Mestizaje*," unpublished manuscript, 2005, 8.

[12]Ibid., 10.

[13]Ibid., 6.

[14]In addition to Elizondo, "*Mestizaje*," see Virgilio Elizondo, "Benevolent Tolerance or Humble Reverence? A Vision for Multicultural Religious Education" in *Beyond Borders: Writings of Virgilio Elizondo and Friends*, ed. Timothy Matovina (Maryknoll, NY: Orbis Books, 2000), 87-97, at 93.

[15]Matthew 11:19 and Luke 7:34.

[16]Elizondo, *Galilean Journey*, 120.

[17]*Dogmatic Constitution on the Church (Lumen Gentium)*, 1.

[18]Virgilio P. Elizondo and Timothy M. Matovina, *San Fernando Cathedral: Soul of the City* (Maryknoll, NY: Orbis Books, 1998), 103.

[19]Elizondo, *Galilean Journey*, 103-14.

[20]See especially Elizondo, *Guadalupe*, for an extended discussion of the theological importance of beauty.

[21]For an overview of Elizondo's work as a "community priest," see Mario T. García, "PADRES: Latino Community Priests and Social Action," in *Latino Religious and Civic Activism in the United States*, ed. Gastón Espinosa, Virgilio Elizondo, and Jesse Miranda (Oxford: Oxford University Press, 2005), 77-95. See also Elizondo and Matovina, *San Fernando Cathedral*, for a discussion of theology embodied in liturgy and ritual at San Fernando Cathedral in San Antonio, Texas.

[22]For a list of Elizondo's video productions before 2000, see Matovina, *Beyond Borders*, 295. The bibliography of Elizondo's work included in that volume also provides an excellent testament to the variety of popular presses with which Elizondo has published. Virgilio Elizondo informed me in a communication on October 25, 2007, of five more recent videos: *A Migrant's Masterpiece—the Life and Work of Archbishop Flores*, a documentary to be shown on PBS television; *Meditation Time*, a thirteen-part series on the psalms for Catholic Television of San Antonio; *Touching God*, a thirteen-part series on the sacramentals for Catholic Television of San Antonio; *Soy Católico*, a thirteen-part series on the Catholic faith for Catholic Television of San Antonio; and *ND Pilgrimage: A Living History in the Land of Jesus*, an eleven-part series for Catholic Television of San Antonio.

[23]See especially Elizondo and Matovina, *San Fernando Cathedral*, 15, for a defense of this method of listening to the *sensus fidelium* of the ordinary faithful, and see throughout *San Fernando Cathedral* for stories of the faith expressed by the people who worshiped at that cathedral. See also Virgilio Elizondo, "Theology's Contribution to Society," in *From the Heart of Our People*, ed. Orlando Espín and Miguel Díaz (Maryknoll, NY: Orbis Books, 1999), 49-53, and Elizondo, *Galilean Journey*, 32-46, for an interpretation of the theology of Mexican-American rituals and devotions.

[24]These and other public rituals are described in Elizondo and Matovina, *San Fernando Cathedral*, 103-13. For a description of explicitly Christian public rituals sponsored by the cathedral, see 81-97.

[25]For Elizondo's description of his intent in developing public rituals at San

Fernando Cathedral, see Elizondo, *Galilean Journey*, 127-29, and Elizondo and Matovina, *San Fernando Cathedral*, 12-13 and 108-9.

[26]Elizondo, *Galilean Journey*, 129.

[27]See Murray, *We Hold These Truths*; Gamwell, *The Meaning of Religious Freedom*, and my discussion of these arguments in Doak, *Reclaiming Narrative for Public Theology*.

[28]For a further defense of these three requirements of religious freedom, see especially my article "Resisting the Eclipse of *Dignitatis Humanae*," in *Horizons* 33 (2006): 33-53.

[29]Murray, *We Hold These Truths*, 155-74.

[30]*Declaration on Religious Freedom (Dignitatis Humanae)*, esp. art. 2.

[31]See García, "PADRES," for an excellent discussion of Elizondo as a "cultural worker."

[32]For studies of the community organizing and empowering organizations of which Elizondo was a founding participant, see, in addition to García, "PADRES," Richard L. Wood, "*Fe y Acción Social*: Hispanic Churches in Faith-Based Community Organizing," in *Latino Religions*, ed. Espinosa et al., 145-58; and Socorro Castañeda-Liles, "Spiritual Affirmation and Empowerment: The Mexican American Cultural Center" in *Latino Religions*, ed. Espinosa et al., 111-25. See also Virgilio Elizondo, "The Ministry of the Church and Contemporary Migration," in *Social Thought* 13 (Spring/Summer): 120-32, and his "The New Humanity of the Americas," in *Beyond Borders*, 272-77.

[33]See for example John Milbank, *Theology and Social Theory: Beyond Secular Reason* (Oxford and Cambridge, MA: Blackwell, 1990), 327.

[34]Elizondo and Matovina, *San Fernando Cathedral*, 108.

Intelligent Design "in the Public Square"

Neo-Conservative Opposition
to Darwinian Naturalism

Anne M. Clifford

During the past decade, a conception of the universe as intelligently designed has been gaining attention in the United States and is therefore a significant factor in contemporary American public life. This paper locates "intelligent design" (ID), a hypothesis that posits that in order to explain life scientifically it is necessary to support the agency of an unevolved intelligence, in the larger context of Christian neo-conservatism. "Neo-conservatism" is used here broadly to name a movement composed primarily of intellectuals, some of whom abandoned formerly held leftist leanings, who have set about exercising influence on American culture by framing public discourse to promote anti-liberal ideas and values. The goal of exercising public influence encompasses every facet of American life, including the education of our nation's future citizens, our children. Intelligent design as a hypothesis put forward as science is not inherently an element of Christian neo-conservatism. However, the negative appraisal by advocates for intelligent design of Darwinian evolution on the grounds that its naturalism has been and is negatively affecting our society and culture—which they have taken into the public square with a fervor one might typify as "evangelical"—locates it under the tent of Christian neo-conservatism.

This article will begin with a brief history of the origins of intelligent design. Attention will be given to ID's goals and strategies for countering the influence of Darwinian naturalism on American culture. It will consider how the ID strategy of inclusion in the science curricula of our nation's schools fared in a 2005 Dover, Pennsylvania, federal court case and the significance of the decision. A critical response to ID with an accompanying proposal will be offered. Since the genre of this paper is theological and not scientific, the author will provide no personal judgments about whether or not intelligent design is a bona fide science. However, some judgments by major scientific communities will be noted.

Origins of Intelligent Design

Spokespersons for intelligent design present it as a new, even revolutionary, science, one that provides a needed corrective to the shortcomings of biological evolution theory. ID advocates question the adequacy of Darwin's account of the descent through modification of millions of species, including *homo sapiens sapiens*, through "natural selection," which is an undirected or "random" process without a scientifically knowable teleology. Darwin himself did not deny design in Earth's plant and animal species, but he did conclude that the functional design that he observed in them resulted from natural processes. Intelligent design proposes that the biological complexity we observe in living species could not have resulted exclusively from mechanisms that are natural and material. It holds that there is evidence of design in nature that can only be attributed to an intelligent agency that is irreducible to natural material mechanisms.[1]

From the standpoint of science, intelligent design is atypical. ID originated not with a new discovery by a scientist, but with the questioning of evolution as a promoter of naturalism by a lawyer and law professor, Phillip E. Johnson. Before he initiated the ID movement, Johnson wrote a sweeping critique of Darwinian naturalism in *First Things* (1990), in which he argued that under the guise of claims that its brand of evolution is a "fact" it promotes a naturalistic dogmatism. The Darwinian creed rules out not only the creationism of biblical fundamentalism but also "*any* [italics his] invocation of a creative intelligence or purpose outside the natural order."[2] Johnson does not delve into the ways to judge design, but does assert that Darwinian evolution cannot account for the perception of intelligence that challenges its insistence on unguided natural forces at work in evolution.

The fact that Johnson has articles on or related to intelligent design published in *First Things* signals his and the ID movement's participation in the broader movement of Christian neo-conservatism in America. Neo-conservatives insist that Christian faith is, in the words of Richard John Neuhaus, founding editor of *First Things*, "in some necessary way 'relevant' to public policy. Christians as Christians . . . have a responsibility to advance a social vision derived from biblical Christianity."[3] Therefore, religious tradition, specifically, Christian belief about God and created reality, must be given a voice in our national life in "the public square." Promoters of intelligent design, like many neo-conservatives, believe that the fragility of the family and the vulnerability of our children to dangerous ideas (for example, Darwinian evolution, which eliminates the uniqueness of humans among other species) require strategies for public activism.

Johnson's major follow-up to the *First Things* article was *Darwin on Trial* (1991), a book in which he gives attention to the demise of creation science's balanced treatment strategy.[4] In 1982, the late Judge William Overton ruled that the Arkansas Balanced Treatment Act violated the First Amendment of the U.S. Constitution because it is a thinly veiled promotion of religion in the guise of science (*McLean v. Arkansas Board of Education*). Overton's decision was reaffirmed in a 1987 Supreme Court decision on a similar balanced treatment act passed in Louisiana (*Edwards v. Aguillard*) and is seen by Johnson to be a disturbing trend. His reason for this assessment is that when Judge Overton presented essential criteria for what counts as science, he placed at the top of the list the notion that science must be "guided by natural law" and must exclude any reference to the supernatural in its discourse.[5] Further, in the *Edwards v. Aguillard* decision, the court ruled that teaching a variety of scientific theories about the origins of humankind to school children might be validly done only "with the clear *secular intent* of enhancing the effectiveness of science instruction."[6]

In *Darwin on Trial*, "intelligent design" appears, but only four times.[7] The term "intelligent design," however, did not originate with Johnson. It can be found in Ferdinand Canning Scott Schiller's *Humanism* (1903), in which he accepts biological evolution as a credible explanation but argues that "it will not be possible to rule out the supposition that the process of evolution may be guided by an intelligent design."[8] Johnson strengthens this supposition without returning to the pre-Schiller idealization of design of William Paley, who in *Natural Theology* proclaimed that in spite of disease and suffering, God desires happiness for creatures.[9] ID does not gloss over "nature as red in tooth and claw." One of the contributing factors in Darwin's abandonment of the natural theology that he studied while a student at Cambridge was the pathos and suffering he observed in nature. Intelligent design advocates, such as William Dembski, account for the abundance of suffering and death in nature by positing: "No real designer attempts optimality in the sense of attaining perfect design. Indeed, there is no such thing as perfect design. Real designers strive for *constrained optimization.*"[10] To explain "constrained optimization," Dembski speaks of the art of compromise between conflicting objectives that we are not privy to because they are known only to the intelligent agency responsible for the design of nature.

Overall, intelligent design advocates accept biological evolution at the micro but not at the macro level. Mutations do occur in natural history to adapt organisms to their environment. Changes do happen within species to enhance survival (microevolution), but mutations are incapable of generating new species and biological systems (macroevolution), which require information-rich structures. Put simply, the evidence for the appearance of new species through the mechanisms that Darwin described is too thin. Macroevolution has yet to be subject to rigorous testing.[11] By not accepting macroevolution ID does not distance itself very far from the "special creation" of species of nineteenth century natural theology and "young Earth creation science."[12] Nevertheless, most ID scientists and spokespersons insist that their science is not an attempt to replace completely biological evolution, but rather to resolve what is lacking in it with a new and superior scientific paradigm.

Although some ID advocates were associated with forms of creation science prior to their affiliation with ID, the warrants for their arguments are not dependent on literal interpretations of biblical creation texts. ID is not concerned with defending a six thousand to ten thousand-year-old Earth. Intelligent design theorists willingly accept the standard scientific dates for the origin of Earth (four to five billion years) and of the universe (twelve to fifteen billion years).[13] Put simply, ID treats the initial chapters of Genesis neither as a scientific text nor as a basis upon which a science can (or must) be built. One might call ID advocates, therefore, "old Earth progressive creationists" whose conception of evolution does not exclude the purposeful intervention of God, the creator of the universe.

Aware that "creation science" promoters have very little credibility within the academy and intellectual circles more generally, ID from its inception has tried to bridge concerns of the educated elite (such as scientists, mathematicians, and persons with degrees in philosophy and law) and the interests of the broader American polis, of which seventy-five percent are at least nominally Christian. Interest in creating and sustaining such a bridge was evident in the Mere Creation Conference held at Biola University, in La Mirada, California, in November 1996.[14] At Johnson's invitation 180 persons, including scientists and scholars, attended and engaged one another in dialogue about their dissatisfaction with the broadly held assumption that evolution is a fact and beyond dispute.[15] A thread joining the wide variety of presentations given at the conference was that from a modest amount of data that supports evolution a grand theory has been created, negatively affecting American society.

Shortly after the Mere Creation Conference, a Center for the Renewal of Science and Culture (later shortened to the Center for Science and Culture) was added to the projects of the already existing Discovery Institute, which was undergoing a process of sharpening its focus on faith in public life.[16] Johnson served as the CRSC's first program advisor and continued his trajectory of rejecting Darwinian evolution because it involves chance mechanisms guided by natural selection.[17] Johnson points out that the establishment of Darwinian evolution in our public schools is "supposedly essential to the improvement of science education, which [he stresses] is in such a dismal state in America that national leaders are truly worried."[18] He further argues that this dismal state is to be expected, since science presents its theories as if they were facts. In Johnson's insistence that Darwinian evolution is merely "theory" and not worthy of the term "fact," he is in company with creation science advocates. His position reflects a popular but not a scientific understanding of these terms. As Eugenie C. Scott points out: "In science a theory is a logical construct of facts [empirical data/observational evidence], hypotheses and laws that explains a natural phenomenon. To the general public, however, a theory is not an explanation but a hunch or guess."[19] Darwinian evolution is a conceptual framework for logically making sense of a wide range of evidence. The "fact of evolution" is that organisms are related by common descent with modification resulting from natural selection.

Intelligent Design on Naturalism

Even more significant than his argument that Darwinian evolution is a mere theory is Johnson's insistence that Darwinian naturalism is identified with a "worldview abhorred by a large section of the American population" that believes in a creator God, either as directly creating discrete species or as guiding evolutionary processes.[20] Johnson has made naturalism's defeat his (and by extension the ID movement's) central objective. For Johnson naturalism rules out intervention or guidance of a creator outside the world of nature. "At most, naturalistic evolution is consistent with the existence of God only if by the term we mean no more than a first cause which retires from further activity after establishing the laws of nature and setting the natural mechanism in motion."[21] He further stresses that the problem with naturalism is that it functions as a worldview that takes a basic premise of natural science and "transforms it into a dogmatic statement about the nature of the universe."[22] For him this dogma is "scientism," which promotes the Godless naturalism/secularism that dominates intellectual life in America and puts theists always on the defensive.[23] To counteract naturalism, Johnson proposes "theistic realism," the term to name his conviction that "God is objectively real and not merely a concept."[24] Nature cannot be rightly understood without acknowledging that God is its creator.

Johnson's understanding of naturalism, however, is not without shortcomings. He speaks of it in inexact ways, referring to it as "speculative philosophy." He does not seem to recognize that "naturalism" is a complex term with multiple meanings. As the Dutch scholar Willem B. Drees notes, naturalism is both methodological and ontological. In the case of methodological naturalism, the emphasis is on what one can know from applying the empirical observational research methods of science. This type of naturalism is "epistemological." In contrast, "ontological naturalism" holds that the natural world is the whole of reality that we can know and interact with in the domain of science. It logically follows that ontological naturalism does not acknowledge a metaphysical or spiritual realm distinct from the natural world because such a realm cannot be known through scientific observation and experimentation. Drees notes that ontological naturalism can be reductive as well as non-reductive. Reductive ontological naturalism operates at the lowest level of physics; for example, protons attract electrons. Non-reductive ontological naturalism comes into play with respect to higher-level entities such as living organisms and their adaptation to a multifaceted environment. In contrast to physics, in biology it is not possible to isolate a single cause when one is addressing the evolution of a species in a complex ecosystem.[25]

Robert T. Pennock, a philosopher of science and a critic of ID, has argued that Johnson conflates the two major types of naturalism—methodological and ontological—and provides only misleading rhetoric, "which serves to polarize the debate [between intelligent design and Darwinian evolution] and undermine the possibility of peaceful co-existence between science and religion."[26] In his response to Pennock, Johnson argues that drawing attention to the distinction between methodological and ontological naturalism implies that Darwinists confine themselves to statements drawn from a naturalistic methodological starting point and refrain from statements of an ontological nature. To strengthen his case, Johnson cites Richard Dawkins, a Darwinist, to demonstrate that this is not the case.[27] Dawkins, who has written, "Darwin made it possible to be an intellectually fulfilled atheist,"[28] is one of Johnson's major foils in his argument that Darwinian evolution's naturalism is fundamentally atheistic.

Although ontological naturalism has been used to promote materialistic reductionism in arguments against the existence of God by Dawkins and others, Drees stresses that methodological naturalism and ontological naturalism, rightly conceived, are neutral where the question of God is concerned. From a methodological standpoint, God can never be a datum of scientific observation. However, ontological naturalism accepts that:

> Nature is, when considered at the level of causal interactions, complete, without religiously relevant holes. The natural world has an integrity which need not to be supplemented within its web of interactions. However, this integrity is not to be confused with self-sufficiency; it does not imply that the natural world owes its existence to itself or is self-explana-

tory. If a religious believer accepts naturalism as integrity, it is still possible to see God as the creator of this framework, the ground of its existence.[29]

Put simply, neither methodological naturalism nor ontological naturalism is necessarily atheistic. Because the neutrality of naturalism is not recognized by ID, Darwinian evolution is judged inimical to a theistic interpretation of the world.

Intelligent Design's Goals and Strategies

The broad and long-range goal of intelligent design, according to Thomas Woodward, is "the replacement of the current evolutionary paradigm with one that is open to both natural and intelligent causes in the history of biological origins."[30] ID advocates believe that for this goal to be achieved not only scientists but also the broader society, which has been influenced by Darwinian rhetoric, must be in its sights. To achieve the long-range goal of ID, the Discovery Institute's Center for [the Renewal of] Science and Culture undertook a two-pronged project and developed an action plan made available to the public in 1999 in a document informally known as the "Wedge Strategy."[31] The Wedge Strategy stated that the center's long-term goals were to create science that would lead to the "overthrow of materialism [naturalism] and its cultural legacies."[32] It further stressed that "Materialistic explanations [in science must be replaced] with the theistic understanding that nature and human beings are created by God."

Wedge is an apt metaphor for the Discovery Institute's project, according to Johnson, who writes: "If we view the predominant materialistic science [traceable to Darwin] as a giant tree, our strategy is intended to function as a 'wedge' that, while relatively small, can split the trunk when applied at its weakest points."[33] That weak point is science education in our nation's public schools. In the course of driving the wedge, Johnson envisions that a space will be made for our schools to "Teach the Controversy." The origin of this slogan is traceable to an amendment added by former Pennsylvania Senator Rick Santorum to President Bush's "No Child Left Behind Act" (a.k.a. "Re-authorized Elementary and Secondary Education Act, 2001"), a federal law that funds state education. The Santorum amendment states: "Where teaching scientific topics generates controversy [many see this as a veiled reference to biological evolution], the curriculum should help students to understand the full range of scientific views that exist [and] why such topics may generate controversy." The conclusion based on the ambiguous "full range of scientific views" reached by the Discovery Institute was that the controversy of Darwinism versus intelligent design could, perhaps even should, be part of science curricula in our nation's schools.

What is the outcome that ID promoters hope for? According to William Dembski, when "Teach the Controversy" is made part of the curricula of our schools, the American people will find ID to be an "instrument for liberation from suffocating ideologies."[34] Freedom from the suffocating ideology of naturalism and materialism can happen only if ID advocates can convince school boards to mandate that teachers present Darwinian evolution and intelligent design in science courses. Therefore, among its current campaigns is to get school boards to insist that evolution be taught from a critical perspective that draws attention to its inconsistencies and the gaps in its supportive evidence. The response of the major scientific organizations is that there is no controversy to teach. The over-arching theory of evolution that ID attacks is beyond debate. Such controversies that do exist concern merely the details of the evolutionary processes.

This brings us to the questions: Does intelligent design offer more than critiques of the naturalistic/materialistic character of Darwinian evolution? Has it presented a body of scientific research with the potential of future development? Although the Center for Science and Culture counts among its fellows scientists and mathematicians with advanced university degrees and experience as college and university professors, its research accomplishments are few. Scientific research questions tend to be very specific, but ID's contributions thus far have been broad and more of a popular nature. The call for renewal of science, by providing new boundaries for what can count as science, allowing room for the inclusion of causes and forces that lie outside the natural world, has not yet been supported by a program of research. Major scientific organizations have not failed to notice this. The American Association for the Advancement of Science's Board of Directors, in the midst of school boards debating whether ID should be taught in Ohio, made public its opposition to the inclusion of intelligent design theory in school curricula on the grounds that its central tenet does not meet the criteria of good science. Mandating the teaching of ID in our nation's schools would undermine the integrity of U.S. science education. Peter H. Raven, chairman of the AAAS Board of Directors and one of the world's leading botanists, has stressed that ID does not fulfill one of the major criteria for science: "Intelligent design theory has so far not been supported by peer-reviewed, published evidence."[35]

Nevertheless, CSC fellows such as Nancy Pearcey believe that ID as a new scientific-cultural movement "shows promise of winning a place in secular academia, while uniting Christians concerned about the role science plays in the current culture wars."[36] While the majority of the participants in the ID movement are Protestants (Johnson, for example, self-identifies as a Presbyterian), among the more noteworthy CSC fellows is Michael Behe, a Roman Catholic who wrote *Darwin's Black Box*. The desire to draw prominent Roman Catholics into ID's participation in the very public cultural war over America's "soul"[37] is evident in a development in the evolving ID story of July 2005. In a *New York Times* op-ed piece by Cardinal Christoph Schönborn of Vienna, entitled "Finding Design in Nature," [38] the cardinal wrote: "Evolution in the sense of common ancestry might be true, but evolution in the [neo-Darwinian] sense of an unguided, unplanned process of random variation and natural selection is not." He further argued that there was ample support for purpose and design in the universe: "The Catholic church, while leaving to science many details about the history of life on earth, proclaims that by the light of reason the human intellect can readily and clearly discern purpose and design in the natural world, including the world of living things."[39]

The cardinal further declared that Pope John Paul II's 1996 address to the Pontifical Academy of Sciences[40] on biological evolution was "rather vague and unimportant." In a follow-up interview, he indicated that he had spoken to Pope Benedict XVI (before his election as pope in April 2005) about his desire for the church to clarify its stance on evolution. He expressed the opinion that students should be taught that evolution is just one of many theories. However, he did make it clear that his positions had not been approved by the Vatican.[41] Judging by a July 2007 statement made by Benedict XVI about the debate between "so-called creationism and evolutionism," it is clear that he supports the position of his predecessor. Benedict called the apparent conflict an "absurdity." "Because on one hand there is a great deal of scientific proof in favor of evolution, which appears as a reality that we must see and that enriches our knowledge of life and of being as such. But the doctrine of evolution does not answer everything and does not answer the great philosophical question: Where does everything come from?"[42]

However, in 2005 statements on intelligent design by a cardinal who is a member of the Vatican's Congregation for Catholic Education, and who played a key role in the development of the official *Catechism of the Catholic Church*, could not be dismissed lightly. U. S. Catholic scholars specializing in theology and science presumed that as a member of the Dominican order, Cardinal Schönborn was associating intelligent design with Thomas Aquinas's so-called fifth "proof for the existence of God," in which Aquinas argued that since nature is ordered in accordance with a discernable purpose, it must be by a superior agent.[43] That the cardinal was involving himself in the controversy about intelligent design as a proposed new science to be taught to America's children backed by the Discovery Institute did not seem to be a reasonable assumption. This assumption, however, proved to be correct. Mark Ryland, a vice-president of the Discovery Institute, and an acquaintance of Cardinal Schönborn through the International Theological Institute in Austria, admitted in an interview that he urged the cardinal to write the op-ed piece in support of intelligent design.[44] Apparently Ryland had solicited the assistance of a cardinal, with impressive Roman Catholic credentials, to become a "point-man" in the Discovery Institute's goal of drawing Catholics (especially those with neo-conservative leanings) into the "public square" at a time when a court case in eastern Pennsylvania with ID as its focus was looming on the horizon.

A noteworthy member of the Pontifical Academy of Sciences, George Coyne, S.J., then the director of the Vatican Observatory, almost immediately challenged Schönborn's dismissive treatment of Pope John Paul II's 1996 address on biological evolution, arguing that science is and should be seen as completely neutral on the issue of the theistic or agnostic implications of its theories. Coyne responded to Cardinal Schönborn in an article that appeared in *The Tablet* of London a few weeks after *The New York Times* op-ed piece. In that article Coyne argued that the Cardinal's treatment of John Paul II's address on biological evolution as "rather vague and unimportant" was a mistake. He referred to the pope's address as an "epoch-making declaration" in which he affirmed

Catholic belief that "evolution is no longer a mere hypothesis and then proceeded, far from any thought of incompatibility, to draw reasonable implications for religious belief from that conclusion."[45] In another article that Coyne made available to the Catholic News Service, he offered an even stronger interpretation of the evolution message of John Paul II, stressing that the pope's position is "fundamental church teaching" and that, "based on the results of modern science and modern biblical scholarship, 'religious believers must move away from the notion of a dictator or designer God, a Newtonian God who made the universe as a watch that ticks along regularly.' "[46] Coyne went on to stress that the God of Christian faith is not a distant designer, but rather a personal and loving God.

Intelligent Design on Trial

The major headline-grabber since Cardinal Schönborn's public support of intelligent design has been the campaign to win support for ID waged by the school board of Dover, Pennsylvania. The plaintiffs filed their suit in October 2004; therefore, the case was already underway when the cardinal's op-ed article appeared in *The New York Times*. At issue was the local school board's policy that required biology teachers to read a statement before teaching the theory of evolution to ninth-grade students that drew the students' attention to "Intelligent Design as an explanation of the origin of life that differs from Darwin's view." Teachers were also directed to refer their students to *Of Pandas and People*, a textbook co-authored by Percival Davis and Dean H. Kenyon, a fellow of the CSC of the Discovery Institute.[47] This policy was challenged by parents of students who attended the local middle and high schools.[48]

On December 20th the presiding judge, John E. Jones III, a Republican appointed to the federal bench by President George W. Bush, argued in his ruling on the *Kitzmiller v. Dover* case that members of the Dover, Pennsylvania School Board, violated the Establishment Clause of the First Amendment of the U.S. Constitution and Art. I, §3 of the Constitution of the Commonwealth of Pennsylvania, which states that "no preference shall be given by law to any religious establishments or modes of worship." The judge found that the board's motives for including ID in the science curriculum in Dover's public schools were religious and not in the interest of improving science education.[49]

The Discovery Institute's web site includes this statement with reference to the Dover decision:

> In December, 2005, a federal trial judge in Pennsylvania made a controversial ruling that it would be unconstitutional to teach the theory of intelligent design in public school science class [sic]. However, the decision in that case, *Kitzmiller v. Dover Area School Board* (M.D. Penn. 2005), was never appealed to an appellate court. Beyond the actual parties to a lawsuit, trial opinions such as Kitzmiller do not have the force of law. Moreover, the decision in the Kitzmiller ruling was based upon evidence and characterizations of intelligent design that have been sharply contested by leading proponents of intelligent design.[50]

The Discovery Institute objects in particular to Judge Jones's view of ID as "essentially creationism." What it does not point out is the extensive research into the history of ID, including the writings of Johnson, especially his *Darwin on Trial*, which provided warrants for the judge to conclude that ID is the progeny of creationism (viz., creation science). ID disclaimers and textbooks were therefore deemed an inappropriate addition to the Dover high school curriculum. In his "Memorandum Opinion," Judge Jones notes that most of the arguments for ID are either negative attacks of Darwin's "gaps" or are based on subjective inference and not testable evidence.[51] He also found fault with the ID text book *On Pandas and People*, because it "distorts and misrepresents scientific knowledge in making its anti-evolution arguments."[52]

Discovery Institute fellows believe that the interpretations of the First Amendment (such as that by Jones and before him by Overton) have turned the intent of the amendment on its head to the detriment of our society, especially our children. According to ID supporters, despite efforts by some of the country's best lawyers to promote applications of the First Amendment that are respectful of the intent of the amendment at its creation, the courts continue to set the establishment and free exercise provisions at odds with each other, to the detriment of individual and institutional religious freedom. In these decisions, the federal Constitution's First Amendment clause that calls for the separation of church and state has been transformed from providing protection of religion from the control of the secular government into a rationale for the "non-establishment" of religion in America. They believe that court decisions against creation science sponsored Balanced Treatment Acts and their own Teach the Controversy initiative have gone beyond the intent of the First Amendment's "no establishment" of religion clause, which originally prohibited Congress from making any law respecting an establishment of religion for the nation or a state, thereby protecting religion from the intrusion of secular government. Now the "no establishment" clause is interpreted as mandating governmental neutrality not only between or among religions but also between religion and irreligion. As a result, the state cannot support religion in any manner. For neo-conservatives, First Amendment state and religion court decisions have contributed to the disestablishment in America of Christianity as a major contributor to the culture,[53] the public square.[54] The result is a tacit promotion of the establishment of secular humanism, thereby allowing its advocates to strengthen the influence of the ideology of "naturalism" in and through science education.

In reaction to "top-down" court decisions that seem to favor irreligious naturalism and secularism, intelligent design advocates are part of a larger "from-the-bottom-up" neo-conservative movement to create a post-secular polis in which evolution theory and its accompanying naturalism would not enjoy a position of unchallenged privilege under the guise of scientific neutrality.[55] It logically follows that a movement set on defeating naturalism would seek to counter secularism and its threat to the rational plausibility of Christian belief and to the role of Christian faith in public life. Although predictions by social scientists and intellectuals who argued that due to the hegemony of science, people would outgrow the need for and commitment to religion have been greatly exaggerated, supporters of the ID movement find in Darwinian evolution a major threat not only to the faith of individuals but also to the influence of Christian churches on American public life and culture.

Conclusion

Intelligent design and its enthusiastic support by a segment of evangelical Protestants and traditionalist Catholics bring into the public square dissatisfaction with naturalistic and materialistic depictions of reality, which they trace to Darwin. A library of books and articles, to say nothing of the 7,940,000 internet sites that a search yielded in November 2007, indicates that ID is getting the attention of the public. The literature either stresses the shortcomings of evolution and advocates for ID or proposes why intelligent design does not meet the criteria for what counts as science. Yet to dismiss intelligent design without attending to the deeper concerns of ID advocates is to miss a possible *kairos* moment that could result in deeper understanding.

Neuhaus and the Christian neo-conservatives associated with *First Things*, including Phillip Johnson and ID advocates, believe that the demands of religion and democracy in America require a wider circle of conversation. So far, the conversation regarding Darwinian naturalism and intelligent design has been debate-driven by imprecise and accusatory rhetoric. This rhetoric comes from both sides of the divide that separates ID not only from advocates of reductionistic naturalism, but also from scientists who have a religious commitment and from many Christians. Included in the latter group are two twenty-first century popes who do not regard Darwinian evolution to be a threat to belief in a creator God.

Conversation, in contrast to argument, is not confrontation and not debate. (It cannot be reduced to winning and losing.) To quote David Tracy: "It [conversation] is the questioning itself. It is the willingness to follow the question wherever it might go."[56] ID, beginning with Johnson, has consistently raised questions about the impact of naturalism on American culture. Granted that Johnson's treatment of naturalism lacks philosophical precision, what is at stake for him and for ID advocates as a whole is clear. If nature is a closed system of causes and effects, then all living beings, including ourselves, resulted from purposeless material processes. If naturalism has hegemony in the public square, then God is reduced to an idea that rose in the imaginations of our pre-scientific ancestors, which has outlived its time.[57] This of course is a big "if."

What we need in the public square is space to allow the questions worth exploring—questions of human meaning and the common good—to emerge so that together we can deal with the issues and corresponding dilemmas that a scientific and technological culture produces, while also resisting narrowly conceived negative judgments and solutions that impoverish the imagination and prevent us from embracing a sacramental naturalism that celebrates the presence of a non-interventionist God whose self gift to the world is life emerging from matter and evolving into newness.

Notes

[1]William A. Dembski, *Design Inference: Eliminating Chance through Small Probabilities* (Cambridge, MA/New York: Cambridge University Press, 1998), 36-66.

[2]Phillip E. Johnson, "Evolution as Dogma: The Establishment of Naturalism," [originally published in *First Things: the Journal of Religion, Culture and Public Life* 6 (1990), 15-22]; reprinted in *Intelligent Design Creationism and Its Critics: Philosophical, Theological and Scientific Perspectives*, ed. Robert T. Pennock (Cambridge, MA/London: A Bradford Book, MIT Press, 2001), 63.

[3]Richard John Neuhaus, *The Naked Public Square, Religion and Democracy in America* (Grand Rapids: Eerdmans, 1995 [1986]), 20.

[4]Phillip E. Johnson, *Darwin on Trial* (Washington, DC: Regnery Gateway, 1991), 3-14.

[5]Opinion of Judge William R. Overton, "McLean v. Arkansas Board of Education," in *Creationism, Science and the Law: The Arkansas Case*, ed. Marcel C. La Folette (Cambridge, MA: MIT Press, 1983), 60. For Johnson's critique of Overton's naturalism, see *Darwin on Trial*, 114-17.

[6]Italics mine. *Edwards v. Aguillard*, U.S. Supreme Court 482 U.S. 578 (1987); http://www.talkorigins.org/faqs/edwards-v-aguillard.html (updated November 6, 2005, accessed November 10, 2007).

[7]Johnson, *Darwin on Trial*, 17 (ID is presented as a replacement for Darwinian "purposeless natural processes"), 119, 146, 205 (in an endnote).

[8]F. C. S. Schiller, "Darwinism and Design Argument," in *Humanism: Philosophical Essays*, ed. F. C. S. Schiller (New York: Macmillan, 1903), 141.

[9]William Paley, *Natural Theology, Or Evidence of the Existence and Attributes of the Deity*, 12th ed. (London: J. Faulder, 1809), 456-57.

[10]William A. Dembski, "Introduction: What Intelligent Design Is Not," in *Signs of Intelligence: Understanding Intelligent Design*, ed. William A Dembski and James M. Kushiner (Grand Rapids: Brazos Press, 2001), 10.

[11]Johnson, *Darwin on Trial*, 116 and *passim*.

[12]The Young Earth Creation Science movement (Earth is 6,000 to 10,000 years old) was founded by Henry Morris and Duane Gish, who were instrumental in creating the Institute for Creation Research in 1970 in Santee, California. ICR channeled its energy into the promotion of the "balanced treatment" of Darwinian evolution and Creation Science in public schools. ICR was instrumental in "The Arkansas Balanced Treatment Act" and other similar pieces of legislation in other states, including Louisiana. The work of the ICR continues from new headquarters in Dallas, Texas. In 2007 an offshoot of ICR, the Bible Science Association, built a high tech Genesis Science museum, featuring YE creation science in Petersburg, Kentucky (near Cincinnati, Ohio).

[13]Two noteworthy ID advocates who are also Young Earth Creationists are Paul Nelson, editor of the ID newsletter "Origins and Designs," and Nancy

Pearcey, a popular ID speaker. See "Our 'Tailor-made' Universe: New Scientific Study Begs the Philosophical Question, 'Who's the Tailor'?" *World Magazine*, 15, no. 34 (2000), http://www.arn.org/docs/pearcey/ np_tailormade090200.htmat (accessed May 25, 2007).

[14]Eighteen Mere Creation Conference papers were published in William Dembski, ed., *Mere Creation* (Downers Grove, IL: InterVarsity Press, 1998). Highlights from the conference are available on the video entitled "Unlocking the Mystery of Life," produced by Illustra Media, 2002, and distributed by Focus on the Family (www.family.org).

[15]The consensus regarding the hegemony of biological evolution within the community of biologists is captured well in the words of Theodosius Dobzhansky: "Nothing in biology makes sense except in the light of evolution" (*The American Biology Teacher*, 35 [March 1973]: 127).

[16]The Discovery Institute originated in 1983 as a Seattle branch of the Hudson Institute (then headquartered in Indianapolis). One of the founders was Bruce Chapman, director of the Census Bureau during the Reagan administration and also an assistant to Reagan advisor Edwin Meese. In 2005 Chapman was president of the Discovery Institute and described ID as the Institute's "No. 1 project." See Chris Mooney, "Inferior Design," *American Prospect Online*, August 10, 2005, http://chem.tufts.edu/AnswersInScience/ Mooney2005-InferiorDesign.htmrom.

[17]Johnson, *Darwin on Trial*, 4.

[18]Johnson, "Evolution as Dogma," 75. Johnson provides no statistics to support his claim. But a recent study of scientific literacy in the United States by Liza Gross concluded that between 1979 and 2006, the proportion of scientifically literate adults has doubled—to a paltry 17 percent. Gross attributes this low percentage to Americans' ambivalence about science, which centers primarily around religion (Liza Gross, "Scientific Illiteracy and the Partisan Takeover of Biology," *Public Library of Science—Biology* [April 18, 2006], http://biology.plosjournals.org/perlserv/?request=get-document&doi=10.1371/journal.pbio.0040167.

[19]Eugenie C. Scott, "Antievolution and Creationism in the United States," *Annual Review of Anthropology* 26 (1997), 278. Scott is the executive director of the National Center for Science Education.

[20]Johnson, "Evolution as Dogma," 69. In this context Johnson cites a 1982 Gallup Poll that indicated that "Only 9 percent identified themselves as believers in a naturalistic evolutionary process not guided by God." In response to Johnson one might argue that the validity of a scientific theory is not dependent on polls, but on evidence. The fact that many Americans are confused about evolution indicates that science education is lacking in quality and not necessarily that evolution is invalid as a scientific theory.

[21]Johnson, "Evolution as Dogma," 64.

[22]Ibid., 72.

[23]Phillip E. Johnson, *Reason in the Balance: The Case Against Naturalism in Science, Law and Education* (Downers Grove, IL: InterVarsity Press, 1995), 8-9 and *passim*.

[24]Ibid.

[25]Willem B. Drees, "Evolutionary Naturalism and Religion," in *Evolutionary and Molecular Biology: Scientific Perspectives on Divine Action*, ed. Robert John Russell, William R. Stoeger, S.J., and Francisco J. Ayala (Vatican City State: Vatican Observatory Foundation, 1998), 306-10.

[26]Robert T. Pennock, "Naturalism, Evidence and Creationism: The Case of Phillip Johnson," in *Intelligent Design Creationism and Its Critics*, 78.

[27]Johnson, "Response to Pennock," *Intelligent Design Creationism and Its Critics: Philosophical, Theological and Scientific Perspectives*, ed. Robert T. Pennock (Cambridge, MA/London: A Bradford Book, MIT Press, 2001), 99.

[28]Richard Dawkins, *The Blind Watchmaker: Why the Evidence of Evolution Reveals a Universe without Design* (New York: W. W. Norton, 1986), 6. Johnson often argues against Dawkins, a former Anglican, who has taught biology at the University of California, Berkeley, and Oxford and has written non-technical science books for the general public that have as their purpose the promotion of an atheistic agenda. In addition to *The Blind Watchmaker*, Dawkins has written *Why the Evidence of Evolution Reveals a Universe Without Design*; *The God Delusion*; and *God, the Devil, and Darwin: A Critique of Intelligent Design Theory*.

[29]Drees, "Evolutionary Naturalism and Religion," 311.

[30]Thomas Woodward, *Doubt about Darwin: A History of Intelligent Design* (Grand Rapids: Baker Books, 2003), 28.

[31]The title of this CRSC strategy, actually a five-year plan, can be traced to Phillip Johnson's critique of Darwinism in *Darwinism on Trial* (1991). The Wedge document is available from http://www.livescience.com/humanbiology/050922 _ID_main.html.

[32]The general concept of the "Wedge" is described in Phillip Johnson's book *Defeating Darwinism by Opening Minds* (1997), 91-92, with further development in his *The Wedge of Truth: Splitting the Foundations of Naturalism* (Downers Grove, IL: InterVarsity Press, 2000). For critical appraisals of the Wedge Strategy see Robert T. Pennock, "Intelligent Design Creationism's 'Wedge Strategy,'" and Barbara Forrest, "The Wedge at Work: How Intelligent Design Creationism Is Wedging Its Way into the Cultural and Academic Mainstream," in *Intelligent Design Creationism and Its Critics*, 1-3 and 5-53, respectively.

[33]From the Wedge document by James Still in "Discovery Institute's 'Wedge Project' Circulates Online" (posted in 1999), http://www.infidels.org/secular_web/feature/1999/wedge.html (accessed May 22, 2007).

[34]William A. Dembski, "Becoming a Disciplined Science: Prospects, Pitfalls, and Reality Check for ID," a lecture given at the International Society for Complexity, Information & Design, on October 28, 2002, http://www.discovery.org/viewDB/index.php3?program=CRSC&command=view&id =1288 (accessed May 20, 2007); see full text at: http://iscid.org/papers/Dembski_DisciplinedScience_102802.pdf.

[35]"AAAS Urges Opposition to 'Intelligent Design Theory' within U.S. Science Classes," American Association for the Advancement of Science

"policy alert" with Board resolution (posted June 11, 2002); http://www.aaas. org/news/releases/2002/1106id2.shtml (accessed May 22, 2006). Of related interest at the same site is a longer excerpt of a statement by Peter H. Raven:

The ID movement argues that random mutation in nature and natural selection can't explain the diversity of life forms or their complexity and that these things may be explained only by an extra-natural intelligent agent. . . . This is an interesting philosophical or theological concept, and some people have strong feelings about it. Unfortunately, it's being put forth as a scientifically based alternative to the theory of biological evolution. Intelligent design theory has so far not been supported by peer-reviewed, published evidence.

[36]Nancy Pearcey, "Opening the 'Big Tent' in Science: The New Design Movement," Access Research Network, http://arn.org/docs/pearcey/np_bigtent30q97.htm (accessed May 22, 2006) (originally published as "The Evolution Backlash," World [March 1997], http://www.worldmag.com/world/issue/03-01-97/cover_1.asp).

[37]The current culture war may be traced to the emergence of the so-called "moral majority" in the early 1980s.

[38]Cardinal Christoph Schönborn, "Finding Design in Nature," The New York Times (July 7, 2005), http://www.nytimes.com/2005/07/07/opinion/07schonborn.html?ex=1278388800&en=95804823e49fb832&ei=5088&partner=rssnyt&emc=rss (accessed May 26, 2007).

[39]Ibid.

[40]Pope John Paul II, "Message to the Pontifical Academy of Sciences on Evolution," Origins 26 (November 14, 1996), 350-352.

[41]Cornella Dean and Laurie Goodstein, "Leading Cardinal Redefines Church's View on Evolution," July 9, 2005, at "Cardinal Creates Controversy," National Center for Science Education, http://www.nytimes.com/2005/07/09/science/09cardinal.html?ex=1278561600&en=0c18381d982e5e77&ei=5090&partner=rssuserland&emc=rss (accessed May 22, 2007); Ian Fisher, citing Pope Benedict XVI, in "About Creation, Pope Melds Faith with Science," New York Times, July 27, 2007, http://topics.nytimes.com/top/news/science/topics/evolution/index.html?query=BENEDICT%20XVI&field=per&match=exact (accessed October 26, 2007).

[42]"Pontiff: Evolution Does Not Exclude a Creator," Zenit.org (July 27, 2007) (accessed November 11, 2007, from http://www.zenit.org/article-20238?l=english).

[43]Thomas Aquinas's fifth demonstration of the rationality of theistic faith in Question 2, Article 3 of the Summa Theologiae I-I is often reduced to a syllogism succinctly stated: Wherever complex design exists, there must have been a designer; nature is complex, therefore, nature must have had an intelligent designer. For Aquinas, this designer was, of course, God, whom Aquinas later identifies as the triune God of Christian revelation.

[44]Mark Ryland said in an interview that he had urged the cardinal to write the essay to clarify the church's position on evolution. The cardinal's essay was submitted to The New York Times by a Virginia public relations firm,

Creative Response Concepts, which also represents the Discovery Institute (Cornelia Dean and Laurie Goodstein, "Leading Cardinal Redefines Church's View on Evolution," *The New York Times*, July 9, 2005, http://www.nytimes.com/2005/07/09/science/09cardinal.html?ex=1278561600& en=0c18381d982e5e77&ei=5090&partner=rssuserland&emc=rss [accessed May 22, 2007]).

[45]George V. Coyne, "God's Chance Creation," *The Tablet*, August 6, 2005, http://www.thetablet.co.uk/articles/1027/ (accessed May 20, 2007).

[46]Catholic News Service [no author given], "Vatican Astronomer Says Evolution Important for Insights into God," posted August 5, 2005, available from http://www.catholicnews.com/data/stories/cns/0504505.htm (accessed May 20, 2007). Five months later, in an interview by Mark Lombard, Coyne stressed that the God of intelligent design is not the God of love revealed by Jesus Christ. See "Intelligent Design Belittles God, Vatican Director Says" (January 30, 2006), http://www.catholic.org/national/national_story.php?id=18503 (cited May 22, 2007).

[47]Percival Davis and Dean H. Kenyon, *Of Pandas and People*, 2nd ed. (Richardson, TX: Foundation for Thought & Ethics, 1993). The first edition speaks of creation science, but the second does not; its focus is intelligent design. Kenyon, a major contributor to ID since the 1996 Mere Creation Conference, coined the term "biochemical predestination" and co-authored a book by that title with Gary Steinman.

[48]The plaintiffs filed a suit challenging the constitutionality of the school board's ID initiative on October 18, 2004; the court case commenced on September 26, 2005. Judge John E. Jones, III, "Memorandum Opinion" for Case 4:04-cv-02688-JEJ, Document 342, filed 12/20/2005, page 2 of 139 (posted December 20, 2005), http://www.pamd.uscourts.gov/kitzmiller/kitzmiller_342.pdf (accessed May 24, 2007).

[49]Associated Press, "Dover ID Case Decided," MSNBC, December 20, 2005, http://www.msnbc.msn.com/id/10545387/ (accessed May 24, 2007).

[50]David K. DeWolf, J.D. and Seth L. Cooper, J.D., "Teaching about Evolution in the Public Schools: A Short Summary of the Law," posted June 20, 2006, http://www.discovery.org/scripts/viewDB/index.php?command=view&id=2543&program=CSC%20-%20Science%20and%20Education%20Policy%20-%20Legal%20Resources (accessed May 25, 2007).

[51]Judge Jones, "Memorandum Opinion" for Case 4:04-cv-02688-JEJ, Document 342, filed 12/20/2005, 81-83.

[52]Judge Jones, "Memorandum Opinion," 84.

[53]This is a major argument in Stephen L. Carter, *The Culture of Disbelief: How American Law and Politics Trivialize Religious Devotion* (New York: Basic Books/HarperCollins, 2003), 105-210.

[54]Richard Neuhaus, *The Naked Public Square* (Grand Rapids: Eerdmans, 1984), *passim*.

[55]This is evident in the goals of the Discovery Institute's Wedge document, especially Phase II, which calls for influencing the popular media, including the Public Broadcasting Service, alongside building a popular base among

Christians, "their natural constituency," and Phase III, which proposes legal assistance in response to the integration of design theory into public school science curricula, in order to draw scientific materialists into open debate with design theorists (http://www.antievolution.org/features/wedge.pdf [accessed November 9, 2007]).

[56]David Tracy, *Plurality and Ambiguity: Hermeneutics, Religion, Hope* (San Francisco: HarperSanFrancisco, 1987), 18.

[57]Johnson, *Reason in the Balance*, 40.

Part III

BROADENING THE HORIZONS

Jus Post Bellum

Extending the Just War Theory

Mark J. Allman and Tobias L. Winright

In *The Wake of War: Encounters with the People of Iraq and Afghanistan*, French journalist Anne Nivat explores what is happening on the ground in the aftermath of the U.S. military "victories" (the scare quotes are hers) in Afghanistan and Iraq. Instead of imbedding herself with the occupying troops, she spent twelve weeks in each country, in remote villages as well as major cities, dressing like the ordinary people, traveling by taxi, and being welcomed into homes for meals and candid conversation. Many persons told her that each invasion had "long-term consequences that are hard to make sense of."[1] Concerns were expressed about a number of postwar problems, including lack of security, increased sectarian violence, destroyed vital infrastructure, widespread corruption, and insufficient reconstruction efforts. "The people of Iraq and Afghanistan," Nivat writes, "have difficulty understanding that such is the price of 'liberation.'"[2]

How should people of faith respond to what is going on in the so-called post-conflict phases in Afghanistan and Iraq? Every four years since 1976, the United States Conference of Catholic Bishops has issued a statement having to do with faith in public life. In their 2003 statement, *Faithful Citizenship: A Catholic Call to Political Responsibility*, the bishops call on Catholics to "bring our moral convictions to public life" and to "apply Catholic principles in the public square."[3] While the bishops identify a number of "fundamental questions of life and death," the issue of war is highlighted in several places, including "international responsibilities in the aftermath of war" and the promotion of "post-conflict reconstruction and reconciliation." Thus the present situation that Nivat describes in Afghanistan and Iraq involves moral concerns that the bishops say warrant the application of Catholic moral principles in the wider public discussion about what ought to be done.

For this reason, in "Toward a Responsible Transition in Iraq," a statement released on January 12, 2006, Bishop Thomas G. Wenski writes, "It is important for all to recognize that addressing questions regarding the decisions that led us to war, and about the conduct of war and its aftermath, is both necessary and patriotic."[4] Here he alludes to the primary overarching categories of the just war tradition, which has long been the gold standard for the ethical evaluation of war. The first category, *jus ad bellum*, addresses decisions that lead to war and includes several criteria: just cause, legitimate authority, right intent, proportionality, probability of success, and last resort. The second category, *jus in bello*, addresses ethical behavior in combat and includes two criteria: non-combatant immunity and proportionate use of force. In most of the tradition, these were the only two major categories of just war principles. However, as evident in Bishop Wenski's statement, attention is now beginning to be given to what justice requires in the wake of war, that is, *jus post bellum*.

The just war tradition, according to British ethicist Charles Reed, "represents a public theology, grounded in Western culture and shaped by historical experience, which provides churches, as one of many actors, with a legitimate public space in which to reflect deeply on the ethics of war."[5] Here Reed highlights the way that the tradition's principles are invoked in the public square by church leaders. This approach is evident in the statement by Bishop Wenski, and it is characteristic of most statements by the United States Conference of Catholic Bishops aimed at communicating with not only the church, which is the bishops' first audience, but the wider society.[6]

Reed also notes that just war is a *living* tradition, developing over the centuries *via* a dynamic intermingling of historical experience and culture, with Christian theological reflection contributing significantly to this nexus. Yet, interestingly, one of the criticisms levied against just war theory is that it lacks "historical thickness."[7] It tends to ignore the larger historical context (namely, the decades preceding the war) and instead looks only to the period immediately prior to conflict. Postwar situations like those in Iraq and Afghanistan highlight the fact that this charge of "lacking historical thickness" now extends into the future, as well. This is not to suggest that the just war tradition has been completely blind to postwar ethics. For centuries, military strategists have talked about exit strategies. Ancient religious versions of the theory prohibit poisoning wells, salting fields, and cutting down fruit and olive trees because such actions extend the effects of war well beyond the period of active combat.[8] Others like Cicero, Augustine, Grotius, Suarez, and Kant have also addressed postwar ethics, but only in passing and not with the same degree of systematic detail that the *jus ad bellum* and *jus in bello* categories enjoy.

Little more than a decade ago, in a brief article appearing in *The Christian Century*, theologian Michael Schuck pointed out this lacuna in the just war tradition.[9] Since then, mostly philosophers, political scientists, and military scientists have treated this neglected dimension of just war, while bishops and theologians have largely been silent on the issue. This essay draws on the nascent literature on postwar ethics that is developing in a variety of disciplines in an attempt to offer a more systematic analysis of *post bellum* ethics. We also hope to answer the bishops' invitation to contribute to the conversation about what a responsible transition in Iraq and Afghanistan might look like. To these dual ends we propose four *jus post bellum* criteria that complement the *jus ad bellum* and *jus in bello* categories of the just war theory: just cause, reconciliation, punishment, and rehabilitation. Postwar ethics are a natural extension of, and share some commonalities with, the *ad bellum* and *in bello* categories. A formal and systematic set of *jus post bellum* criteria is essential to the future of the just war tradition, especially if Catholics are going to contribute to the public discussion about what to do in the wake of wars such as in Afghanistan and Iraq.

The Just Cause Principle

Centuries ago Augustine noted that the *telos* of a just war is not simply victory on the battlefield, but the *tranquillitas ordinis*, the tranquility that comes from order, in other words, a just and lasting peace. Classical just war theory identifies self-defense, defense of human rights (for example, humanitarian intervention), restitution (regaining what was wrongfully taken), redress (taking possession of what is wrongfully withheld), and legitimate punishment as the only "just causes" for going to war.[10] It follows that the end of any just war must be the accomplishment of the objectives that served as the grounds for "just cause" in the *ad bellum* phase.[11] Moreover, satisfying the just cause demands is different from returning to the *status quo ante bellum*. As Michael Walzer notes, the *status quo* before the war is precisely what leads to war in the first place.[12] The goal of a just war must be to establish social, political, and economic conditions that are substantially more stable, more just, and less prone to chaos than what existed prior to the fighting.

The just cause principle has three primary objectives. First, it holds the party claiming to fight a just war accountable. It requires that party to complete the objectives that were identified as the legitimate reasons for going to war in the first place. As Gary Bass observes:

> *Jus post bellum* is connected with *jus ad bellum* . . . in that the declared ends that justify a war—whether stopping genocide or preventing aggression—impose obligations on belligerent powers to try, even after the conclusion of the war, to bring about the desired outcome. If a state wages war to remove a genocidal regime, but then leaves the conquered country awash with weapons and grievances, and without a security apparatus, then it may relinquish by its postwar actions the justice it might otherwise have claimed in waging the war.[13]

This principle makes parties claiming to fight for a just cause stay the course until the mission is accomplished.

In the U.S. invasion of Iraq some of the reasons cited under this principle were: to liberate the people of Iraq from a violent dictator, to eradicate a safe haven for global terrorists, and to bring democracy and stability to the Middle East. However, as the cost of the war in terms of dollars and lives mounted, popular support for the war evaporated and Americans began calling for a pullout. To do so, though, would be a direct violation of this principle. The supposed "just cause" has not been accomplished. Iraq is in a state of anarchy and the region is more unstable. The U.S. has a *post bellum* responsibility to provide security until it has accomplished the mission(s) it claimed as its objective(s). Furthermore, considering that bringing democracy and regime change are dubious just causes from an *ad bellum* perspective in the first place, this only makes the *post bellum* responsibilities that much greater.

In short, the U.S.'s *post bellum* responsibilities under the just cause principle demand greater U.S. involvement in Iraq—until it can finance and support a responsible transition to the Iraqis or an international third party—regardless of the cost to the U.S. in terms of dollars or U.S. soldiers' lives.

Second, this principle restrains parties from seeking additional gains. To go beyond what was identified as the just cause would be an act of aggression. The just cause principle prohibits shifting rationales for going to war after the conflict has begun. Once a nation has achieved its declared mission, the conflict must end. For example, let us assume (for the sake of illustration) the 1991 Gulf War met the *jus ad bellum* criteria. President George H. Bush was criticized for not marching to Baghdad once the Iraqi forces were driven beyond the Kuwaiti border. The allied forces had the advantage and it is reasonably assumed they could have toppled the Hussein regime. However, to do so would have been rightly condemned as an act of aggression because the rights of the Kuwaiti people (the just cause of the war) had been vindicated. Any additional gains would be unjust.

Third, this principle seeks to ensure proportional (meaning measured and restrained) *post bellum* behavior by the victors. As philosopher Brian Orend (a principal architect of *post bellum* ethics) observes, it prevents "war from spilling over into something like a crusade, which demands the utter destruction of the demonized enemy. The very essence of justice in and after war is about there being firm limits and constraints upon its aims and conduct."[14] A proportionate *post bellum* response only accomplishes the just cause it seeks; it does not go beyond its declared objectives, and it constrains zealotry.

The practical implications of the just cause principle are clear. Any unjust gains made during war (such as through acquisition of land, capital, and war booty, or seizure of financial assets or natural resources) must be returned to their original owners. And an unconditional surrender cannot be made a provision of ending the conflict because it violates the demands of proportionality.[15] In short, the just cause principle acts as a tenet of restraint and accountability. The remaining criteria of *jus post bellum* ethics are the natural consequences of the just cause principle and are best characterized as phases in that they are not only moral principles, but also include concrete steps necessary for achieving *jus post bellum*.

The Reconciliation Phase

If the primary objective of a just war is a just and lasting peace, then there can be no peace without reconciliation. The goal of reconciliation is to transform a relationship of animosity, fear, and hatred into one of tolerance, if not respect; to turn enemies into friends and to bring emotional healing to the victims of war. There is a parallel between the sacrament of reconciliation and *jus post bellum* reconciliation.[16] The reconciliation phase contains the basic elements of the sacrament of reconciliation: admission of guilt, absolution, penance, and the return of the offending party to full communion. The goal of reconciliation, be it sacramental or *jus post bellum*, is justice tempered by mercy.

Davida Kellogg and others object to making reconciliation an aim of the *post bellum* phase. Seeking or forcing reconciliation, they argue, trivializes the brutality of war by reducing the crimes of war to an area of disputation and fails to recognize war as a violent crime. Forcing or even pressuring the victims of war to reconcile with their perpetrators is akin to expecting the rape victim to forgive her rapist. "It is the height of presumption" to imagine that victims of the crime of aggression and of war crimes should ever forgive their attackers.[17] Instead, they argue, prevention should be the primary aim of *post bellum* ethics.

Such detractors operate out of an impoverished understanding of reconciliation, seeing it primarily as a "forgive and forget" approach, whereas a richer understanding of reconciliation demands acknowledgment of guilt, reparations (penance), and only then absolution. If, as Kellogg admits, the purpose of a just war and in particular of the *jus post bellum* phase is "the establishment of a lasting peace," then the need for reconciliation is paramount, lest the punishment phase be nothing more than retribution. They also fall into a dualist trap, seeing the choice as reconciliation or prevention, as opposed to reconciliation and prevention. While reconciliation might seem a lofty ideal, the relationships between the Allied Forces of World War II and Germany, Italy, and Japan reveal that adversarial relationships can be reconciled in a relatively short period of time. The success of truth and reconciliation commissions, such as those used in South Africa and Guatemala, provides further evidence of the power of admission of guilt, apology and forgiveness.[18] Practically speaking, the reconciliatory aims can be attended to by paying attention to three key areas: cease-fire agreements, postwar celebrations, and postwar settlement processes coupled with apologies.

Typically the *post bellum* phase begins with a cease-fire agreement, an armistice, or surrender. Rear Admiral Louis Iasiello stresses the importance of an honorable surrender in creating "a healing mind-set." The surrender of the Confederate Army at the end of the U.S. Civil War serves as the paradigm of honorable surrender. Union soldiers, at the command of General Grant, extended military courtesies including a marching salute to their defeated former enemy. Grant acknowledged the reconciliatory aim of the *post bellum* phase when he said to his troops, "Gentlemen, the war is over; the rebels are our countrymen again."[19]

Restraint in postwar celebrations can also contribute to the reconciliatory aims of this phase. Plato warned that constructing monuments to victors can harden the hearts of the vanquished.[20] Michael Schuck makes a similar observation.[21] It is normal to celebrate the end of the war and the return of soldiers; however, when victors celebrate not only the end of the war but the defeat of their enemy as well, they fail to recognize the moral and nonmoral evils that accompany all war, including just wars. Postwar victory celebrations that laud the killing of others gloss over how the death of an enemy—even though the killing may have been justified—involves a (non-moral) evil, meaning that a creature of God now lacks being and no longer exists. Celebrating the return of soldiers is understandable, but to rejoice in the defeat of enemies turns killing itself into a good. Instead of celebrating the defeat of the enemy, the honorable behavior, valorous acts, and sacrifices made by all sides need to be respected and honored. The little good that can be found in war needs to be publicly acknowledged so all sides might come to see that their former enemy includes decent, kind, brave, and virtuous people.[22]

In order to blunt the pernicious effects of rumor, to quell seething resentments, and to ensure that peace agreements enjoy popular support, the postwar settlement process must be as public and transparent as possible and negotiated by parties widely recognized as having the authority to do so. Victors in battle ought not to assume that they, by virtue of victory, are the most competent authority to negotiate postwar settlements. To prevent settlements from appearing excessively punitive or vindictive it is better for independent authorities (such as international bodies like the UN,

NATO, the European Union, the African Union, or a third party state) to negotiate the postwar settlement process.

If the primary goal of a just war is a just and lasting peace, and if the primary goal of the reconciliation phase is to transform adversarial relationships into ones of respect, trust and ultimately friendship, then a formal apology is a necessary condition of the settlement process. Just as there can be no forgiveness without an admission of guilt, so too, formerly warring parties cannot reconcile without admissions of wrongdoing. Obviously, the unjust aggressor needs to apologize for the crime of aggression and for any offenses committed *in bello*; likewise the victors ought to apologize for any crimes, offenses, and insensitivities shown in the course of the conflict. Admissions of guilt are not the same as admissions of criminal activity, which must be punished. Admissions of guilt at this phase can be broadly construed, saving the prosecution of specific war crimes and the details of compensation agreements for the punishment phase. Mutual admissions of guilt are a necessary first step and augment the long-term healing process of reconciliation.

The Punishment Phase

While reconciliation aims at rebuilding relationships, the punishment phase's primary objectives are justice, accountability, and restitution. The legitimacy of punishments depends on: publicity and transparency (for example, punishments ought to be meted out *via* public forums to which many, if not all, have access), proportionality and discrimination (appropriate punitive measures ought not be excessively debilitating and must make distinctions based on level of command and culpability), and competent authority (such as assigned by an authority recognized as legitimate by all sides). In all likelihood, the legitimacy of the punishment phase depends on an independent authority in order to avoid even the appearance of victors acting as judge, jury, and executioner of the vanquished. The punishment phase comprises two principal parts: compensation and war crimes trials.

Compensation

Restitution is a demand of justice. The unjust aggressor owes compensation to the victim. However, the most contentious issues regarding restitution concern proportionality and discrimination ("How much and to whom?"). There is no calculus to determine what an unjust aggressor owes the victim of its crime. It is relative to the nature and severity of the crime and to the ability of the aggressor to pay.[23]

As the example of the Treaty of Versailles aptly illustrates, compensation agreements that cripple aggressors so severely that they never return to a functioning civil society only sow seeds of resentment. Compensation agreements need to be proportional: enough to make restitution more than a token gesture and enough to serve as a penalty that satisfies (at least in part) the victims of the crime, but not so severe that the vanquished can never recover. Bass rightly points out that reparations have their limits, "Economic reconstruction can only do so much," and no sum of money can compensate for death of a loved one or for rape and torture; as such, "reparations should be compensatory, not vindictive."[24]

Concerning who ought to pay, due care needs to be exercised to ensure that the civilian population of the unjust aggressor nation does not bear the burden of decisions made by political and military leaders over which they had no control. Walzer and Orend agree that the political and military elite of the unjust aggressor nation bear the primary responsibilities of compensation and that the personal wealth of the architects of the aggression should be seized in order to compensate the victims of their crime. Walzer, however, argues if the private wealth of these architects is not enough, then it is legitimate to tax the population of the aggressor nation. He considers postwar taxes on the populace of the aggressor the price for maintaining national sovereignty. Bass rightly expands the list of who ought to pay to include the profiteers of an unjust war.[25] Orend disagrees with Walzer: "Respect for discrimination entails taking a reasonable amount of compensation only from those sources that can afford it *and* that were materially linked to the aggression in a morally culpable way."[26] For Orend, taxing the populace amounts to guilt by association.

Walzer also questions whether the personal wealth of the architects of aggression could ever be enough to serve as legitimate reparation. Orend responds by noting that frequently these architects of aggression are tyrants who have amassed small fortunes. Orend, however, fails to take into account that the personal wealth of tyrants is often unjustly acquired (such as the misappropriation of development funds, bribes, illegal activities, and so on), which is properly owed not to the victims of the aggression but to the victims of the tyrant's theft and other illegal activities. Paying the victims of a tyrant's aggression with wealth stolen from other victims of the tyrant's bad behavior is tantamount to making one victim pay another victim.

Trade is an additional source of revenue that could compensate the victims of the aggression but has been largely ignored. Trade agreements that are deliberately favorable for the victims of aggression (such as no tariffs for goods flowing from the victim nation to the aggressor and higher, but non-crippling, tariffs for goods flowing from the aggressor nation to the victim) can be sources of tremendous revenue and hasten postwar reconstruction efforts. While tariffs on goods are still a form of taxation, tariffs are less direct than postwar taxes on the populace.[27] Other constituents (such as ally nations of the victims and the aggressor, other regional parties, and international trade organizations) could also establish short-term favorable trade policies that help the victims recover. Trade has the added benefit of being relational and potentially reconciliatory. Nations that cooperate with each other through trade are more likely to eventually see their former enemy as a new partner because they share common economic interests.

The motivating principles behind compensation are restitution (returning whatever one has unjustly seized and paying for what one has unjustly destroyed) and the practical concern that war, just like any other crime, ought not to pay.[28] While reparations have a notorious history, they can serve as a powerful disincentive for aggression. By forcing the architects and profiteers of unjust aggressions to compensate their victims and by constructing reparation agreements in a way that does not unduly burden those who were not "materially linked to the aggression in a morally culpable way," the crime of aggression can, in part, be properly punished and effectively discouraged in the future.

War Crimes Trials

If war always involves crimes, then the perpetrators must be brought to justice. War crimes trials are an essential and long-standing component to postwar justice, for without them, the just war theory is a dog without teeth. In short, war crimes trials are about accountability. Typically, war crimes fall into two categories: *jus ad bellum* crimes and *jus in bello* crimes.

Jus ad bellum crimes include unjust aggression or what Nuremburg prosecutors called, "crimes against peace," such as "planning, preparing, initiating and waging" a war of aggression, genocide, and crimes against humanity.[29] *Jus ad bellum* war crimes trials are essential to postwar justice because they "strip away the veneer of statehood to reveal human beings making choices."[30] States (like corporations) do not commit crimes. People acting in the name of the state make decisions, give orders, and act in ways that are criminal. As such, the architects of unjust aggression ought to bear the greatest punishment. Prosecution of *jus ad bellum* crimes must discern (discriminate between) those who orchestrated the crimes from those who carried them out, from those who were mere pawns.

In theory, all crimes of unjust aggression ought to be vigorously prosecuted. Failure to prosecute war crimes is a form of passive endorsement and violates the just cause principle.[31] Yet a dose of realism is needed to temper this idealism. Sometimes perfect justice must be sacrificed on the altar of peace. War is frequently ended by negotiating with the architects of the unjust aggression who often demand immunity as part of the peace settlement. Such compromises, while imperfect, are a proportionate response because without immunity the architects of the aggression have no incentive to seek an end to the conflict and may prolong the violence in the hope of victory. If the aim of a just war is peace, then granting immunity along with other conditions may in fact be the best solution. "But," as Bass stipulates, "the fact that sometimes one must reluctantly sell out justice for the sake of peace does not mean that there should never be justice."[32] In contradiction to the adage, "Justice delayed is justice denied," sometimes war criminals must be engaged and prosecution of their crimes *delayed* in the name of the greater good, peace. Nevertheless, the crimes ought not be ignored or excused. Making a deal with the devil is not the same as excusing the devil's behavior.

Jus in bello crimes include such acts as disproportionate uses of force, failure to discriminate between soldiers and civilians, or engaging in inherently immoral acts (rape, torture, using civilians or POWs as shields, and so on). On a practical level prosecution and punishment of *in bello* war criminals is necessary for *post bellum* justice simply because it "gets the thugs off the streets." It is also a basic demand of justice. The principal architects of these war crimes bear the greatest responsibility, especially the military, police, paramilitary, and political leaders who ordered the crimes and those soldiers who committed them. Commanding officers, by virtue of their rank, experience, and training should be held to a higher level of responsibility than lower-ranking soldiers in the field.[33]

In the postwar period, victors face the temptation to prosecute only *jus ad bellum* crimes, thereby avoiding the ugly reality that all sides commit crimes *in bello*. In order to avoid claims of victor's justice, the prosecution of all war crimes is best left to an independent third party (such as international war crimes tribunals or a third party state). *Post bellum* justice must not simply execute justice, but be publicly acknowledged as independent and free of prejudice.

Again the just war theory's lack of robust *jus post bellum* criteria is evident. While most scholars and jurists readily identify *jus ad bellum* and *jus in bello* crimes, none identify *jus post bellum* crimes. If there are *ad bellum* and *in bello* crimes, then there must also be *post bellum* crimes. While space does not permit a lengthy exploration of types of *post bellum* crimes, it is safe to say that failures to meet *post bellum* responsibilities as delineated throughout this essay ought to be codified and ratified by the international community in a manner similar to what *ad bellum* and *in bello* crimes currently enjoy. War leaves a wake of destruction. It wreaks havoc on people, cultures, the environment, and the social, political, and economic infrastructure. Those that engage in war must be held responsible for the effects of their actions.

The Restoration Phase

Recalling that the principal aim of a just war is a just and lasting peace, then the goal of a just war is not simply the cessation of violence, but political, economic, social, and ecological conditions that allow citizens to flourish. In other words, a just war ends with the creation of an environment that permits citizens to pursue a life that is meaningful and dignified. A just war can be fought unjustly, and an unjust war can be ended justly. Obviously, if a war is unjust (*ad bellum* or *in bello*), then the obligations *post bellum* are all the greater. There are five components to the restoration phase: security and policing, political reform, economic recovery, social rehabilitation, and environmental clean-up.

Security and Policing

According to Kenneth Himes, "an expansion of the principle of restoration" would entail "the work of securing domestic peace through protection of civil liberties and human rights, as well as helping to organize police and judicial institutions so that the necessary social space is created for men and women to begin the work of restoring public life."[34] Concerning postwar Iraq, Bishop Wenski observes, "Stability remains elusive and rebuilding efforts are uneven, inadequate and frequently undermined by the lack of security."[35] Nivat's Iraqi and Afghan interviewees reported that, more than anything, "a lack of security" leaves them with "an absence of faith in the future."[36] Basic security is a necessary condition for stability and development. Institutions are needed to secure domestic peace, which allows other restoration tasks—including rebuilding roads and developing other elements of a defeated nation's infrastructure—to proceed.

In the political science, international relations, and human rights literature, the "rule of law" is a component of post-conflict security and peacebuilding. According to Vivienne O'Connor, "The rule of law is recognized as an inherent element in ensuring long-term sustainable peace, economic and political development in post-conflict states."[37] Graham Day, a Canadian peacekeeping expert, believes that once the actual fighting stops, "the efficacy of the military dramatically diminishes . . . [and] the need for civilian peace-building tools—the agencies of law and order: the police, judiciary, penal system, and body of law—increases."[38] While the police, judiciary, and prisons are the three primary related prongs included under the rule of law, the "police force is responsible for upholding and enforcing the law," writes political scientist Rama Mani, "and is the most publicly visible pillar of the rule of law to citizens in their daily life."[39]

To establish the rule of law, Day suggests developing a rapid-deployment "blue force" consisting of civilian police from the region and international community. A victorious nation probably should not handle this responsibility itself, but should invite and financially underwrite such a police force to secure the rule of law in the defeated nation. According to Day, the blue force would be responsible for "policekeeping," which includes routine police work, the arrest of war criminals, security for refugees, and the process of vetting, restructuring, and training the local police of the defeated nation once the period of active combat has ended.[40] The blue force's role would incrementally diminish until governance and responsibility for the rule of law has been transferred to and assumed by local authorities.[41]

Day and Mani agree that the rule of law should not entail a return to the *status quo ante*, but instead should seek a just peace, where human rights flourish. According to Day, in a post-conflict country, the transition to a just peace proceeds in three phases: order, law and order, and finally, law and order with justice.[42] For her part, Mani distinguishes "positive peace," which includes justice and human rights along with order and security, from "negative peace," which is merely enforcing law and order. Indeed, negative peace can be oppressive and unjust, such as in a police state. In Mani's view, if "the rule of law is treated primarily as a mechanism to restore order and security and to maintain and enforce negative peace . . . the police may backslide towards the use of excessive force."[43] She worries this temptation may arise when police are regarded primarily as law *enforcers*, as the coercive arm of the state, rather than more positively as guardians of the peace.

The police about whom Mani is concerned are not necessarily the international or regional police that Day sees as doing most of the law and order work at the front end of the post-conflict situation. Rather, she is worried about the restored or rebuilt police of the defeated or post-conflict nation itself. As international legal scholar Hurst Hannum puts it, "In many countries, incompetent or inadequate police forces, biased or corrupt courts, inhumane prisons not only perpetuate human rights violations but also undermine attempts to introduce stability and accountability to newly formed governments."[44] For these reasons, Mani makes a number of suggestions for reforming the police institution. A crucial step involves de-linking the military and police in the transition from conflict to peace, especially since in many countries the two institutions were closely merged prior to or during the hostilities.[45] Also, she expresses some reservations about allowing new recruits to come from demobilized, unemployed soldiers, or rehiring police who were implicated in earlier abuses. Mani emphasizes, moreover, that police need training in human rights and some "exercises that bring police and communities closer to each other, so that the police's genuine commitment to generating and upholding the rule of law is made evident to a fearful, distrustful public."[46] Similarly, Day believes that cooperation between local populations and the police is "paramount."[47]

Any *jus post bellum* efforts at restoration, with regard to security and policing, should take into account this growing body of literature on the subject. Establishing and securing a just rule of law is essential for other components of the restoration phase.

Political Reform

The question of political reform revolves around what to do about the power vacuum left in war's wake. According to Orend, the answer depends on the type of regime that was responsible for the aggression and the range of options presented by the cultural-political context. In the immediate post-conflict period some type of demilitarization is necessary (for example, buffer zones, curtailing military capabilities, reorganizing military/police command structures, education of military/police personnel, and so on). Minimally, demilitarization needs to be pursued to the point that the vanquished aggressor no longer poses an immediate threat, but it cannot be pursued to the point that the vanquished become vulnerable to reappraisal attacks from others or cannot maintain law and order within their own borders.[48] During this period of protectorship, the victor also assumes responsibility for reconstruction and maintenance of systems necessary for life (water, sewage treatment, health care, electricity, and so on). Finally, the victor should also work bilaterally or multilaterally in order to avoid charges of victor's justice.

Bass, drawing heavily on Walzer and Rawls, identifies sovereignty, territorial integrity, and political autonomy of the vanquished as key concerns of political reform. Since sovereignty is "the bedrock of international relations," victors must limit their occupation to the shortest possible period, but not end it prematurely, meaning before internal and external security are established and a functioning civil society is in place.[49] Furthermore, victors must exercise restraint. "Once the war is over, the enemy country must be seen in a radically different light. Its sovereignty must be respected. . . . Victorious states have no right to impose puppet regimes, or reconstruct a polity for the victor's economic, military, or political gain."[50]

Orend finds this apprehension toward political restructuring overly cautious:

"There should be a presumption *in favor of permitting reha-bilitative measures* in the domestic political structure of the de-feated aggressor. But such rehabilitation does need to be propor-tional to the degree of depravity inherent in the political structure itself."[51] He agrees with Walzer that particularly heinous regimes (such as Nazi Germany) warrant complete dismantling and repre-sent exceptional cases.

> But comparatively minor renovations—like human rights education programs, police and military retraining pro-grams, reform of the judiciary and bureaucracy into account-able institutions, external verification of subsequent election results, and the like—are permitted in *any* defeated aggres-sor, subject to need and proportionality.[52]

Walzer, Bass, and Orend disagree in degree, not in substance. The goal of political reform cannot be the *status quo ante bellum*. Pro-portionality is the guiding principle of political reform. The van-quished do not surrender their sovereignty, territorial integrity, or the right to self-determination. The political, policing, and mili-tary structures of the vanquished aggressor need to be reformed to a degree that eliminates the conditions that led to the aggres-sion and removes new threats, but not to a degree that leaves them vulnerable.

Economic Recovery

War is destructive by its very nature; it is also very expensive. In our section on punishment, compensation was cast largely as a means of reprimanding the unjust aggressor, but it is also part of the restoration effort.[53] War interrupts normal commerce, manu-facturing, transportation, and financial markets and forces a host of industries to shift their production efforts to accommodate the war effort. In the *post bellum* phase steps need to be taken to retrofit the economy to a non-wartime model. If a conflict has waged for decades, then countries face the possibility of a workforce that knows no vocation other than soldiering. In such situations vocational training is paramount for peace.

As Pope Paul VI noted decades ago, "Development is the new name for peace."[54] A concerted effort by governmental and non-governmental agencies, international aid groups (such as the World

Bank or the International Monetary Fund), and private industry must be courted to invest in infrastructure reconstruction and development (including roads, ports, electrical grids, and so on) and vocational training. Such endeavors are a necessary precondition for postwar peace. Private industry is legitimately apprehensive about investing in volatile areas. An unskilled workforce that is physically and emotionally scarred by war is equally unattractive to investors. Therefore, other incentives are required to attract private investment in a postwar economy. Reconstruction of the economy is absolutely essential. Work, a normal human activity whereby persons feel they are sustaining themselves and contributing to the common good, is essential for returning to a prewar life.

Social Rehabilitation

Louis Iasiello, a U.S. Navy chaplain, is unusual in his attention to social rehabilitation and *post bellum* ethics. He identifies the need to safeguard the innocent/vulnerable and to pay attention to warrior transition as two vital components to *post bellum* social rehabilitation. In particular, children, the elderly, the sick, and some groups of women may lack the ability to defend themselves in times of war and are easily overlooked. Furthermore, the long range psychological effects of war are especially damaging to children. Refugees and internally displaced populations pose additional burdens. Lacking shelter, sustenance, water, or health care, they become easy targets of physical and sexual abuse, slavery, and forced conscription in regular armies, militias, and guerilla groups. They also can become the unintended targets of munitions left behind after the war, such as landmines and cluster bombs, which will be addressed below.[55]

The preferential option for the poor, a biblically based Judeo-Christian moral principle, provides the most vigorous moral argument for the defense of the innocent. Ideally, armed forces protect civilians. History, however, teaches that these vulnerable groups often bear the heaviest burdens of war. All post-war restoration efforts ought to begin by evaluating the needs of the weakest and most vulnerable.

Iasiello is also concerned with soldiers attempting to reintegrate into society.[56] While the emotional destruction of war has always been painfully obvious (including shell shock and battle fatigue), only recently has it received significant clinical attention (for example, post traumatic stress disorder). For example, the U.S. Department of Defense found that 30 to 40 percent of the soldiers returning from the current conflict in Iraq suffer from some form of psychological trauma and that the military was not providing basic mental health for these soldiers due to lack of trained personnel and funding.[57] When a nation sends its citizens off to war, it turns ordinary men and women into killers. In so doing, nations should assume the responsibility to assist warriors in their transition back to civilian life once the fighting has ended. This includes rehabilitation for physical injuries sustained in combat, as well as emotional disabilities. We call for a return to the medieval practice that encouraged soldiers returning from war to make a retreat in order to repent for the sins of war and to heal from the psychological and spiritual damage inherent in combat.

Environmental Clean-Up

A new class of weaponry compels the just war theory to develop *post bellum* criteria. These weapons of long-term destruction (WLTDs) extend the pernicious effects of war well into the future. Chemical, biological, and nuclear weapons, as well as antipersonnel landmines and cluster bombs, claim victims decades and possibly centuries after the formal battle has ended. Two examples of WLTDs are sufficient for illustration. The U.K. Atomic Energy Authority estimates that a half-million people in Kuwait and Iraq could die from the use of depleted uranium shells in the first Gulf War alone.[58] A thirty-year study by Humanitarian International found that cluster bombs have claimed over 100,000 lives, with 98 percent of the victims of cluster bombs being civilians (mostly children), due to the fact that the munitions leave unexploded bomblets on the ground, which civilians later detonate by accident.[59] WLTDs challenge the just war theory to consider the countless future victims of war, most of whom are civilians and some of whom have not yet even been born, thereby extending the effect and moral responsibilities of war well beyond active combat.

The principle of restoration requires that those who employ WLTDs be held responsible for postwar clean-up efforts. Those who resort to WLTDs must return the environment (e.g., soil, water, and animal and plant life) to its prewar condition and make every effort to rehabilitate those affected by WLTDs. Restoration is a logical consequence of the aim of all just wars, namely a just peace. A nation cannot return to a state of affairs that encourages its citizens to flourish when its land remains unusable or when people are severely physically debilitated, are plagued by cancers, or suffer chromosomal defects for generations. On practical grounds, such a requirement would discourage the use of such weapons since the clean-up efforts are prohibitively expensive. The cost-benefit analysis of the use of WLTDs ought to accurately reflect the true cost of resorting to such weaponry. This would force military leaders to consider whether or not the effectiveness of WLTDs is worth the clean-up costs.

Collectively, these restoration obligations are expensive and laborious. That is a good thing. Waging war is one of the most destructive and evil human activities. By burdening those who engage in war, whether for just cause or not, with security and policing, political reform, economic recovery, social rehabilitation, and environmental clean-up, the true cost of war would be taken into account and perhaps the often feverish rush to war might be quelled. War is and ought to be expensive.

Conclusion

Traditional just war theory assumes that moral responsibilities dissipate with the smoke of the battle field. A more comprehensive just war theory appropriate for the twenty-first century, however, considers not only events preceding combat and behavior on the battlefield, but the long-term effects of war as well. According to Hugo Slim, Policy Director at the Centre for Humanitarian Dialogue, Jesus Christ is a source of hope and comfort before, during, and after times of trouble. "In the gospel, he seeks to call people away from disaster before it happens, to be with them as they suffer and to remake lives anew after they have been shattered."[60] The church, as the body of Christ, carries on this mission. If Catholics—be they laypersons, theologians, or bishops—wish to contribute to the wider public debate concerning what ought to be done for a just peace in postwar Afghanistan and Iraq, then the moral principles that they bring to bear, as part of their public theology, which includes the just war theory, need to be extended to include *jus post bellum*.

Notes

[1] Anne Nivat, *The Wake of War: Encounters with the People of Iraq and Afghanistan*, trans. Jane Marie Todd (Boston: Beacon Press, 2005), xiii.

[2] Ibid., 284.

[3] United States Conference of Catholic Bishops, *Faithful Citizenship: A Catholic Call to Political Responsibility* (Washington, DC: United States Conference of Catholic Bishops, 2003), 3.

[4] Thomas G. Wenski, "Toward a Responsible Transition in Iraq," http://www.usccb.org/sdwp/international/iraqstatement0106.htm (updated January 12, 2006). For a follow-up letter by Bishop William S. Skylstad, president of the United States Conference of Catholic Bishops, see "Call for Dialogue and Action on Responsible Transition in Iraq," available at http://www.usccb.org/sdwp/international/iraqresponsibletransition.pdf (updated November 13, 2006).

[5] Charles Reed, *Just War?* (New York: Church Publishing, 2004), 1-2, 5. In this essay, "just war tradition" and "just war theory" will be used interchangeably, even though distinctions could be made about each of these ways of referring to just war ethics. See Peter S. Temes, *The Just War: An American Reflection on the Morality of War in Our Time* (Chicago: Ivan R. Dee, 2003), xi-xii. In response to the objection that just war theory tends not to be a public language during times of war in the U.S. or that the theory tends to be abused, we would urge, as did John Courtney Murray, for a recovery of just war discipline. While Murray acknowledged that "the traditional doctrine was irrelevant during World War II," and that it had "not been made the basis for a sound critique of public policies, and as a means for the formation of right public opinion," he added that all this "is not an argument against the traditional doctrine. The Ten Commandments do not lose their imperative relevance by reason of the fact that they are violated. But there is place for an indictment of all of us who failed to make the tradition relevant" (John Courtney Murray, S.J., "Remarks on the Moral Problem of War," *Theological Studies* 20, no. 1 [March 1959]: 53-54).

[6] Kristin E. Heyer, *Prophetic and Public: The Social Witness of U.S. Catholicism* (Washington, DC: Georgetown University Press, 2006), 146.

[7] John Kelsay makes this claim in "How to Refine and Improve Just War Criteria," in David R. Smock, *Religious Perspectives on War: Christian, Muslim and Jewish Attitudes toward Force after the Gulf War* (Washington, DC: U.S. Institute for Peace Press, 1992), 28-29.

[8] Smock, *Religious Perspectives on War*, 19.

[9] Michael Schuck, "When the Shooting Stops: Missing Elements in Just War Theory," *The Christian Century*, October 26, 1994, 982-83.

[10] Although there are differences between the "classical just war tradition" and the "contemporary just war tradition" with regard to what constitutes just cause, it does not diminish or significantly affect this essay's logical extension of the just cause principle into *jus post bellum*. For more on the

differences between the classical and contemporary versions of just war theory, see chap. 2, "War and Peace: Parallel Traditions," in *Just War, Lasting Peace: What Christian Traditions Can Teach Us*, ed. John Kleiderer et al. (Maryknoll, NY: Orbis Books, 2006), 17-30.

[11]Brian Orend, *"Jus Post Bellum*," *Journal of Social Philosophy* 31, no. 1 (Spring 2000): 128; "Justice after War," *Ethics and International Affairs* 61, no. 1 (2002): 46; "Kant's Just War Theory," *Journal of the History of Philosophy* 37, no. 2 (April 1999): 346.

[12]Michael Walzer, *Just and Unjust Wars* (New York: Basic Books, 1977, 2000), 119-21. See also Orend, *"Jus Post Bellum*," 122-23; and "Justice after War," 45.

[13]Gary Bass, *"Jus Post Bellum*," *Philosophy and Public Affairs* 32, no. 4 (Fall 2004): 386.

[14]Orend, "Justice after War," 46.

[15]Since it could force the defeated party to fight to the bitter end. See Walzer, *Just and Unjust Wars*, 263-68, and Orend, "Justice after War," 46.

[16]Mark Allman, "Postwar Justice," *America*, October 17, 2005, 11.

[17]Davida Kellogg, *"Jus Post Bellum*: The Importance of War Crimes Trials," *Parameters* 32, no. 3 (September 22, 2002), 93. See also Anthony Ellis, "What Should We Do with War Criminals?" in *War Crimes and Collective Wrongdoing: A Reader*, ed. Aleksander Jokic (Cambridge: Blackwell, 2001): 97-111.

[18]For more on reconciliation see Andrew Rigby, "Forgiveness and Reconciliation in *Jus Post Bellum*," in *Just War Theory: A Reappraisal*, ed. Mark Evan (New York: Palgrave MacMillan, 2005), 177-200; Walter Wink, *When Powers Fall: Reconciliation in the Healing of Nations* (Minneapolis: Fortress Press, 1998); and James Turner Johnson, "War Crimes and Reconciliation after Conflict," in *Morality and Contemporary Warfare* (New Haven: Yale University Press, 1999), 191-218.

[19]Samuel Eliot Morison, *The Oxford History of the American People* (New York: Oxford University Press, 1965), 700, quoted in Louis Iasiello, *"Jus Post Bellum*: The Moral Responsibilities of Victors in War," *Naval War College Review* 57 (Summer/Autumn 2004), 38.

[20]Iasiello, *"Jus Post Bellum*," 38.

[21]Schuck, "When the Shooting Stops," 982-83.

[22]Allman, "Postwar Justice," 11.

[23]Orend, "Justice after War," 48-49.

[24]Bass, *"Jus Post Bellum*," 409.

[25]Ibid., 408.

[26]Orend, "Justice after War," 49.

[27]In a similar vein, The Network of Spiritual Progressives has called for a "Global Marshall Plan" that is like the original Marshall plan in which 1.5 to 2 percent of the U.S. gross domestic product was allocated toward reconstruction of Europe in the wake of the Second World War (The Network of Spiritual Progressives, "An Ethical Way to End the War in Iraq: Generosity Beats Domination as a Strategy for Homeland Security" and "What Is the

NSP's Global Marshall Plan?" Available at http://www.spiritualprogressives. org/ (updated February 26, 2007).

[28]Bass, "*Jus Post Bellum*," 410.

[29]Walzer, *Just and Unjust Wars*, 292-301. See also Orend, "Justice after War," 53.

[30]Bass, "*Jus Post Bellum*," 404.

[31]As Kellogg contends: "If in fact the only acceptable reason for going to war is . . . to do justice—then stopping short of trying and punishing those most responsible for war crimes and crimes against humanity which either led to the war or were committed in its prosecution may be likened to declaring 'checkmate,' and then declining to take your opponent's king. It makes no strategic sense, since the purpose for which war was undertaken is never achieved. It makes no legal sense, since the criminal activities the war was undertaken to rectify or curtail are allowed to continue unchecked. What is worse, it makes no legal sense since justice is not done for the victims of atrocities in such an outcome to war. Declining to do full justice for those who have been most grievously wronged by aggression . . . leads to the perpetration of further moral injustice on both the victims of war crimes and on innocents. . . . Sweeping these injustices under the dusty rug of history, whether to keep a fragile peace or in a foredoomed effort at reconciliation, only continues their abusive treatment as non-persons who do not even register on the radar screen of international justice" ("*Jus Post Bellum*: The Importance of War Crimes Trials," 88-89).

[32]Bass, "*Jus Post Bellum*," 406.

[33]Orend, "Justice after War," 54.

[34]Kenneth Himes, "Intervention, Just War, and U.S. National Security," *Theological Studies* 65, no. 1 (March 2004): 156.

[35]Wenski, "Toward a Responsible Transition in Iraq," 1.

[36]Nivat, *In the Wake of War*, 91.

[37]Vivienne O'Connor, "Rule of Law and Human Rights Protections through Criminal Law Reform: Model Codes for Post-conflict Criminal Justice," *International Peacekeeping* 13, no. 4 (December 2006): 517. See also Rama Mani, "Restoring Justice in the Aftermath of Conflict: Bridging the Gap between Theory and Practice," in *International Justice*, ed. Tony Coates (Burlington, VT: Ashgate, 2000), 264-69.

[38]Graham Day, "After War, Send Blue Force," *Christian Science Monitor*, May 30, 2001, 11.

[39]Rama Mani, *Beyond Retribution: Seeking Justice in the Shadows of War* (Cambridge: Polity Press, 2002), 57. See also Rama Mani, "Balancing Peace with Justice in the Aftermath of Violent Conflict," *Development* 48, no. 3 (September 2005): 27; Rama Mani, "Contextualizing Police Reform: Security, the Rule of Law and Post-Conflict Peacebuilding," in *Peacebuilding and Police Reform*, ed. Tor Tanke Holme (London and Portland, OR: Frank Cass, 2000), 10; and Leslie Vinjamuri, "Order and Justice in Iraq," *Survival* 45, no. 4 (Winter 2003-2004): 136, 138.

[40]Day, "After War, Send Blue Force," 11; Graham Day, " 'Policekeeping'

Critical to Rebuilding Iraq," *Mondial* (May 2003): 3-4; Graham Day and Christopher Freeman, "Policekeeping Is the Key: Rebuilding the Internal Security Architecture of Postwar Iraq," *International Affairs* 79, no. 2 (March 2003): 299-313. For a helpful grid of definitions for peacekeeping, peacebuilding, and so on, see Roland Paris, *At War's End: Building Peace after Civil Conflict* (Cambridge and New York: Cambridge University Press, 2004), 38-39.

[41]Graham Day and Christopher Freeman, "Operationalizing the Responsibility to Protect—The Policekeeping Approach," *Global Governance* 11 (April-June 2005): 142.

[42]Day, " 'Policekeeping' Critical to Rebuilding Iraq," 4; Day and Freeman, "Policekeeping Is the Key," 305, attributing this insight to Michael Dziedzic in *Policing the New World Disorder: Peace Operations and Public Security* (Washington, DC: National Defense University Press, 1998).

[43]Mani, "Balancing Peace with Justice in the Aftermath of Violent Conflict," 30; Mani, "Contextualizing Police Reform," 10, 17.

[44]Hurst Hannum, "Peace versus Justice: Creating Rights as Well as Order out of Chaos," *International Peacekeeping* 13, no. 4 (December 2006): 589. See also Rama Mani, "Rebuilding an Inclusive Political Community after War," *Security Dialogue* 36, no. 4 (December 2005): 515.

[45]Mani, *Beyond Retribution*, 58. Reforming state institutions, including the police, is referred to as vetting or lustration, which political scientist Jens Meierhenrich argues "must factor in considerations of justice after war, or *jus post bellum*" (Jens Meierhenrich, "The Ethics of Lustration," *Ethics & International Affairs* 20, no. 1 [April 2006]: 102).

[46]Mani, *Beyond Retribution*, 63; also, Mani, "Balancing Peace with Justice in the Aftermath of Violent Conflict," 29-30; "Contextualizing Police Reform," 20, 26.

[47]Day and Freeman, "Policekeeping Is the Key," 309.

[48]As discussed in the previous section, this may require the victors to provide internal and external security to the vanquished aggressor (a costly endeavor in terms of lives and finances), until the vanquished can defend themselves and provide law and order (see Orend, "Justice after War," 49-50).

[49]Bass, "*Jus Post Bellum*," 387.

[50]Ibid., 390.

[51]Orend, "Justice after War," 51.

[52]Ibid.

[53]As such, what was said earlier about trade also applies in this category.

[54]Pope Paul VI, *Populorum progressio*, ##76, 87.

[55]Iasiello, "*Jus Post Bellum*," 39.

[56]"Combatants are not amoral agents or machines. . . . Warriors are persons—they are body-mind-spirit. They are complex moral agents who must live and fight within the context of military protocol and duty. . . . While warriors submit to the authority of their superiors, they never submit so completely that they surrender or forfeit their moral personhood. . . .

Warriors are soldiers, marines, sailors, and airmen who must kill when legally ordered to do so, but must live with those decisions the rest of their lives" (Iasiello, "*Jus Post Bellum*," 45).

[57]Defense Health Board Task Force on Mental Health, "An Achievable Vision: Report of the Department of Defense Task Force on Mental Health," http://www.ha.osd.mil/dhb/mhtf/MHTF-Report-Final.pdf (updated June 15, 2007).

[58]Depleted uranium has a radioactive half-life of 4.5 billion years and maintains 60 percent of natural uranium radioactivity. The health risks associated with it include: chromosomal damage, stillborn births, renal collapse, infertility, leukemia, and a host of cancers (Allman, 10-11, and Doug Westerman, "Depleted Uranium—Far Worse than 9/11," http://www.globalresearch.ca/index.php?context=viewArticle&code=20060503&articleId=2374 [updated May 3, 2006]).

[59]Tobias Winright, "Compunction over Cluster Bombs," *The Cresset* 70, no. 1 (September 2006): 45-47; and Richard Norton-Taylor, "Civilians Cluster Bombs Main Victims," http://www.guardian.co.uk/armstrade/story/0,,1938494,00.html [updated November 3, 2006]).

[60] Hugo Slim, "The Christian Responsibility to Protect," in *The Responsibility to Protect: Ethical and Theological Reflections*, ed. Semegnish Asfaw et al. (Geneva: World Council of Churches, 2005), 21.

Living as "Risen Beings" in Pursuit of a Reconciled World

Resources from Jon Sobrino

Ernesto Valiente

While reconciliation has been a central theme of Christian faith since the days of the apostles, Christian understandings of the meaning of reconciliation have expanded and deepened over time. As the German theologian Geiko Muller-Fahrenholz notes, traditional Protestant and Catholic teaching and spirituality have "tended to address only the sinner and lost sight of the many who were 'sinned against.' "[1] In the same vein, Christianity's conventional emphasis on the personal character of reconciliation—chiefly understood as the reconciliation between God and the individual soul—has been accompanied by a neglect of the social dimensions of reconciliation and, by extension, their political implications.

However, in the last thirty years, global political changes that opened the possibility for initiating processes of social reconciliation,[2] as well as tragic conflicts in countries like South Africa, El Salvador, Bosnia, and Rwanda, have prompted some theologians to re-examine the Christian understanding of reconciliation and the discipleship that ensues from it. Such theological reconsiderations strive to appropriate God's reconciling work as a model for how human beings are called to relate to one another, overcome their conflicts, and seek reconciliation.[3] With different emphases, these theologies agree that social reconciliation demands three critical and interrelated moments: 1) a truthful uncovering of the events and sources of conflict; 2) the pursuit of a justice that responds to the claims of the victims and engages in the task of constructing a socio-political order that fosters communal life; and 3) a forgiveness led by the victims, who relinquish certain legitimate rights to retribution in order to open the possibility for reconciliation.

This paper examines how an authentic Christian spirituality can help us overcome one of the most critical obstacles in this process of reconciliation, namely, how to attend to both the demands of social justice and the value of forgiveness. It proposes that Jon Sobrino's Christology and particularly his interpretation of Jesus' resurrection offer important theological resources for the development of a spirituality that fosters social reconciliation as well as a ministry of reconciliation capable of successfully integrating the values of social justice with personal and social forgiveness.[4] The essay is divided into three parts: 1) a brief consideration of the problem that prompts this reflection; 2) an overview of Sobrino's Christology and its implications for how Christians should fundamentally engage historical reality; and 3) the impact that his interpretation of Jesus' resurrection has on informing a Christian discipleship that promotes an enduring social reconciliation.

Stating the Problem

The widespread use of political amnesties in Latin American countries[5] has shown that even when enough political and social will is mustered to uncover the truth of what actually happened, these initial reconciling efforts are often derailed by an overemphasis on forgiveness. In many instances, the value of forgiveness has been manipulated to promote a cheap reconciliation that trivializes the demands of the victims and ignores the roots of the conflict and thus fosters a climate of political impunity. Alternatively, the events that transpired in Rwanda and Bosnia show how the value of justice can also be used to rationalize an unwillingness to forgive, the demonization of the oppressor, and the transformation of the victim into an avenging victimizer.

Hence, while each one of the reconciling moments enumerated above is indispensable to the reconciliation process, in the contemporary context particular attention should be placed on the relationship between the second and the third moments—the pursuit of justice and the need for forgiveness. By focusing on Christian spirituality I want to suggest, with the South African theologian John de Gruchy, that "reconciliation is . . . an action, a praxis and movement before it becomes a theory or a dogma, something celebrated before it is explained."[6]

Sobrino's Christology: Kingdom, Anti-Kingdom, and the Christian Task

Like other theologies that emerge from the so-called Third World, Sobrino's theology is shaped by and responds to an immediate reality of oppression, conflict, and widespread suffering. Writing from El Salvador—a country still ravaged by the effects of a twelve-year civil war—Sobrino stresses that human salvation takes place in history[7] and contends that through the mediation of Jesus, God has been revealed to us as a merciful liberator who reacts with compassion and justice to the suffering of the victims. As Sobrino notes, "It is this primordial mercy of God that appears concretely historicized in Jesus' practice and message."[8] This mercy informs Jesus' demand for justice as well as his denunciations of those who produce suffering.

Sobrino also underscores that, according to the gospels, at the center of Jesus' mission is the proclamation and ushering in of God's Kingdom as the ultimate reality that will transform and reconcile our conflicted world. The Kingdom, which is first offered to the victims of history, stands as the chief eschatological reality in which truth, justice, and forgiveness converge. As Jesus' ministry, passion, and death clearly indicate, God's Kingdom is not ushered into a neutral or receptive landscape but breaks into our world over and against a reality infused with the effects of sin. This sinful reality, which Sobrino describes as the anti-Kingdom, fosters deception, injustice, and conflict. More significantly, it produces the suffering and death of millions of victims.

Sobrino's Christology offers a sobering diagnosis that describes current historical reality as existing in a state of crisis and conflict—a reality in which the forces of the anti-Kingdom are in constant struggle with those of God's Kingdom. Here the fundamental line of demarcation is not between nature and grace, or the natural and the supernatural, but rather between sin and grace. Sobrino explains that, on the one hand, history encompasses "the true God (of life), God's mediation (the Kingdom) and its mediator (Jesus)" and, on the other, "the idols (of death), their mediation (the anti-Kingdom) and mediators (oppressors)."[9] The idols are those social and political realities—such as national security, wealth, and unbridled ownership of private property—that stand behind the oppressors and to which they have wrongly ascribed the ultimate-ness and absoluteness that belong only to God.[10]

For Christians the implications of this diagnosis are both clear and serious since it tells us that we cannot remain passive observers in a conflicted world. Our collaboration in ushering in God's Kingdom calls for a spirituality—a way of living out our faith—that corresponds to God's revelation in history. Sobrino proposes a Christological spirituality that seeks to incarnate Jesus' values, praxis, and mission in our own historical context. Thus, as followers of Jesus, we are called to prophetically unmask the presence of sin and seek to transform our conflicted reality into one that approximates the reconciling values of God's Kingdom. For Sobrino this following of Jesus in the present should be structured in such a way that it sets forth "the correct mode of human relationship with history, and thereby with God and the personal aspect of God."[11] In other words, Christian spirituality must enable us to engage historical reality as Jesus did: with honesty, responsibility, and hope.

The task of reconciling reality demands, first, that Christians be "honest about the real" and accept historical reality for what it is, resisting any attempt to cover it up or manipulate it. This honesty means recognizing that while historical reality is grounded in God and thus has the capacity to mediate God's presence to us, it has been vitiated by the sinful choices of human persons, and is therefore a reality "weighted" by sin and conflict. Moreover, Sobrino insists that an honest engagement with reality necessarily elicits from us a compassionate response toward those who bear the consequences of sin and against all that negates the primacy of life.[12] Hence, honesty with reality also means responding with mercy to reality's tangible needs. Indeed, Sobrino contends that "The great question, the invitation and demand for mercy, is concrete reality itself. When we respond with mercy, we are being honest with reality."[13] Second, Christians are called to be "faithful to the real"—to persevere even at great personal cost in their original honesty by fostering what is positive in reality and striving against that which is negative (sin). This faithfulness leads Christians to engage in a process that Sobrino calls the "forgiveness of sinful reality"; that is, the liberation of reality from the sinfulness that permeates its historical structures and denies God's reconciling will for humanity. Third, Christians should embrace reality mindful that history is not only sheer negativity but also contains a liberating promise, a "more" that we cannot fully comprehend but that will lead to the ultimate reconciliation of humanity.[14] In other words, for all its brokenness reality calls us to have hope. "But the hope it calls for is an active impulse. . . ." Sobrino continues, "It is a hope bent upon helping reality become what it seeks to be. This is love. Hope and love are but two sides of the same coin: the conviction, put into practice, of the possibilities of reality."[15]

Thus, for Sobrino, an authentic Christian spirituality must seek to engage reality guided by the compassionate desire to liberate and reconcile it. To be sure, developing a spirituality that engages reality honestly, responsibly and hopefully demands a radical deepening of one's faith analogous to the personal transformation of the first disciples after the Easter event. As Sobrino notes, it was only after the resurrection that the disciples began to radically shape their lives according to Jesus' life, take up his mission, and become his witnesses even at the cost of their lives.[16] Hence, our efforts to transform our conflicted reality into one that approximates the values of God's Kingdom must be informed and fueled by an active faith—a following of Jesus that has appropriated the power of the resurrection.

Living as Reconciling "Risen Beings"

The cross confirms the underlying historical structure of a reality framed by the conflicting forces of sin and grace. It also reveals Jesus' death as the culmination of a faithful, exemplary, and authentic human life that is pleasing to God. No less significantly, the cross unveils a merciful God who is willing to suffer in order to enter into solidarity with and offer communion to an alienated humanity.[17] The cross, however, should not be understood as an isolated event, but as one that is deeply interrelated with the event of the resurrection. By itself the cross does not fully explain who God is for us, Christ's Paschal event, or the potential of humankind. Rather these three find a fuller revelation when the cross and the resurrection are taken as a single event[18] that represents an irruption of the eschatological into history and the victory of the God of life over the forces of death and the anti-Kingdom. In the act of raising Jesus, God responds to the unjust and meaningless reality of a crucified victim, reveals Godself as a just liberator of victims, and ushers in a reconciling hope for all, but particularly for the least of this world.

Sobrino approaches the resurrection from the perspective of

those who are the victims of history because, for him, Jesus' cross reveals that their world offers the most appropriate place from which to grasp the Easter event.[19] In the cross the fate of the crucifiers is handed over to the crucified one, and it is this same crucified one who is later resurrected. This insight unveils the essential relationship that exists between the cross and the resurrection and underlines that the victims are the only ones capable of extending forgiveness and welcoming the persecutors to a reconciled community.

Sobrino also examines the resurrection with an eye toward how this may affect our lives today. While he acknowledges that Jesus' resurrection is a unique eschatological event that took place beyond history, he argues that because this event was encountered and perceived in history it must be capable of transforming our present lives. Sobrino insists that it would be paradoxical and even absurd if the resurrection could remain as something extrinsic to the human condition since "this would suppose that the eschatological had come about in history but that it had no effect in our present life—except in hope."[20] In the same vein he speculates that in some analogous and limited way we must be able to share today the experiences enjoyed by the witnesses who first encountered the risen Christ.[21] Hence, Sobrino puts forward that inasmuch as the followers of the crucified Jesus make the risen Christ present in their lives, they may live as "risen beings" today.[22]

But in order to understand what it means to live as risen beings, Sobrino argues that we must first grasp the meaning of the resurrection—a meaning that is most fully unveiled when we assume a particular stance and a particular way of being in the world.[23] Moreover, since faith in the resurrected Christ impinges on how we engage reality in its totality, this stance must be as encompassing as possible and must include the different human dimensions with which we confront reality. Hence, Sobrino adapts Immanuel Kant's three famous anthropological questions that map out the whole field of reality—What can I know? What ought I do? For what can I hope?—in order to identify the proper stance that allows the human person to grasp the resurrection and thus live as a risen being.[24] To Kant's questions, Sobrino adds one of his own: What can we celebrate in history today? Sobrino's responses to each one of these questions illuminate the impact a "risen" way of living has on fostering a Christian discipleship that advances social reconciliation and successfully integrates the pursuit of justice with the need for personal forgiveness.

Hope: The Power of God and Justice

To the question what kind of hope allows us to grasp the resurrection, Sobrino insists that it is one that stresses not only the victory of life over death but also the victory of justice over injustice. It is ultimately a *"hope in the power of God over the injustice that produces victims."*[25] Sobrino explains that the Israelite notion of the resurrection emerges from the Old Testament apocalyptic tradition. Surrounded as they were by oppressing empires, the Israelites understood that the Lordship of God and their communion with God had to extend beyond death because neither the passage of time nor death could obstruct God's justice. Thus, they not only expected that God would defend them against tyrannical forces throughout history, but also hoped that at the end of history God would resurrect the dead and correct all injustices. As such, the Israelites' concept of resurrection is imbued with a concern for ultimate justice, and from this concern emerges a communal hope rooted in the fact that God is just and that God always takes the side of the victims.[26]

Building on this insight, Sobrino insists that our hope in the resurrection cannot be a hope just for "me"—for my own survival; it must also be a hope that includes the other, particularly the victims of history. Moreover, from a Christian perspective, this de-centered hope calls for the profound conversion of all—both non-victims and victims—since our capacity to share in the hope of the resurrection is linked to our participation in the life and death of Jesus, and by extension to our partaking in the hope of the victims. In other words, we may share in the hope of the resurrection insofar as our hope resembles Jesus' hope and thus incorporates the just aspirations of the victims. Thus, Sobrino claims that "the Christian courage to hope in one's own resurrection depends on the courage to hope for the overcoming of the historical scandal of injustice."[27] This hope demands a profound shift in our worldview and in the way we engage a reality distorted by sin. It leads us to embrace, subjectively and through our actions, a preferential option for the victim. As such, this de-centered hope calls non-victims to a self-forgetfulness that places us in solidarity with the victims, prompts us to make their hope for justice our own, and propels us to work for it, even if in the process we become victims ourselves.

That the victims share their hope with us does not mean that we should expect them to warrant our newly acquired hope through moral or religious uprightness. Many will and some will not, but that is not the issue. Ultimately, we make the option of partaking in the victims' hope because we desire to embrace the same hope that Jesus embraced, because we are moved to love them, and because we believe in a just God whose gratuitous love has always shown a predilection for the weak and the victims of history.[28]

Holding to the hope of the resurrection also enables the victims to make an authentic option for themselves. For victims, holding to this hope means, first, taking heart that God is on their side and that justice will be done; second, holding on to their own aspirations and thus rejecting the alienating values of the dominant group, including the desire to impose upon their opponents the conditions of oppression imposed upon them;[29] and, third, extending to their persecutors the forgiveness that God first offers to us in the cross. Implicitly, this de-centering hope demands that we do not give up on the oppressors trapped under the weight of sin, nor on the possibility of their conversion.[30]

Thus, a Christian ministry of reconciliation shaped by a resurrected hope defies the apparent success of hostility and injustice, and hopes against hope that a different world—a just and reconciled one—is possible. Emboldened by the resurrection and led by the aspirations of the victims, we hope that justice will overcome injustice, and we hope for the miracle of conversion that steers the oppressor into God's reconciled Kingdom.

Praxis: Living the Cross and Resurrection

Moving now to the question of what type of praxis allows us to grasp the resurrection and live as risen beings, Sobrino answers that it is a praxis constituted by actions that concretize the hope ushered in by the Easter event. He tells us that our actions must be, in their formal and substantial dimensions, analogous to God's raising Jesus from death.[31] Formally our actions are analogous to God's when we try to make possible what seems impossible in this world, for instance, when we attempt to overcome structures that perpetuate oppression and conflict. Content-wise, our actions are analogous to God's resurrecting action when we seek justice for the victims of injustice. In other words, our Christian praxis must be rooted in eschatological ideas and seek to remove the victims of history from their crosses through transformative political and social actions. Sobrino notes that these actions are historical signs—partial and limited resurrections that disclose God's preferential love for the victims and generate hope in the final resurrection.[32]

As Sobrino rightly puts forward, in a conflicted world a Christian praxis of reconciliation must first seek the eradication of structural sin and the corresponding humanization of its victims.[33] Secondarily, our praxis must seek the rehabilitation of the oppressor. When Sobrino describes the Christian task of taking responsibility for the sinfulness of reality, he speaks of both overcoming and redeeming its evil.[34] While overcoming sin stresses that we must use the different means at our disposal to confront and oppose the forces of evil, Sobrino uses the redemptive language of the cross to emphasize that eradicating the sin and injustice that permeate our social relationships is not something we can fully accomplish from a distance.[35] As agents of reconciliation Christians must also take upon their shoulders the weight of sin by placing—incarnating—themselves in the world of the victims and exposing themselves to the perils of such a world. "This incarnation," Sobrino states, "is hard, but it is a conversion which leads to solidarity with the poor and seeing reality in a very different way, overcoming the mechanisms we use to defend ourselves from reality."[36] By taking on the weight of sin, Christians engaged in the ministry of reconciliation make themselves vulnerable to sin's fury and thus accept the likely possibility that they will also experience its destructive force in the forms of persecution and death. For Sobrino, then, a ministry of reconciliation calls for a "fundamental spirituality of personal selflessness, radical self-giving, and radical love, hope put to the test and thus triumphant, true faith—true because it is victory over trials—in God who is the holy mystery."[37]

The chronological priority that the praxis of reconciliation gives to the struggle for social justice stresses that our reconciling efforts must begin with what is most urgent and serious—addressing, albeit imperfectly, the causes of widespread oppression, conflict, and suffering. Such priority, however, does not exclude the central role that forgiveness plays in a reconciliation process, nor does it assume that full social justice must be achieved before forgiveness can be extended. Rather it presumes that our pursuit of justice is already informed by our willingness to extend forgiveness.

God's act of raising Jesus arrives without reprisal to those who abandoned or betrayed the resurrected one, nor does God await their conversion to act. In the same vein, the appearances of the risen Christ to his disciples are both a sign of God's forgiving love as well as commissioning events in which the disciples are accepted back into the community and entrusted with Jesus' reconciling mission. As Sobrino notes, "The freely forgiven one is the grateful one. And it is *the gratitude of knowing oneself to be accepted that moves a person to a de-centering from self . . .* to a life of eager striving that the love of God that has been experienced may be a historical reality in this world."[38] Although the victims are the forgiving subjects who are asked to extend pardon to their oppressors, forgiveness is necessary for both the victims and the victimizers. God's forgiveness opens the possibility for the victims to liberate themselves from their own limited reality—one often characterized by justifiable but poisonous feelings of resentment, or worse, a crippling internalized sense of worthlessness due to prolonged victimization—and turn their attention to the oppression into which the oppressors themselves have fallen.

While Christian forgiveness acknowledges the truth of prior injustices and the need for a new relationship between victims and perpetrators, as Sobrino notes it also "[stresses] the gratuity, unreason, and defenselessness of love . . . we do not forgive out of any personal or group interest, even a legitimate one, but simply out of love."[39] The apparent impossibility of such an action, evident to those who have worked closely with victims of oppression, highlights the centrality of a particular faith in Christ—one permeated with the eschatological ideals of love, justice, and communion, and thus informed by the ultimate-ness of the reality revealed in the Easter event.

Thus, a Christian praxis of reconciliation that actualizes the hope of the resurrection must seek to do the justice that overcomes injustice and to extend the forgiveness that heals the guilt of the sinner. But this praxis must also be informed by the eschatological purpose of God's actions—the drawing of all into a just and reconciled communion.[40]

Knowledge: Knowing and Accepting Reality

This leads to the third question regarding the type of knowledge that allows us to grasp the resurrection and live as risen beings. Sobrino contends this knowing is one that accepts reality as a gratuitous mystery given to us.[41] He notes the resurrection can be understood as a promise that points to the future, or as a future reality that seeks its becoming in the present.[42] Key in both of these approaches is that something has already happened in the present that now points to the definitive future. Sobrino prefers to see the resurrection as a promise—"an offering that proclaims a reality that does not yet exist."[43] More significantly, the resurrection means that we cannot understand reality's future as a simple extrapolation of the present with all of its conflict and negativity. Rather, the resurrection irrupts into history as a hope that defies and confronts such negativity. Hence, Sobrino explains that to grasp the resurrection we have to grasp reality as a promise, and this grasping demands both that we relinquish the desire to fully control how reality unfolds and that we remain open to God's unexpected grace. While we are called to accept reality honestly, as it is given to us, and while we must be faithful to this reality by assuming responsibility for it, we are also called to be mindful that there is a "more" to reality that we cannot fully grasp in the present.[44]

This intellectual stance of openness to grace and epistemological modesty is critical as we engage in a ministry of reconciliation that will remain ambiguous and incomplete until the end of time. Although necessary, no human project of reconciliation coincides with God's Kingdom and thus no human effort can offer us a complete and final reconciliation. Consequently, the provisional character of our reconciling endeavors must be duly weighted and our efforts must make room for the likely interruption of God's grace— a grace often mediated through the voices and lives of the victims but also present in the unexpected conversion of the oppressors. Hence, appropriating the power of the resurrection enables us to engage in a ministry of reconciliation that, because it is mindful of its limitations, opens itself up to the unexpected gifts of God's reconciling grace.

Celebration: New Life in Freedom and Joy

In sketching the particular hope, praxis, and knowledge with which we are to follow Jesus, Sobrino is advancing the core of a Christian anthropology that mediates the risen Christ and allows us to begin living as risen beings today. But what does the triumph of the resurrection add to this following of Christ? What can we celebrate in history today? And how does this celebrating influence our ministry of reconciliation?

The capacity to live as risen beings does not remove Christians from history or from the anguish, hopes, and grief that it entails. On the contrary, it encourages us to a fuller incarnation in history. What this capacity consists of, Sobrino tells us, is adding a dimension of victory to our following of Jesus and to our stance on behalf of the victims of history. Ultimately, it transforms us by disposing us to follow him and to engage reality with a new freedom and a new joy.[45]

Our following of Jesus and our efforts to work for a reconciled world demand a radical love let loose by a radical freedom. Yet different kinds of historical attachments often impair the effectiveness of our love. These attachments are particularly evident among the persecutors, whose ambitions for power and wealth frequently bind them to a life that generates conflict. They are also noticeable in the victims, whose deep-seated feelings of anger and resentment often preclude them from extending forgiveness to their persecutors. Some types of attachments, however, are also present in non-victims who engage in the ministry of reconciliation. The ties to our families, careers, or political and religious associations, although legitimate, often elicit priorities and commitments that may limit the effectiveness of our reconciling love. In contrast, Sobrino suggests that Christians who have appropriated in their lives the power of the resurrection manifest in their lives a freedom that enables them to love "without anything putting limits on or standing in the way of this love."[46] He points to Archbishop Oscar Romero—a man who offered his life for the reconciliation of the Salvadoran people—as an example of a contemporary person who lived the latter part of his life with the freedom of a risen being. Thus the type of freedom that emerges from the resurrection is a freedom that enables Christians to rise above their ties in order to love without barriers and become utterly available to God's will and work. Indeed, this is the freedom manifested in the lives of the Christian martyrs whose self-offering bears the effects of a conflicted world, breaks the cycle of violence, and generates concrete hope for a reconciled humanity.

The martyrs not only underscore the cost of staying faithful to a ministry of reconciliation and to the following of Jesus, they also shed light on what is critical and ultimate in the Christian life. They tell us that our Christian freedom is always a freedom to love and to serve. Moreover, for Sobrino, their openness to martyrdom "shows the most radical meaning of Christian existence as a journey," since "that walking toward God—if it is like Jesus' journey—follows the pattern of liberation-martyrdom, of kingdom-cross."[47] Hence, a Christian ministry of reconciliation that manifests the triumph of the resurrection involves appropriating a radical and heroic freedom that enables us to love others without limits, even when this love will invariably lead us to the cross.

For Sobrino, living with joy is the second dimension that reflects the victory of the resurrection. Such joy, central to our living as risen beings, implies that even today Christians have reason to celebrate life, not in a fashion that is a mere diversion to entertain us while also alienating us from reality, but in a way that is deeply mindful of the grace-filled mystery life offers to us. This joy refers to our being able to celebrate all that is positive in the world—for even in the midst of conflict we can celebrate the presence of grace manifested in the life of our martyrs as well as in partial moments of justice, forgiveness, and fraternity. In Sobrino's words, "It is the joy of communities that, despite everything, come together to sing and recite poetry, to show that they are happy [when] they are together, to celebrate the eucharist."[48]

The celebrations that express the joy of the resurrection are critical for a Christian spirituality committed to a ministry of reconciliation because they generate solidarity, strengthen our Christian hope and identity, and anticipate our eschatological communion. Moreover, they are rooted in a joy that recognizes with the deepest gratitude that alongside the negativity and conflict of reality there is also a reconciling goodness—a grace—actively present in it. In a world of pervasive conflict and in the midst of a history that has generated millions of crosses, such celebrations are fueled by the recognition—and the joy—that the reality of the resurrection has somehow reached us, and our reconciling efforts are guided by the "promise of a 'more' that touches us and draws us despite ourselves."[49]

Conclusion

The efficacy of any reconciliation process demands that it be mindful of the complex historical, cultural, and social context within which the conflict emerged. To be sure, recent efforts to address existing conflicts have shown the daunting challenges that every particular attempt at reconciliation entails: how to contend with the different parties' opposing interpretations of both the causes of the conflict and its painful effects; how to define what constitutes justice and forgiveness in this specific situation; how to address the all too common absence of repentance among the offenders and those who benefited from the situation that generated the conflict; how to deal with the victims' unwillingness to extend forgiveness; and so the list goes on.

In the same vein, the relevance of any theological reflection on reconciliation depends in large measure on how attentive it is to the particular context it is addressing and how appropriately it responds to the challenges of a given reality. In Latin America, where the effects of large-scale social conflicts still reverberate throughout most of the continent, liberation theologians have rightly stressed the contextual character of theology and the need to attend to the signs of times. Hence, they have vigorously attended to the oppressive situation of the victims and the urgent need for an integral liberation, which implicitly incorporates the need for reconciliation. Nonetheless, little has been formally written on the subject of reconciliation, and no systematic theology of reconciliation has been published from a Latin American liberationist perspective.[50] This essay shows that Latin American liberation theology, and particularly Jon Sobrino's work, offers a significant contribution to a problem that is as complex as it is pressing. It also points to how theologians like Sobrino have begun laying the ground for a more explicit systematic theology of reconciliation from the Latin American liberationist perspective.

Finally, this essay proposes a basic agenda for a constructive theology of reconciliation rooted in Sobrino's Christology. First, such a project will need to explore the context within which he has done his theology—his surrounding socio-historical conditions, personal experiences and intellectual influences—in order to identify and examine the sources that have stimulated and shaped the development of his theological thought. Second, it will outline in detail the three dimensions (honesty about reality, fidelity to the real, willingness to be led by the "more" of the real) that, according to Sobrino, structure the human person's relationship with reality and thus ground his or her spirituality. Third, this basic structure is fleshed out with those elements in Sobrino's Christology that are important for developing a spirituality capable of fostering a theology and a ministry of reconciliation: his treatment of

Jesus' life, message, death, and resurrection interpreted from the perspective of the victims and the hope in God's Kingdom as the hermeneutical principles that allow us to draw closer to Christ's reconciling revelation. Fourth, the Christian spirituality of reconciliation that emerges from Sobrino's Christology then becomes the foundation for a theology and a ministry of reconciliation and for the stance with which the followers of Christ and Christian theology may engage the process of a) truthfully uncovering the events and sources of conflict; b) pursuing a justice that responds to the claims of the victims and seeks the construction of a more harmonious socio-political order; and c) fostering the necessary forgiveness that restores communal life. Ultimately, this theology and ministry of reconciliation will prompt us to live as risen beings, to make concrete the promise of a reconciled humanity, and to become more credible signs of hope and sacraments of love for the victims, the bystanders, and the oppressors of this world.

Notes

[1]Geiko Muller-Fahrenholz, *The Art of Forgiveness: Theological Reflections on Healing and Reconciliation* (Geneva: World Council of Churches Publications, 1996), 15.

[2]Robert J. Schreiter notes a dramatic increase in possibilities for initiating processes of reconciliation beginning in the late 1980s as a consequence of the end of military dictatorships and civil wars in Latin America, the collapse of the Berlin Wall, and the resurgence of indigenous people with the United Nations Year of the Indigenous in 1992 ("Source and Resource for Reconciliation," in *Reconciliation in a World of Conflicts*, ed. Luiz Carlos Susin and María Pilar Aquino [London: SCM Press, 2003], 109).

[3]See, for instance, John D. de Gruchy, *Reconciliation: Restoring Justice* (Minneapolis: Fortress Press, 2002); Robert J. Schreiter, *Reconciliation: Mission and Ministry in a Changing Social Order* (Maryknoll, NY: Orbis Books, 2001), and *The Ministry of Reconciliation: Spirituality and Strategies* (Maryknoll, NY: Orbis Books, 2004); and Miroslav Volf, *Exclusion and Embrace: A Theological Exploration of Identity, Otherness, and Reconciliation* (Nashville: Abingdon Press, 1996).

[4]While Sobrino has not developed a systematic treatment of reconciliation, he has written several insightful articles on the subject. See "Christianity and Reconciliation: The Way to a Utopia," in *Reconciliation in a World of Conflicts*, ed. Susin et al., (London: SCM Press, 2003), 80-90; "Latin America: Place of Sin and Place of Forgiveness," and "Personal Sin, Forgiveness, and Liberation," both in *The Principle of Mercy: Taking the Crucified People from the Cross* (Maryknoll, NY: Orbis Books, 1999), 58-68, 83-102.

[5]Roy H. May notes that "amnesty has been decreed to protect human rights

violators in Chile (1978), Brazil (1979), Honduras (1981), Argentina (1983), Guatemala (1982), El Salvador (1987, 1992, 1993), Surinam (1989), and Peru (1995)" ("Reconciliation: A Political Requirement for Latin America," *Annual of the Society of Christian Ethics* [1996]: 54).

⁶de Gruchy, *Reconciliation*, 21.

⁷Jon Sobrino, *Jesus the Liberator: A Historical-Theological View*, trans. Paul Burns and Francis McDonagh (Maryknoll, NY: Orbis Books, 1993), 46.

⁸Sobrino, *The Principle of Mercy*, 17.

⁹Sobrino, *Jesus the Liberator,* 162. This theologal-idolatric interpretation, however, also has its limitations. While it is helpful in offering an overall religious interpretation of historical reality in which the categories of evil (sin) and good (grace) are clearly demarcated, it does not account for the fluidity that characterizes the functioning of social structures and the ambiguity of the human condition and our often inconsistent behavior. Our personal experiences tell us that we often tread on both realties at once—e.g., we are often both oppressive and oppressed.

¹⁰For instance, in examining the situation of the Salvadoran society in the late 1970s, Archbishop Oscar Romero, who worked closely with Jon Sobrino, saw the idolatry of wealth and private property as the source of the country's unequal economic structures and the root cause for the country's conflict. "Above all," preached Romero, "I denounce the absolutization of wealth. This is the great evil of El Salvador: wealth—private property as an untouchable absolute" (Archbishop Oscar Romero in his homily "El Divino Salvador, Carne para la Vida del Mundo," preached in San Salvador on August 12, 1979, in *Su Pensamiento VI* [San Salvador: Imprenta Criterio, 1988], 162, my translation).

¹¹Sobrino, "Presuppositions and Foundations of Spirituality," in *Spirituality of Liberation: Toward Political Holiness*, trans. Robert R. Barr (Maryknoll, NY: Orbis Books, 1985), 22.

¹²Sobrino, "Spirituality and the Following of Jesus," in *Mysterium Liberationis: Fundamental Concepts of Liberation Theology*, ed. Jon Sobrino and Ignacio Ellacuría (Maryknoll, NY: Orbis Books, 1993), 682-83. Sobrino further elaborates on the centrality of mercy as the authentic human response before reality: "Mercy is the primary and the ultimate, the first and the last, of human reactions. It is that in terms of which all dimensions of the human being acquire meaning and without which nothing else attains to human status" (682).

¹³Ibid., 683.

¹⁴Sobrino, "Presuppositions and Foundations of Spirituality," in *Spirituality of Liberation*, 14-22.

¹⁵Ibid., 19.

¹⁶Jon Sobrino, *Christ the Liberator* (Maryknoll, NY: Orbis Books, 2001), 105-7. Sobrino sees a certain discontinuity between the disciples' "first faith" in Jesus and their faith after Jesus' resurrection. In fact, he does not feel totally comfortable speaking about the disciples' faith before the resurrection and argues that the Easter event added two critical aspects to the disciples' original

faith: "The first, obviously, is *definiteness*. The other and perhaps more important, is having *to integrate the reality of the cross* into this new faith, this 'second' faith" (*Christ the Liberator*, 102, italics in the original).

[17]Sobrino, *Jesus the Liberator*, 227-46.

[18]For Sobrino, the resurrection reveals three new theological insights: God the Father is revealed as Trinity, Jesus is revealed as being in unity with God, and human persons are revealed as having received the Holy Spirit (*Christ the Liberator*, 21-22).

[19]Sobrino notes that the cross is "the prime *locus theologicus* for understanding the resurrection and other *loci* will be so to the extent that they analogously reproduce the reality of the cross" (*Christ the Liberator*, 14, italics in the original).

[20]Ibid.

[21]Sobrino acknowledges the difference between the Easter experience and those experiences that we may have of the Easter event today. He notes, "The essential difference between them is that the Easter experience, besides being the first, has fullness as its content, in the sense of anticipated fulfillment of the end of history, while experiences throughout history clearly depend on that first one for being understood as analogous Easter experiences; their content would make them experiences of finality, but without the distinction of referring to the finality of the end time" (ibid., 66).

[22]Ibid., 12.

[23]Sobrino builds this argument aided by the insights of Rudolf Bultmann, Willi Marxsen, Wolfhart Pannenberg, Karl Rahner, and Leonardo Boff. From the European theologians two of these insights are particularly important to us. First, we cannot speak of the resurrection assuming, in advance, that we fully know what we are speaking about. Nonetheless, while it seems extremely difficult to speak about the resurrection, we should be able to do so; otherwise the fact that this revelation took place would not make sense. In other words, why would God offer a revelation if we cannot understand it, even if only partially? Second, it is clear that the New Testament texts assume certain anthropological presuppositions in those who were granted the experience of the resurrection, for instance, a certain trust in an ultimate hope, openness to grace, and affinity between our lives and that of the resurrected one. From Boff, Sobrino gathers how a hope understood in its communal sense and a praxis informed by "a hope of justice for the weak and a life lived for justice" are necessary hermeneutical principles to grasp the resurrection. See ibid., 22-34.

[24]Ibid., 35-36.

[25]Ibid., 42, italics in the original.

[26]Ibid., 37-41.

[27]Ibid., 44.

[28] For an excellent treatment on the reasons for the preferential option for the poor, see Gustavo Gutiérrez, "Option for the Poor," in *Mysterium Liberationis*, 235-50.

[29]Volf writes eloquently on the victims' need for conversion. He notes that

the victims' repentance offers the opportunity to finally break humanity's cycles of violence and the possibility of developing *"social agents that are shaped by the values of God's kingdom and therefore capable of participating in the project of authentic social transformation"* (*Exclusion and Embrace*, 118, italics in the original).

[30]It should be clear that understanding the hope of the resurrection as one that stresses the victory of God's justice over injustice does not mean that the hope for the resurrection becomes de-universalized, but that this hope demands certain conditions and a particular setting—the world of the victims—from which it embraces all, victims and non-victims. See *Christ the Liberator*, 43.

[31]Ibid., 47-48.

[32]Ibid., 49.

[33]Sobrino draws from the Latin American bishops' conferences at Medellín and Puebla to stress the serious effects of structural injustice in Latin America and to argue that Christian praxis must first seek to convert this reality (*The Principle of Mercy*, 59-62).

[34]Sobrino, "La Teologia y el Principio de Liberación," *Revista Latinoamericana de Teologia* 35 (1995): 135.

[35]Sobrino tells us, "Sin cannot be eradicated from outside ourselves, simply by opposing its destructive force with force of our own, even though . . . this must also be done" (*The Principle of Mercy*, 62). Elsewhere speaking of God in the cross, Sobrino affirms that "What this crucified God reminds us of constantly is that there can be no liberation from sin without bearing of sin, that injustice cannot be eradicated unless it is borne" (*Jesus the Liberator*, 246).

[36]Sobrino, *The Principle of Mercy*, 62.

[37]Ibid.

[38]Ibid., 96, italics in the original.

[39]Ibid., 64.

[40]Ibid., 63.

[41]Sobrino, *Christ the Liberator*, 52-53.

[42]Ibid., 51-52. These two positions correspond to the approaches developed by Jürgen Moltmann in *Theology of Hope: On the Ground and the Implications of a Christian Eschatology* (London: SCM Press; New York: Harper and Row, 1977), and Wolfhart Pannenberg in *Theology and the Kingdom of God* (Philadelphia: Westminster Press; London: Search Press, 1974).

[43]Moltmann, quoted in Sobrino, *Christ the Liberator*, 52.

[44]Ibid., 53.

[45]Ibid., 76.

[46]Ibid., 77. Sobrino notes that Romero's tireless work for a peaceful reconciliation in El Salvador was informed by a radical love for the victims— a love not even restricted by the constant threats to his life or to the institutional church.

[47]Sobrino, "From a Theology of Liberation Alone to a Theology of

Martyrdom," in *Witnesses to the Kingdom: The Martyrs of El Salvador and the Crucified Peoples* (Maryknoll, NY: Orbis Books, 2003), 117-18.

[48]Sobrino, *Christ the Liberator*, 77.

[49]Ibid., 78.

[50]Some Latin American bishops have proposed a theology of reconciliation that endorses a return to the same social conditions that originated the conflict, eschews the need for the change in social structures, and conceives itself as an alternative to liberation theology (Gregory Baum, "A Theological Afterword," in *The Reconciliation of Peoples: Challenge to the Churches*, ed. Bregory Baum and Harold Wells [Maryknoll, NY: Orbis Books, 1997], 188). For an example of this approach to reconciliation, see Cardinal Alfonso Lopez Trujillo, *Liberacion y Reconciliacion: Breve recorrido historico* (Lima: Editora Latina, 1990).

Communal Penance and Public Life

On the Church's Becoming a Sign of Conversion from Social Sin

James T. Cross

The Introduction to the church's present *Rite of Penance* (*RP*)[1] contains a number of statements that reflect the relationship between the sacrament of penance and public life. Two of these statements read as follows: "In fact, people frequently join together to commit injustice. But it is also true that they help each other in doing penance; freed from sin by the grace of Christ, they become, with all persons of good will, agents of justice and peace in the world" (*RP* 5); and "The people of God accomplish and perfect . . . continual repentance in many different ways. . . . Thus the people of God become in the world a sign of conversion to God" (*RP* 4).[2] Both of these statements also contain terms and teachings of the Second Vatican Council—fittingly so, since this Council's *Constitution on the Sacred Liturgy* (*Sacrosanctum Concilium*) calls for the revised Rite of which the statements are parts (*SC* 72).[3] The first statement quoted above especially resembles the Council's *Pastoral Constitution on the Church in the Modern World* (*Gaudium et Spes*), including the latter's reference to what is now called "social sin" (*GS* 25),[4] as well as the latter's insistence that faith and public life are intertwined (*GS* 38, 43).[5] The second statement quoted above includes three terms that are outstanding in the Council's *Dogmatic Constitution on the Church* (*Lumen Gentium*): "people of God" (*LG* 9); "continual repentance" (*LG* 8); church as "sign" (*LG* 1).[6]

Given these statements in the *Rite of Penance*, and given their roots in conciliar concerns, I propose that the postconciliar church is to become in the world a sign of conversion from social sin, and that it cannot fully become such a sign without further developing and celebrating various forms of communal penance. Indeed, if living the faith of the church can (and should) improve the moral quality of public life, then it will do so insufficiently if the church does not prophetically and symbolically—via catechesis and liturgy[7]—address social sin, which includes the evil mindsets, attitudes, systems, structures, situations, conspiracies, and omissions that constitute the "dark side" of public life.[8]

In this essay I will first provide an overview of magisterial and scholarly understandings of social sin that have been put forth since the closing of the Second Vatican Council. Then I will explain how three postconciliar Catholic documents significantly inspire and inform ecclesial responses to social sin. Finally, I will recommend ecclesial—particularly catechetical and liturgical—responses to social sin that have not sufficiently, or have not at all, been pursued in the life of the church.

Social Sin

Social sin is a designation that arose in Christian theological discourse only in the twentieth century.[9] Although they did not refer to this designation in their works, Walter Rauschenbusch and Reinhold Niebuhr were among the first Christian theologians to have recognized and described this type of sin.[10] After receiving its initial recognition by the Roman Catholic magisterium in *Gaudium et Spes*,[11] social sin has continued to receive attention in both magisterial and scholarly writings.[12]

An often quoted and influential magisterial treatment of social sin is that of John Paul II in his Apostolic Exhortation *Reconciliatio et Paenitentia*.[13] In that document, as in others,[14] he understands social sin as harmful acts committed by an individual against a community, by a community against an individual, or by one community against another (*REP* 16). However, despite acknowledging such sin, John Paul II ultimately diminishes its significance when he invokes a pre-modern distinction made by Thomas Aquinas: "Sin, in the proper sense, is always a *personal act* . . . and not properly of a group or community. . . . Hence if one speaks of *social sin* here, the expression obviously has an analogical meaning" (REP 16).[15] After admitting that situations, systems, structures, and institutions can be sinful, and that social groups, societies, nations, and nation-blocs can commit sinful "collective behaviour," he then devalues the term "social sin" when he concludes that "such cases of *social sin* are the result of the accumulation and concentration of many *personal sins*. . . . The real responsibility, then, lies with individuals" (*REP* 16).

Thus, John Paul II leads a school of thought that views social sin as subordinate to individual sin. Allied with him—but more extreme—is neoconservative Richard John Neuhaus, who believes that the structure of "the [free] market has no morality of its own; it simply reflects the morality and immorality of those who participate in it."[16] This school cannot deny the complexity and interconnectedness of human activities and relationships in the modern world, which inevitably includes a collective experience of evils; it, therefore, must somehow come to grips with the existence of social sin. At the same time, this school cannot move beyond its favoritism of the individualistic model of sin (and penance) that came to be canonized by the Roman Catholic Church in the thirteenth century.[17] It is as if this school prefers to stand upon the shore of individualism[18] while occasionally dipping its toes into the ocean of communitarianism.

A number of contemporary theologians have challenged such an individualistic view of social sin. One of these, Thomas F. Schindler, reverses the former argument, maintaining that sin is primarily a social experience. Schindler sees individual persons as participating in and contributing to a social and historical human opposition to God's reign.[19] Supporting his assertion is a groundbreaking theologian of social sin, Gustavo Gutiérrez. Liberation theology, which owes so much to Gutiérrez, is based upon an initial consciousness of evil social situations.[20] As Aquinas helped to move Christian theology away from Platonic dualism via the hylomorphism of Aristotle, so Gutiérrez helped to move Christian theology away from individualism via the socialism of Marx.[21] Such theologians do not share John Paul II's ambivalence about "reading the signs of the time" (*GS* 4) via Marx's lens.[22] They do not agree that attributing a primacy to social sin constitutes a slippery slope toward "the watering down and almost the abolition of personal sin"(*REP* 16). A magisterial view of social sin reflecting this school of thought is that of the Latin American bishops, to be discussed later.

A moderate school of thought between the two prior extremes includes theologians such as Rosemary Radford Ruether, who argues that our hamartology is seriously distorted if we ignore the interconnection between the individual and social dimensions of sin: "The larger [sexist] system still entraps us and limits our choices. We await that massive repentance of all humanity. . . . It demands the conversion of all, not only as individuals, but as a collective system."[23] Ruether, and others,[24] would probably join Mark O'Keefe in reexamining the necessity or validity of the afore-mentioned Thomistic distinction between proper sins (meaning mortal sins committed by individuals) and sins by analogy: per-haps social sin is not merely analogical, suggests O'Keefe, but is rather co-essential (in other words, simultaneous or interdepen-dent) with personal sin. Such a claim logically follows when one's hamartological point of departure is not Aquinas's isolating fac-ulty psychology, but is, instead, the experience of sin as being si-multaneously chosen yet externally influenced.[25] Patrick McCormick and Russell Connors, who identify racism, consum-erism, and militarism as examples of sinful beliefs and practices that are shared, also support this co-essential hamartology.[26] An example of this hamartology operative in magisterial teaching is the following statement by the U.S. bishops in *Brothers and Sis-ters to Us*: "The structures of our society are subtly racist, for these structures reflect the values which society upholds. They are geared to the success of the majority and the failure of the minor-ity; and members of both groups give unwitting approval by ac-cepting things as they are."[27]

Whether social sin is seen as being subordinate to, primary over, or co-essential with individual sin, it is clearly a type of sin that has become a distinctive and enduring concern in both magisterial and scholarly theological writing.[28] Three official postconciliar documents are especially inspiring and informative in respect to social sin.

Three Challenging Documents

As mentioned above, what came to be called social sin was ini-tially recognized by the Roman Catholic magisterium in *Gaudium et Spes*. Within eight years, three more official Catholic documents would devote significant attention to this type of sin. In a sense, *GS* 25 both enables and is further developed by these documents. The Latin American bishops' document *Justice (Med-JU)*,[29] the synodal document *Justice in the World* (*JW*),[30] and the *Rite of Penance* each contain prophetic statements that inspire and inform further ecclesial responses to social sin.

At their conference in Medellín, Colombia in 1968, the Latin American bishops produced multiple documents, one of them entitled *Justice*. More than half of this document's endnotes refer to *Gaudium et Spes*, particularly to the latter's realized eschatology (*GS* 38), to its rejection of a faith vs. morality dualism (*GS* 38), to its *diakonia* ecclesiology (*GS* 42), and to its insistence upon the universal destination of earthly goods (*GS* 69).[31]

The bishops also incorporate the vocabulary and concerns of fellow Latin Americans, such as the aforementioned Gutiérrez and educator Paulo Freire.[32] Structural injustice is condemned as a serious sin to be eradicated since this world is to be perfected and its inhabitants are to be liberated (*Med-JU* 2, 3, 5). In this document, these bishops see their pastoral mission as essentially a service of *concientización*—an indispensable education of consciences "ordered to changing the structures and the observance of justice" (*Med-JU* 23). Valuing collegiality and collaboration, they promise to lead all of the people of God toward supporting "the downtrodden of every social class so that they might come to know their rights and how to make use of them" (*Med-JU* 20). Although this document never identifies the sacrament of penance as a potential means of *concientización*, the bishops' emphases of conscience education and universal moral conversion (*Med-JU* 3) imply such a possibility.[33]

Three years after the Medellín conference, at the 1971 Synod of Bishops, the sacrament of penance was clearly identified as a means of conscience formation and education in social justice. Advancing this position was Archbishop Paul Grégoire, who specified communal celebrations of penance as superior for such conscientizing.[34] The Synod's eventual document, *Justice in the World*, embraces this position in the following statement: "The practice of penance should emphasize the social dimension of sin and of the sacrament" (*JW*, chap. 3). This statement must be read in the context of the document's theological centerpiece: "Action on behalf of justice and participation in the transformation of the world fully appear to us as a constitutive dimension of the preaching of the Gospel, or, in other words, of the Church's mission for the redemption of the human race and its liberation from every oppressive situation" (*JW*, Introduction). This sentence reflects the

1971 Synod's agreement with the Medellín conference that liberation from social evils is an essential part of the church's mission—a mission that depends, in part, upon the sacrament of penance.

Two years after this Synod, the Congregation for Divine Worship promulgated the *Rite of Penance*. *RP* 7 classifies actual sins as "grave" or "venial" sins committed by individual persons. However, other sections of *RP* include acknowledgment of social sin and call for communal responses. One of the most obvious of these is given in *RP* 5, which is quoted at the beginning of this essay. Another is present in *RP* 22: "Communal celebration shows more clearly the ecclesial nature of penance. The faithful listen together to the word of God, which . . . invites them to conversion; at the same time they examine the conformity of their lives with that word of God and help each other through common prayer."

The *Rite of Penance* offers three possible forms of sacramental reconciliation, as well as a nonsacramental communal penitential liturgy. The communal rites—also labeled as Rites "B" (*RP* 22-30) and "C" (*RP* 31-35)—are the first new forms of penance in a millennium.[35] Their being offered prepares for the fulfillment of *SC* 27 and 72, wherein the Second Vatican Council urges communal sacramental and liturgical celebrations, including communal penance. Although *RP* still allows a centuries-old juridical paradigm to dominate our ecclesial pursuit of conversion and reconciliation, nevertheless the options offered in *RP* also reflect the influence of a liturgical model: the revised rites and the penitential liturgy are centered upon prayer and the word of God, and they are to be a work of all the people (*RP* 4, 8, 22).[36]

The encouragement of participation by each and every person in the community is evident in *RP* 26, which states that a communal examination of conscience, an examination that may be led by a lay minister, may take the place of an ordained minister's homily. Lay ministers may also preside at nonsacramental communal penitential celebrations (*RP* 36),[37] liturgies that are "very useful in places where no priest is available" and that "are very helpful in promoting conversion of life and purification of heart" (*RP* 37). Furthermore, the lay persons in the community may assist ordained priests in choosing texts and adapting penitential services to the needs of the community (*RP* 40).

Justice, Justice in the World, and the *Rite of Penance* are not the only postconciliar documents that challenge the church to respond in a significant way to social sin. These were chosen as examples since they are especially prophetic and since together they form a foundation for postconciliar development.

Recommendations

Having briefly looked at social sin and at some particularly challenging documents that call for and inform responses to social sin, I would now like to recommend some possible responses. Whichever responses are pursued, they must both catechize and symbolize as regards social sin. Both of these needs can be met in Rite B, Rite C, or the penitential celebration.

Prophetic catechesis about social sin—*concientización*, if you will—can be experienced via common prayers, homilies, and communal examinations of conscience. Regarding the latter, I would not limit conscience examinations to those led by an ordained or lay minister in the midst of an assembly. Additionally, I urge that every fully initiated person in the assembly would at least have the opportunity to contribute to *dialogical* examinations of our individual and communal consciences. In the past, when a juridical and individualistic paradigm of sin and penance was considered adequate, the lone ministry of an ordained confessor was considered sufficient to form each penitent's conscience. Now, due to the inclusion of a liturgical and communitarian model of sin, penance, and reconciliation in *RP*, and due to the church's professed solidarity with all humanity in a complex modern world (*GS* 1-10), each penitent needs to both proclaim and hear prophetic moral challenges within a pluralistic community of dialogue partners. Supporting such dialogical examinations is Monika Hellwig, who asks each assembly member to listen with the same compassion that confessors have traditionally been expected to exercise: "A good way to do this in a communal penance celebration, because sin is revealed in suffering, is by letting the suffering of others speak to us, by giving such suffering a voice in our assembly . . . by stories of particular individuals or groups, by descriptions, even by simple economic or political analyses."[38] Such conscience examinations would also help to fulfill conciliar teachings on conscience, such as: "It is by these means [instruction, communication and dialogue] that men share with each other the truth they have discovered, or think they have discovered, in such a way that they help one another in the search for truth."[39]

As for the symbolic dimension, in the very gathering at a communal penitential liturgy, the church is more obviously and more meaningfully symbolizing its conversion as well as the conversion from unjust habits and practices that human persons generally desire and pursue. Applying Karl Rahner's theology of worship is very helpful here: the church's penitential liturgies, in mediating and celebrating moral awareness and conversion among penitent Catholics, are explicit realizations of the "secular liturgies" of justice and reconciliation implicitly celebrated in public life.[40]

These prophetic/catechetical and symbolic/liturgical needs can be met in the alternatives provided in the *Rite of Penance*. The question is: will these alternatives be utilized? Given the extraordinary status assigned to Rite C in *RP* itself (*RP* 31), its practical unavailability must be, temporarily at least, endured. Much harder to accept, however, is the minimal utilization (only during Advent and Lent) of Rite B and the nonsacramental penitential celebration. Neither of these, unlike Rite C, is classified as extraordinary. *RP* 13 recommends the season of Lent as "most appropriate for celebrating the sacrament of penance," but the same paragraph begins by stating that this sacrament "may be celebrated in all liturgical seasons and on any day." Theoretically, Rite B could be celebrated once a month, even once a week, as could the penitential celebration. Even if such frequency is impractical, shouldn't a church presumably committed to conversion from social sin catechize and symbolize that conversion more often than once or twice a year? Are not voters in November, for example, too far removed from the one socially conscious penitential liturgy they may have been challenged by during a February in Lent?

The development of dialogical examinations of conscience is a possible response to social sin that could be pursued within the liturgies given in *RP*. Another possibility is a noteworthy proposal of Peter Fink: a liturgy celebrating a Christian Day of Atonement.[41] Inspired by the Jewish Day of Atonement, Fink's proposed ritual would span the weekend of Christ the King, asking communities to pray for healing and forgiveness of their collective sins, the sins of the universal church, and the sins of the world. Both those who are aware of and those who are ignorant of social sin need such a ritual. Fink explains:

> Where the consciousness of social sin is strong, a ritual of this kind can serve to keep before people *both* the challenge to do whatever they can to undo it *and* the power of Christ's own

surrender to social evil where they can do nothing else. . . . On the other hand, where the consciousness of social sin is not strong and where people are comfortable simply to acquiesce in it, a ritual of this kind can serve a prophetic function, a call to consciousness and an assault on the very acquiescence which is evil's own victory.[42]

Yet another ecclesial response to social sin that deserves recommendation is one that has already been and continues to be pursued: the Journey to Justice process.[43] This structured process was designed by the Catholic Campaign for Human Development to effect conversion, especially among those who are more economically advantaged. This repeatable process can be initiated in any Catholic diocese. It includes a weekend retreat where conversion from social sin is conscientized and symbolized. The post-retreat phase of Journey to Justice includes forming small faith communities and partnerships with empowered low-income groups. As a component of the Catholic Campaign for Human Development, Journey to Justice is committed to empowerment, a goal urged by the United States Conference of Catholic Bishops[44] and consistent with modern Catholic social teaching.[45]

Conclusion

Just as the church would be less obviously a "sign of communion" if we considered communal celebrations of Eucharist to be optional, so the church will be less obviously a "sign of conversion" from all sin—including social sin—if we continue to consider the communal celebration of penance as optional, and as a ritual wherein social sin need not be addressed. The Catholic Church's response to social sin—the dark side of public life—continues to be inadequate catechetically, liturgically, and morally; it is also an example of a type of social sin previously unrecognized: the sin of a community against *itself*. Whether we utilize the liturgies in the *Rite of Penance*, or, like Fink and the Catholic Campaign for Human Development, develop adaptations of them, it is imperative for the church to commit universally to regular and more frequent celebrations of communal penance. Such celebrations will help to increase the joys and fulfill the hopes of the church and the publics it seeks to serve.[46]

Notes

[1]Congregation for Divine Worship, *Ordo Paenitentiae* (Editio typica: Rome: Typis Polyglottis Vaticanis, 1974). Throughout this essay I refer to the English translation of the *Rite of Penance* (ICEL: 1974) in *The Rites of the Catholic Church*, vol. 1 (Collegeville, MN: Liturgical/Pueblo, 1990), 517-629. Hereinafter, *RP* refers to the *Rite of Penance*. Citations will refer to section numbers in *RP*. The aforementioned Introduction is contained in *RP* 1-40. *RP* was promulgated on December 2, 1973.

[2]I here quote *RP* 4 after *RP* 5 so that the quoted material climaxes with the phrase "sign of conversion," a phrase obviously central to my proposal.

[3]All citations of documents of the Council are taken from Austin Flannery, ed., *Vatican Council II: The Conciliar and Post Conciliar Documents* (Northport, NY: Costello Publishing Co., 1975). As with *RP*, citations will be made parenthetically and refer to section numbers in the documents. *Sacrosanctum Concilium* was formally approved on December 4, 1963.

[4]This reference to social sin in *GS* 25 begins: "It cannot be denied that he [man] is often turned away from the good and urged to evil by the social environment in which he lives and in which he is immersed since the day of his birth." It concludes by drawing a distinction between original sin and social sin: "As it is, man is prone to evil, but whenever he meets a situation where the effects of sin are to be found, he is exposed to further inducements to sin." *Gaudium et Spes* was formally approved on December 7, 1965.

[5]Exemplifying this insistence in *GS* 43 is: "One of the gravest errors of our time is the dichotomy between the faith which many profess and the practice of their daily lives."

[6]*Lumen Gentium* was formally approved on November 21, 1964.

[7]The catechesis to which I refer can and should take place within these various forms of communal penance (as well as by other means). Supporting this assertion is section 47 in Paul VI's 1975 Apostolic Exhortation *Evangelii Nuntiandi*. See the English translation in David J. O'Brien and Thomas A. Shannon, eds., *Catholic Social Thought: The Documentary Heritage* (Maryknoll, NY: Orbis Books, 1992), 320.

[8]John Paul II sees the desire for profit, the thirst for power, and the idolatry of money, ideology, class, and technology as the worst social sins. See his 1987 encyclical *Sollicitudo Rei Socialis* 37 in O'Brien and Shannon, *Catholic Social Thought*, 420. Peter Henriot has provided some specific examples of social sin: a welfare system that includes minimal payments; a tax system with loopholes for the wealthy; a trade system that exploits workers. See his article "The Concept of Social Sin," *Catholic Mind* 71 (1973): 38-53. In American public life today, the lack of universal health insurance and unjust immigration policies are prominent examples.

[9]J. Milburn Thompson points out that the concept of social sin is "deeply rooted in the theology of the Hebrew prophets who accused Israel of infidelity

and who functioned as the conscience of the nation." See his *Justice and Peace*, 2nd ed. (Maryknoll, NY: Orbis Books, 2003), 198-99.

[10]Walter Rauschenbusch, *A Theology for the Social Gospel* (New York: Macmillan, 1917); Reinhold Niebuhr, *Moral Man and Immoral Society: A Study in Ethics and Politics* (New York: Charles Scribner's Sons, 1932).

[11]See *GS* 25. Such magisterial recognition may be implicit in John XXIII's 1961 encyclical *Mater et Magistra*. See O'Brien and Shannon, *Catholic Social Thought*, 84-128.

[12]Examples of both of these kinds of writings are offered throughout this essay.

[13]John Paul II, Post-Synodal Apostolic Exhortation *Reconciliatio et Paenitentia*. I refer to the English translation *On Reconciliation and Penance in the Mission of the Church Today* (Washington, DC: United States Catholic Conference, 1984). Hereinafter this document will be referred to as *REP*, since *RP* refers to the *Rite of Penance*. *REP* was promulgated on December 2, 1984, commemorating the eleventh anniversary of the promulgation of *RP*. *REP*'s treatment of social sin—in the lengthy section no. 16—is the only source referred to in the treatment of social sin given in the current *Catechism of the Catholic Church* (*CCC* 1869)—a sign of how influential John Paul II's understanding is. The *Catechism* is available at http://www.vatican.va.

[14]See, for example, *Sollicitudo Rei Socialis* 36-40 in O'Brien and Shannon, *Catholic Social Thought*, 419-24.

[15]Proper vs. analogical meanings of sin are distinguished in Thomas Aquinas, *Summa Theologiae* I-II.88.1. See the English translation by the Dominicans of the English Province (New York: Benziger, 1948; reprint, Westminster, MD: Christian Classics, 1981).

[16]Richard John Neuhaus, *Doing Well and Doing Good: The Challenge to the Christian Capitalist* (New York: Doubleday, 1992), 59. The appendix of this book is a condensation of John Paul II's 1991 Encyclical *Centesimus Annus* (*CA*). Neuhaus's condensation of *CA* 38 (297-8) excludes a rather important passage on social sin. Such an exclusion is evidence of Neuhaus preferring an individualism even more extreme than that of the late pope. Regarding this and related differences between John Paul II and neoconservatives, see John Sniegocki, "The Social Ethics of Pope John Paul II: A Critique of Neoconservative Interpretations," *Horizons* 33 (2006): 7-32. For a similar critique, also see David L. Schindler, *Heart of the World, Center of the Church: Communio Ecclesiology, Liberalism, and Liberation* (Grand Rapids: Eerdmans, 1996), 89-142.

[17]This canonization took place in 1215 at the Fourth Lateran Council when the Council established annual integral private confession as obligatory for all Roman Catholics. Later in the same century, the Thomistic distinction referred to in note 16 (above) added a scholarly rationale to such moral and sacramental individualism. See Kenan B. Osborne, *Reconciliation and Justification: The Sacrament and Its Theology* (Mahwah, NJ: Paulist Press, 1990), 84-93. Furthermore, such individualism is reinforced whenever the Confiteor

is prayed. It is somewhat ironic to note that the individualistic Confiteor is always followed by a communal absolution at Eucharist.

[18]This moral (and penitential) individualism in the Catholic tradition is not identical with the radical individualism that Robert Bellah and his colleagues see as a "language" opposed to the pursuit of the common good in American life. Nevertheless, these two forms of individualism are similar and complementary, to the point where, I contend, private celebration of penance can contribute to such disintegrating individualism in public life. See Robert N. Bellah et al., *Habits of the Heart: Individualism and Commitment in American Life* (Berkeley: University of California, 1985; reprint, New York: Harper & Row, 1986), 219-49.

[19]Thomas F. Schindler, *Ethics: The Social Dimension*, Theology and Life Series, vol. 27 (Wilmington, DE: Michael Glazier, 1989), 129-49.

[20]See Gustavo Gutiérrez, *A Theology of Liberation: History, Politics and Salvation* (Maryknoll, NY: Orbis Books, 1973), 174, where he writes: "In the underdeveloped countries one starts with a rejection of the existing situation, considered as fundamentally unjust and dehumanizing."

[21]In 1984, the same year in which the Congregation for the Doctrine of the Faith formally expressed its concerns about liberation theology in its first instruction on that field, Gutiérrez published the article, "Teologia y ciencias sociales" (theology and social sciences), where he wrote:

Once the situation of poverty and marginalization comes to play a part in theological reflections, an analysis of that situation from the sociological viewpoint becomes important, and requires recourse to the relevant disciplines. This means that if there is a meeting, it is between *theology and the social sciences*, and not between theology and Marxist analysis, except to the extent that elements of the latter are found in the contemporary social sciences, especially as these are practiced in the Latin American world. (Reprinted in James B. Nickoloff, ed., *Gustavo Gutiérrez: Essential Writings* [Maryknoll, NY: Orbis Books, 1996], 47)

[22]Gutiérrez has commended a different papal document of John Paul II due to its call for change of unjust economic structures. See Patricia A. Lamoureux, "Commentary on *Laborem exercens*," in *Modern Catholic Social Teaching: Commentaries and Interpretations*, ed. Kenneth R. Himes (Washington, DC: Georgetown University Press, 2005), 409. Donal Dorr has suggested that some of John Paul II's papal teaching may be compatible with Marxist tenets. See his *Option for the Poor: A Hundred Years of Vatican Social Teaching*, rev. ed. (Maryknoll, NY: Orbis Books, 1992), 308-12. Dorr's suggestion deserves consideration, given John Paul II's encouragement of the struggle for social justice, given his defense of workers, and given his occasional employment of inductive method.

[23]Rosemary Radford Ruether, *Sexism and God-Talk: Toward a Feminist Theology* (Boston: Beacon Press, 1983), 183.

[24]Gregory Baum, *Religion and Alienation: A Theological Reading of*

Sociology (New York: Paulist Press, 1975; reprint, Maryknoll, NY: Orbis Books, 2007), 193-226; Norbert Rigali, "Human Solidarity and Sin in the Apostolic Exhortation, *Reconciliation and Penance*," *The Living Light* 21 (1985): 337-44.

[25]Mark O'Keefe, *What Are They Saying about Social Sin?* (Mahwah, NJ: Paulist Press, 1990), 23.

[26]Patrick T. McCormick and Russell B. Connors, *Facing Ethical Issues: Dimensions of Character, Choices and Community* (Mahwah, NJ: Paulist Press, 2002), 22-24.

[27]National Conference of Catholic Bishops, *Brothers and Sisters to Us: U.S. Bishops' Pastoral Letter on Racism in Our Day* (Washington, D.C.: USCC, 1979).

[28]See, for example, Benedict XVI's 2005 encyclical, *Deus Caritas Est* 27-29, where social sin in the form of structural injustice is implicitly condemned. Available from http://www.vatican.va.

[29]Second General Conference of Latin American Bishops, *Justice* (Medellín, Colombia, September 6, 1968). See the English translation in Joseph Gremillion, *The Gospel of Peace and Justice: Catholic Social Teaching since Pope John* (Maryknoll, NY: Orbis Books, 1976), 445-54.

[30]1971 Synod of Bishops, *Justice in the World*. See O'Brien and Shannon, *Catholic Social Thought*, 288-300.

[31]Five of the eight references to *GS* are made in *Med-JU* 4-5, the latter paragraphs being situated in a section entitled "Doctrinal Bases." The Latin American bishops obviously saw their teaching at Medellín as being continuous with that of the Second Vatican Council.

[32]See Alfred T. Hennelly, *Liberation Theologies: The Global Pursuit of Justice* (Mystic, CT: Twenty-Third Publications, 1995), 11, 17. Also see Nickoloff, *Gustavo Gutiérrez*, 3-4 and Dorr, *Option for the Poor*, 208-9.

[33]Considering the sacrament of penance as a means of *concientización* is also implicitly supported in the Medellín document *Peace* (no. 24). See Gremillion, *The Gospel of Peace and Justice*, 462.

[34]James Dallen, *The Reconciling Community: The Rite of Penance* (Collegeville, MN: Liturgical Press, 1991), 264.

[35]Ibid., 230. See also Osborne, *Reconciliation and Justification*, 223, on seeing the form to be used when death is imminent (*RP* 64-65) as a fourth form.

[36]While Dallen, *The Reconciling Community*, 298-348, emphasizes the liturgical character of *RP*, Michael G. Lawler supports my claim that *RP* simultaneously perpetuates the age-old juridical paradigm of sin and penance. See Lawler's *Symbol and Sacrament: A Contemporary Sacramental Theology* (Mahwah, NJ: Paulist Press, 1987), 117-21.

[37]*RP* inconsistently calls these "celebrations" and "services." David Coffey claims that these expressions are meant to be synonymous because the original Latin consistently uses the word *celebratio* (celebration). See David M. Coffey, *The Sacrament of Reconciliation*, ed. John D. Laurance (Collegeville,

MN: Liturgical Press, 2001), 170 n.28. Coffey also urges the necessity of these celebrations because they fulfill an essential objective (i.e., the promotion of contrition), which is different from that of the sacrament proper (153-55). Also see Dallen, *The Reconciling Community*, 235, for an understanding of how these nonsacramental celebrations are "not completely extrinsic to the sacrament."

[38]Monika K. Hellwig, *Sign of Reconciliation and Conversion: The Sacrament of Penance for Our Times* (Wilmington, DE: Michael Glazier, 1984), 153-54.

[39]Second Vatican Council, *Dignitatis Humanae* 3. This declaration was formally approved on December 7, 1965. Perhaps such examinations of conscience could be followed by a communal version of the Confiteor, beginning "We confess to Almighty God and to one another that we have sinned. . . ."

[40]See Karl Rahner, "On the Theology of Worship," in *Theological Investigations*, vol. 19, *Faith and Ministry* (London: Darton, Longman & Todd, 1983), 141-49. Note that in *RP* 4 the church is to "become in the world a sign of conversion." This reflects a sacramental theology and an ecclesiology that *peritus* Rahner helped to contribute at the Second Vatican Council, and contributed again as a member of *RP*'s first draft committee (of two). Regarding the latter, see Dallen, *The Reconciling Community*, 209-15.

[41]Peter E. Fink, "Liturgy for a Christian Day of Atonement," in Peter E. Fink, ed., *Alternative Futures for Worship*, vol. 4, *Reconciliation* (Collegeville, MN: Liturgical Press, 1987), 127-45.

[42]Ibid., 144-45.

[43]Available from http://www.usccb.org.

[44]National Conference of Catholic Bishops, *Economic Justice for All: Pastoral Letter on Catholic Social Teaching and the U.S. Economy* (Washington, D.C.: USCC, 1986), 188, 200-1.

[45]Dorr, *Option for the Poor*, 378.

[46]I would like to thank Bill Collinge and the anonymous referees for their very helpful comments.

Contributors

Mark J. Allman is an associate professor in the Religious and Theological Studies Department at Merrimack College (North Andover, Massachusetts). His main areas of interest include the ethics of war and peace, political and economic ethics, globalization, poverty, Catholic social thought, and business ethics. He earned his M.A. in theology from The Catholic University of America and his Ph.D. in theology (Christian ethics) from Loyola University of Chicago. He is currently finishing *War and Peace: A Continuum of Approaches in Christianity and Beyond* for St. Mary's Press.

Anne M. Clifford is an associate professor of theology and director of the University Core Curriculum at Duquesne University and the president of the College Theology Society. Among her publications are sixteen articles on theology and science and ecological theology in monographs, encyclopedias, and journals. She is the author of *Introducing Feminist Theology* and co-edited *Christology: Memory, Inquiry and Practice*, the CTS Annual Volume 48 (Orbis Books). Her *Man, Woman, Earth: Christian Anthropology* (Orbis Books) is forthcoming. She thanks the Wimmer Family Foundation for a grant that helped to make the Intelligent Design article in this volume possible.

William J. Collinge teaches at Mount Saint Mary's University in Emmitsburg, Maryland, where he holds the Knott Professorship in Theology and a joint appointment to the philosophy department. He is the author of *The A to Z of Catholicism* (Scarecrow, 2001) as well as publications on St. Augustine, the Catholic Worker movement, and the American theologian John S. Dunne.

James T. Cross is an assistant professor of theology at Carroll College in Helena, Montana. He received his Ph.D. in systematic theology from Duquesne University. His research interests include moral theology, especially modern Catholic social teaching and thought, the relationship between sacraments and the moral life, and documents of the Second Vatican Council.

Mary Doak is an assistant professor in the Department of Theology and Religious Studies at the University of San Diego. She received her Ph.D. in systematic theology from the University of Chicago, and her main areas of research include public and political theology, theological method, eschatology, and ecclesiology. She has published *Reclaiming Narrative for Public Theology* (SUNY Press, 2004) and is currently working on a book in feminist ecclesiology.

Harold E. Ernst is a Ph.D. candidate in the Department of Theology at the University of Notre Dame, where he is completing a dissertation on the doctrine of divine providence in the theology of Thomas Aquinas. His interests lie in systematic and historical theology, particularly in such topics as creation, grace, theological anthropology, and method. His recent publications include "New Horizons in Catholic Philosophical Theology: *Fides et ratio* and the Changed Status of Thomism" (*Heythrop Journal*), and "The Hierarchy of Truths in the Thought of John Henry Newman" (*Irish Theological Quarterly*).

Coleman Fannin is a Ph.D. student and instructor in theology at the University of Dayton. His research interests include church and state, ecclesiology, and ethics, and in his dissertation he is exploring the Protestant conception(s) of religious liberty in conversation with Catholic Americanism. He is a graduate of the University of Georgia (B.A.) and Baylor University (M.Div., M.A.) and the author of several encyclopedia entries and journal articles as well as a chapter in Terrence W. Tilley et al., *Religious Diversity and the American Experience*.

Dennis Hamm, S.J., is a professor in the Department of Theology at Creighton University and holder of the Amelia B. and Emil G. Graff Chair in Catholic Theology. His most recent book is his commentary on the Acts of the Apostles (Liturgical Press, 2005) in the New Collegeville Bible Commentary series.

Patrick Hayes is an assistant professor in the Department of Theology and Religious Studies at St. John's University in New York. His doctorate is from The Catholic University of America, with a focus on Catholic ecclesiology. His present research interests revolve around the question of Catholic identity in America. He is at work on two books related to Catholic intellectual life and the impact of Catholic miracle narratives in the nineteenth century. Hayes is also the review editor of H-Catholic, a listserv for those interested in Catholic studies.

Elizabeth Newman is a professor of theology and ethics at the Baptist Theological Seminary at Richmond. She has recently published *Untamed Hospitality: Welcoming God and Other Strangers* (Brazos, 2007). She has also published articles in theology and science, Christian identity and higher education, and various ecclesial practices. She received her Ph.D. in theology and ethics from Duke University and wrote her dissertation on the Russian Orthodox theologian Alexander Schmemann.

Michael J. Perry is the Robert W. Woodruff Professor of Law and Senior Fellow, Center for the Study of Law and Religion, Emory University. He is a specialist in the relation of religion and morality to the law, in particular, the U.S. Constitution. His nine books include *Toward a Theory of Human Rights: Religion, Law, Courts* (Cambridge, 2006), *Under God? Religious Faith and Liberal Democracy* (Cambridge, 2003), and *Religion in Politics: Constitutional and Moral Perspectives* (Oxford, 1997).

William L. Portier holds the Mary Ann Spearin Chair of Catholic Theology in the Religious Studies Department at the University of Dayton. He is the author of more than thirty books and articles and co-edited *American Catholic Traditions: Resources for Renewal*, the CTS Annual Volume 42 (Orbis Books, 1996).

John Sniegocki is an assistant professor in the Department of Theology at Xavier University (Cincinnati). His main areas of interest include Catholic social teaching, globalization, the ethics of war and nonviolence, grassroots social movements, ecology, and contemplative spirituality. He received a Ph.D. in Christian ethics from the University of Notre Dame. His dissertation has recently been revised for publication as a book, tentatively entitled *Catholic Social Teaching and Globalization: The Quest for Alternatives.*

Ernesto Valiente is a Salvadoran-born doctoral student of systematic theology at the University of Notre Dame. His main areas of scholarly interest include political, liberation, and U.S. Latino theology. He is currently working on his dissertation, tentatively entitled *Truth, Justice, and Forgiveness: Reconciliation in the Christology of Jon Sobrino.*

Tobias L. Winright is an assistant professor in the Department of Theological Studies at Saint Louis University. A former law enforcement officer, he has also taught ethics at the Des Moines Regional Police Academy and the Saint Louis County and Municipal Police Academy. He earned his M.Div. from Duke Divinity School and his Ph.D. in Christian ethics from the University of Notre Dame. His main areas of interest include the ethics of war and peace, just policing, capital punishment, Catholic social teaching, and environmental theology.